PRAISE FOR *UNLEASH THE DRAGON WITHIN*

"*Unleash the Dragon Within* is an artful and intelligently written book about life, not just about martial arts. It's about the human experience and how we all can discover our best selves through discipline, focus, concentration, and determination. Macramalla sets us on that path, with storytelling that is insightful, knowledgeable, and informative."

—HOMER HANS BRYANT, artistic director of Chicago Multicultural Dance Center

"Ch'ien-lung has provided my body with a vocabulary of movement and spirit, a poetry of bows and forms. With his dual backgrounds in psychology and martial arts, Macramalla is that rare individual who can not only bridge the gap between Eastern and Western ideas, but who can write about them with delightful clarity."

—JON PEARCE, professor, Department of Computer Science, San Jose State University

"*Unleash the Dragon Within* is a beautifully written, practical book on personal development through the art of Ch'ien-lung kung-fu. Macramalla takes you on a fun and body-centered journey into your own way of being to better cope with everyday life. If you want to have better relationships, a calmer mind, a firmer grasp on your own emotional responses as well as be fitter, more flexible, and toned, you really should buy this book."

—SARAH TURNER, alternative medicine researcher

"Steven Macramalla bridges Eastern philosophy, martial arts, and ancient wisdom to modern life. He provides deep insight to the Western mind and awakens our inner psychology to the amazing possibilities life has to offer. He gives new insight and perspective on how to live more fully and how to ignite our human potential."

—LEE HOLDEN, author, TV personality, producer, and qigong master

"Discovering and studying Ch'ien-lung changed my life drastically, in the greatest of ways. It has given me tools for every area of my life, which I still use on a daily basis. I have learned the fluidity to change perspectives in a number of important ways, and to respond to my environment creatively and openly. If you want to explore and transform your inner and outer world in the most astonishing of ways, I highly recommend this book."

—PETER IRISH, six-time world hacky sack champion, award-winning juggler, and artist

"Steven Macramalla expounds a revolutionary new perspective on an ancient path forward by which we may better understand ourselves, others, and our relationship to our environment. This book invites us to profoundly shift the way we see our world. At the same time, it provides a practice framework that enables us to access the vitality, potency, and poignancy available to each of us through this strange and beautiful thing we call life."

—VALERIE MOSELLE, author of *Breathwork: A 3-Week Breathing Program to Gain Clarity, Calm, and Better Health*

"The Animals of Ch'ien-lung straddle both personal-level archetypes and representations of the building blocks of nature itself—texture, weight, flow, weather patterns, and the elements of fire, water, and earth. You are deeper than your personality, deeper than archetype even, and, as an Animal, you are little more than a loosely bound-together collection of attributes."

—EMILIA SANDILANDS, massage practitioner and movement teacher

"For those who are looking to embody the greater version of their self that is waiting just around the corner, I highly recommend that you read this book!"

—SIFU KELLY RYAN LAKE, daoist priest, doctor of medical qigong therapy, acupuncturist, and instructor of Chinese martial arts

"The Ch'ien-lung Animals practice enriched my work as a young dancer and continues to do so now as an international show director. Macramalla has brought to life an exciting and unique fusion of science and art that will inspire any artist with ideas and themes for a lifetime."

—SUSAN GAUDREAU, show director, Cirque Du Soleil Entertainment Group

"Academically precise and lyrically passionate, Steven Macramalla's insights combine animal symbolism with a pragmatic approach to changing human behavior, all in a mesmerizing style. Dr. Macramalla offers a rich, poetic analysis of martial arts that is as intellectually refreshing as it is daring. I highly recommend it to any reader."

—SERGEY MAKARENKO, Project Director II, State of California, DGS EO OS, internationally renowned instructor in Systema

UNLEASH THE DRAGON WITHIN

TRANSFORM YOUR LIFE WITH THE KUNG-FU ANIMALS OF CH'IEN-LUNG

Steven Macramalla, PhD

Published by
Blue Snake Books
Berkeley, California

Cover design by Rob Johnson
Book design by Happenstance Type-O-Rama

Images of the bows, mudras, and seated positions © G. Craig Hobbs, Associate Professor, San Jose State University.

Diagrams of the skeletons © Meann85 on Fiverr; the stances © Anshue on Fiverr.

Photographs of Constantine Darling © Robin Yeh, Soul Visuals.

Printed in Canada

Unleash the Dragon Within: Transform Your Life with the Kung-Fu Animals of Ch'ien-Lung is sponsored and published by the Society for the Study of Native Arts and Sciences (dba North Atlantic Books), an educational nonprofit based in Berkeley, California, that collaborates with partners to develop cross-cultural perspectives, nurture holistic views of art, science, the humanities, and healing, and seed personal and global transformation by publishing work on the relationship of body, spirit, and nature.

North Atlantic Books' publications are available through most bookstores. For further information, visit our website at www.northatlanticbooks.com or call 800-733-3000.

The following information is intended for general information purposes only. Individuals should always see their health care provider before administering any suggestions made in this book. Any application of the material set forth in the following pages is at the reader's discretion and is his or her sole responsibility.

Library of Congress Cataloging-in-Publication Data

Names: Macramalla, Steven, author.
Title: Unleash the dragon within: Transform your life with the kung-fu animals of Ch'ien-Lung / by Steven Macramalla.
Description: Berkeley, California : Blue Snake Books, [2019] | Includes bibliographical references and index.
Identifiers: LCCN 2019002357 (print) | LCCN 2019009342 (ebook) |
ISBN 9781623173661 (ebook) | ISBN 9781623173654 (pbk. : alk. paper)
Subjects: LCSH: Kung fu—Philosophy. | Martial arts—Philosophy. |
Animals—Symbolic aspects.
Classification: LCC GV1114.7 (ebook) | LCC GV1114.7 .M33 2019 (print) |
DDC 796.815/9—dc23
LC record available at https://lccn.loc.gov/2019002357

1 2 3 4 5 6 7 8 9 MARQUIS 24 23 22 21 20 19

North Atlantic Books is committed to the protection of our environment. We print on recycled paper whenever possible and partner with printers who strive to use environmentally responsible practices.

Dedicated to my wife, Veronica, and

to the future generations of this planet.

The climate will change.

The mores of our humanity will not.

CONTENTS

ACKNOWLEDGMENTS

I would like to thank my wife, Veronica Tonay, who provided moral and material support. Dear Santa Cruz, you will never know how much darkness she dispels.

There are more training partners than I can name who played a big role bringing this work to light. In one way or another, you are in this book. Thanks to Alisoun Payne, Jean-Paul and Dory Thuot, Dana Peterson, Susie Gaudreau, Kassandra Jewall, Laura Bergstrome, Barbara Poggemiller, Lynda Raino, Blaise Eagleheart, Irma Soltonovich, Cameron Avery, Cindy Smith, Dave Philips, Rick Abermyck, Gerry, Christo, and the Munnuke clan, Robert Birch, Melissa Whipps, Marcus Mcdonough, Chad Iocovetta, Scott Hunter, Jon Pearce, the Ashland Crew of Justin Thyme, Heather Hill, Peter Gross, Jasmin Patten, and Destino Das. Thanks also go to the whole crew from Salt Spring Island, Matthew Horn, Serena Vaillancourt, Emma Yardley, and Craig DiAngelis; and to my brothers and sister in arms, David Rabby, Peter Irish, Robin Yeh, Orion and Silas Radies, Ocean Hellman, Sameer Gupta, Alper Caglayan, and Terri Salvatore. Thanks also to my aikido teachers, Linda Holiday, Glen Kimoto, Aimen Al-Refai, Mary Heiny, and Yoshi Shibata, and to the whole aikido family. Thank you to the incomparable James McNeil and Little Nine Heavens Kung-Fu for your example of tenacity and integrity. Thanks to Brian Lynn for teaching Feldenkrais and opening a world of systematic investigation. To Homer Hans Bryant, Marlise McCormick, Clara Roberts, Sarah Turner, and Emilia Sandilands for your support! From Systema, thanks to Sergey Makarenko, Gene Smithson, and Casey Lake; and from Bagua and Daoist mysticism, Kelly Lake. Thank you to Grace Darling, Peter Jonassen, Gabrielle Ciceri, and Beth Niernberg for being family. To my advisor in grad school, the late Bruce Bridgeman. To Dacher Keltner, a leader in the field of Positive Psychology, who helped me take the plunge into writing the Seven Steps for each chapter. Thanks to friends of the pen, Chad Sampanes, Jeff Reed, Ben Preston, Crystal

Tanaka, Dr. David Anthony, and Andy Couturier, for your edits and moral support. And, of course, to Mom, Maggie, Esmat, and Hany. To Michael and Lesley Colgan, thank you for planting the seeds.

A special thanks to Deng Ming-Dao, whose advice was as bountiful as wise.

Thank you, Pam Berkman, for saying "yes" and to Louis Swaim, Lily Miller, Emma Cofod, and Alison Knowles for the follow-through. Thanks to copyeditor Rebecca Rider; they don't pay you enough.

Photo credits of the bows and mudras go to wizard of digital arts, Dr. Craig Hobbs of San Jose State University; thanks to Fiverr artists Anshue for the stances and Meann85 for the skeletons.

Thank you, Constantine Darling, for all the dreams.

PREFACE

The chatter in the auditorium of 400 college students in the Psychology of Human Sexuality is about to give way to a moment of silence. The professor had invited me to talk about sex from the point of view of Animal* archetypes from the kung-fu martial art Ch'ien-lung—a practice with roots in Daoist alchemy. Naturally, this involves demonstrating the kung-fu moves of an Animal before explaining its approach to sex.

First—always—Tiger: forceful and explosive. To see the movements of Tiger is like watching fresh lava being forced through the arms and legs, and to hear Tiger's intense breathing is like hearing the whine of a jet engine trapped in a mason jar. My demeanor hardens, my posture squares up, my gaze burns. All my muscles pull in opposite direction from each other, my hands make the shape of Tiger claws, like I'm digging my nails in the bark of a tree to mark my territory. My movements are imbued with the hundreds of memories of when becoming Tiger has helped me attain goals at work and strive for honesty and courage in my relationships. When I finish the demonstration, the students applaud appreciatively. Riding the momentum, I segue into describing Tiger's disciplined personality, the power of his concentration in meditation and competitive sports, and how Tiger approaches sex: passionate, committed, loyal, and intimate, with that edge of ownership when you recognize you and your partner belong to each other. I see heads nod and looks of recognition scattered in the crowd. The students are abuzz. They see their own inner Tiger expressed in my movement. I allow them a few

---

* I will be capitalizing the word *Animal*, along with the names of the individual Animals, like *Tiger* and *Black Panther*. This avoids confusion when talking about, as happens occasionally, an actual animal, and emphasizes that these Animals are dynamic systems that process information in a particular way.

moments to chatter among themselves, and then I call for their attention through the din to tell them I am demonstrating Boa next.

Boa is the opposite of Tiger. She is soft, lyrical, flowing, full of locks and dodges unseen by the untrained eye, but who cares, it's damn pretty. Again, I embody the Animal; my gaze softens, my posture rounds; the arms make gentle arcs, palms open as if ready to shake hands. The crackling of Tiger gives way to the billowing clouds of Boa's loving embrace. There's always a moment when I *become* the Animal. When it happens with Boa, I feel vulnerability pervading my entire body, like I'm holding my own newborn for the first time. The movement and breathing evoke recollections of vulnerability enriching my life. I'm not just recalling these times, I am moving through them. The hypnotic sequence ends. The students applaud and listen attentively as I describe Boa's empathetic nature—how she can walk into a room and feel the emotional nuances of all the people who were there ten minutes ago; a good listener, she makes an incredible therapist, absorbing and letting go of feelings without any compulsion to do something. In sex, she is vulnerable, surrendering, flowing fully with the moment. I conclude, and there is an elevated buzz of chatter in the lecture hall. I answer questions. Do I see when I am being Tiger or Boa in my own relationships? Yes. Do I see them in others? Yes. Does knowing the difference between them help me to change from Tiger to Boa? Yes.

Then I say I am going to demonstrate White Leopard. Now, here, comes the moment of silence: the auditorium of over 400 students goes abruptly and absolutely quiet to see the next Animal I transform into. The students don't have words for it, but they viscerally respond to how I change from one Animal to the next. I have done the demonstration hundreds of times and people respond, in varied ways, to the same thing: I morph before their eyes, and it is undeniable, consistent, and intense. The proof is in the silence.

Ch'ien-lung is genius, and simply far too good, too fun, and too needed to let it disappear into the night. Ch'ien-lung is not only an endless trove of fitness and training ideas, but it speaks to the psychological shock and needs we will be confronting in the coming years with climate change as we seek to find a new way to relate to nature, to the planet, and to each other. My hope for this book is to kindle an interest in the public for martial arts and to stoke in martial artists a remembrance of beauties past, when pantheons of masters taught students that their skills were equally apt for healing as for fighting, for scholarship as for competition, and for uplifting the spirit as for containing conflict. This book will teach you how to use the Animals of Ch'ien-lung to bring zest and insight to every nook of your life. The archetypes heal: the psyche through reflection, the body through movement, and our relationship to the planet through our relationships to each other.

Tapping into archetypal forces can help, and remains for many people an underdeveloped resource. In my over thirty years of practicing and teaching hundreds of students, I can swear as to how people find the Animals incredibly useful. You will gain insight into the motivations, strengths, and weaknesses of others as well as your own; you will better track how others are growing, often unbeknownst even to themselves. You will add a dimension to your physical workouts and spiritual practices while making them more fun. If you are an artist, congratulations! This book is a trove of ideas, textures, and themes that will last you fifteen lifetimes.

This book will show you how to draw on your potential for each Animal and bring these inner treasures to life. Each Animal has its own standalone chapter. The chapters are organized along a spectrum, from the deepest levels of the unconscious to the highest levels of thought and wisdom. Each chapter attunes you to the symbolic meaning, or *mythos,* of the Animal in consciousness: its anatomy, its neural function, and its relationship to Earth. The chapters describe how the symbolism translates to practical application, or *logos,* in martial arts, as well as all kinds of sports and physical activities, and finally, how the Animal symbols help us weave a coherent narrative of our transformation, the *morphos.*

You begin the journey of discovering your inner Animals with the Seven Steps at the end of each chapter, which include visualized breathing and contemplative practices. You can practice any or all of the steps as little or as much as you like. Ch'ien-lung can be practiced at any age, and it is a lifetime practice that evolves as you do. Possible side effects include greater peace of mind, clarity, creativity, purpose, and the ability to articulate the wisdom forged of the fires you have passed through.

1 THE LIFE ART OF CH'IEN-LUNG

Man's physical survival depends on technology.
Man's psychological survival depends on mystery.

—ATTRIBUTED TO JOSEPH CAMPBELL

Our teacher, Constantine, affectionately called me a lunatic for the exercises I concocted and then subjected myself to in the pursuit of practicing Ch'ien-lung both on and off the mat. When I worked as a dishwasher, which was mind-numbing and messy work, I practiced Python mental juggling, simultaneously counting up to 100 by twos, and down from 99 by threes. I biked home late at night in the cold, pouring rain, toasty warm as I practiced Tiger breathing, focusing energy on the area of my belly; I delivered advertising flyers, running in White Leopard from house to house, lightly and quickly, in the style of parkour, jumping over hedges like hurdles.[1] Once, as I returned to the studio after a Python breathing practice, Constantine jokingly asked me to remember a phone number, which he presently rattled off in a flurry. To the astonishment of both of us, I repeated it back to him verbatim. Perhaps the greatest benefits resulted from Boa meditations, taking the time to open up while listening, to slow down and breathe before speaking. I learned all the forms and all the internal practices, did the homework he assigned, internalized the Animal archetypes, and made every part of my life a part of my practice.

Constantine often asked me to take new students to a coffee shop and explain the Animals. As I spoke, I shifted into each of the Animals, from the airy Boa to the burning Tiger to the slinky Black Panther, right before their eyes.[2] The new students always commented not only on how I shifted, but also on how the space around us changed. It was as if embodying these archetypes was like a lighting cue in a stage production, changing the ambience of the setting and the mood of the students at the table. In demonstrations at high school gyms, I invoke White Leopard's cool, light movement, imagining the feeling of high-altitude air improving my depth perception and strings that are lifting me up into the air as I float and glide. From there, I shift into Python's heavy, whip-like and dissembling motion. My shoulders drop and roll, and now it feels like my bones have had iron poured into their marrow and that they are connected by chains, like a sectioned staff; in Python, my mind simultaneously tracks the dramatic arc of the demonstration, monitors the upcoming sequence of whip kicks, and checks off the conceptual points of the lecture. I use the Animals in research, switching from deliberate reasoning to purposeful imagination; in my workouts, shifting from power to finesse; in conversations with friends and strangers, shifting from strong and forceful, to soft and empathetic, creating new dynamics in conversation in the service of developing deeper connection. This shifting often yields tangible fruits, such as greater meaning, creativity, and a sense of freedom from within.

Ch'ien-lung (pronounced "chin" and "lung") is a kung-fu, like its cousins Taiji and Qigong. The word *kung-fu* (sometimes spelled *gongfu*) usually connotes to the Western mind exotic fighting styles full of twisting strikes done with the grace of ballet and the power of gymnastics. But the word *kung-fu* has little to do with fighting. Its meaning derives from "labor" and "strength" and connotes great effort over time. It refers to any practice done over a long period and with such devotion that it becomes part of the person, the lens through which they see the world. What turns a martial skill into a kung-fu is when the practice is taken into the real world and put into everyday use. When you walk to the store, you practice moving your hips like you would for a kick; when you stand in line for a movie, you practice using your peripheral vision to be cognizant of your surroundings. Ch'ien-lung has a wealth of off-the-mat practices that make it not just a martial art, but as Constantine called it, a life art.[3]

Our Western language has poor choices for what to call this volitional change. It could be called *shape-shifting* ... but no. It could be called *Daoist alchemy* or *Tibetan shamanism,* as it has roots in these practices, but these terms include an entire world-view of religious beliefs and cultural knowledge that do not clarify what type of change is being made. The word *transformation* is too general, and *ontology* (the study of what makes a thing what it is) is too narrow. *Simulated proprioception* comes close and sounds scientific, but it is one small part of a greater art.

The phrase that best defines my thinking is, perhaps, *embodied metaphysics,* and this phrase, though clunky, comes closest to conveying how the body is our intimate partner in the transformation of how we perceive the world and act in it. Embodied metaphysics is a language spoken in feeling, breath, and movement used to shift your perspective and perception of reality. Your presence and actions change the world and are changed by the world. You cannot control all these changes on this two-way road of transformation, and you don't really want to, but the Animals of Ch'ien-lung can help you to own the changes in a language that is evocative and fun. Embodied metaphysics captures something we naturally do when we give our all. Whether you are a dancer embodying an emotion, an athlete getting into the zone, an actor invoking a character, a yogi delving deep into selflessness, or a businessman putting on your game-face, you become bigger than what you are. As a life art, the question is how to bring that presence to other parts of your day. The answer lies in connecting with your Animal archetypes.

The Dragon in Our Genes

Archetypes are psychological DNA. Traditionally, they are conceived of as patterned thoughts, feelings, and images that hang together. They are general outlines for how to act, celebrate, survive, and thrive under specific circumstances. They are superstructures of the psyche. We share them in common, and yet they make us unique, just as birds have an instinct to make nests, yet each nest differs from the next.

Everybody can embody an archetype. If you knew nothing about Ch'ien-lung and called on yourself to be more "Tiger," I am sure you would have no difficulty in summoning its powerful, indomitable, fiery, and fearless spirit. Knowing nothing of the Animals, if you were asked to draw on your "Black Panther," I bet you would invoke with glee its sleek, sexy, and deadly mystery. People would respond to you differently, too. The moment you started to invoke the quality of a Panther, people would at once be drawn to you as you exuded a heightened awareness of your surroundings while also being taken aback by your intensity. Each archetype you embody brings to life different facets of who you are. Together the archetypes provide a map to the psyche that you can use to draw on strength, balance, and well-being.

Each of the Animals has a stereotypical physique—an idealized body type with facial features that is emblematic of the Animal spirit. Ch'ien-lung is an embodied art, so it is not important that you possess the physique but that you *imagine what it would feel like* to possess them. I have often heard reports from my students who are strong in one Animal—say, the soft Boa—highlight their strength in another—say, the competitive Tiger—by imagining they possess that body type and adopting the posture, tone, and gaze that go with it.

But why do this? Why become Boa? How does being White Leopard help you? This deep power to call on archetypes is your birthright. The Animals are tools to spur the imagination, promote wonder, and revere mystery. The Animals provide a holistic map to the mind-body connection. They bridge art and science, East and West. Working with archetypes, you will find that every new idea, every novel flavor, and each surprising cultural practice you encounter will have a place to hang its hat. They offer a radically different perspective on relationships, illuminating and making them richer. The exercises at the ends of the chapters will help you tap into this deep power we all possess.

Archetypes: The Art of Yin and Jung

In the mythology of Ch'ien-lung, the Animals symbolize energies born at the birth of the cosmos which then, in turn, formed Earth, organized life, and shaped our minds. An Animal represents an energy, and in

Ch'ien-lung, the energy gives rise to the rest—from the natural features of Earth to the anatomy of the body, and the regions of the brain to the personality types and behaviors. The archetypes are *transgressive,* which means that although you need to know whether you are talking about a forest, a brain, a personality quirk, or a style of interior decoration, the Animal archetypes symbolize the quality those very different things share in common. As a transgressive symbol, an archetype can symbolize not just what you are, but what you do and how you do it, which may be distinct from one another. A person may be engaged in the Python profession of law, be a creative White Leopard by nature, and perform their daily tasks in the manner of an empathic Boa. They represent developmental stages. Panther is the dawn or first stages of growth, Tiger is the zenith or height of power, and Leopard and Cobra are the sunset and final stages. These transgressive qualities apply to individual personalities as well as to the characters of entire nations, cultures, works of art, and institutions. A music genre or movie character is Tiger, a Cirque du Soleil show expresses Leopard, a motorcycle stunt captures Panther, a head scarf as a fashion accessory invokes Cobra's mystery, and the US is Tiger to India's Boa.

The Animals express opposing elements of the psyche: conceptual versus concrete, granular against holistic, active compared to receptive. In Ch'ien-lung mythology, two opposite Animals combine to create the Dragon. Part of the practice to understand the tensions created when combining archetypes is to assign gender to the Animals.

Sex and gender are different, of course. Sex is biological, male or female, and gender is psychological, masculine or feminine. We tend to put people in a box, expecting a male to be masculine and a female to be feminine. Closer to the truth, gender and sex are not lock-step; and, as the transgender movement and research in psychology teach us, gender is a spectrum where you can proactively interpret your fit. In my experience teaching Ch'ien-lung, every person carries archetypes for *both* masculine and feminine behaviors—where labeling a behavior as gendered is sometimes a complete social construct; at other times is grounded in the irrevocable division of labor in sexual reproduction; and sometimes shifts according to personal preference or evolution.

The archetypes exist on a spectrum from masculine to feminine where the Cats are mostly masculine and the Snakes are mostly feminine.

Tiger and Panther are both masculine archetypes, but Panther is more feminine than Tiger; Python and Boa are both feminine, but Python is more masculine than Boa. This book uses the masculine pronoun *he* for the Cats and the feminine pronoun *she* for the Snakes, to be consistent with the archetype. But it's with the understanding that a person of any sex and gender can embody any of the archetypes. The gender of the Animal pales in importance compared to other attributes; the gender is there not because it is important to the Animal but because it challenges the student to confront their own personally held assumptions about masculinity, femininity, and the gamut between and beyond. In the mythology, the Dragon is created by the pressure of opposing forces. These sometimes include resistance to societal or personally held beliefs around gender. The Dragon is the archetype of a person who, among many other things, has integrated both masculine and feminine within themselves and transcends these labels.

The Animals in you grow and mature. For example, an immature Tiger pushes for power, whereas a mature Tiger stands for principles. They journey through four stages, described in the section on personality in the Animal chapters, that are based on Jung's four stages of the inner masculine, which he called the *animus,* and the inner feminine, called the *anima*. The Animals are a symbolic language of how all sorts of psychological attributes, including masculinity and femininity, are first affirmed and then transcended.

Martial Arts as Life Arts

Every martial art leads a double life—the first as the martial art practiced on the mat and the second as a life art touching every part of your day. Ch'ien-lung, to be sure, has a practical side. Constantine taught self-defense to the Israeli army, and Ch'ien-lung is full of eye-gauges, throat-rips, groin-kicks, joint-locks, and breaks for all 206 bones of the human body. But often as not, halfway through a class on these techniques, Constantine would sit us down for a chat. He explained that in ancient times martial arts consisted of three elements. The fighting skill, what in the West is called the *hoplology* (*hoplot* is Greek for warrior), the science of inflicting pain, causing damage, and breaking balance. The second element was a healing art. You were expected to be able to heal the damage you caused (especially so as not to run out of training partners). The third element was some kind of artistic expression, like calligraphy, music, or poetry, with the deepest being the meditative arts. The art helped to vent the ardors of training, hone the spirit, and develop ideas that eventually cross-pollinated with the martial practice, creating a cycle.

These three elements together make a life art. The concept of a *life art* is not new. For centuries the Japanese, for example, have turned numerous arts and skills into practices of crafting mindfulness and presence. You can hone character and refine spirit by arranging flowers (*kado,* "way of flowers"), performing tea ceremonies (*sado,* "way of tea"), or practicing martial arts (*budo,* "way of the warrior"). The Japanese character for *budo* includes a symbol for "spear" with that of "stop," literally meaning "stop spear" or "means of peace" or "way to stop violence." The same brush strokes make up the first part of the related Chinese calligraphy for *wushu* (lit. "martial art").[4] In both cultures, the symbols imply a way to grow a whole person.

As a life art, Ch'ien-lung inspired me to pursue a doctorate in *cognitive psychology,* the science of how the brain processes information and generates the illusion of your reality, studying how the multiple systems of the brain compete and integrate information with each other the way the Animals do. To round out my understanding of life art principles, I study how they are expressed in other styles, practicing aikido (second-degree black belt) as well as Systema, Bagua, and Taiji. It is my own Dragon quest of sorts, studying life arts taught by instructors of other styles, and I can assure you, I continue to endlessly rediscover the principles Constantine taught. This book shares the knowledge gained along this path. My hope is that *life art* puts into words something long-time martial artists have felt, which they will now be able to share with beginners more easily.

Mythos, Logos, Morphos

Any practice can be made into a life art—whether it is yoga, football, or cooking—wherein it teaches a person how to transcend through a repertoire of skills. What makes a life art is how it teaches a person to engage with *conflict.* Conflict here is taken to mean not just physical fights, but any tension and tradeoff between opposites, whether it is in the theatre of war or in a scene at the theatre. Life is filled with conflicts and risk, and although we may not handle the conflict perfectly or always beat the odds we take, having an approach to conflict and uncertainty means we can get better at dealing with them over time.

Martial arts (and all life arts, really) offer three important elements to engaging in conflict: a *mythos,* a *logos,* and a *morphos.* The *mythos* provides a worldview that answers questions about how the world came to be and who you are in it. The word *mythos* comes from the Greek meaning tale or story, with connections to the words *mystery* and *initiation.* Mythos precedes conflict, providing the rationale and terms of engagement. The second element is the *logos,* and it addresses the realities of implementation. *Logos* comes from the Greek word for reason, from which we derive *logistics.* Logos pertains to the event of the conflict, from the biomechanics of hand-to-hand combat to the principles underlying strategies and tactics. The third element is the *morphos,* the Greek word for shape or structure, from which we derive the word *metamorphosis.* Morphos follows a conflict and has to do with how we have been changed by the conflict and its outcome, and, especially, how we integrate the event of the conflict into a coherent and meaningful part of the narrative of our own life. Martial arts become life arts when they prepare you for the moment before the fight, during the fight, and after the fight by providing a mythos, logos, and morphos. Every martial art has a different way of approaching each.

In the mythos of the Chinese arts, like Bagua and Taiji, the world follows natural laws that are dynamic and fluid in ever-varying cyclic patterns. The logos of these fighting arts reflect this worldview in the fluid, continuous, dynamic spirals of their movement and breath work. In the morphos after the fight, those same natural principles are applied to heal internal organ damage and mend broken bones, through the use of natural herbs, acupuncture, moxibustion, and energy work.

In the mythos of Aikido, the Japanese art of peace, people train to come into alignment with *kami* (the gods; divine nature), and so bring peace to society. The logos of the art reflects this in the circular arcs of motion used to dissipate force, allowing them to sidestep and blend with their opponents in order to disarm and neutralize the attack without destroying the attacker, putting a stop not just to the fighter but to the fighting. In the morphos, they turn to their Shinto roots of prayer and purification.

The worldview of the US military is through the historical and legal lens of the Constitution, and that America is more than just a country but an idea, the American mythos. The logos is enshrined in the hierarchical structure of decision-making that assesses cost and benefits, matching the means to the ends aligned (hopefully) with national interests and strategies. Veterans return and are, ideally, taken care of by the country they served, in the morphos, reminding all that they and we leave no one behind, and that courage makes all other virtues possible as we seek a more perfect union.

The mythos of the martial art of Systema is deeply rooted in its Russian culture, which values deep-feeling intelligence blended with an understated power and a history of appreciating the mystical. The logos of the style emphasizes a natural posture, flowing movement, and skilled use of breath; Systema fighters are known for their dissembling blends and counterstrikes, which are delivered with shuddering depth all the while looking perfectly casual. In their morphos, they train fighters to recover through breath control and the same flow of natural movement, offering a freedom from the fear of pain.

Fighters in mixed martial arts (MMA) abide by a warrior mythos of authenticity, discipline, and courage, supporting each other in fellowship through the difficulties of training and performance, cultivating values they find missing in an increasingly childproof world. The logos is reflected in their no-nonsense techniques that they hone and test using the cultural norms of research in Western science they have absorbed by osmosis their entire lives. In the morphos, immersed in Western culture as they are, some parlay their success into television, film, or product placement, while others pass their hard-won lessons on to the next generation through coaching.

In the mythos of Ch'ien-lung, the Animals symbolize energies born at the birth of the universe. These energies shaped Earth, the body, and our consciousness. In the mythos, the Animal consciousness and Animal anatomy draw strength from places of Earth rich with the Animal energy. For example, the Boa's respiratory system, empathy and unconscious mind draw energy from the wind currents over the ocean. In the logos, the Animal anatomy and psyche produce the Animal strategy and proprioception (what the movement feels like). For example, the Boa's empathy and breath awareness allow her to blend with her opponents as she applies chokes. And though the techniques are cool, more importantly, they are an extension of the Boa energy found in wind and open empty spaces. In the morphos, movement and breath heal the psyche and the body by drawing Animal energy from Earth. For example, Boa breathes and moves in soft graceful arcs invoking the energy of wind and ocean currents to restore feelings of empathic connection. In each example, the Animal's psyche, the techniques, the anatomy, the natural elements and the path toward wholeness represent a type of energy from our cosmic origin. And in morphos, as we draw on movement and Earth energy to heal and create a coherent narrative of our transformation through conflict, we inevitably draw on the opposite Animal energy to create something new: the Dragon.

Movement as Medicine

Walking in pain, again, she grabs my arm. "Please, can you show me an exercise to help my hip?" Her name is Mary-Anne, and she is fifty, feisty, and fit. She takes her supplements, does her cardio, does weight-bearing exercises, and practices yoga ("Because I like the philosophy," she says). And, in general, she revels in her health—all, but for her hip.

"Let me look at you walk," I request. From one corner of the room to another, she takes a teetering stride. After three passes, I see the strong feet of a dancer, well-toned legs, straight back, and even relaxed shoulders. The only problem is a frozen lower back. "OK, now stop walking and stand straight. Could you please try to flatten your lower back." She presses her hips forward. "No, No. Feel as though your tailbone is being pulled straight to the ground," I say. She tries again, this time leaning back.

"No, not quite. Imagine your back is up against a wall and is completely straight ... Tuck your bum under ... Feel your rib cage over your hips ... Imagine a string pulling you up by the top of your head, and one string on each hip pulling them down." To every instruction she shifts, curves, hunches, stiffens, all in the futile attempt to straighten her lower back.

It becomes clear what the problem is. Although she is not paralyzed and would feel a pinch on her skin, she has no kinetic awareness of her lumbar vertebrae. She isn't aware of them, does not feel them, and does not move them. This habitual laziness is causing the rotators and adductors (inner thighs) to shorten, leading the psoas and abductors to overwork, which results in pain.

Drugs are not the answer. Painkillers will dope and dull the mind, abuse the liver, and could lead to a downward spiral of needing more drugs to help other drugs control the side effects of the first drugs. Chiropractics help to correct, but the problem recurs because Mary-Anne does not know how to make the correction permanent; the same is true with her acupuncture treatment. She has an inkling that strengthening will help, so she's done leg extensions and leg presses, hoping against hope that sheer muscle force will rig the joints back in place. But she does not need legs with more strength; she needs a lower back with more proprioceptive feedback. "You're my last hope. If this doesn't work, you can take the old horse out back and shoot her!" she jokes. I tell her I liked *Animal Farm* too, and then ask her to lie down on her back.

I speak in a conversational tone, guiding her through various exercises. One set of exercises comes from Python, where I get her to lie on her back and make small circles with her pelvis, relaxing every muscle that does not need to be involved. Relaxed movement of the full range of motion redraws the brain's map for the joint, and with the full range outlined, the brain returns the joint to the middle where motion is inherently most efficient. Normal breathing produces collateral movement in other joints and tissue as they accommodate the expanding and contracting volume of the lungs. The body depends on those small but regular pulses to maintain health. Her muscles are tight from pain, stopping up that natural motility. A second set of exercises comes from Boa, where she accentuates the rise and fall of her head and arms to her breath, resetting the body's wired responses to its own breathing. Another exercise draws from Panther, using movement to organize the connective fascia tissue, the plastic goo that is shock absorber, glue, and viscous grease for muscle, bone, and organ. The movement is the medicine, and each Animal provides part of the treatment.

As we progress through small circles of movement, relaxing muscle tension, and following the breath, the changing look in her eye tells the whole story. She starts with an anxious gaze caused by the pain. As she listens to the instructions, her gaze tells how preoccupied she is. The vacant stare tells how she is applying the instructions superficially. I give her refinements and corrections. The vacancy gives way to a focused look, as though she is zooming in for a closeup. Finally, she closes her eyes, mumbles something about "surprisingly difficult," and summons every ounce of concentration. Finally, she moves her back. Two virtually frozen vertebrae now press into and lift off the floor. Tension drops from her face. When she finally does open her eyes, they are larger and seem to be taking in her surroundings more. "We won't be visiting the glue factory, then?"

Breath, Movement, and Imagery

Mythos, logos, and morphos turn a martial art into a life art, framing the reason for engaging in conflict, the means by which to resolve conflict, and a process to integrate the conflict into a coherent narrative. You embody the changes each stage brings in your breath, movement, and mental focus. As a life art, Ch'ien-lung brings a unique language of breath, movement, and imagery with which to embody the changes in these stages.

The deliberate use of imagery makes the mind and spirit more supple to change and is what makes this a metaphysical art. There are two types of visualization this book focuses on. The first is called *ideokinetics,* combining the Greek *ideo,* meaning image, idea, or thought, with the Greek *kine* for "movement," and it literally means "image of movement." I use the term *ideokinetics* to refer to the deliberate use of imagination in guiding motion. Ideokinetics can be directional, like "Imagine a string pulling your head straight," or textural, like "Move your arm like a flame." Ideokinetics cue subtle postural adjustments faster than you can alter them by deliberately articulating each joint. Ideokinetics is a powerful tool in creating consistency in the movement of an athlete or artist the same way careful use of imagery in writing creates thematic consistency in the mind of a reader.

The second type of imagery is visualization of the breath, a recurring exercise throughout the book. We tend to think of breath as simply going in and out of the lungs, but many life arts treat the breath as though it can enter and leave any part of the body. Depending on the archetype, visualizing breath can refer to using the air to influence the mechanics of movement (as with the Melon exercise in appendix C) or to a mental focus that guides revitalizing properties of oxygen to chosen areas of the body. The term *ideopneuma* is technically appropriate but awkward, so *visualized breathing* and *breath visualization* will do. *Breath visualization* is a voluntary use of imagination, which can include the Western practice of mindfulness, where the observer acts like a neutral witness to the breath. Both deliberate visualization and neutral witnessing make up the "Follow Your Breath" exercise in the Seven Steps of an Animal at the end of Chapters 2 through 8.

Visualizing breath covers a range of nuanced interpretations where it can refer to oxygenation or to more subtle energy, like *prana, ki,* or *qi,* which connote consciousness-like qualities. Similar to Eastern traditions like Chinese *neiqong* (directing energy without movement) and *qigong* (directing energy with movement) and yogic *niyamas,* Ch'ien-lung incorporates breath visualization with subtle energy. Sometimes the flow of subtle energy is subsumed with the breath, being one and the same, whereas in more advanced practices, the subtle energy is independent of the visualized breath. The energy follows circuits typically running from one source point, usually Earth, passing through an anatomical system, to an endpoint, again usually Earth. Each archetype has one basic circuit, which can be found in "Step Seven: Use the Plaques" near the end of each chapter. Start with the basic circuit, but after you gain familiarity, explore. The circuits usually start and end with Earth to provide grounding but also to nourish and affirm the Animal. The "Follow Your Breath" exercise in the Seven Steps offers additional ways to connect Earth to the Animal through breath.

An Animal's ideokinetics and breathing visualization are used across the mythos, logos, and morphos. In meditation, you can breathe through the tendons into the groin to connect to the Panther mythos, use the same breath visualization when practicing the ground kicks of the Panther logos, or breathe that way to calm the adrenalin rush from a confrontation in the Panther morphos. The outward movements and the visualization remain the same, but the impact varies with intention and context. Working with the ideokinetics in this book will help improve movement; breath visualizations will help to manage attention, inwardly and outwardly; and energy circuits are a contemplative way of affirming spiritual growth.

Constantine had a rich and unique brand of ideokinetics, visualized breath, and energy circuits, which this book shares. Readers are encouraged to select the elements that best suit their needs. My hope is that a martial artist of any type can adapt these ideokinetics, breath visualizations, and energy circuits to their own style; that dancers find inspiration and interpretative depth in this language of imagery; that athletes find the imagery and archetypes useful in their training and performance; and that from this use of imagery, yogis or others on a spiritual path can incorporate a growing vocabulary of tones in the mind-body connection.

Tales of the Dragon

Ch'ien-lung made its way from China to the borough of Queens in New York, where my teacher, Constantine Darling, learned it. Knowing some of his story can help us grasp principles running through Ch'ien-lung. Constantine was an incredibly dynamic person. He was, in his own words, a New York Jew from Queens who, as a child, wanted to take dance lessons, and "with a name like Connie Darling," walking to and from dance classes carrying ballet shoes, he had to fight every day. One day, he got home bloodied from a fight and went crying to his father about it. His father kicked him out of the house and told him not to return until he "had the blood of the kid" who did that to him on his fists, which is what Connie did. It was an event that marked his interest in martial arts, but it also marked an uneasy compact with what he called his Beast.

Connie learned a variety of styles—Jujitsu, Kajukenbo, Shorinji Kempo, and other Japanese and Chinese arts. In those days, it was not uncommon for traditionalist teachers to teach the nuances of the art only to students of the same race, leaving others to fend for themselves. Constantine was a kinesthetic genius, a Mozart of movement, and he learned to grasp the inner mechanics of the moves he observed. He often talked of "stealing technique," of being able to reverse-engineer the kinematics. The moment a senior student demonstrated a new skill or nuance, Connie "empathed it," and it was his. By the end of a year, he often ended up better than many of the senior students of the school.

For Constantine, intention was everything in martial arts. Early on in his journey, he had a conversation with a Chinese medical doctor that he recounted often; it was about *pressure points,* areas on the body that, when struck, cause pain or paralysis. Constantine pointed to a spot that could be used to damage the liver, and the doctor smiled and said it was also a point used to heal the kidneys; Constantine then pointed to the spot used to damage the kidneys, and the doctor replied with a smile that it was also used to heal the lungs; Constantine touched one point he knew was used to damage the stomach, and the doctor laughed saying that it was also used to relieve cramps. Every point that Constantine used to hurt, the doctor used to heal. The difference between life-giving and taking was not in the location of the strike but in the intention and in the energy. For a naturally kind-hearted person such as Constantine who, when pressed, could loose his Beast to terrible effect, it was a profound insight—the very means he used to inflict damage could also be used to heal. That insight permeates the whole art.

Mystical and near-death experiences came early and often to Constantine. When he was eight, he fell from a third-story balcony, witnessing himself fall as if on three split screens. In the first, he watched as the ground came toward him; in the second, he watched himself falling, as if from a distance; on the third, he watched how he would roll out of the fall and run back up to his grandmother, who had startled him when she called his name, causing him to fall in the first place. He had numerous close calls, including flying through the windshield in a head-on truck collision. He had shared out-of-body experiences; transmitted and received telepathic images under controlled conditions; studied the Kabbalah with his grandfather; and played awareness games in the nursery of the Gurdjieff group where his mother studied. These experiences and others like them raised questions for him about the limits of consciousness. The Animal meditations were meant to explore the limits and ground the abilities these experiences suggested.

The galvanizing event of his life, defining the individualistic and humanitarian values he taught, was being drafted as a conscientious objector into the Vietnam War. He went to boot camp and said he "actually enjoyed the training," and even appreciated "learning how to shoot," but at some point, he made it clear that if ordered to use his weapon to harm someone who had not personally harmed him, he would refuse.[5]

His superiors tried to wear him down, but Constantine discovered another trait that was a hallmark of his life: his humor. When his superiors barked "Darling!" he replied, "Yes, Dear?" He had the rest of his company in stitches at first, until they were all punished for his impudence; then they turned against him. Finally, one night, three superior officers took matters into their own hands; they took him behind the barracks and started to "work [him] over pretty hard." At first he didn't resist—Gandhi was one of his heroes—"but then [his] Beast turned on." By the end of it, he put all three officers in the hospital. He was arrested, court-martialed, and sentenced to twenty years in the brig. By chance, the only remaining friend he had on base turned out to be the driver who was assigned to transport him to the military prison. As Connie tells it, his friend's face was inscrutable so that Connie thought that even this friend had turned against him. But at the last possible exit before the prison base, his friend drove the truck into a ditch, unlocked Connie from the hold, and told him to get out of the truck and get out of the States.

First in Montreal, then in Victoria, Connie started dance troupes, founding *Les Ballet Jazz de Montreal,* and taught martial art classes. He was an impresario who, at the height of his career, presented such world-renowned groups as Alvin Ailey, the Kirov Ballet, Mikhail Baryshnikov, and his White Oak Dance Project—all in the small town of Victoria, British Columbia.

What drew many of us to his classes was Constantine the magus. The second day I met him, he reminded a young lady of a dream *she* had the night before. On a camping trip, a friend, Sandra, had a dream wherein she vividly recalled Constantine saying a certain phrase directly to her. The next morning, by a river, she looked up to see Constantine, who looked her straight in the eyes and repeated the exact same phrase from the dream. Sometimes he shifted in appearance right before our eyes. One night, he was starting a class series for street fighting. In those days, he taught his dance and martial art classes back to back. He ended the dance class, turned, spoke to the person at the reception desk, and then turned around to teach the martial arts class—and he was a shorter, stockier, more muscularly compact version of himself. Several of us confirmed our perceptions with each other after the class. It was as if he had morphed into a street-fighter version of himself to teach the street-fighting class. There were many other such instances among those of us who spent time with him.

Our training with him was so diverse that it would be hard to call it exclusively martial arts. Our workouts seemed ahead of their time. Since the '90s, I have watched fitness trends rapidly overtake—eccentric contractions, Pilates, fitness balls, Tae Bo, kettlebells, interval training, bodyweight calisthenics, every shade of yoga—and I have thought, "We used to do that with Connie." Our classes delved into areas of mysticism, chanting, and meditation; role playing, dream interpretation, and dancing. The two most frequently used words in our studio were *energy* and *attention*. Our classes were permeated with symbolism. A spinning kick was not just a kick—it reflected the cosmic spirals of the universe; a kick to the groin was to uproot an opponent's instinctive connection to Earth; a low stance was a way to connect to the core of Earth. Moving the body was just a way to pray.

Why our workouts included everything from Feldenkrais to sparring on obstacle courses was because the man who could shift between the Beast, the magus, the dancer, the impresario, and the mystic had stuffed this martial art with every aspect of himself. He turned his martial art into a kind of alchemical notation, a sort of periodic chart of personal transformation. He loved to shift—it was his joy—and he used the martial art to describe how he shifted between each embodiment. Breath, energy, and quality of attention were the key ingredients in his embodied practice; and the Animals were a shorthand description of how he combined various elements to shift and a map for what he was shifting to and from.

Constantine was an incredible person who was also incredibly flawed. Many of his students can attest to his larger-than-life compassion, which was always psychologically informed and socially progressive; his shamanic-like abilities, matched by his genius in choreography, zest in movies, and good food; and his insatiable curiosity. But he also was culpable in defrauding people financially and sleeping with and entering into romantic relationships with his underage students. At the time, this smacked more of scandal than crime, and it was not until ten years later, when I began studies in psychology, that I grasped the full extent of the abuse and damage his behavior had wrought. I did not speak up at the time because the simple truth is that I desperately needed someone like him. He took me under wing and protected me, and in this art, gave me the gift of a life I love. He likely saved me from suicide. But his behavior was also the corrosive force that eventually repelled me and led to the prolonged disintegration of our school. It was one of the most painful periods in my life, in which the things I loved and needed were destroyed by things I did not yet understand and that disgusted me.

In the aftermath, we parted ways; he embarked on a journey where he reflected on his behavior, and he came to repent and make amends. He apologized to me and to any who would receive his amends, and he was forgiven by many. In July of 2011, he perished from the throat cancer for which he refused treatment. According to the code he lived and died by, the cancer was a manifestation of his own guilt for misusing his voice to persuade and manipulate people, as well as the guilt he felt for failing his daughters as a parent. "This is the gift life is presenting me with, I'm not going to resist it," he answered several times when asked why he would not seek treatment. He did change his behaviors, but he left behind a trail of broken hearts and broken triangles. He was larger than life, stuffed as he was with every vice and virtue. If he were alive today, he would, as I had seen so many times when he was alive, open himself to legitimate grievances against his behavior, reflect upon them, learn from them, alter course, and then wish for us to learn from his mistakes. And he would have used the Animals to help us understand those lessons.

He loved this art of mutability; it was his laboratory wherein he interconnected ideas from science, social relations, and spirituality. The principles of cell heritability underpinned the recurring patterns of romantic relationships; the principles of good societal governance reflected the principles of mental self-care; the principles of dream interpretation applied to interpreting art and mass media. "As above, so below" was a common refrain, and though a little axiomatic, the end goal was always to take the study of these life principles and embody them. He wove his ideas and his personal growth into his dance choreographies and into his martial arts. The Animal metaphors were a way to annotate and transpose principles among science, art, and self-knowledge. It was an embodied metaphysical study, and he challenged his students to do the same, to discover all the parts of their own makeup and embody them at will with skill.

2 THE ANIMALS

Vocatus Atque Non Vocatus, Deus Aderit
Bidden or Unbidden, the Gods are Present
—QUOTE ABOVE CARL JUNG'S DOOR AT BOLLINGEN

We get in trouble when we are out of balance. Athletes and artists eat, sleep, and breathe their art or sport to make it to the Olympics or Carnegie Hall, but they also need to find the fun that makes their training sustainable and their performance transcendent. A religious leader needs to stay connected to earthly pleasures, or else he loses the very empathy he is trying to pass on. The businesswoman must remember to be charitable, the teacher must remember to learn, and a leader must remember to serve. Ch'ien-lung is a language of balancing opposites, spoken in breath, imagery, and movement, using archetypes.

The Animals of Ch'ien-Lung

In the mythos of Ch'ien-lung, the energies that created the cosmos also shaped the planet and organized the mind, as though the psyche were a microcosm of the planet and the universe. Table 2.1 features the archetypes and the facets of the psyche they each represent.

TABLE 2.1: The Animal Archetypes and Their Consciousness

Tiger	Intention; desire and linear will
Black Panther	Instinct, sensuality, and the subconscious
White Leopard	Intuition, abstract thought, and creativity
Cobra	Psychic and transcendent perception
Boa	Empathy and the unconscious
Python	Studied observation and manipulation; the connections between the unconscious, subconscious, and conscious mind

Whether or not you practice Ch'ien-lung, you engage these facets of the psyche. At work, you exercise willpower to set and attain objectives (Tiger); on a date, you celebrate sensuality and your instinct performs myriad social calculations (Black Panther); in doing research, you manipulate conditions and observe results until a pattern or hypothesis emerges that you are compelled to test (Python). These shifts between the facets of the psyche happen automatically; it is how we are designed. The Animals are not required for that. But the Animals do make it easier to notice the shifts because of the added distance they provide, and they make it easier to embody the shifts because of the license they give. They help you to deliberately shift mental states when you can and follow the shift when you must, in body, heart, and mind. The Animals express their energies in recurring patterns and motifs across a wide variety of domains:

- Anatomy
- Brain
- Personality development and preferences
- Quality of movement and breath
- Natural environments
- Sexuality
- Artistic themes
- Spiritual practices and energetic qualities

Each Animal has a theme for these categories, which makes up the mythos of the Animal, and which each subsequent chapter covers in detail. The Animal mythoses are rich and complex, just like the real world, so they make great shoes for any path you take. Any new idea, sensation, or cultural practice you encounter will have a place to hang its hat and will help cultivate the archetype in you. The Animal mythoses bridge art and science, East and West, and map the mind-body connection. The next section explains the guidelines for applying this embodied art that you can adapt to suit your needs using the Seven Steps listed at the end of chapters 2 through 8. Where do you start? Right where you are now.

The Game Board

Every person possesses each of the Animal psyches and has usually developed one or two of them, at least in part. You begin with the Animal you naturally are. How do you know which one that is? By reading the descriptions in this book, using the Animal Inventory Questionnaire on our website, and watching videos of the forms online.[1] The one you most resonate with is your starting point.

In Ch'ien-lung, the practice begins with articulating the Animal you most resonate with. You learn to completely articulate one Animal first, and then you move onto its opposite, developing each facet to an equal level of depth. A natural momentum will develop, catalyzed by external circumstances, and the archetypes will begin to integrate, forming the Dragon. A Dragon is the combination of a Cat and a Snake. I can still recall the first time I heard Constantine introduce this system:

> *The Cats represent masculine aspects and the Snakes represent feminine aspects. When a Cat and a Snake marry, they create the Dragon, which is an enthusiastic "YES!" to all aspects of life.*

When you have selected your Animal, familiarize yourself with its mythos. Learn about the archetype's anatomy, brain region, consciousness, and nature power spots. In its mythos, each Animal has a personality type with favorite music, food, movies, books, art, and physical, spiritual, or energetic practice. To develop the Animal within, you adopt its preferences as you would the character of a play. You walk the way it walks, talk the way it talks, eat the foods it likes to eat, and do the things it likes to do.

For example, if you want to develop Tiger, you would listen to the music of a military parade, eat steak and potatoes, and work out in a gym doing power lifts for your legs, glutes, and chest. If you want to develop Panther, you would eat red, red meat and chocolate cheesecake, preferably at the same time, listen to Afro-Cuban drumming, and run obstacle courses through a forest, preferably by sense of smell alone.

Here is where mythos turns to logos, where the expression and motifs of the Animal begin to be embodied. As you immerse yourself in the Animal, allow the expression of the Animal character to inform the ideokinetics and breath visualization of your movement. For example, part of the Python mythos is its ability to juggle, mentally and literally. In your exploration, you experiment with juggling. After some practice with a little gain, you recognize a loose dexterity in your arms. The looseness becomes an ideokinetic cue to incorporate in your embodiment of Python at other times. For example, in sparring, juggle the feint of a kick with the fake of a punch to land the strike. If basketball is your thing, keep your arms loose as if you are juggling while you dribble and dodge opponents on the basketball court. But even walking with your arms loose as though juggling while simply going for a stroll is embodying Python. Or perhaps, you notice a calm, open focus when you juggle. You can visualize your breath going to the areas in your brain where you feel that calm openness as though breathing into it will spread the calm sensation throughout your whole brain. With Python, you monitor your senses like a neutral observer, as if from the center of where all the senses converge, a technique you may find refreshes your meditation. Each Animal chapter is packed with examples of how to express the Animal with internalized kinesthetic cues.

As you become familiar with an Animal, you will recognize that several points must be satisfied in order for the Animal to be complete. We possess the potential for each of the Animals, but very often, a person develops only one or two of the Animals, and often only in part. For example, a person may have a strong Tiger physique but still needs to develop Tiger's linear focus; another person has a strong Tiger focus but a weak physique; a third has an open, loving Tiger heart but does not have physical strength or focus. The goal is to make your inner Tiger whole and strong.

What makes Ch'ien-lung fun are the *crossover points*. Each Animal has a physical and energetic connection to another Animal. Constantine called them "entry points," which carried other connotations with it, so I have settled on crossover; he was forever challenging us to discover these points on our own. While watching a documentary or reading a book, we would happen on an interesting candidate for a crossover and approach him. He would give us his thumbs up or down, always providing a coherent rationale that often captured our still-unformed thoughts on the matter. Thinking about what the crossover points could be was a riddle it would take us years to answer, but it made us self-sufficient in understanding the Animals. The crossover points are important because they grease the wheels when you are shifting from one archetype to another. When ideokinetics and breath visualization involve a crossover point for one Animal, it primes the other Animal sharing the crossover. This requires quality time spent with the breath visualization and ideokinetics of both Animals, but with practice, the crossover points turn the archetypes of Ch'ien-lung into a metaphysical system.

There is also a push-pull tension between the archetypes that gives the system energy. For example, if you engage Tiger's willfulness, then you drive Boa's yielding underground. Engage Leopard's abstract reasoning, and you suppress Panther's subconscious. Often, a person is authentically one Animal but uses another as a defense mechanism or coping strategy. A person who is authentically a soft, sensitive Boa uses the hard outer shell of Tiger for protection; a courageous, disciplined Tiger uses the hedonistic Panther to let go and luxuriate. Exercising one pushes the others to recede, and if you go to an extreme (as I have done often), the others push back. Fortunately, if engaging one Animal pushes the others away, the crossover points act to keep them together.

The Animals are complex, but the practice is simple: return to breath, movement, and imagery. With time, the motifs, personality, and expressions of the Animals along with the ideokinetics and visualized breath will inform each other, and you will begin to *articulate* the Animal. A fuller explanation of articulation is provided in chapter 9, "Becoming Dragon," under the subheading "Purifying," but for now, articulating an Animal means to *breathe, feel,* and *move* your body the way the Animal does, to focus *on the objects in the world* the Animal focuses on, and to focus on them *in the cognitive style* of the Animal. When you can do these at the same time from one situation to another, you can be said to articulate an Animal.

To help you embody the archetypes in your own life, this book details *Seven Steps.* Along with embodiment exercises, the Seven Steps include the *bows,* the *plaques,* and the *keys.* The *bows* are short movement sequences, timed to the breath. During the bows, you visualize breath and energy drawn from Earth and directed into the anatomical and brain areas of the Animal. The bows include a subset of practices Constantine called *keys. Keys* are a set of finger, hand, eye, tongue, and seated positions for the Animal. The bow and keys are featured at the end of each Animal chapter. The *plaques* are simple, colored, geometric shapes symbolizing the metaphysical quality of the Animal. There is a brief instruction on how to focus on the plaque for an archetype at the end of each Animal chapter, and a full set of instructions on the accompanying breath pattern called the plaque work appears in appendix A. Along with the other exercises in the Seven Steps, the bows, keys, and plaques will build strong associations between the anatomical, energetic, psychological qualities, and crossover points of the archetype. Using the Seven Steps, you will begin to make of the archetypes a life art.

How to Train Your Dragons

There are numerous possible Cat-Snake pairings. In some pairings, the Cat and Snake share some affinities in common, while in other pairings they are diametric poles. The practice in Ch'ien-lung emphasizes the Dragons formed by the diametrically opposite Animals. Table 2.2 shows these pairings and the respective Dragons they create.

TABLE 2.2: Animal Pairings

CATS	SNAKES	DRAGONS
White Leopard (Creativity)	Cobra (Psychic Ability)	Celestial Dragon
Tiger (Will)	Boa (Empathy)	Earth Dragon
Black Panther (Instinct)	Python (Manipulation/ Skill)	Sub-Earth Dragon

What do Dragons do? The Dragon burns away limiting habits, fears, and old beliefs to instigate growth in others. The last chapter, "Becoming Dragon," introduces principles of developing the Dragon. But the first step toward the Dragon is *to be aware of the transition between Animals.* Being mindful of the transition from one Animal to the next prepares the ground for the integration of opposites into the Dragons.

The Practice: All You Need Is Bows

The wind is sweeping white caps toward the curving, wide, sandy shores of the giant aquatic food bowl that is Monterey Bay, California. In this ideal setting, we do the Boa bow. "Inhale and let your in-breath curl your spine up for you," the instructor says. "Breathe in through every pore of your body ... feel like you are hugging the entire Bay ... feel your empathy touching all shores of the Bay at once ... feel as though you can extend your empathy to hug the ocean floor.... Feel the deep unconscious the ocean represents ... the sea and blood have the same salinity; feel this connect the unconscious and feminine aspects of the ocean with your own ... soften ... exhale ... hold the mudra ... keep a soft, unfocused gaze." With that, the students gradually open their eyes. Their focus and bodies have softened, as though they have been given a full-body massage.

Each Animal has a *bow,* a signature movement synchronized to breath, which is the stylized expression of the Animal. If all you know are the bows, you can practice Ch'ien-lung.

The bows are embodiments of the archetypes. The bows combine the visualized breath, energy, anatomy, and psyche of the Animal. In the bows, your embodiment of the Animals has a chance to set; they are like pushups for personal transformation. For example, in the Black Panther bow, you visualize sending breath into the groin, coccyx, and brainstem; at the same time, you visualize energy going into the centers located at those respective points—*svadhisthana,* the procreative center at the groin; *muladhara,* the energetic ground wire at the tailbone; and the *Jade Pillow,* the "storehouse of instincts" at the brainstem. When the ideokinetics and the visualized breathing and energy circuits are combined in the bow along with your expression of the instinct and sensuality, you begin to embody the Panther. Each chapter details the rich repertoire of imagery for the Animal bows.

The bows are meant to be practiced in nature. For those of us who practiced Ch'ien-lung, some of our fondest memories are of doing the bows together in the wilds. Whether in the rain forests of British Columbia, on the sandy beaches of Northern California, or in the sage-drenched air on the dusty floor of the Grand Canyon, Constantine would gather us in a circle to talk, and he had a gift in evoking in anyone who listened a feeling that Earth was a living, intelligent organism. "Why would I be given a body if I was not meant to enjoy feeling everything the planet offers? In cultures that shame the body, heaven is up and out of reach, but in cultures that have a healthy relationship to the body, heaven is on or under Earth," and "We drill for oil, we dump pollution in the ocean, but she keeps giving us the best she can ... She's like us, she goes through her own emotions, but the planet provides the same sustenance and support for all forms of life, no matter who you are," and "she not only gives us food but also takes our waste. Earth takes our emotional waste and recycles it as compost, giving us energy" to restore balance to our interpersonal relationships. Through bows, Constantine taught us his unique connection to Earth and to make our own connection.

Ch'ien-lung is intertwined with nature, where Earth is an intelligent partner in the bows. When doing the bows, we breathe and draw energy from Earth as an organism with a psyche parallel to our own, but of course on a scale far exceeding our own, where we connect our Animal psyche to the equivalent of Earth's.[2] Earth possesses empathy and an unconscious that you can draw on for your Boa; Earth has emotions that can help counsel your Tiger heart; Earth has dreams like Panther, psychic impulses like Cobra, and like White Leopard, draws intuition from the cosmos and protects us from harm with the auric layers of her magnetic field. It is a metaphysical and mystical view of human consciousness as a microcosm of planetary sentience embodied and celebrated in the bows.

It was a conversation that also extended to masculinity and the femininity of the Animals. The earth fosters and transcends both.[3] Ch'ien-lung looks to nature to model examples of masculinity and femininity, how to play with them, and how to transcend them. When you do Tiger bows standing on sheer cliffs overseeing verdant plains as lightning bolts crash in the distance, you express Tiger's masculine sense of dominion and power; when you do the Boa bow on the beaches of Monterey Bay, you connect to the life-giving spirit of the feminine; and when you do the bows on top of the Jackson Hole in Wyoming, when winds blow the muscle right off your bone, you know White Leopard's cosmic indifference to trite labels.

This is a time when people are finding a new balance of power between men and women and between humans and Earth. The violence committed against the planet and the violence committed against women comes from the same source, what Constantine called *separation.* Call it narcissism, psychopathy, sociopathy, immaturity, Western patriarchy, or environmental alienation, it is a quiet rage of separation that divorces feeling from thinking. Separation inverts the power between body and mind where the body is made to serve the mind when it is the job of the mind to serve the body, causing us to act against our own best interests. It is in separation where we solve problems of We with Me, of Us with Them, and of Ours with It. When we see ourselves as separate from the environment, we fail to recognize how people and ecology mutually influence each other. Ch'ien-lung provides a poetry in breath, movement, and symbolic imagery to mend our connection to the masculine, the feminine, and Earth so that a cathedral of trees and a forest of people inspire the same awe and love.

The bows are also performed with the intention of giving a gift to Earth. It is difficult to convey to someone who has not experienced something similar to this, but doing the bows in nature while holding the intention of expressing gratitude to Earth elicits a unique sense of connection and communion. It was done by doing the bows while invoking the energy of an entirely different place, like doing Boa bows at the bottom of the Canyon while evoking the energy of the beaches in Santa Cruz, giving the desert floor the gift of the ocean.

The keys are a set of practices that, for each Animal, include a specific eye, finger, tongue, and seated position. These will be familiar to people who practice yoga as *mudras, bandhas,* and *asanas,* and they are also found in other Eastern arts. In Ch'ien-lung, they are used in seated meditation and plaque work. We called them *keys* because, over time, the association to the Animal becomes so strong that doing the practice—say, making the finger shape—kicks the Animal psyche into gear the same way a key turning the ignition starts a car. More discrete than the bows, keys can be used during the day to reaffirm the archetypes and are an excellent form of embodied practice.

The Blind Shall See

Blind work forms an important part of Ch'ien-lung. We often trained doing forms, sparring, or moving like the Animals out in nature with our eyes closed. In the pristine evergreen forests north of Victoria, British Columbia, we started by doing the Animal bows as a warm-up. Then, after a few games involving sticks or hacky sacks, we started along a trail in pairs. One person led with open eyes, walking ahead about ten feet, snapping their fingers intermittently to provide direction to their blind partner. Once in a while, the leader issued a verbal command to stop or course correct, but on the whole, the blind walkers were left to make their way, reaching out ahead with their senses.

At first, people were tentative, but they gained confidence with surprising rapidity and sometimes with dramatic results. A student would start off by probing the ground with their feet, as though walking on thin ice. They would reach out in front of themselves with hands to guard against bumping into a rock or a tree. The first hundred yards were travelled slowly in this fashion, but it did not take long for confidence to build and the pace to pick up. Soon, they found themselves going almost at their regular walking speed. Constantine would challenge us to push further. Arriving at a fallen tree over a ditch, he would direct us to traverse it blind; or if we came to a small three-foot bluff or a tall stump, he would guide us to the top and then tap the ground where we were to land, with eyes closed, and without signing waivers.

From experience, keeping the eyes closed makes anticipating the jump worse than the jump itself, and the jolt from the landing seems to come earlier than expected. But very quickly, the legs take on the right amount of tension to absorb the landing, and the body takes on the mid-air neutral posture for absorbing the shock. Soon, people jumped with prowess and landed with grace.

After a walk of a mile in this fashion, and continuing on after switching roles, we would return to playing games. We would spar, blind or eyes open, making very light contact. It was not sparring with the goal of getting a shot in or scoring a point. It was sparring done with the quality of providing a service to the partner, of showing the blind spots or openings that were easier to discern because of the heightened awareness and easier to correct because blind work has a way of stimulating kinesthetic intelligence.

In one class, a student named Jason and I were blind sparring in the Black Panther and White Leopard styles, respectively. We squared off, and closed our eyes. We exchanged minor jabs and blocks. Then something out of a movie happened. With our eyes still closed, Jason dropped low to the ground doing a Panther backward sweep, a technique that essentially turned his leg into a helicopter propeller to knock my feet right out from under me. Though blind, I sensed something and leapt forward over the sweep, into a Leopard flying side-thrust. Jason, realizing he missed his mark and sensing a looming figure over him, tucked and rolled in Panther right under me as I flew over him in the opposite direction. He came up from his roll, and I stuck the landing as silently as I could. Both of us turned and faced each other square-on, arms at the ready—all with our eyes closed. The student who was watching burst into shouts, which prompted us to stop and then listen in surprise as he recounted what had happened.

Blind work invariably frees people up. Our sparring, for example, became fluid, more like a conversation than a clash, more dance than fight, which was the spirit with which Constantine taught the art. The effects would carry over into the evening when we would end up at a crowded pub for dinner. Little things would happen: one person on the way to the bathroom seamlessly weaved through the throngs on the crowded floor; another person caught a pen as it rolled off a table only to look at it after he caught it; another let a peanut slip from his hand as he was popping it into his mouth and then snatched it mid-air before it reached his waist. These small acts of preternatural dexterity marked our progress.

Blind training in nature is a regular and important part of our practice in Ch'ien-lung. It breaks a reliance on vision and forces the other senses to work, a shift in gears that is otherwise out of conscious control. But developing feral senses, while exhilarating, is not an end unto itself. Blind works strops perception, but it also changes our relationship to perception, and the change in relationship is occasionally tied to our associations about gender. To listen for the forest path, a go-getting masculine Tiger has to find his quiet, more patient, feminine Boa side. An introverted Boa closes her eyes to the overstimulating world to find that when she is not distracted by it, she can respond to it with the feline grace of her more masculine Panther nature. Blind work immerses you where the imagery of nature and the archetypes and their gender meet within your psyche. Blind work is not one of the Seven Steps per se, but it can be incorporated into the practice of the bows with the exercises at the end of the Cobra chapter (chapter 8).

The Plaques

The Animals are each represented by a *plaque,* a geometric symbol of the Animal used as a tool for internal work. Each plaque is composed of a triangle, circumscribed by a circle, inside of a square (see Figure 2.1). The square is always white, whereas the triangle and circle differ in color for each Animal. The triangle represents the person, the circle represents Earth and the world from the perspective of the Animal, and the square stands for universal laws, like those of time, space, energy, and karma or causality.

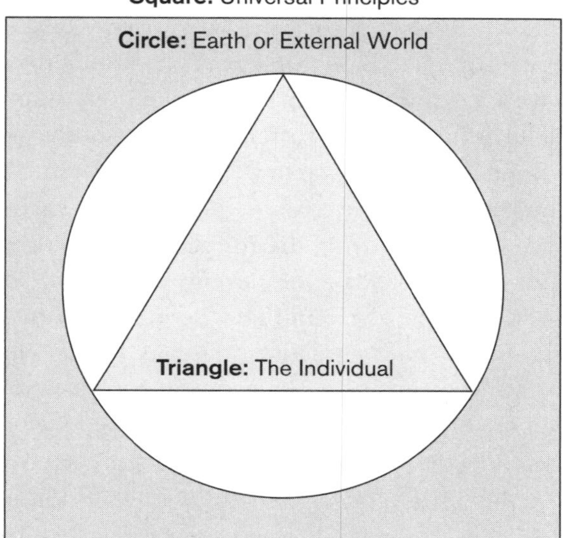

FIGURE 2.1: Each Animal is represented by a triangle, circle, and square. The square is always white, but the circle and triangle change color. Contemplating the meaning of the shapes and colors for an Animal develops its mindset.

The plaques are important for two reasons. First, the plaques are like a good bean dip—they're layered, where each layer represents one of the physical, psychological, and energetic expressions of the Animal. For example, at the first level, the three points of the Tiger triangle represent the mythos of his physical expression, the heart, the muscles, and the forehead; at the second level, the triangle represents his psychological expression through desire, intention, and action; and at the third level, the triangle points represent his energy centers at the belly (*manipura*), the heart (*anahata*), and the frontal lobe. The plaques organize the key expressions of the Animals and the crossover points among them, like a sort of metaphysical street map.

Second, the plaques are used in internal work to embody the Animal. The plaque work incorporates visualized breath and energy circuits, as well as practices of *concentration, meditation,* and *contemplation,* which have specific meanings in Ch'ien-lung, as taught by Constantine, and are detailed in chapter 9. Most of the time when people talk about meditation, what they really mean is *concentration.* So, I will use the generic term *meditation* in the plaque work making specific references as needed.

In the plaque work, you concentrate on the perimeters of the shapes while, at the same time, breathing in a rhythmic pattern. The eye movements and the breathing pattern are the same for each Animal and are performed while embodying the Animal. Embodying an Animal in a contemplative practice adds an important element of *tone* to meditation work. In meditation, the mind may be quiet, but it still has tone. *Tone* is a perpetual renewal of active presence. Just as embodying the Animal imbues movement with character, so too does embodying an Animal imbue meditation with a tone. The instructions on how to use the plaques are detailed in appendix A, whereas "Step Seven: Use the Plaques" at the end of chapters describes the tone for the Animal.

The Seven Steps

The following chapters will help you use the Animals as a life art. Each chapter starts with one of Constantine's allegories of an Animal. From there, each chapter details the motifs, expressions, and patterns of the archetype's mythos and explains how to embody the mythos through ideokinetics and visualized breathing. The chapters outline how each Animal archetype matures as a personality (therefore, how it matures within you) to become ready to integrate with its opposite to form the Dragon. The chapters spend a little time talking about how the Animals approach sex and how to recognize their themes in art, particularly movies. Each chapter includes instructions on the bows and brief directions in embodying tone with the plaques.

All this information comes together in the Seven Steps at the end of each chapter. These were exercises Constantine assigned us and that I have practiced for the better part of my life. They do not need to be done together. Rather, you can rotate through them, doing a few one week, and then switching to others the week after. The Seven Steps incorporate the bows, the plaques, and the keys, along with ongoing mindful practices for each archetype. They are a beginner's first step, requiring no martial art or fitness experience. You can choose to do as much or as little of any combination of the Seven Steps listed here.

Step One: Follow Your Breath (Ongoing Mindfulness Practice) The practice of Ch'ien-lung begins and returns with the breath. Following the breath incorporates both directed breath visualization and neutral breath witnessing. Following your breath means you notice which areas of the body carry tension as you breathe, and the tempo, depth, and the mood or attitude of your breath. For example, if you were a character from a movie or book, and that character was breathing the way you are now, what would that say about the character? How would the Animal you are practicing breathe at this moment?

Python breath, for example, follows the marrow of the bones. To embody Python, actively visualize energy circulating in and out of your bone marrow as you inhale and exhale, and at other times, passively witness your breath while feeling its connection to the marrow. You can set aside dedicated time to follow the breath of an Animal, but it falls in the category of an *ongoing practice,* one that you do throughout the day.

Step Two: Recall Your Day (Daily/10 Minutes before Sleep) Constantine assigned this exercise early on in our practice. Review the day from the perspective of the Animal to gain insight into the Animals and how to embody them more fully. This is done at the end of the day prior to bed to prepare for dreams the same way a host tidies the house prior to guests arriving. For example, Panther will review the day for the sensual pleasures, while Tiger will recall the day in terms of goals, obstacles, and progress.

Step Three: Scan Your Body (Daily/10 Minutes before and after Sleep) Scanning your body should follow the review of your day and bookend your sleep. Visualize an area of the body in your mind's eye while feeling the body area at the same time. For example, with Cobra, before falling asleep and upon waking, take a few minutes to visualize and feel the nerves of the body, starting at the feet and working your way to the top of the head. You can do this for one or all the Animals.

As this is a book on an embodied art, each chapter provides information about the anatomy relevant to the archetype, but such information is rudimentary, and with great enthusiasm I encourage you to seek additional sources on anatomy.

Step Four: Do the Bows in Nature (Weekly/10–15 Minutes) Again, if all you know are the bows, you can practice Ch'ien-lung. The Animals resonate with different elements and expressions of nature. So, the bows are done in nature for inspiration, of course, but also for the abundance of natural elements that are drawn as if magnetized into the body and the Animal energy circuit. Each bow is a signature movement of arms and legs, timed to breathing, and explained at the end of each of the Animal chapters.

Step Five: Adopt the Animal Personality (Ongoing Practice) The best way to learn the Animals is to roleplay them. Eat, drink, dress, and play the way the Animal would. Makeup is optional, but highly recommended.

Step Six: Remember Your Dreams (Daily/10 Minutes upon Waking) Bringing an archetypal world to life means building a bridge to the realm of the unconscious where they reside. Recalling dreams is an excellent way of building the bridge. Constantine regularly interpreted dreams, drawing on various methods. A thorough explanation of dream interpretation techniques is beyond the scope of this book, but a general description of how each archetype approaches dream interpretation is provided.

Step Seven: Use the Plaques (Daily/20 Minutes) The plaque involves a pattern of focused eye movements in synchrony with the breathing that the Animals share. The instructions for the plaque work are detailed in appendix A, with a brief description of the tone at the end of each Animal chapter.

3

BOA: THE DEPTHS OF THE UNCONSCIOUS

In one drop of water are found all the secrets of all the oceans.

—KAHLIL GIBRAN

THE BOA WAITS DRAPED on the branches of a tree overhanging a forest path, in complete trust that Life will provide. An animal full of vitality passes unaware below her, rousing her, for she is only drawn to that which has the most energy. She drops down upon her prey. It struggles, striking, clawing, and slashing, but like quicksand, every move entangles it further into Boa. She ensnares and begins to constrict, stealing the breath from her prey. She consumes its breath and energy, then the physical body to be complete with the laws of nature, letting pass what she cannot digest.

Boa Consciousness: Empathy, Collective Unconscious, Breath

Boa is the meditative quiet, the void you find at the bottom of the collective unconscious. Boa is deeply connected to everything through empathy, and for her, space is an intelligent thing, possessing memory; for Boa, space is a dynamic medium acting as a container and conductor of sentience. You experience Boa during moments when you feel your breath as the intimate link to the cosmos and all that was, is, and will be; you're in Boa when you experience the cycle of your breath as one instance of the universal law that all things come to pass in cycles ... within cycles. You are in Boa when you directly feel the emotions, attention, and energy of people, plants, or animals. Empathy and breath make the Boa a sponge for feelings that flow and pass through without judgment. It is peace, but the peace of a vacuum in deep space, the total quiet that elicits truth from deep within you, the kind of silence harrowing to someone who is uncomfortable when left alone with their own thoughts. The Boa experience is to feel pregnant with all of life without compunction to do anything with it. For Boa, all life, animate and inanimate, is sentient, awash in its own awareness, and united by the need for breath.

Boa Anatomy: Lungs, Lymph, and Skin

In the mythos of Boa, the respiratory and circulatory system reflect the importance of the breath as a connection to all things. With Boa, everything breathes: we breathe, plants breathe, and forests breathe. The seasonal change in daylight means the Amazon forest produces more oxygen during the long summer days and more carbon dioxide during the long winter evenings, essentially causing the planet to breathe.[1] Not only are we bound to the entire biological kingdom by the function of breath, but by the atoms that make it up—each breath you take carries one atom from Julius Caesar's last breath.[2]

The diaphragm relaxes with every exhale, driving the relaxation of the whole body. Relaxing unnecessary tension is important to Boa mind and movement. Billowed by the diaphragm, the exchange between oxygen and carbon dioxide occurs at the soft round sacs of the alveoli. The surface area of alveoli sacs covers the equivalent of a three-car garage.[3] Here, carbon dioxide, stress, and fear are traded for oxygen, relief, and freedom. Boa breathes not just to oxygenate, but to let go. An often neglected but equally important organ of Boa respiration is the skin, the body's largest organ. Our bodies are more like porous sponges than vacuum-sealed gourds. If you placed some garlic on the skin of your foot, you would taste it in your mouth five minutes later.[4] Boa visualizes breath to any part of the skin, especially the tiny arcade-shaped capillaries in the subcutaneous layers.

Her capacity for empathy can be so powerful that Boa can be overwhelmed by feelings. Boa lets experiences flow through her and then lets go of what she cannot digest. Hence, Boa represents the digestive system as well as the lymphatic system, which cleans up your body's metabolic waste. The lymphatic system does not have an active pump of its own like the heart. Passive, it relies on voluntary muscle contractions to pump lymph through channels, delivering commandos of white blood cells to fight infection and illness. To embody Boa, follow your breath moving through the skin, lymph, lungs, digestive, and circulatory systems, associating them with empathy and the unconscious. In the ideokinetics of Boa, move as though you are guided by empathy and the unconscious as breath passes through skin, lungs, and lymph, as though the movement originated from the digestive system, sightless but guided, with deep spiral contractions of the core. Additional visualized breathing exercises are provided in Seven Steps at the end of this chapter.

Boa Brain: Medulla Oblongata, Ventricles, Mirror Neurons

It was the greatest neuroscientific breakthrough ever owed to the casual attitude of a monkey. It happened at the Department of Neurophysiology, at the University of Parma, Italy, at the lab of Giacomo Rizzolatti and his colleagues, who were studying the neurons that were active in monkeys when they were reaching and grasping.[5] The scientists had placed electrodes in areas of the monkey's brain known to be involved in reaching. When the monkey reached, the neurons fired electrical impulses amplified on a speaker: taratatatata. Put a banana in front of the monkey, monkey reaches, taratatatata. Place an apple in front of the monkey, monkey reaches, taratatatata. One day, after setting up the experiment, a graduate student reached to adjust the fruit—and the electrode fired, taratatatata. But the monkey had not moved.

After ruling out alternative explanations, they realized that these neurons fired not only to trigger an action but also in response to seeing the same action executed by another. Thus was made the discovery of *mirror neurons,* the "monkey see, monkey do" nerves of the brain. Mirror neurons will fire, for example, when you rip a piece of paper. They will also fire when you can see but not hear someone else rip the paper and when you can only hear the ripping sound.[6] Mirror neurons are the prime candidates for the neurological basis of empathy.[7] Empathy, of course, is central to the Boa psyche, but mirror neurons are also an important crossover point to the other Animals. They make possible imitation (Panther and Python) and reading other people's intention (Cobra).[8] In one of the early studies, one group of neurons fired only when the monkey watched the graduate student grip an apple to put it into his mouth, and another group of mirror neurons only fired when the student gripped it to put into a cup, and the two groups never got confused. So, the mirror neurons not only seem to code for the action, but to code for the goal.[9] Coding for the goal makes them an important crossover point between Boa and goal-directed Tiger in creating the Earth-Dragon. Exercises to cultivate imitation and empathy, and hence your mirror neurons, are listed in the Seven Steps at the end of this chapter.

Besides empathy, the Boa mythos revolves around the breath and motifs of yielding to the unconscious—themes captured by the medulla oblongata and the ventricles. The *medulla oblongata* sends waves of neural impulses to regulate functions outside of your conscious control, like breathing, blood vessel constriction, and the peristaltic (wave) action of the digestion system.[10] Reflecting the theme of empty space in the Boa mythos, the *ventricles* are cavities located in the middle of the brain that are filled with cerebrospinal fluid and lined with cells that monitor changes in metabolite and hormone levels.[11] The cavities themselves are, like Boa, passive yet crucial in providing the space for life's vital functions. The Seven Steps include exercises for visualizing the medulla-regulating breath along with exercises for the mirror neurons and ideokinetics based on the ventricles.

Boa Personality

If ever there was an empath, it was Sandy, a long-time student of Ch'ien-lung. If she sat in a chair that someone with a headache sat in ten minutes ago, she would get up with a headache herself. It is the blessing and the curse of the Boa personality to feel fully, an ability that progresses through stages. When young, Boas have a natural inclination to project themselves into the other's experiences—whether that means the feelings of people, animals, trees, art, rocks, or razors. Today we usually define empathy as "feeling other people's feelings as your own"—and that is a part of it—but for Boa, it is more. Boa's empathy is empathy for sentience; she feels the intelligence, the awareness, of other things directly. At her early stages, her personal boundaries are nebulous, so things around her feel like they are happening directly to her body. Early on Boa learns that to watch movement is to be moved, to see is to feel, to feel is to become. She learns that the body picks up on small differences in mood, emotion, power, movement. Such empathy makes for great mimics and actresses, but it also requires Boa to learn to let go what is not of her, relax, and release tension through breath.

When young, Boa indiscriminately absorbs from all around her like a sponge; she is sensitive to the plants in her garden, the secrets of a house, and the political tone of a country. Feelings to her are like a virus—in her, but not of her. When young, Boa exudes a natural authenticity untainted by dogma, and she possesses a strong, rich, inner life, drawing from a deep well of introspection. Her kind of empathy is dynamic. She empathetically bonds with experiences across time and place. For her, emotions are motion; everything moves in emotions. She doesn't just perceive facial expressions of happiness or sadness; she feels the energy of the emotions fling through her body, ripple around her, well up through her chest—she can feel your emotions as though they were moving in her body. The experience is intense, opening her up without making her fragile.

At this early stage, Boa makes the critical discovery that she needs time to digest her experience. She needs the quiet, dark, and comfortable space of meditation to reflect upon an experience without the encumbrance of words. Cost-benefit analysis is jarring. Occasionally, you will come across a gregarious Boa type; her personal energy fills up and quietly influences the entire room, sending out waves of emotions. At this stage, she likes to wear loose-flowing earth-toned clothes, although she tends to wear black clothes that smack of mourning when she is feeling hurt. If she can't get silence, she would prefer vocal acoustic music or chanting. Buddhist chanting, Loreena McKennitt, Sarah McLachlan, and powerful, evocative singers such as Ella Fitzgerald and the great Egyptian singer Oum Kalthoum, who brought concert halls full of adults to tears with her voice, are examples. Boa enjoys reading T. S. Eliot, Sartre, and Camus, where mere existence is a mysterious and heroic act.

When it comes to foods, the Boa type prefers a freshly juiced drink teeming with antioxidants and nutrients promoting oxygenation: think spinach and fruit smoothie. But it's not so much what she eats as how she eats. In her mythos, Boa takes the breath of her prey and consumes it whole, leaving behind what cannot be digested. She focuses on the energy of the food, drawing out all the life force from the meal, and then consumes the physical remains, to be in harmony with the law of nature that nothing be wasted. And so it goes for how she digests experiences—she takes everything in without judgment and lets go of what does not serve her. This ability to empathize without judgment allows her to immerse herself in the world of another. She superbonds like an actor who practices the speech and mannerisms of a character, not letting it go even during breaks, as was said of Jim Carrey playing Andy Kaufman in the *Man on the Moon* or the late Philip Seymour Hoffman as Truman Capote in *In Cold Blood.*

At the second level of development, the gift to empathize and absorb turns into reflecting or mirroring others back at themselves. Boa is the kind of person people are compelled to tell their problems to because "she is just such a good listener," "she always gets it," and she ends up voicing your feelings better than you do—not that she has to talk, as more often than not, a glance or a change in expression or posture will convey everything for her. As Boa matures, she becomes the life-companion, the soft glue holding people together; she does not focus on or tackle problems directly. Rather, she keeps a soft awareness, embracing the context in increasingly larger concentric circles, which creates an environment in which others resolve the problem themselves. At this stage, she discovers in herself the gift of yielding, surrender, and sacrifice, and she grows through the hard realities these often bring but is nonetheless empowered.

At this stage, she grows more discriminating in what she empathetically bonds with. She is more selective, choosing things that are healthiest for her in terms of body and soul. As she gains strength in herself, claiming her space, she fosters a sense of space in others. Around her, people find they have a place where their talents can grow. It may be the safe space of a counselor's office or the judgment-free zone of a brainstorming session, but Boa has a knack for making a container where growth can happen.

At the second stage, her capacity for empathy grows more dynamic. It broadens into what psychologists once called *aesthetic empathy,* the kind of feeling an artist would use to "imagine what it is like to be such things as a contorted beaten shovel."[12] Her empathy enlarges and enriches her life in extraordinary ways. These are not flights of fancy or imagination, but a connection to a feeling that rises up from deep within the unconscious as she drops down deep into her world through meditation and contemplation. She empathetically bonds with experiences across time and place, projecting herself into the Queen of Sheba's first kiss, a lawyer pleading with Henry VIII, a forest in need of a fire, and the waters around Fukushima, connecting to what is, was, and always will be.

As she matures into the third stage, she becomes a spiritual sojourner flowing in the tidal forces unifying all life. The collective unconscious guides and nourishes her, irresistibly relinquishing her control. Her quietude allows her to witness the unconscious in nonverbal feeling-impressions. And in the unconscious, she comes into contact with the source of life. Everything rests in the unconscious, for it contains everything—everything she has been, and will be, and was not, everything she hates and loves. It washes over her, and there is nothing to do in the unconscious but to let go, to let herself be where she is, letting the denizens of the deep, the leviathans, roam as they will. She gets so deep and quiet she forgets to breathe.

Once you touch that place you cannot go back. You see yourself as a very small part of a flow of life that has a pulse of its own and over which you have no control; the only power you can exercise is acceptance. And when you reemerge from there, you are bigger, and you are attuned to the cycle of breath; you are attuned to the unconscious through the breath. Here, everything has a season, and you witness each season pass as with each breath. What the Boa of the spirit discovers is that this profound yielding and acceptance of the unconscious allows her to ride the forces of the unconscious without resistance, it allows her to ride them like a wave, and the more she can relax and allow the wave to fully express through her, the more empowered she is, the more life flows through her.

Peace Pilgrim, who renounced her real name in 1953 before she started to walk across America for peace, embodied the sojourning Boa. She fasted unless she was offered food and did not sleep unless she was offered shelter. By the time of her tragic death twenty-eight years later, she had walked 25,000 miles for peace, inspiring thousands of people with her simple message: "This is the way of peace, to overcome evil with good, falsehood with truth, and hatred with love." The Friends of Peace Pilgrim compiled a book about her that inspired thousands. In one story that explored how she faced being tested, she agreed to accompany a young boy who wanted to walk with her. Everyone was scared of him because he suffered violent psychological issues and had even put his mother in the hospital. In her recounting of her journey with him, they had climbed a hilltop when a thunderstorm broke, and though everything had been fine up to then, the boy was "terrified" and "went off the beam."[13] He was big and burly and began striking Peace Pilgrim, who was a "little old lady." He struck her, and in keeping with her love of peace, she did not fight back or struggle. After a few moments, he stopped, and said, "You aren't hitting me back. My mother always hit me back."

The example is in extremis, and not appropriate for everyone to emulate, but it fit with her temperament and purpose and is an excellent example of Boa. In her telling, had she not trusted that there was good in him and trusted in life to take care of her, he never would have seen his own anger. The boy, she notes, went on and grew up to be a happy and productive citizen. She describes the elements in her transformation from a life companion to the spirit of peace, and it reads like a how-to manual for training in Boa and has indeed guided my own Boa practice: relinquish self-will, relinquish feelings of separateness, relinquish all attachments, relinquish all negative feelings, and bring your life into harmony with the laws of the universe.

At the fourth stage, Boa has grown ready to give birth to the Dragon. She is no longer just Boa. She has absorbed so much; she contains the imprints of so many empathically absorbed experiences. Like a good mimic who has internalized all the great mannerisms of the times, she now spontaneously regurgitates something novel from the amalgam. But even here, she is not fully in control of the new creation; it requires combining with the forces of her opposite, Tiger.

The Dark Side of Boa: Self-Numbing Collapse

We live in a harsh and brutal world for a sensitive Boa type; it is filled with overstimulation and violence, both emotional and physical. The sensitive Boa type seeks protection by closing down her empathy, tuning out, withdrawing, and silencing herself. Over a prolonged period of time, cut off from her own feelings, resenting herself and others for this self-silencing, her anger turns inward, leading to depression. She exudes the pathos of the victimized. Where the healthy Boa expands and lets go, the unbalanced Boa collapses in on herself. The tragedy is that because of her underlying nature to draw and absorb, she has an uncanny ability to attract the very things that cause her grief. In breath-like rhythm, she draws in events and people that exacerbate her wound. The hardship for Boa is not the abuse itself, but the chatter and negative self-talk the abuse produces, which corrupts the silence that is her strength.

Boa Movement: Breathing Spirals and Vulnerable Undulations

How do you turn the Boa mythos into the logos of technique? Boa's mythos centers around the breath, a quiet mind, and vulnerability. So, too, does the embodied expression of her logos. The ideokinetics for Boa invoke breath, wind, waves, spirals, and undulations. When you move in Boa, your mantra is "How can I connect my breath to my movement more? How can I let my breath and movement be more natural?" Natural movement means something different to each Animal, and Boa's natural movement reflects the spiral flows found in nature. Like the movement of galaxies, Boa moves in spirals within spirals, cycles within cycles. It resembles the way the Moon orbits Earth, which spins on its own axis, orbiting the Sun, in a solar system that spirals around a galactic center point, in a breathing universe that expands and contracts. You embody Boa by reflecting nature's concentric spirals in your own movement, where the rotation of a small joint begins and ends within the period rotation of a larger joint, which cycles in turn with the rotation of the core. For example, in most every style of arm block, you will likely find the wrist rotating at the same time as you rotate the shoulder, at the same time you rotate the hips. Although each joint rotates a different number of degrees, usually on multiple planes at once, the rotations all start and stop on the same beat, giving your motion a sense of completion and wholeness.

The spirals are propelled by the breath. As you inhale, the shoulders and arms want to rotate out; as you exhale, they want to rotate in. Breathing shifts the thoracic vertebrae, causing a subtle undulation. To deepen joint rotation in response to breath, do the Double-Wrapping exercise in appendix D. Double-wrapping will help develop extreme coordination and joint articulation. It is based on the principle that the body moves in opposing spirals, the same way your arms swing opposite each other when you walk. In martial arts and many other sports, you can increase the power of one arm rotating in one direction by rotating the other arm in the opposite direction. Oppositional spirals compel power through the structure of the body with an easy flowing grace, Boa's hallmark.

Boa spirals in waves, like a twisting and undulating snake. To cultivate the undulatory power of the spine, do the Melon exercise in appendix C. In the ideokinetics of the melon, you have a ball of air the shape of a watermelon at the base of the spine, which spins and expands as you inhale. Your belly should be popping out in each direction with the swelling melon, and when it has expanded to its fullest, you roll the melon up the body from the base of the spine to the base of the neck. Although this sounds quixotic, the melon will ground your movement and reduce overextending from your center of gravity. I took this image for granted, even began to deride it until a few years after I began training with Constantine. I joined an aikido class, and a beloved teacher, Mary Heiny Sensei, who had no connection with Constantine whatsoever, walked to the front of class and instructed us all to press "air in the shape of a football" into our lower backs. Together, the Melon and Double-Wrapping exercises will amplify your body's articulation.

The cycling of spirals makes your movement structurally integral, with an easy flowing power. In martial arts, soft styles or internal styles like Taiji and Bagua harness these natural flowing spirals of Boa. The words *soft* and *internal* are misleading. Putting aside the image of elderly people in a park waving their hands slowly through the air, Taiji is regarded as one of the most devastating forms of self-defense—especially in the hands of a master. One moment they are caressingly redirecting an attack with the gentlest of touches, and then the next they are crushing internal organs with a fearsome, heavy blast. And this is all with the natural flow of a falling leaf—courtesy of the cyclic spirals and undulations. Natural spiral and undulations have practical application in martial arts. Many arts make use of joint locks, where resisting the lock causes additional pain and damage. It is better to flow first with the lock; then spiral with, then around the tension to relieve the pain from the lock; and then to reverse it, turning it back on the aggressor. Surprisingly, force is counterproductive. The tension from the effort in reversing a lock signals your intention, which will que the opponent's countermeasure. A key ingredient is to be able to relax and soften and move following the natural arcs of the body. Boa helps to cultivate the relaxation and the absorption that can reverse a lock. These same elements of flow make the staff a remarkable weapon, and Boa's favorite. A symbol of the connection to life through breath, the staff in the hands of a Boa is a formidable weapon. Like her breath, it fills the space wherever it is needed. Though made of wood and without an edge like the sword you are using against it, you will not be able to cut it. But in any art, what makes the movement metaphysical is doing the movement and connecting it to an aspect of consciousness through imagery and mindfulness. In the case of Ch'ien-lung, you associate Boa ideokinetics and breath visualizations of waves and spirals to the unconscious aspects of the mind.

You cannot connect to the Boa's meditative void and become attune to its life-breath in a state of mental tension and forced expectations. One must be mentally relaxed, and this turns into the somatic expression of Boa's relaxed and released quality. Taiji folk, in particular, may appreciate this principle of being relaxed and released, called *Song* or *Sung*, with a variety of ideokinetics used to foster it, such as hair, string, rope, seaweed, even cooked noodles. I have heard teachers of soft styles who will refer to muscular tension, saying "be more Sung." One teacher explained it, "Relaxed but not collapsed, and strong but not rigid." Adam Mizner, a remarkably clear Taiji instructor with exceptional videos on YouTube, uses the image of hair, saying, "When hair hangs down loose, it is relaxed and released. If you tie the hair up in a bun, it is still relaxed, but it is not released. To be released it must be allowed to hang down. So, too, the muscles must be relaxed and allowed to release to their full, natural length."[14] Constantine frequently evoked an image for Boa—to imagine every limb draped in seaweed. Imagining this always had the effect of slowing, and smoothing movement; it encouraged a slight bend in the knees for a lower center of gravity, with the practical advantage of dropping the elbows to protect the ribs. This was another ideokinetic used by Constantine. Years later, I was stunned to hear Mary Heiny Sensei use the image independently. The Tree Pose in appendix E is an excellent way to develop the relaxed and released quality of Boa-like soft styles, letting your arms droop as if they are weighed down by wet seaweed.

Boa is vulnerable, and her vulnerability is her power. To convey this, I am going to give an example that may well make some readers uncomfortable or dismissive: move like a pregnant mother (Figure 3.1). I had two teachers, Barbara Poggemiller and Lynda Raino, who, on separate occasions, mounted their own one-woman show at seven-months pregnant. The performance, called *Moondance,* was about motherhood; they acted, danced, and sang, and then even spun while hanging off the ground from a gymnastic ring. "You know, a lot of people are going to be really uncomfortable seeing a pregnant woman doing this [twirling on a gym ring]," said the director to Barbara one day. And that was the point, she said, to have people walk away with their ideas changed about what mothers, and women in general, could do or be. In the same way, Boa challenges our ideas of what fighting can be—that vulnerability, softness, and sensitivity have a role in resolving conflict.

Of course, no one is suggesting pregnant mothers enter an octagon, but to capture the healing quality of Boa's movement, imagine you had to ward off or avoid an aggressor as though you were with child. With your lower center of gravity, you would take aware and deliberate steps to maintain balance and fluidity; you would deeply contract your own body, moving to slip, when possible, out of harm's way or the line of attack;

breathing fully, you would move gently out of concern for the life you harbor but also out of a newfound reverence for all life, including that of the opponent whose energy you are drinking in to the core in order to understand and stop it. This is Boa at its fullest.

FIGURE 3.1: Young mother-to-be doing Boa soft style: This image captures the feeling to aim for when doing the Boa bow.

How does Boa heal hurt? Boa's gift in your transformation is to help you yield into healing through vulnerability, softness, surrender, and (as always) breath. The morphos of Boa is best encapsulated in a story about the magician and the warrior.

A magician and a warrior were strolling together in the garden one day, when suddenly a terrible demon appeared. The warrior exclaimed he would defeat the demon and stepped forward to slay the monster. The magician asked him to wait, and he stepped before the demon. The demon began to attack the magician, laying blows and trying to devour him. The magician humbly accepted every blow and bite of the demon as gifts, and in this way, the demon became less powerful, and the magician began to take the demon into himself. Finally, there was nothing left of the demon. The warrior asked the magician why he let the demon attack him, why he did not fight back. The magician said that before, the demon was separate and antagonistic, but now the demon was a part of the magician and made him more whole. In the same way, the morphos of Boa is to become more by letting in and letting go.

You can use the Boa archetype to build your own repertoire of practices to empower self-care. You can create your own Boa-inspired practices like Contact Improv, or in martial practices, Sticky Hands; both consist of keeping one shifting point of contact between both partners while playing with tension and connection—dancing in Contact Improv and aiming to land a strike in Sticky Hands. Both are Boa practices of healing through movement, but should you feel lazy and want to be more passive, you will be relieved to know saunas, hot tubs, massages, and luxurious spa treatments make for lovely Boa rest and relaxation. You can do a spiritual art and still look and feel fah-boo-lous! Boa's surrender allows us to integrate hurt and heroism into a narrative tapestry of our own without rending its fabric.

Embodying Boa turns movement and breath into emotional medicine and physical therapy. Boa ideokinetics of airy lightness and softness turn any movement into a healing massage that you can explore in the Boa bows at the end of this chapter. You can also look to the foundational exercises of Ch'ien-lung called the Basic Breaths, in appendix C. The visualization in the Basic Breaths draws elements up from Earth, through the body, up into the heavens, then down through the body and back into Earth. The Basic Breaths are Boa's pushups, but instead of the goal being a six-pack, it is to soften and feel the body respond to visualized breath entering and leaving any part of the body. The ideokinetics are of the body as one large sponge, and you can willingly contract and expand any part of the sponge to draw breath in or out. The practical benefit to beginners of martial arts of this breath practice is in cultivating situational awareness in all six planes around the body.

It may seem whimsical at first, but this sponge-like breathing has serious healing benefits as practiced in other martial arts. In Systema (a Russian martial art taught by former Soviet Special Forces), for example, you breathe in and out from any part of the body in order to relieve fear and pain. I got to discover the utility of the Basic Breaths when I attended a few Systema seminars where participants take heavy blows to various parts of the body and use rapid-fire breathing techniques to recover from the shock and pain. It is a rare example of practicing and drilling the morphos. I do not pretend to claim proficiency, but my previous practice with the Basic Breaths provided me with a starting point for dissipating the impact of the strikes. This seemed corroborated when I was pleasantly surprised by the comments of senior students who said I was doing surprisingly well for a beginner. Like in Systema, Boa can breathe through any part of her body to release pain and fear, the same way you wring water out of a sponge. Of course, in the process of morphos, why stop at fear and pain? Boa uses the breath to release anger, resentment, blame, impatience, and pride. In the mythos, Boa is drawn to the thing with the most energy, eating it whole and letting go of what she cannot digest; she lets go in morphos through breath.

Boa Sex: The Small Death

Boa yields and surrenders. She relinquishes attachment. In sex, you can experience this Boa state of mind during *le petit mort,* the little death, the moment during and slightly after climax when you cannot think and there is no separation between you and your lover. Behind Tantric practices and their catalogs of strokes, pokes, and positions, the reason for all the special breathing and the timed eye gazes and tongue positions is to prepare your psychological and spiritual wiring for further union with your partner, to prepare you for what can be the shuddering surrender.

When two Boa lovers meet, they stand before each other, feeling each other's presence, savoring the space between them without being consumed by the anticipation of closing it, of filling it. A Boa texture in lovemaking is gentle, receptive, sometimes passive, other times hungry, sometimes receiving, other times actively drawing in, entwining. The caresses are light and airy, the hands hover over the body just enough so the lover can feel their warmth without feeling the hand itself. The whole body is teased and massaged. As passion grows, both partners' breathing finds one natural rhythm, where the exhalation of one coincides with the inhalation of the other, as if each were an extension of the other's breath in a continuous cycle. Yes, the breath, along with well-timed muscle contractions worthy of a break-dancer, can lead to longer orgasms for women and longer periods of excitation for men, but the Tiger, Panther, or Python would care more about the implementation of these pleasuring techniques. For Boa, the breathing in sexual union is absolutely authentic. It is the result, not the cause, of creating a deeper union.

Boa in the Arts

Knowing how to recognize themes related to Boa can help cultivate a quiet, meditative, or yielding empathy. These themes are found around you in books, film, and music. How can you tell a painting is by a Boa? When you look at it, you are stopped by your reflection and feel for the canvas. The poems of T. S. Eliot, like "The Love Song of J. Alfred Prufrock," for example, capture the author's struggle with contrived social rules.

When you encounter the essence of yourself, there is an instant when you perceive the filters through which you perceive the world. Constantine called these "Boa stops the world," when you apprehend the oneness of life. Poems like William Blake's "Auguries of Innocence" capture this sense of apprehending unity.

To see a world in a grain of sand,
And a heaven in a wild flower,
Hold infinity in the palm of your hand,
And eternity in an hour.
. . .
A Horse misused upon the Road
Calls to Heaven for Human blood
Each outcry of the hunted Hare
A fibre from the Brain does tear

—*William Blake, "Auguries of Innocence"*[15]

The subject of Boa art revolves around the principle that all things breathe: people, plants, even Earth in its cycle of producing and reabsorbing atmospheric carbon dioxide, or the universe in its cyclic contraction and expansion. There is a place where emptiness is harrowing and meaningless, and another where emptiness is peaceful and fulfilling—the space of Boa contains both.

The Seen Anima: Boa in the Movies

It says something about our society that movies often portray empathy as a superpower. Rogue, in *X-Men,*[16] sucks the life force, including the powers of other mutants, with whom she comes into physical contact. George Malley, played by John Travolta in *Phenomenon,*[17] locates a child suffering from food poisoning like an empathy bloodhound, moving ever closer to the source of pain.

Star Wars is probably one of the few films where male characters, such as Luke and Obi Wan, actively show empathy in negotiating relationships.[18] Parodies of Obi Wan feeling "as if millions of voices suddenly cried out in terror and were suddenly silenced" or of Luke when he tells his father Darth Vader that he can feel the good within him speak to how powerful, intriguing, and threatening the ability to feel with accuracy is. The movie portrayed empathy as an acceptable way for a father and son to seek connection and find redemption in an otherwise emotionally gridlocked relationship.

Meryl Streep's breadth, depth, and communication of feeling is a good example of Boa artistry. In each of her performances, her emotions flow seamlessly, arcing across a spectrum of human feeling from comic to tragic with a quick grace. One review describes her performance in a play as drawing broadly from influences floating around her in the zeitgeist; she channels the comic timing from a broad array of inspirations including the Marx Brothers and Lucille Ball, and the haughty reserve of Marlene Dietrich, just as a Boa would do.[19]

Jacques, a free diver (who goes to depths of 400 feet within a minute without an oxygen tank) in the movie *Big Blue,*[20] is a character who richly succeeds in portraying the dreamy, sweet, sensitive, vulnerable-but-strong quality of a Boa type person. In the movie he is scientifically monitored for his ability to slow his heart rate and oxygen use while underwater, mimicking states found only in dolphins. While others seek glory in an international diving competition, he dives out of a spiritual quest, so that by film's end, he is taken in by a pod of dolphins as family, immersed as he is in the world of feelings. This autonomic control is just a physical manifestation of his profound meditative connection to states of being that touch the unconscious and universal forces that bring the characters of the story together as they seek out the inner quiet he possesses in their own ways.

Becoming Boa

As with each of the Animals, developing Boa means breathing, thinking, feeling, and moving like a Boa. It can be an eye-opening experience to wear the clothes, taste the foods, listen to the music, try the hobbies—all with the goal of affirming the consciousness of Boa's empathic and soft awareness. You've likely already done it. Perhaps you have practiced yoga, and after a session of lengthening poses, rhythmically timed breathing, and deliberate mindfulness, you felt less like the world has engulfed you and more like your awareness has engulfed the world. Perhaps you have taken walks through the woods, breathing the energized air of the forest trees, feeling as though you are in the company of giants, and that they are as aware of you as you are of them. Or perhaps you have been in love and felt that moment of vulnerability and gratitude, the moment when you realize you have let someone else into your life, their entrance irrevocable.

So, how do you live your day in Boa? How, exactly, do you relax into your center, develop empathy, and tap into the collective unconscious? In all things Boa, let your breath be your guide, starting with the plaque work described below.

The Boa Plaque

The plaque of the Boa is a black triangle on a green circle (see Figure 3.2 in this book's color insert). The black symbolizes her ability to accept all things, which is best illustrated in a story from *Mister God, This Is Anna.*[21]

In this book, a young girl explains how God would not shine like a white light, but rather, would appear black. You see, she explains, when you look at the color of a thing, what you see is not the color it possesses, but the reflected light of the color it does not have. The colors it possesses, it absorbs, the colors it does not possess, it reflects back to our eyes. Therefore, as objects reflect light, we see the colors they don't have. And so God (she argues in a way that would make Aristotle grin) who is all things, must be all colors, and thus would not reflect any light back, but be black: deep, dark, loving, always-been-home black. Hence, for similar reasons, the triangle for Boa, the triangle for the all-consuming, all-embracing, all-enveloping Boa is black. (See color insert Figure 3.2.)

Although the black of the triangle represents the receptive quality of the individual, the green circle represents the vital energies of nature in flow with each other. The green of the circle evokes the opposing sides of growth and decay in their natural cycle. On the one hand, the color green captures the oxygen-rich verdure of temperate rainforests, lush gardens, and jungles, while on the other, it also captures the sickly hues of rot, mold, and disease, all of which make up the cycle of life. All of this is just energy to the Boa, and like the serenity prayer, it knows what to accept, what to absorb, and what to let go, and it allows the difference between them.

In the plaque work, the triangle for the psyche suggests Boa's meditative quality, and the anatomy triangle provides areas toward which you should direct visualized breath. The energetic triangle highlights the importance of breath as life-giving and intelligent, and it includes energetic anatomy called the *empathic fields* and *membranes.* Most people are familiar with *auras,* layers of energy emanating from the body, each one corresponding to an aspect of consciousness. But you may not be familiar with the further dissection of auras. Separating each aura are narrow transition layers called *empathic membranes* that connect and cushion the auric layers. The *empathic field* is separate from the aura, not really fixed to any region, and changes shape depending on what the person is feeling; it can be an ideokinetic tool for actors and dancers. The pumps and membranes are detailed fully in appendix B.

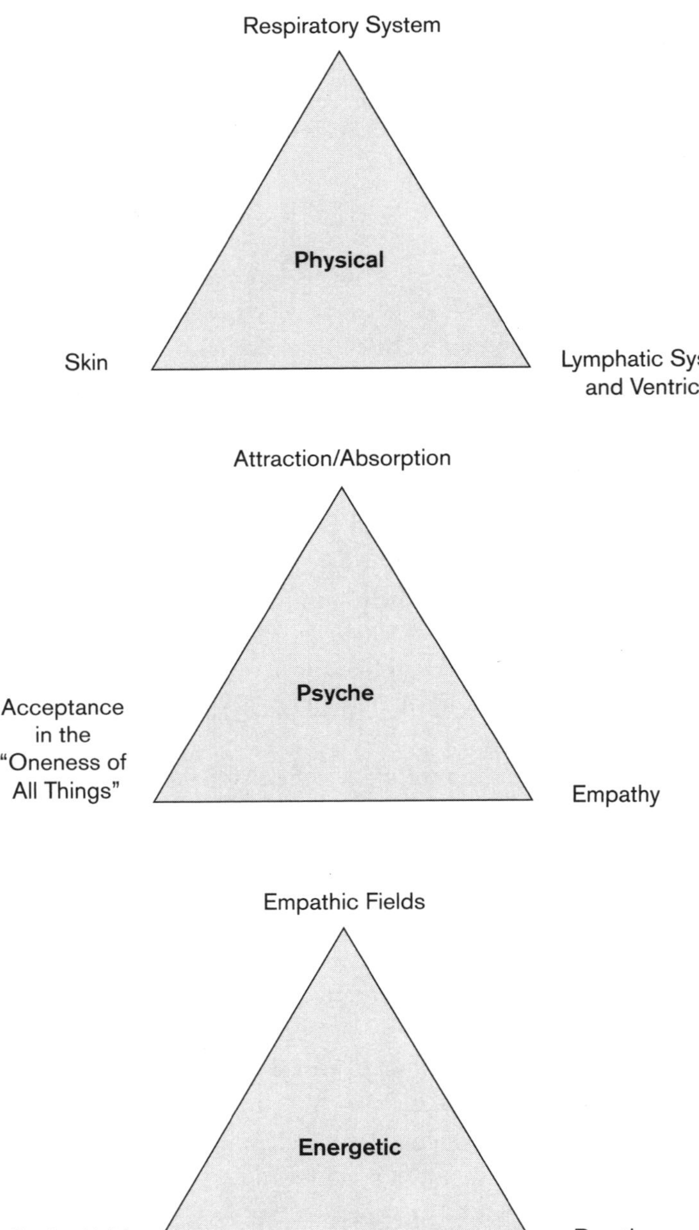

FIGURE 3.3: The symbolic meaning of the triangle points for the Boa

Seven Steps to Embodying Boa

The exercises for the Animals are organized into seven steps. The steps are time-limited or ongoing mindfulness practices and either internal (awareness) or external (behavior) practices. They are designed to help you embody each Animal. The exercises require no martial art or fitness experience. You can choose the number of steps you wish to adopt. The steps are prioritized by accessibility, according to my experience with students, and you should feel free to choose the combination of steps that works for you:

Step One: Follow Your Breath (Ongoing Practice)

Step Two: Recall Your Day (Daily/10 Minutes before Sleep)

Step Three: Scan Your Body (Daily/10 Minutes before Sleep)

Step Four: Do the Bows in Nature (Weekly/0–15 Minutes)

Step Five: Adopt the Animal Personality (Ongoing Practice)

Step Six: Remember Your Dreams (Daily/10 Minutes upon Waking)

Step Seven: Use the Plaques (Daily/20 Minutes)

Step One: Follow Your Breath (Ongoing Mindfulness Practice)

The practice of Ch'ien-lung begins and returns with the breath. Following your breath means noticing which areas of the body carry tension as you breathe: notice how deep and how shallow you are breathing; notice the mood or attitude connected to the way you are breathing right now; if you were a character from a movie or book, and that character was breathing the way you are now, what would that say about the character? How would the Animal you are practicing breathe at this moment?

Following the breath involves a liberal dose of directed imagination. Assume your breath is not limited to the expansion and contraction of your lungs, but that you can breathe into any body part you choose, expanding and contracting it at will. To start your practice, simply pick an anatomical system of the Animal, and imagine it expands and contracts as you breathe directly in and out from there. Following your breath in Boa means visualizing that you can breathe deeply and slowly into your:

Skin Imagine you can feel your skin respiring, letting oxygen in and carbon dioxide out. As it does, let your skin relax and open. A heated sauna or light effleurage is particularly effective at leaving your skin feeling alive, which you can follow up with Boa bows. The skin is the largest organ of the body and a major excretory organ, ridding toxins through sweat; rich in proprioceptive receptors, it dominates your sense of movement and balance. Ideokinetics: Move the body as though the skin is inflated like a porous sponge. Move as if the breath passing in and out of the pores of the skin causes you to move. Scan the body while you move; visualize breath moving from the places with sensation to the places without much. Connect the skin to the thin film of life on Earth, connecting the breathing skin to the breathing trees and grasses.

Pulmonary system Feel the breath enter and caress the tissue of the lungs all the way down to the small alveoli where the exchange of carbon dioxide and oxygen occurs. Following the breath in and out of the lungs restores calm and perspective. Ideokinetics: Move as if the lungs originate motion. Expand and contract with the breath, letting the air of your lungs lift your limbs as if a helium balloon were under each joint. Connect the lungs to the giant breathing forests of Earth. Connect to the wind and jet streams.

Circulatory system Five gallons of blood with the same salinity as the ocean flows through your circulatory system carrying life-giving oxygen and the energy Boa draws ever-more into herself. Visualize breath moving with the blood coursing through the large veins and arteries to and from the heart and the small capillaries, just large enough to allow one blood cell to pass through them at a time. Visualize energy carried by the blood, relaxing and dropping tension as it flows. Ideokinetics: Move as if the fluid dynamics of the blood cause you to slosh, ripple, and pulse. Connect to river systems and aquifers.

Lymphatic system Feel the network of nodes throughout your body. Imagine you can feel the lymph, filled with immune cells, clearing the body of metabolic debris and the collateral byproducts of fighting infections. The lymphatic system is not pumped by a central muscle like the heart. Instead, lymph is pumped by skeletal muscles. This passivity is analogous to how we are moved by the unconscious, worthy of contemplation in plaque work. Visualize breath moving with the lymph. Ideokinetics: Move as if deliberately circulating lymph, as if movement is cleansing the body. Connect to the sentience of bacteria, insects, and scavengers that play the critical role of cleaning up waste and debris.

Ventricles of the brain These fluid-filled cavities in the middle of the brain are lined with cells monitoring for levels of sugar, salt, and proteins, all in an effort to make sure the body has what it needs. You have no feeling receptors in these ventricles, but imagine feeling them do their job; visualize the breath circulating the fluids. The process of exercising empathy is similar to how ventricles do their job: a quiet and dark space subtly responds to changes in the environment. Ideokinetics: Move as if you are floating in the womb, completely submersed and in the dark, vulnerable in all directions. Connect to subterranean caves where residues build formations over eons.

Digestive system Boa takes in everything and lets go of what she cannot digest, a theme shared with the digestive system. Imagine you can breathe into your digestive system–the stomach, the large and small intestines. Imagine their walls filling and emptying of breath, relaxing as they do. Ideokinetics: Move as if the digestive system is the center of your movement. Women include the uterus, not only because it cues a low center of gravity, but also because it brings to mind the nurturing and floating quality of the Boa. Connect to the cycle of life and decay in nature.

Medulla oblongata Imagine, especially in the plaque work, that you can feel the rhythm-setting of the medulla as it regulates the tempo of your heart, breathing, and peristalsis, the wave-like contractions of your intestines. Following the breath's rhythm will cultivate the soft Boa consciousness you embody. Ideokinetics: Move as if you can feel the rhythm set by all your pulses.

Mirror neurons These neurons, located on both sides of the head, halfway between the temples and the ears, fire when you imitate and empathize. There are no receptors to feel them, but they go to work when you imitate or empathize. Ideokinetics: Move as if you are imitating your opponent or partner; this is known as *blending* in martial arts and *following* in dance. Connect to the genius for imitation in children.

Empathy Imagine your empathy takes up space, like a magnetic field, filling and surrounding you. Imagine you can emotionally resonate with any form of sentience that falls in that field, whether it is in the form of a person, animal, or plant or the emotional charge of a photograph or dented toaster. Imagine breathing into that empathic space. Ideokinetics: Move as if you respond to shifts in your empathic field as feelings pass through it. Connect to Earth and send the feelings you have no use for into Earth for recycling.

Step Two: Recall Your Day (Daily/10 Minutes before Sleep)

Before going to bed, remember the high and low points of your day, recalling them as though you cast a blanket over them, capturing them all at once–this is Boa's way of remembering the day as a whole. Let these memories flow in no particular order; let one trigger the next. Boa is fluid and continuous, so just let go when you find yourself stuck on a particular moment, regardless of intensity. Practicing Boa allows the mind to naturally associate your memories in a flowing way, without judgment or criticism. If chatter or criticism arises, let it pass like a cloud drifting across the sky; let go like Boa.

To hone your empathy, review your day for moments of feelings that were in sync with others or moments when you felt a subthreshold level of imitating another person's actions, when you could imagine what it would feel like to do or behave in their manner, even if you did not imitate them explicitly.

Step Three: Scan Your Body (Daily/10 Minutes before and after Sleep)

At night before going to sleep and upon waking, scan the systems of the Boa body: skin, respiratory and circulatory system, lymphatic system, digestive system, and the neural areas of the medulla, mirror neurons, and ventricles.

Step Four: Do the Bows in Nature (Weekly/10–15 Minutes)

Each of the Animals resonates with an ecological environment, and your connection to an Animal can be strengthened by doing the bows in nature. You can learn a great deal about the undulatory movement of Boa from the ocean. Imitate the undulatory action of the waves with your limbs and spine. If you have been to the ocean, you have felt the powerful undercurrent of the water rushing back to the sea after a wave has crashed; in much the same way, while your arms are moving in one direction, your hips are also moving in an opposing spiral, providing a powerful counterforce. The ocean represents the deep unconscious–unfathomable, full of unseen, living things, touching all shores at once–and can be used as an inspiration to understand your own unconscious. If you want to contemplate Boa's unconscious, go out on a moonless night and look out onto the vast ocean under the darkness of the night sky.

The ocean waves are obvious to see, but the ideokinetics of Boa echo the breath and wind. There is a light touch, an expanding and airy quality to Boa movement. Boa moves like the wind, with currents of flow, and invisible eddies and spirals. Boa moves in a cyclical manner, with each movement creating a vacuum to be filled by the next. You can study the wind and ocean waves to better learn how Boa moves.

When you practice Boa in nature, you want to extend your empathy out. You want to experience the emotional state or the consciousness of the plants, animals, and landscapes around you. You will have moments when you feel the communication between trees, or feel energy pouring off lush ferns, or even feel yourself being watched by an unseen animal.[22] Let your bow include your environment. Connect the expressions of Boa's anatomy to the Earth: feel the wind as your breath the small rivers, streams, and underground waterways as the lymphatic drains of the Earth.

Boa Bow

The bows are simple movements to timed breathing with the ideokinetics and visualized breathing of the Animal. The bows cultivate the Animal psyche and strengthen your connection to Earth. Doing the bows out in nature is a wonderful way to enjoy the outdoors and will deepen your Animal practice.

FIGURE 3.4: Stand feet together, arms as if holding a beach ball down at the belly. Feel layers of empathic fields around the body. Fingers in mudra position.

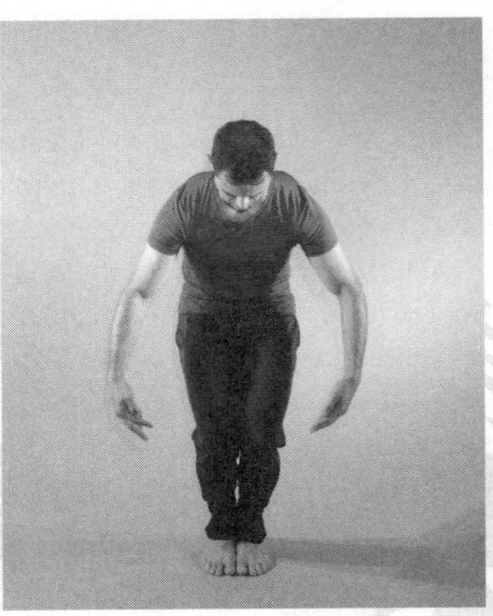

FIGURE 3.5: Exhale, let go of the beach ball, curl over, dropping into the unconscious. Be empty of breath at the bottom.

FIGURE 3.6: Start to inhale, elbows point to the back, as if pressing forearms against the inside of a barrel.

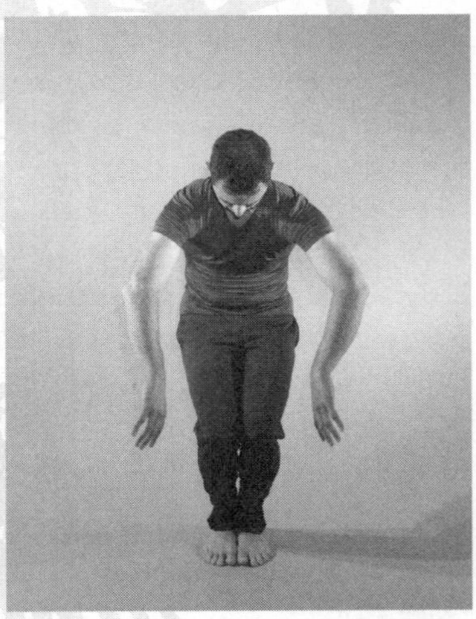

FIGURE 3.7: Continue inhaling. Bring the arms to the front, the back of the forearms toward each other. Envelop in a cocoon of soft breath.

FIGURE 3.8: Continue inhaling. Curl the spine up as if Earth sent a wave of breath through your body, raise the hands, keep the elbows dropped, fingers in front of the midline. Brush away stagnant energy, and clear the empathy fields.

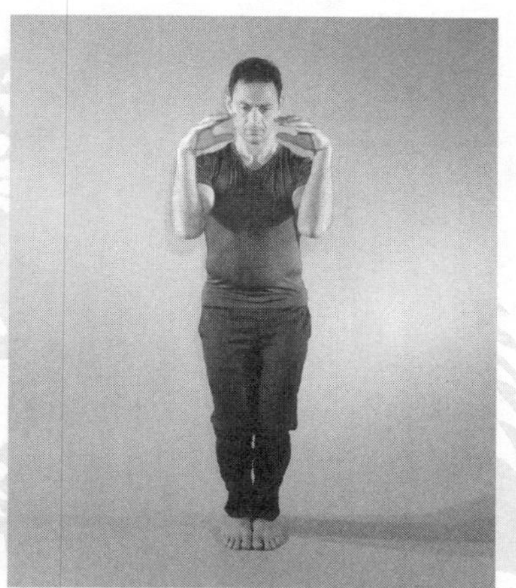

FIGURE 3.9: Continue inhaling. Curl up to straight, elbows pulled straight down as the hands rise to the face, as if brushing cobwebs from the eyes, clearing the windows of perception with the breath.

FIGURE 3.10: Continue inhaling. Arms go out to the side, opening and softening.

FIGURE 3.11: Hold the breath, the arms hold a large beach ball at chest level. "Stop the world," cease all mental chatter, rest in the unconscious.

FIGURE 3.12: Keep holding the breath, bring the fingers in toward the chest. Keep the elbows pointing down. Bring energy in empathically.

FIGURE 3.13: Hold the breath. Fingers come up the throat, elbows keep pointing down.

FIGURE 3.14: Exhale, bend the knees. Let go of the energy, pouring the breath into the palms.

FIGURE 3.15: Finish exhaling, relax completely.

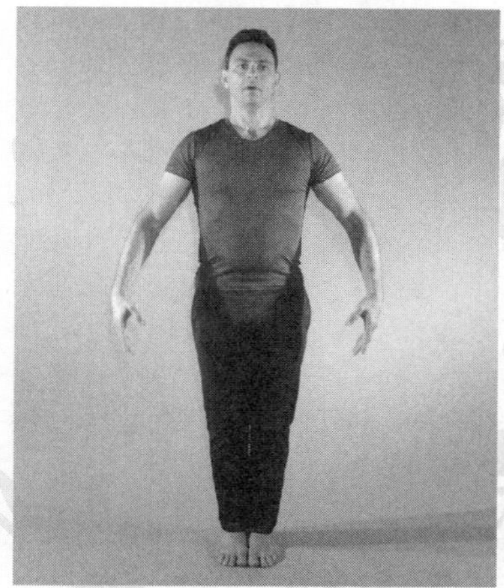

FIGURE 3.16: Inhale, fill up, and rise. Start the next bow.

FIGURE 3.17: Finish bows, and place the arms like they're holding a beach ball. The other Animals make triangle shapes after the bow, but Boa makes a rounded shape. Soften, relax, release. Connect to the breath of Earth and the unconscious. Fingers in mudra position.

Step Five: Adopt the Animal Personality (Ongoing Practice)

Adopting the personalities and preferences of the Animals makes them more fun and accessible. In your Boa practice, wear loose, flowing clothing that conveys a sense of how Boa likes to move—as though your limbs are floating on billows of air.

When it comes to eating, Boa enjoys leafy greens or fresh-made vegetable juices rich in energy and oxygen. But more important than what Boa eats is how she eats it. When you practice Boa, prior to eating, take a moment to feel the vitality of what you are about to consume, taking in that vital energy before you eat the physical form of the food.

The sounds that cultivate Boa involve a natural vocal quality—like Gregorian or Buddhist chanting, or the singing of a musician like Enya—soothing, lyrical, hypnotic, a quality that takes the listener on an internal journey. That said, Boas are more than comfortable with silence.

Boas read about meditation, and then become it. Movies that inspire Boa are powerful, internally driven dramas, starring actors and actresses with a seemingly endless range of feeling conveyed with easy nuances. They enjoy forms of physical exercise like yoga, Qigong, or Taiji where they feel the energy of their body fill in all directions, the same way the ocean touches all shores at once. They also delve into marathon and distance running, which expresses the incredible endurance of Boa, and the power of breath at its most basic. Boas' strong capacity for empathy causes them to care about environmental issues–their empathy is so strong, they feel environmental degradation happening as though it was happening to their own body or to a close friend.

Empathy is central to Boa. You can deepen your empathy by giving and receiving massages, which has the added benefit of building friendship and community and facilitating meaningful dialogue.

Imitation exercises help activate your mirror neuron system and expand your breath awareness. Explore empathy through exercises like acting classes: take poetic license in pretending to be other people or, for that matter, any living or inanimate object like a tree, a shovel, or the color purple.

When you watch people with the intent to mimic them, you will experience what we call in psychology *subthreshold firing*. This is neural activity that fires in the same pattern as the action you want to execute but does not fire strongly enough to actually execute the action. As you watch the person or thing you want to imitate, feel your body for the areas where you experience the subthreshold firing. Move from those impulses to start your imitation. Then, when you are done, feel those same areas and relax them through breath, as though letting go of the pattern.

At first, choose from a broad range of people, animals, and objects to imitate. As you mature, do as Boa does and pick the ones with a lot of energy. If you practice a physical art or skill, like dance, martial arts, or yoga, and you cannot successfully reproduce what the instructor demonstrates, watch someone who is only a little more advanced than you are and imitate what you see them doing.

In my own experience, Boa imitation has practical use in sparring as a check-and-reset for tension. I will do a momentary flash mirroring of my sparring partner's posture, rhythm, or stance. I do this very quickly, but it has a relaxing effect on my body, cues those valuable skills in situational awareness I practiced during training, and helps me absorb information about my opponent.

Empathy in conversation is gold. When speaking with others, check in with the emotional experience they are having *without imposing your own interpretation*. Ask them how they feel and *listen to the response,* rather than telling them how they should feel or how you would feel in that situation. These conversation tips can be helpful, but words are not where Boa feels comfortable. For Boa, words are tags to track *the motion in the emotion* behind what is said. When you connect to the feelings of others, you may notice one person's happiness elicits an upward spiral, another's gives you a feeling of calmness or bubbliness, and suspicion causes an inward drop on your right side. Empathy extends not just to emotions. For example, the ideas in the class Introduction to American Literature may make you feel warm or cold, expanding or contracting, earthy or watery, each of these carrying a quality of motion with it. Notice how your breathing changes in response to the emotions, feelings, and aesthetic impressions surrounding you.

For a person who is a Tiger, White Leopard, or Python with strong analytical skills, you may find it easy to put words to feelings, and the idea of an exercise in which you articulate impressions may seem superfluous. Your emphasis will be on paying attention to prevent analysis from cutting you off from the immediate experience of empathy. If you are ready with words, then your challenge will be to *wait for a genuine feeling response from within yourself and steep in the feeling before putting words to it.* For those who are strongly Boa, Cobra, or Panther, and speaking is not your strong suit, it can be beneficial to exercise being explicit for a time.

Step Six: Remember Your Dreams (Daily/10 Minutes upon Waking)

Although you may not dream of a boa per se, Boa qualities may appear in dreams in other ways. First, practicing Boa will bring up deep feelings, and one of the universal symbols for deeply felt emotions is water as well as animals in water.[23] Notice lakes, oceans, streams, steam, or ice, and try to feel the emotion these evoked in the dream. Second, Boa is the most feminine of the Snakes and resembles an archetype Jung called the *anima.* The anima is the internal feminine. She is deeply connected to the sum total of all feelings across the psyche and transcends the individual. Watch for characters in your dreams represented as female with deep wells of feeling tied to the rawness of life. The feminine archetypes communicate important transitions where you may need to let go like Boa.

Third, Boa represents the unconscious, and on occasion, you may experience dreams that are more intense and vivid and that carry an important message, which Jung called *archetypal dreams.* These differ in quality from everyday dreams. Having an archetypal dream is directly experiencing the unconscious of Boa. Regardless of their interpretation, recalling archetypal dreams will develop your sense of how Boa lives in you.

As you recall your dreams, there will be a point at which you cannot recall anymore. Rather than becoming frustrated, recognize that the dream is a part of you and continues to exist in your unconscious, in the realm of Boa. Feel like you are sending out an invitation into the unconscious for the dream to make itself more explicit in your waking life. Simply acknowledge that you cannot recall any more and that you will allow your unconscious to guide you to greater wholeness and completion. During the course of the day, watch for subtle feelings of familiarity that echo themes and issues you are working on in dreams. Boa does not need to interpret the dreams, and in some ways, does not even need to recall the dream, but she trusts that the dream is part of an ongoing process.

Step Seven: Use the Plaques (Daily/20 Minutes)

When doing the plaque work (see appendix A) for Boa, pay attention to the pause between the exhalation and the inhalation, where Boa "stops the world." Use the Boa single-handed mudra, tongue position, and asana. Use Boa's soft general gaze to follow the contours of the triangle. Boa's eyes are lidded, halfway covering the pupils, and relaxed, with a soft, fuzzy focus. Your eyes do not focus hard on the edge of the shapes so much as they *feel* the edges, as though your gaze was a tendril caressing the perimeters. At deeper levels of meditation, you will feel the shapes as though they are in your body. With practice, you maintain the gaze on one shape while allowing your empathy to wrap and feel the other shapes.

Boa Energy Circuit

The Boa energy circuit is more of a cloud. Visualize the breath coming in through every pore and orifice of the body, including tear ducts, breathing into the essence (where breath and attention meet). The exhale is the same.

People often ask, "How do I know it is working or if I'm doing it right?" With Boa, you will have a sense of timelessness or of time slowing down, as though the intervals in a beat have expanded. You will feel a deep sense of relaxation and effortless self-correcting of posture, sitting or standing straighter without forcing it. After the meditation and during the normal course of your day, you will be calmer, startle less, and be more mindful of your surroundings with less mental chatter. Your reaction times will be the same, but your physical motion will be smoother, following natural arcs, buying you more ease and presence of mind.

Boa vs. Animals

As constrictor Snakes, Boa and Python focus on breath; whereas the pragmatic Python emphasizes breathing into the marrow, Boa breathes into the essence, where the breath and attention meet. Boa and Tiger are clearly opposites, but it can be easy to confuse empathy and heart. Empathy feels in emotion and as though sensations have direction and movement. Boa feels deeply but does not really care. She moves on. It takes Tiger's heart, the courage to act, to turn the insight from empathy into effective compassion.

Often in martial practice, a beginner student of hard Tiger arts will outdo a beginner student of soft Boa arts, but the soft-style student who has trained for many years will outdo the hard-style student of equivalent years.

Boa Keys

The keys are a set of finger, hand, eye, tongue, and seated positions for the Animal. You use them during the plaque work and (with the exception of the seated position) after performing the bows. You can also use them to adopt the Animal personality. With practice, when you casually make the finger shape, tongue position, or eye-glance, it will trigger the cumulative associations you have built around the archetype, bringing it to life, the way turning the key in the ignition brings an engine to life.

The Boa eye-gaze: Your eyes are half-lidded and relaxed, with a soft focus.

The Boa tongue position: The tongue is relaxed on the floor of the mouth, as you breathe naturally.

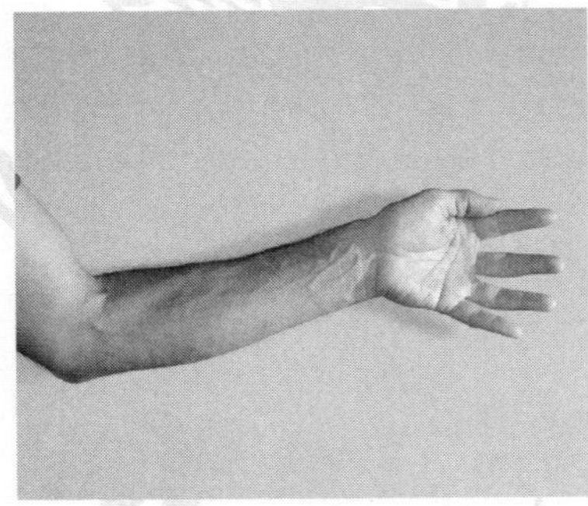

FIGURE 3.18: The Boa single-handed mudra is simple; place the thumb on the second joint of the index finger and softly cup the hand, like cupping a sparrow. Use the mudra in meditation or during your day to invoke your Boa's empathy and connection to breath and the unconscious.

FIGURE 3.19: Boa asana is ideally a full lotus, but half-lotus or simply sitting with crossed-legs is acceptable.

Table 3.1 summarizes the Boa archetype.

TABLE 3.1: Boa Summary

Consciousness	Accepting the oneness of all things, empathy, active absorption, and embrace
Nature	Rain forest trees, wind, Amazon river, Ganges river, the Nile, ocean currents and waves
Anatomy	Skin, respiratory and circulatory (esp. capillaries), lymphatic system, digestive system

Neural regions	Medulla oblongata, ventricles, cerebrospinal fluid
Energetic system	Empathic membranes, *qi/prana/ki/* breath
Favorite foods	Fresh-made juices, raw foods *(anything filled with vitality and life-force)*
Music	Silence, meditative chanting, Gregorian or Buddhist chanting, Enya
Sports and martia arts	Yoga, Taiji, Qigong
Hobbies	Meditation, massage
Clothes	Loose and flowing shawls, sari

PYTHON: THE BRIDGE BETWEEN

One way to open your eyes is to ask yourself, "What if I had never seen this before? What if I knew I would never see it again?"

—RACHEL CARSON

CAMOUFLAGED BY THE DENSE brush, Python has watched her prey for three days. Python knows the habits of her prey: the paths it takes to and from its lair; the times when it feeds, drinks, sleeps. She watches for moments of inattentiveness in that routine. She notices it pays little attention when it comes around the large stump on its way toward the watering hole at dusk. She places herself there a few moments before and waits for her prey to do the rest.

Python Consciousness: Observation, Manipulation, the Bridge Between

We live in a self-organizing cosmos where interconnected principles engender patterns out of chaos. These principles of the natural world underpin the arc of waterfalls, the shape of honeycombs, the path of blood vessels, and the workings of the mind. Nature's laws have left their footprints in our souls all the way through from our genes to our imagination. We are tuned by nature, and we naturally resonate, chase, and explore the recurring natural laws of which we are composed—we learn the chords, and we pluck the strings ourselves.

The Python consciousness detects patterns, churning patient observation into premeditated action: what she observes, she must manipulate; what she imitates, she must improve; what she can conceive, she must design; and what she can calculate, she must engineer. When you experience Python, you feel like your scientific mind has met the vital forces of life and is compelled to test its understanding through experimentation. The interlocked principles that make nature tick have produced brains capable of bearing witness to themselves. At our best, we are the dedicated effort of the cosmos to chase its own tail.

Python represents the bridges between the unconscious, the subconscious, and the conscious minds. The manipulation of breath, through careful diaphragmatic control, slides our attention along the spectrum of consciousness, from deep sleep and dreams to creative flow. For Python, awareness and timing of breath acts like a drawbridge between the lands of the conscious and unconscious realms.

Python, in its most raw form, feels like pure *salience:* the potential for meaning. Deaf and blind Helen Keller said that in the moment she learned to hand-sign the word *water,* it was not only the word she understood, but it was as if a whole world of meaning suddenly opened up to her.[1] This feeling—of a world of meaning to be leveraged, a world of laws, patterns, and potential opening to be "handled"—is the experience of Python in its purest form.

Python Anatomy: Lungs, Bones, and Joints

Python observes and manipulates structure, so we go to the skeletal system for the ideokinetics to embody her. Bone is fascinating tissue. We normally think of healthy bone as rock hard. In fact, skeletal tissue is soft like Jell-O until each cell absorbs a mineral.[2] In response to weight-bearing pressures, bone cells migrate to positions that optimize their integrity. The shape of your bone changes gradually over time, your skeleton molding itself to fit the demands you impose upon it, in the same way cowboys riding horseback for years grew bowlegged thigh bones. This metaphor of bone captures the gift of Python's morphos, which is the transformation of self through expertise. We become changed as we develop expert knowledge, absorbing millions of bits. And as we amass and organize them, they give us shape. Over time, we grow more dynamic as we absorb more knowledge. Python's observations are the fixative of our transformation.

Python and bone multitask. The skeleton supports locomotion, for although muscle provides drive, without the anchor of the skeleton, you'd writhe like an octopus. The skeleton protects the brain and vital organs; it enables hearing via the tiny middle-ear bones of the stirrup, anvil, and hammer. The *otoliths,* tiny rocks of the inner ear, enable our sense of equilibrium; the hyoid bone floats in front of White Leopard's throat center and anchors the tongue to facilitate speech and swallowing. The raw materials of the bone are like the body's own savings account for minerals from which it makes calcium deposits and withdrawals for all sorts of homeostatic processes. Such mineral stores can be depleted by drinking too much soda.[3] To embody Python's cunning, consider a problem from an equally diverse number of angles as the multiple functions of the skeleton.

Python is dissembling, hiding her intentions and actions. She is like a magician misdirecting your attention with one hand while, with the other, she steals your wallet, winds your watch, and changes the password on your electronic device—all at the same time. Python does not let you see what she is really up to. *She does so by leveraging the space between things:* transitions, connections, gaps, bridges, intervals, beats, pauses, fulcrum, and levers. She asks, like a good lawyer, "What is missing?" She is like Portia telling Shylock that the contract lets him take a pound of flesh but that it does not stipulate blood. So, too, when embodying the metaphysics of Python, the lure is the solid skeleton, but the real prize is the *negative space of the skeleton.* This is why the ideokinetics and breath visualizations for Python emphasize the spaces between the joints. A house has walls, but what makes the house livable is the space inside;[4] in the same way, what makes the skeleton dynamic is not its rigidity but the space between the joints.

In Ch'ien-lung, the joints possess small energetic centers, like mini chakras, called *pumps* (see appendix B). Like billows, the pumps circulate energy within the joint and along the limb from one joint to the next. Visualization of sending energy through the marrow from one pump to the next is an important Python practice and complements other *qigong* and *tuina* (bone cleansing or bone strengthening) practices.

Boa and Python are constrictor Snakes, stealing the breath, and they cross over at the respiratory system. For both, but especially for Python, the breath starts in the marrow of the bones, where oxygen-carrying red blood cells are produced.[5] Boa and Python relate differently to the breath and the unconscious. For Boa, it's as though the breath emanates from the unknowable energy of life, and by resting in a meditative void, she can respond to this unconscious force by being responsive to the breath. Python studies and leverages the breath as the bridge between the conscious and the unconscious. In the words of Sergey Makarenko, Systema Instructor at Norcal Systema, it is the one vital function that is under both voluntary control (holding your breath) as well as involuntary autonomic control.[6] Breath manipulation pervades all sports. Athletes exhale on a jump to maximize height or distance, and sharpshooters hold their breath and pull the trigger between heartbeats when their arms are steadiest from the pulse of the brachial artery. Systema teaches you to breathe out the mouth to clear the body and in through the nose to clear the mind. Meditators have long known a regular breathing pattern *entrains* consciousness—it synchronizes brainwaves, getting brain areas to fire synchronously as a conductor does an orchestra.[7] Both Boa and Python link to the unconscious through the breath, but whereas Boa and the breath are one, sinking deeper and broader within the unconscious, Python experiments with breath to leverage the conscious mind's access to the unconscious, to harness it in meeting the needs of the moment.

Python Brain: Corpus Callosum

In 1964, the neuroscientist Roger Sperry was summoned by Pope Paul VI for a debate at the Vatican. The topic: Do people have two souls?[8] The controversy arose from Sperry's experiments with split-brain patients who had undergone a surgical procedure called a *corpus callosumectomy*. The procedure prevents epileptic seizures from spreading throughout the brain by cutting the corpus callosum, the band of 250 million neurons that bridges the left and right hemispheres. Patients with a severed corpus callosum appear perfectly normal, except when their arms start to wrestle each other over a difference of opinion, giving the appearance of two people coexisting in the same mind. Cutting the corpus callosum severs communication between the two halves of the brain, resulting in humorous outcomes. One split-brain patient pushed away her husband with one hand while signaling him to approach with the other.[9]

Python's manipulations are deep because she lets her observations soak into her unconscious and subconscious, which gives the hundreds of observations the necessary time to build connections among themselves until a coherent whole emerges. Real neural pathways are required for those connections to be made. Although there are numerous bridging structures, the star among them for Python is the corpus callosum, which bridges the left and right hemispheres.

The corpus callosum (along with the *anterior commissure*) connects the two hemispheres, helping them to communicate—a good thing too, because while the two hemispheres collaborate together on every spoken word or intended goal, they focus on different parts of the jobs they share. The left half of the brain loves to work when changes are coming in fast and furious. If there are many changes in light in a given small space, or many changes in sound in a brief moment, the left hemisphere analyzes them, turning them into the surface textures that help you tell fur from feather, or into the different sounds that help you tell a *boot* from a *beet*. Meanwhile, the right-hemisphere loves picking up clues that are more spread out in time and space. It does its best work over large pieces of space or broad windows of time, which means contours, profiles, and context. The left specializes in seeing the small granular details, whereas the right sees the big picture; the left sees the trees for the right's forest. The two hemispheres combine their information to generate the illusion of your reality, courtesy of the corpus callosum. In any technological device there are always two components that share information or transfer power between them, yet they have to be separated in order to do their specialized jobs—and so it is with the hemispheres of the brain. The Python within you finds this important because any bridging link may become the soft spot that acts as the fulcrum, where a little pressure at the right angle causes a chain reaction, turning the machinery against itself.

How do you get two sides of a split-brain patient to wrestle each other? By showing each hemisphere a different image. Imagine a widescreen television with the image of a snowman on the left half of the screen and a rooster head on the right. Now, you may have heard that people are *contralaterally organized*, meaning the left hemisphere "sees" the right side of the world and vice versa. That segregation would be a problem, except the sides communicate to each other via the corpus callosum to cobble together a whole image. But this is not so in split-brain patients. If you flash the image fast enough (before the individual eyeballs can glance at both sides), the left hemisphere sees a rooster head (on the right side of the screen) and the right hemisphere sees a snowman (on the left side of the screen)—and neither side knows what the other side saw. But the wrestling does not start until you ask the patient what they saw.

In order to make sense of what happens next, it helps to remember the division of labor between the hemispheres. The left half of the brain controls speech. It controls speech production, vocabulary, and grammar and, to add to all that, it controls the right half of the body, including the right hand. The right hemisphere controls the left side of the body, and although it recognizes *prosody* (the information conveyed by emotional tone), it does not control speech. It's a mute. So, the left side of the brain sees the rooster and can talk about it and, in a lineup of pictures, can point to a picture of a chicken claw with the right hand. Meanwhile, the right hemisphere sees the snowman, but all it can do is point to the picture of a snow shovel in the lineup with the left hand.

As the right hemisphere tries to communicate what it sees, you will watch the left hand, which controls point with increasing insistence to the image of the snow shovel. To add to it, the right hemisphere gets the gist that the left hemisphere is giving a "wrong" verbal answer (of rooster) because the sound of the verbal response bounces to both ears. Then you witness the type of behavior that gets the Pope to convene a summit. The left hand (right/mute hemisphere), like a disgruntled co-worker, reaches over to the right hand (verbal/left hemisphere) to forcibly drag it over to the image of the snow shovel. The right hand pulls itself out of the grip of the left like a bullied sibling and continues to point to the rooster claw. And back and forth it goes. Because of the removal of the corpus callosum, the right and left hemispheres fail to communicate within the brain, so they take the fight "outside."

Python loves mental jobs that require switching thinking styles or mental skills that require communication to travel to all areas of the brain, and more often than not, across the corpus callosum. A game of chess, for example, means using spatial skills to imagine possible moves while using your language skills to keep in mind the rules of the game. These structural bridges integrate experiences into a whole that is greater than the sum of its parts. For Python, the practice is to look for moments of mental stretch, of the "tapping your head and rubbing your stomach" variety, and deliberately embrace combining diametrically opposed elements. If you can do this while breathing rhythmically and holding a cool-headed, calm center, then you have done your first official Python exercise.

Python Personality

Captain Sir Richard Francis Burton traveled the world as a secret agent for the Honorable East India Company, and as a Python *par excellence,* he blended in seamlessly wherever he went. Meticulously dressing in the region's clothing, he immersed himself in the area's religious practices and scriptures and even got circumcised for travel in Arab countries. He became the first Westerner to enter the forbidden cities of Harar, Medina, and Mecca masquerading as a Muslim, for which the penalty of discovery is death. He was a linguistic chameleon, blending in with the phonemic soundscape of his hosts. He devoted hours to his study of languages and was so well practiced that he was regarded by many from a multitude of backgrounds as a native speaker in their own language and a devoted disciple of their faith. He chanted the Koran in Arabic, was given the hereditary title of Brahmin by the Hindus, and read from the Torah in Jewish synagogues. In exchange, he brought to the English language the words *pajama* and *safari* along with translations of the *1001 Arabian Nights* and the *Kama Sutra.* By the time of his death, he was able to speak thirty languages in numerous dialects with a perfect accent.[10]

He is also considered by historians the paradigm of a cold-blooded secret agent in a war of cultural imperialism who pitted a people against their very own customs. He broke into these cultures the way spies break codes. For while he was immersed in languages and religions, he only wore the garb of their worldview. The Python hallmark is to be in the world but not of it, and Burton kept coolly detached. He once said, "The more I study religions the more I am convinced that man never worshipped anything but himself."[11] For the Python type, cultures are codes protecting the secret agreement made mutually and unevenly between the oppressive and the oppressed groups of a society, notarized deep in the psyches of all its citizens. And for Python, codes—numerical, linguistic, or psychological—are meant to be broken.

A Python personality prefers the complex, covert, and cool-headed. In music, Python likes jazz for its intercutting rhythms. Python dresses in the required camouflage, blending in with the natives to disappear in plain sight. At dinner, the Python sommelier pairs the wine to the meat to counterpoint nuances of flavor; designs menus with contrasts of hot, cool, sweet, and sour; and embeds the plate's presentation with the ambient décor, all the while making methodical calculations on the ratio of protein to fat and cataloguing the missing micronutrients so as to supplement them with vitamins.

You can grow your Python by reading and watching movies. When Python reads, detective stories or nonfiction works on science and politics will do, but her joy leaps with authors who invent a complete and self-contained world with its own languages, physics, and social structures, like J. R. R. Tolkien, C. S. Lewis, Frank Herbert, and J. K. Rowling.[12] There is no such thing as a casual viewing when it comes to her watching movies. She tracks the lighting, sound, casting, scriptwriting, and special effects, analyzing each production element for its innovation in the field of cinema and for its power in communicating the sociopolitical meaning of the movie. But as the bridge between the unconscious and conscious mind, she sees movies as messages to the masses from their own collective unconscious and interprets films using the same methods used to analyze dreams.

In her hobbies, she is drawn like a magnet to the levers of nature. She is the geneticist or breeder who grafts and splices characteristics from one species onto another to produce a new breed of rose, dog, or cattle. She loves the mental peace that comes from methodically organizing and cataloging, following her breath as she collects and sorts through stamps, butterflies, or words from other languages conveying sentiments absent in our own. What games does Python like? Games of strategy, like Spock's three-dimensional chess board in *Star Trek,*[13] or curling and billiards where she revels in playing angles off one another, adding a hustle to sweeten the game. All poker players calculate the probability of the next hand, but Python goes a step further. She uses her observation skills to read her opponents, announcing to her table that she will lose for at least the first hour. During the hour, she watches her opponents for tells. She's not frozen; she's gestating. Her losses are investments, each debt purchasing a secret message. At the end of an hour, you are pegged and lulled into a false sense of security, at which time she starts a relentless and accelerating winning streak.

There is something cool and calculating about a Python. In organizations, she does not hold the key decision-making position—she is never the face of the organization—but she knows how to exert influence on the one who is. How do you recognize a Python? The Python person is right in the middle of things yet remains unseen—she *is* camouflage. She blends in, works behind the scenes, whether as a schemer or an administrator, and is an utter pragmatist. The Python type knows the rules, the theories, the principles, and orchestrates the subtle forces that produce startling consequences, like turning a minority of popular votes into a majority of electoral votes.

Like the other Animals, Python matures in stages. During the first stage, Python is born in a world where a new language is emerging, and she spends time absorbing the patterns of the new language. At this stage, like Boa, she seems passive, even inert. But her passivity is a tranquility that allows her subconscious and unconscious to digest her observations. The job of the subconscious is to mull, whereas the job of the unconscious is to contain the flood of related feelings that would fry the conscious mind if it were to analyze each one individually. Together, the subconscious and unconscious pass information back and forth to each other in a combinatorial way, and in the quiet, Python can hear the sets of observations that resonate according to a larger pattern. Like Boa, Python absorbs, but where Boa absorbs feelings and emotional energies, Python absorbs observations of habits, preferences, and methods. At this first stage, her hypnotic quiet is the womb in which her observations gestate into meaningful patterns, even before she can form the thought of what to look for.

During this first stage, Python becomes an expert. I once had a music teacher explain transcription training. When he was a student, his instructor played a melody for the class to transcribe on the fly. They worked through single melodies, then melody and accompaniment, then two melodies at once, and so on, until they could transpose entire songs at once. My teacher said, from then on, he always visualized the notes to the music he heard, and his experience was completely different: he felt he had actually *listened* to music for the first time.

Psychologist Paul Ekman trained himself to read other people's emotions. He started by studying the muscles of the face in an anatomy atlas and learning to move each muscle in isolation.[14] He studied hours of slow-motion videos of spontaneous emotions in courtroom hearings. With careful study, he could accurately interpret the emotions of others with approximately 90-percent accuracy when most everyone, including police officers and judges, hovers around 50 percent. He commented that once you trained yourself to have the skill, it was difficult to turn off, as though there was a computer in the brain at work.

These stories capture the feeling of developing Python and what it feels like to develop expertise. To develop your inner Python, you need to develop expert observation skills, whether in music or emotional facial expressions. You need to break things down into smaller components to reveal underlying principles that are richer in meaning when resynthesized. It's laborious at first, but when you gain fluidity, the skill becomes automatic, like automatically registering words as a whole rather than adding up the letters while reading.

At the second stage, Python evaluates, discriminates, and seeks meaningfulness. Like Boa, Python has a knack for affirming the deep poetry of things, but where Boa simply holds those values as being self-evident, Python feels compelled to test them. So this is the stage when she becomes adept at manipulation. At the University of California, Santa Cruz, between 2001 and 2005, Dr. Mara Mather conducted research on memory and aging. She designed two experiments, one inside the other. In the world of psychological research, front-loading is king, and a tremendous amount of work goes into planning a study before you ever gather data; you create the right task (a job or game that targets memory) under the right circumstances, selecting the type of data to be analyzed. On top of that, you can't let your subjects know what the experiment is about. So, to lead them astray—and to make the job a little tougher (and really get the brain to work hard for clear results)—you give your subjects a distractor task. I will never forget Mara's presentation when she showed results from the two studies. The second study, a shorter task, was the distractor within the first longer study—she made this experiment part of a second larger experiment, which resulted in two journal articles, a researcher's coup. It was the experimental version of Russian dolls and is an example of the kind of design complexity Python loves.

The main challenge during the second stage for Python is to see the forest for the trees. It is easy for a Python to be too clever for her own good; overwhelmed by the minutiae of detail, wrangling every angle, anticipating every contingency, she never completes the action. Whereas Tiger will bulldoze his way to the goal and miss the sights along the way, Python, at this stage, can suffer from the opposite problem. Trying to map every detour and sideshow, she might never cross the finish line.

But if she overcomes this tendency, she works to uncover nature's secrets. At this stage, she works hard, asking lists of systematic questions, verifying her assumptions, taking methodical measurements, testing falsifiable hypotheses, and taking educated gambles. Here, she devises tools out of her own ingenuity. All this work leads to discovering that the principles she is studying out in the world extend into her as well. She discovers secrets and patterns within herself that are planted there by the very same forces of nature that she is studying outside herself. It's like being a master thief in the middle of your career break-in realizing you have been asked to break into your own house. Seeing herself as a smaller pattern within a larger pattern is what makes her manipulations so shuddering and overwhelming and what builds the bridge between the unconscious and conscious and helps Python to mature to the third stage.

At the third stage, the Python's skills in observation and grasp of principles grow to yield deep insights. The insights touch on the sacred, but this is not a spirituality from above and outside, but rather from within and up-from-underneath. This is the crone or witch who knows the properties of the roots, stems, leaves, and seeds of every medicinal plant, the dosages to heal and poison, the times of season to gather them, and how to prepare and how to store them. This is the Python who has strong bridges between the unconscious and conscious minds; her powers of observation, and her contemplation of them, yield deep insight. Psychoanalyst and physician Sabina Spielrein, for example, was first to write about the unconscious drive for sex as containing both the instinct for destruction and the drive for transformation. She earned this insight from observations she made as a mother during the butchery of WWI, having suffered her own schizophrenic episodes. She worked toward healing with Jung, and became a great psychoanalyst, planting the seeds of the death instinct in Freud's ideas and the seeds for the ideas of individuation and transformation in Jung's work.[15]

At the last stage, Python has delved with such depth into the laws of nature that she is touching its pulsing source. She is now ready for Panther, her counterpart in creating the Dragon. Where Python observes, Panther is immersed; where Python understands, Panther experiences, and where Python manipulates, Panther responds. Python is fascinated by Panther's rawness and seeks union between comprehensive analysis and wild impulse.

The Dark Side of Python: Ineffective and Machiavellian

With Python, there are always many variations, and so there are several shades of gray when she turns toward the dark. Out of balance, Python falls for the means, forgetting the ends. Pythons can be easily diverted from their final objective, lured in by the points of interest along the way, seduced by their own fascination, enthralled by their own breadth of knowledge; rapt into inaction, they'll study, prep, and rehearse, but fail to close the deal, seal it with a kiss, or go for the jugular, as nearly happened with Darwin, who sat on his *Origin of the Species* for some twenty years before publishing it.[16]

If you go a little darker, Python is Machiavellian. She is selective about whom she lets know certain secrets; she uses competition between her subordinates to keep them productive but in their place; she uses the carrots and sticks of institutional incentives playing on vanity and fear. Sure, a Tiger or even a Panther will use these tactics, making them great bullies and petty dictators, but Python will employ these with greater depth and nuance while staying out of the public eye. What separates Python from the other Animals here is that her manipulations recruit the system.

At her darkest, she is the psychopath. Do yourself a favor and read Robert Hare's *Without Conscience* and inoculate yourself against psychopaths for life. At its most sinister, the Python-psychopath manipulates with an ease that freezes the blood. They are glib, grandiose, and display superficial emotion; they are likeable masters of image management, gain confidences easily, figure out what people need, and play to those needs, insecurities, and fantasies. They take advantage of our drive for meaning in life; they "seem sane, skating on the surface of emotions," and playing the right role at the right time to the right audience.[17]

The Python-psychopath embodies our worst nightmares of manipulation. The psychopath understands that we "sheep," the people the psychopath preys upon, feel emotions like guilt, shame, embarrassment, and regret—feelings they do not have—and to avoid these feelings we will act against our own self-interest. On the other hand, Python-psychopaths, unhampered by conscience or empathy, are free to lie, cheat, bilk, and defraud with slick ease (and without the bite of remorse or the hurt that comes from knowing they have caused pain to others). And they possess an uncanny talent for blaming the victim. In the eyes of the Python-psychopath, if we are too stupid to look out for ourselves, well then, we deserve to be sheared—we might even learn from it if we try hard enough.

Python Movement: Whips, Breath, and Structure

The python (the actual species) is the only snake to have once had legs, and it still retains the vestiges of a pelvic bone—it's the only snake with hips.[18] I imagine long ago Python approached the gods with a petition. She explained that her understanding of how to move the skeleton like a whip in crashing waves of action was so strong, she found the extra limbs just got in the way. She could do so much more by observing the patterns of her prey's behavior and lying in wait at their moment of greatest inattention. The details of her prey's habits would seep down into her unconscious and then rise into the subconscious as a web of opportunities from which she would consciously choose the time, place, and circumstance and generate a full-bodied wave, shattering the internal structure of her foe. So, she asked if the gods could remove her legs. The gods granted her wish, and she has been practicing the art of doing more with less ever since.

Python ideokinetics, like the mythos, invoke the skeleton moving like a series of whips lashed to each other, where one wave cracks the next, and so on down the line. A natural wave travels up from Earth, through the arched trampoline of the feet, through the legs, the keystone arch of the pelvis, which swivels and sways with freakish liberty, through the spine into the arms—which, in turn, propel the legs. If you watch a Python type going for a jog, you will see a loose, long gait as each of her limbs swings like a pendulum.

Good posture amplifies strength, speed, and balance. Python studies the space between the bones, the angular ranges of the joints that make for natural and powerful movement. Python joint articulation feels like it is happening as deep inside the socket as possible. In this modern world, natural movement, strangely enough, must come with practice, and it involves working to unlearn poor habits. Space precludes a full list of relaxation and alignment techniques; however, appendix C has two Python skeletal alignment exercises, Rock 'Round the Clock and the Spinal Roll. They involve lying on the floor and letting your weight fall as you make small movements. Lying on the floor provides the kinetic equivalent of a soundproof chamber against which the dumb giant of your body can listen to the proprioceptive feedback from your joints. As you move a joint from one end to another of its range of motion, the brain creates a map of the movement and chooses the midpoint of the two extremes as the resting place, which happens also to be the soundest position structurally. This is a good example of how Python leverages natural forces while seeming passive. Allowing the weight of her body to fall into the floor while drawing small circles with the hips, she lets the supercomputer of proprioception chug along.

The Python logos emerges from the depths of this mindset. In conflict, she uses all means at her disposal to misdirect attention; camouflage, subterfuge, infiltration, espionage, ambush, counterespionage, and sabotage are all part of her trade-craft. Her mythos in moving herself is a revelation when you see how she moves others. The Queen of Disarming and Applying Locks, she uses the force and strength of her opponents against them, as they often find themselves hanging from their own rope. She enjoys jujitsu and other arts that focus on disrupting skeletal structure. She juggles multiple attackers, using one against the other, and she loves the complex interplay of rhythm, angles, and planes of motion in double stick fighting, like Escrima. Regardless of what martial art you practice, here are two Python tips: imagine that fulcrums are at points of contact and that levers as longer than they are. For example, imagine your arm crossed with that of an opponent, the arms making an X like two swords. If you both merely push each other at the point of contact, the contest devolves into arm wrestling. But if you imagine a ball sandwiched at the point of contact acting like a fulcrum around which you can leverage, then suddenly, you can effortlessly wield around your opponent's arm to strike or unbalance. Conversely, you can imagine a longer lever. Still think about crossing your arm like a sword with that of an opponent's; if you think of your arm as ending at your shoulder, you end up arm wrestling. But if you extend the lever of the arm through the shoulder blade down to the center of the back, then a small action at your center results in a large change at the point of contact, moving the person as though they are drawn by a magnet.

The mythos of hiding to study the pattern of her opponent turns into dissembling techniques. Python styles have a "soft" side that emphasizes *blending* with the motion of their opponent. *Blending* in a martial art is a little like going from following to leading in partner dancing; you match the speed of your opponent, staying not so close that you crash into them, but not so far away that you create a gap for them to chase across after you. You start by going in the same direction as the limb of your opponent and then guide their center in a new direction. Take the trajectory of a fist or arrow as an example. If you stay on the trajectory line, you will be shot or punched, but if you move off the line, and at first glide along with the arm or the shaft, you can apply a gentle nudge to redirect the line of the strike or the trajectory of the archer's aim. The redirection does not require much force. In fact, in martial practice, the use of force alerts your opponent to your intention and escalates the fight. The key is to steer gently, with a calm, relaxed posture, and trust in the natural spirals of the body. To the opponent, it feels like they are being inexplicably and irresistibly drawn. One second they are attacking, the next they are on the ground and have no idea how they got there. If you train with a master in a martial art with strong Python elements like jujitsu, judo, aikido, or Systema, you may have the good fortune to experience this sense of dissembling.

Sure, Python can win a fight, but "you have to win two fights. The first one, on the street. The second one, in court."[19] But for Python, like the great general Sun Tzu, getting into a fight is a sign of failure. You should be able to study, strategize, influence, disrupt, and position your way to victory. It's best to avoid the cycle of retribution altogether. And the only way to succeed in this is to grasp her own weaknesses as well as those of the opponent. Python's morphos is transformation through recognition: seeing in herself those same patterns she observes in others. She recognizes that the tensions she reacts to in the world are a reflection of tensions she holds in herself and that she must use the same cunning and patience to confront both. So, although Python shares breath with Boa in healing, where Boa seeks empathic union and energetic wholeness, Python strives for a narrative unity, not about how an opponent was foiled, but about how the forces propelling them to confront each other were neutralized.

The energy of Python's morphos visited a friend of mine around a campfire one night. He had gone camping with some martial arts friends and other friends from various walks of life—two dojo teachers, a police trainer, an old street fighter turned high school teacher, a military sharpshooter, a nurse, and a lawyer. The two martial arts teachers started talking shop about techniques on the mat, trading stories, which quickly escalated with the police trainer and the old street fighter adding theirs. The stories varied from stupidly funny mistakes in drills, to intense tests and simulations, to real confrontations with multiple assailants. They reached their culmination with stories from the sharpshooter. Then, from the dimly lit part of the campfire circle, the nurse started to go into what it is like at the hospital to treat a gunshot wound and other emergencies. She explained how the internal organs never really fully recover from a gunshot, how people get migraines for the rest of their lives from a concussive punch as a teenager, or how they are hobbled for the rest of their lives from a fractured vertebra that they got from falling too hard to the ground. The lawyer then chimed in to speak about cases where a man was sued for *stopping* a child molestation, or when using your martial art training turns your self-defense into assault with a deadly weapon in the eyes of the law or causes the loss of friends who just see you in a different light because you used violence. My friend felt at that moment that he was witnessing the entire narrative of conflict from training to consequences in all its gradations of intensity, and he felt his experiences gel in a *1001 Arabian Nights* kind of a story. He said after that trip, his training and his relationships took on a new depth.

The bridge between the conscious and the unconscious is built by breath and narrative. Not just stories, but *narratives*. Saying we are made up of stories is not just a quaint comment but actually has some theoretical basis.[20] Stories compete in our minds for dominance, and the one that wins is the one we are. But such stories do not exist in a vacuum. We have to decide what a story will be about, and when we have many, what their relationship to each other will be. Narratives are metastories—they are a story about the stories. A narrative is about how we choose what a story will focus on and what stories belong together. The stories from the campfire I mentioned earlier center on themes of how to cope with violence. When taken together, all the perspectives from around the campfire make up the narrative. The Python bridge between the conscious and unconscious is made by how we weave the many individual stories into a single coherent narrative.

Python never forgets the narrative. Every confrontation has a prelude and an aftermath, and she works to win the rights to tell the story. The narrative is everything. The narrative may be told in the language of aiki, dao, physics, Washington, or Hollywood, but it is always about the process of transformation, how we became what we are, how the mythos leads to the morphos.

In morphos, Python is a formidable healer because, to paraphrase Gilbert and Sullivan, Python is the model of a modern major generalist. She works across all systems of the body, leveraging their built-in gifts for self-repair. She heals the muscles by focusing on eccentric contractions; tones fascia and tendons and ligaments through full range of joint movements on multiple planes; realigns the skeleton using methods like Feldenkrais or the Alexander Technique; promotes the health of organ tissue through proper nutrition; and ties all this to the breath. Dr. Michael Colgan is an excellent example of Python integrating multiple systems; he has written comprehensive tomes on nutrition, power, flexibility, posture, and mental balance. You will know the Python morphos by the subtle methods she uses, like craniosacral therapy, where a gentle touch at the bottom end of the spine adjusts the top. You will recognize Python by how she goes deep when treating wounds, physical and psychological. She will fortify the body with *Tui na,* or bone cleansing exercises, and she will heal the psyche starting with Freudian and Jungian psychoanalysis, working up through the layers to behavioral and cognitive therapies, before she finishes with humanistic approaches.

Python Sex: Buttons, Buttons, Buttons

Sensuality is calculated. What places to touch, when to touch them and, most importantly, how to time the touch with one's breath make up Python's "sexpertise," but it is a double-edged sword. Instead of pleasing and fulfilling your partner, you may just as easily turn love-making into a performance. The master observer, Python understands body language, from the split-second glance when attraction starts, to the mannered mimicry that indicates interest and liking, to the paced breathing of growing intimacy. She notes the shape of the lips and fingers, and from that, she can tell the shape of the erogenous organs.

Python in the Arts

Python authors revel in creating entire worlds, complete with socio-geopolitical-economic realities and an invented language. J. R. R. Tolkien created languages and songs for each species inhabiting *The Hobbit* and *The Lord of the Rings* trilogy.[21] His adventures depict the struggles between the extremes of industrialization and connection to nature. Orcs, elves, hobbits, and dwarves illustrate the psychological costs of where we choose to place ourselves on the spectrum between relating to and exploiting nature. Frank Herbert borrowed from Arabic culture and language to create the world of *Dune.*[22] In his book, the development of the planet's ecology parallels the political development of its people and the development in consciousness of the main characters. The charm of J. K. Rowling's books is to have the wizarding world hidden in parallel—parked in plain sight of the normal world,[23] but it is the Latin in her magic spells and the recasting of creatures from classical mythology that give her magic an exotic yet familiar feel. She charts the psychological progress of the hero, Harry Potter, who gradually integrates his personal shadow, the traits he shares in common with his nemesis, Lord Voldemort, while he learns to be part of his adoptive society, the wizarding world. The wizarding world must, in turn, also integrate *its* collective shadow, the festering moral and political issues of slavery, racism, authoritarianism, genocide, war, and child abuse—taken to an extreme by the Death Eaters but tolerated passively by everyday citizen witches and wizards. These are the kinds of books Python likes to read and write.

Because of its technical complexity and rich artistic potential, film is a medium ideally suited for Pythons. The production designer must match historical accuracies to the tone and mood of the film; the writer surgically juggles character, dialogue, setting, and plot; the director, the Python-in-Chief, balances all of these elements into a cohesive whole. Audiences love a strong Python character like Sir Arthur Conan Doyle's Sherlock Holmes and Keyser Söze in *The Usual Suspects*.[24] Python actors tend to have lanky body movement and laconic vocal work, like John Malkovich.

An all-time great Python character is Hannibal Lecter in *Silence of the Lambs*.[25] Hannibal personifies the Python's formidable power of observation, the ability to track each sensory modality in parallel for clues in the intrinsic makeup of a person. As Jodie Foster's character, Clarice Starling, walks the twenty feet to Hannibal's cell from the block entrance, Hannibal has already tracked her by the sound of her gait (the rhythm is clumsy because she's not used to wearing heels) and her smell (the perfume she's wearing today is masking the cheaper one she usually wears). Her concealed twang betrays her poor, West Virginia upbringing. He pegs her socially, and in Python fashion, uses this as leverage to get inside her head. Like the Python, Hannibal "The Cannibal" literally preys on people when they are unaware. But with Starling, he can figuratively feed on the insight she has into herself (and which he cannot bear himself). Starling reveals to him her motivation for being an FBI agent—her need to save victims today to assuage the crying of the spring lambs set for slaughter so many years ago, when she was child, fresh after the murder of her Marshall father when her mother sent her away to her uncle's farm. There, she tried to save the panicking lambs but couldn't, and she still hears their cries in her sleep. That she could walk back and forth on the bridge between the unconscious motivations from the past and the conscious interrogation of the present business is what elevates her in the eyes of the master Python.

Equally important to the Python nature of Hannibal was his modus operandi. During the movie, we watch him trap his jailors while they are inattentive, symbolically asleep. What does it take to be a prison guard or a warden? To be an oppressor, which is the symbolic meaning of a prison guard, you have to forget who you are; you have to fall asleep while still remaining awake. You have to forget that you and the oppressed share a common humanity. It is the deepest form of sleep. Hannibal preyed on those who were inattentive, asleep and, unlike Starling, did not have the courage to face themselves.

What makes Hannibal so threatening, and such a good example of Python, is his focus on essential nature. Pythons distill the essential function of a thing or action. For example, Hannibal helps Starling psychologically profile Buffalo Bill, a serial murderer on the loose. He helps her recognize that the motivation of his murders is driven not by hate or lust, but by covetousness. From there, he infers the serial killer needed to make visual contact to identify desirable victims.

Python Turning Toward Dragon

Python plaque exercises, with practice, will leave you alert and relaxed, and with a meta-awareness of attention—not only do you pay attention more easily, you are aware of shifts in your attention.

The Python Plaque

Python's plaque (see Figure 4.1 in this book's color insert) focuses on themes of integrating natural laws and principles. Her plaque is a green triangle inside a brown circle inside a white square. The triangle, circle, and square represent the person, the world, and the cosmos, respectively. The green of Python's triangle symbolizes the cyclic laws of nature that oscillate between growth and decay with the rhythmic regularity of breath. For Python, the triangle that represents the person is green because she sees herself as an extension of the same natural laws she observes and internalizes. (See Figure 4.1 in color insert.)

Any five-year-old with finger paint will make a dirty brown by swirling many colors together. In much the same way, the Python's brown circle symbolizes the sum total of natural laws waltzing through stars and cells. It can be tempting, if you made a plaque out of glue and construction paper, to think of the green triangle as stuck on top of the brown circle. But a hard-earned secret of long-time meditators is that static mandalas are actually dynamic and animated, and the green triangle emanates out from the brown circle the same way colors emanate from a rainbow.

Like each of the Animals, the Python plaque has levels of meaning. The first level, the points on the triangle, captures the Python anatomy discussed earlier, the skeleton, respiratory system, and the corpus callosum. In the next layer, we find the cornerstones of Python's psychology—sensory awareness, observation, and manipulation. You can focus on each one at a time or together. And lastly, there is the energetic layer. In this layer, Python shares the pumps and breath it has in common with Boa, emphasizing breath visualization of the bone marrow.

The *breath* refers to vital energy, like *prana, ki,* or *chi,* that, for Python, not only invigorates the body, but *carries information.* At the very least, a rhythmic breathing keeps your mind (more) open under stress. You are more in touch with your awareness of the situation. But on a deeper level it is as though, for Python, the breath contains direct knowledge and insight, as though the breathing is directly drawing in insight.

The *pumps* refer to an energy system located at the joints of the skeleton. In Ch'ien-lung, the joints are treated like mini chakras or centers, and the pumps are energetic membranes that act like bellows, circulating energy throughout the joint. You don't strengthen the pumps so much as tone them by extending and relaxing as fully as you can while doing the bows or other physical exercise. *Marrow energy* refers not only to the yellow and red marrow of the skeleton, but to the brain as well, which Chinese medicine calls the *sea of marrow.* When doing the Python bow, you draw energy into the marrow to invigorate and tone it. The marrow is like a cell battery offering an added boost of vitality when needed.

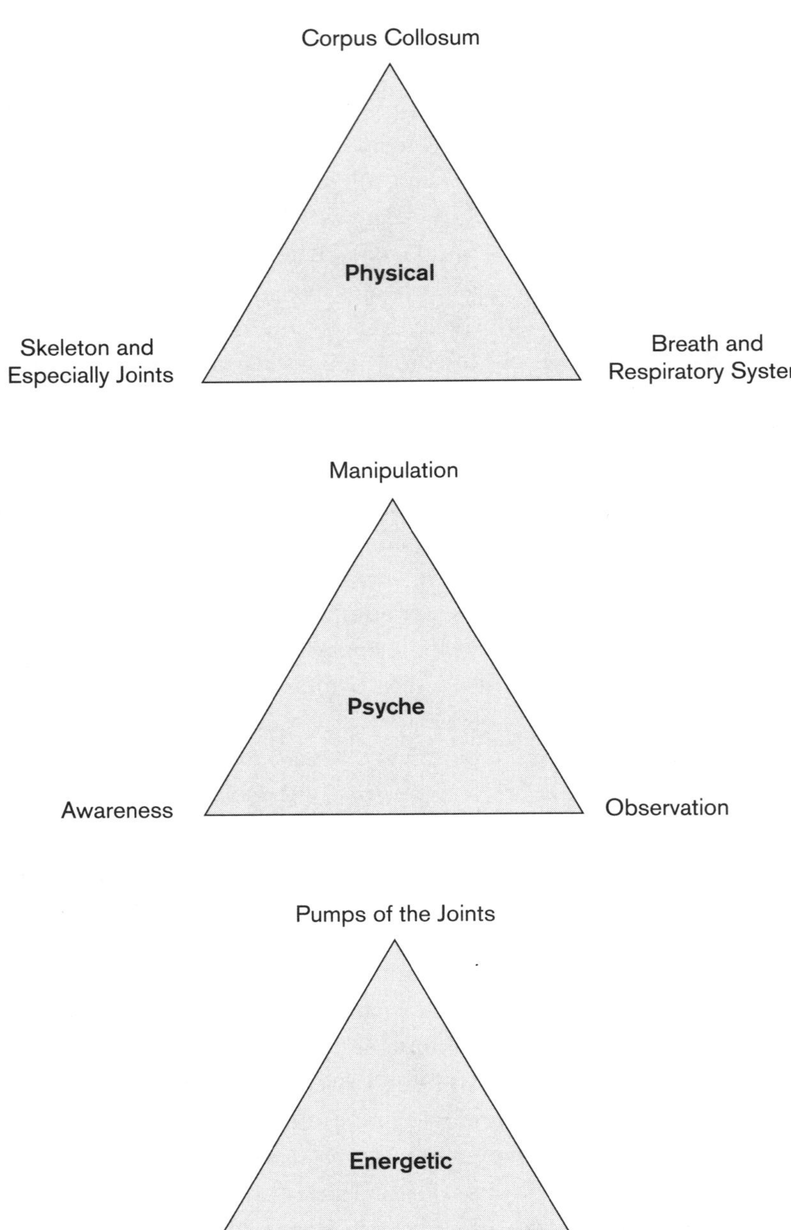

FIGURE 4.2: The symbolic meaning of the triangle points for the Python

In the plaque work, Python sits down in meditation not as an individual, but as an embodied extension of the laws of nature. By engaging the dynamics of nature through synchronized breath and attention, Python starts off a Möbius strip of feedback and self-tuning. What kinds of concentration exercises does a Python do?[26] There are myriad variations that usually fall into one of four main types: 1) multimodal tracking, 2) attention games involving covert and overt attention, 3) deep language, and 4) mnemonics. In multimodal games, you keep a regular breathing pattern while explicitly noting what you observe in each sensory modality, as though each sense has its own track in an eight-track recorder.

Python plays with attention like kids play with cardboard boxes, especially in monitoring the shift between overt and covert attention. *Overt attention* basically means you can tell what a person or animal is paying attention to through movement, like a shift in eye-gaze during a conversation or the way a dog's ear turns toward an unexpected sound, whereas *covert attention* means to watch "out of the corner of your eye" without physically orienting. Overt attention allows you to move your eyes over the words on this page to take in their meaning; covert attention allows you to pay attention to the sounds in the room while you are reading. Python plaque exercises for covert and overt attention are detailed later in this chapter.

Python loves crossword puzzles and word games, and like a good lawyer, she can use a question like a scalpel. But when it comes to plaque work, Python takes the opportunity to ask what she chooses to use language *for.* This is about approaching your life with a poet's eye, like a literature professor, analyzing the so-called mundane details for metaphors and symbols. It is about interpreting the mythos of your life, which then alters the way your words frame that world. The following section shares Python exercises for deep language.

Finally, memory exercises cultivate Python's acumen. Observations stick with a good memory. Memory can be trained with peg-word associations and by reviewing your day, one of the seven steps for the Animals. Both go a long way to developing a better memory.

Seven Steps to Embodying Python

Step One: Follow Your Breath (Ongoing Mindfulness Practice)

Of all the Animals, Python has the most complex relationship to breath. To embody Python, play with breath, observing how rhythm influences movement and attention. Following your breath in Python means visualizing breath in your

Bone marrow Imagine you can breathe into the red marrow, which produces red blood cells that, in turn, carry oxygen and the breath. Red marrow is located in the flat bones of the pelvis, sternum, cranium, ribs, vertebrae, and scapulae, and in the "spongy" ends of the long bones such as the femur and humerus. Ideokinetics: Move as if the spongy marrow absorbs impact. Move as if you can pack sensory information into the marrow to store it as energy and raw material for contemplation. Connect to Earth's structure, from the molten core up through the geological layers to the edge of the atmosphere. Connect to Earth's rich deposits of minerals and oils.

Corpus callosum The Python represents bridging structures. There are numerous bridges in the brain, but the Python centers on the corpus callosum, which bridges the left and right hemispheres of the brain. Imagine your breath traveling along these neural fibers, connecting the left and right hemisphere. Ideokinetics: Move as if deliberately using the left and right sides of the body to counterbalance each other.

Joint space Pick one joint or a set of joints (i.e., knees, elbows, etc.), and feel the space of the joints expanding as you inhale and contracting as you exhale. Make sure to include the bones with fused joints, such as the pelvis and the skull, imagining you can breathe directly into the sutures of these fused bones. You can practice this while standing in line, sitting in a waiting room, or jogging. Ideokinetics: Move as if the expansion and contraction of the space inside of the joints drives your motion. Move as if the bones are tethered by ropes, each limb a segment of a six-sectioned staff (two arms, two legs, spine, and head).

Respiratory system Like Boa, Python also represents the breath. Like Boa, feel the breath enter and caress the tissue of the lungs all the way down to the small alveoli where the exchange of carbon dioxide and oxygen occurs. For Python, there is an emphasis on the movement of the skeleton from breathing, like the movement of the ribcage and, especially, the miniscule shift in the fused bones of the pelvis and skull. Ideokinetics: Move like Boa, expanding and contracting with the breath with special attention on the pulse of the sutured bones. Connect to the fault lines between the tectonic plates and fissures in rocks. Connect to forests and jungles of Earth, the winds, jet streams, hurricanes, and tornadoes.

Rhythm of breath Pay attention to each of the phases of the breath. Notice the duration of the 1) in-breath, 2) the pause between the in- and out-breath 3) the length of the out-breath 4) the pause before the next breathing cycle. You may find introspection easier on the in-breath, and that it is easier to get rid of tension and focus outward on the out-breath. In my personal experience, it is easier to move attention on the exhale and while holding the breath but more effortful on the in-breath. Ideokinetics: Move your body as if in sympathy with shifts in your attention caused by changes in your breath.

Language Keep a steady breath, pick a word to say mentally, and track where the word originates; that is, feel where in your brain the words are forming. Monitor your speech to break unconscious linguistic habits, like avoiding swear words, or not using contractions, such as don't, could've, or it's; Python attenuates the strengths of statements, saying upset rather than angry, and proposes suggestions rather than simply stating directions. For Python, vocabulary is power. Pick a word of the day or resolve to look up any word you don't know in a dictionary, appreciating nuances in meaning. Language reflects power. Examine how your language assumes privileges that society confers upon or withholds from you, merited or not. Look at the labels you use–whether someone is a "freedom-fighter" or an "insurgent," for instance–and deconstruct them; tear them apart to look at all the assumptions the labels contain, and actively experiment with countering them. Ideokinetics: Move as if the semantic articulation translates to joint articulation.

Step Two: Recall Your Day (Daily/10 Minutes before Sleep)

Before falling asleep, review your day's events applying a Python perspective. Look at the day in terms of measurable differences and identifiable patterns. How have you grown and matured as a person? Put today in the context of psychological, social, economic, and political trends; what quantifiable differences did you notice today? And if there are none, observe this objectively as well. Do you notice a difference if you compare this day to one from a week, month, season, or year ago?

Review your day for moments when you made a keen or insightful observation and acted on the observation in an indirect way undetected. Notice how you felt. If you did not act on it, file away the memory in your bones for future use. Review your observations from a granular left hemisphere view for details and from a holistic right hemisphere view for context.

Step Three: Scan Your Body (Daily/10 Minutes before and after Sleep)

Before going to sleep at night, scan your skeletal system, feeling the marrow on the inside and the epithelium skin on the outside of the bone, and imagine being able to feel the space between the bones. Imagine you can feel the corpus callosum sending signals back and forth between both hemispheres.

Step Four: Do the Bows in Nature (Weekly/10–15 Minutes)

Python is the most complex of the Animals, so it is the relationships among types of geography rather than any particular one that inspires the Python bows. Fault lines and subduction zones inspire Python, who is just as much about the space between the tectonic plates as she is about the space between the bones.

She is also about layers and loves to read rocks, from Precambrian to Holocene. When I do Python bows, as I am curling my spine up to a stand, I imagine I am straightening up through geological layers. In geology, the deeper down you go, the further back in time you are. As I curl up, I feel the passage of time in millions of years, rising from the core of Earth up to the surface.

Python is the bridge between the unconscious and conscious, so deep water wells, geyser systems, and natural springs emerging from underground water tables are great places to do bows.

Python loves studying geography, reading how land formations mold the local ecosystem, absorbing how life adapts to estuaries, desert rocks, swamps, forests, jungles, or cave systems. Pythons love to track, so no den, nest, print, or trail where you practice goes unnoticed.

Python Bow

FIGURE 4.3: Stand with the feet together, arms by the side; hold the mudras.

FIGURE 4.4: Release the mudra and begin to curl down on the exhale, as you imagine dropping down through layers of consciousness and Earth.

FIGURE 4.5: At the bottom, begin to curl up on the inhale, rising up through layers of consciousness and layers of Earth.

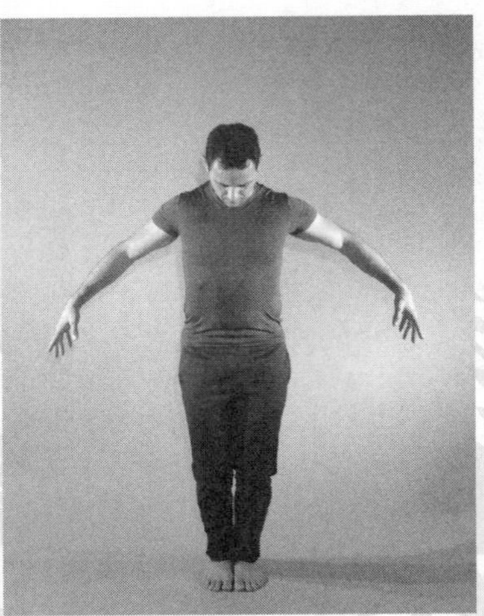

FIGURE 4.6: As you curl up, let the breath raise your arms out to the side, rising up through layers of consciousness and from the core of Earth to the top of the atmosphere.

FIGURE 4.7: Continue to raise the arms.

FIGURE 4.8: Hold the breath in when the arms reach the top.

FIGURE 4.9: Raise the heels off the ground.

FIGURE 4.10: Stomp the heels into Earth, and pack the energy into the marrow of the bones.

FIGURE 4.11: Begin to exhale, and relax the arms as they drop down in front of your body, passing the head.. Keep the palms facing each other.

FIGURE 4.12: Continue relaxing and dropping the arms, down to the collarbones.

FIGURE 4.13: Relax and let the arms fall to the level of the belly button. Bring the palms to face each other, with the hands about a fist's distance apart, and keep the elbows close together and aimed toward the floor.

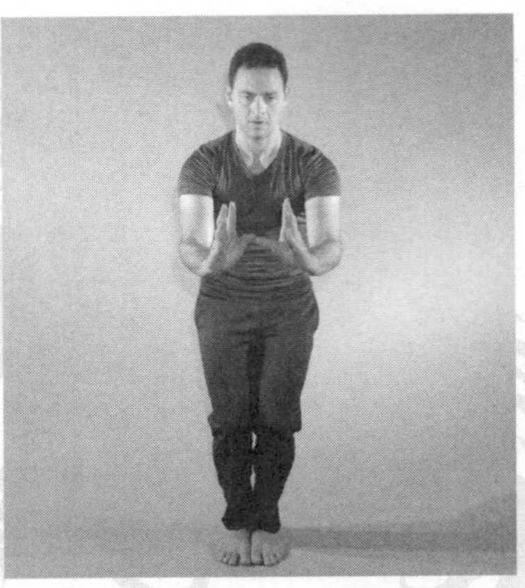

FIGURE 4.14: Keep exhaling: Rock the hands up and forward, with the pinky edge of the hand leading the motion.

FIGURE 4.15: Continue the forward and upward motion. The hands arc up with the pinky edge of the hand pressing forward like a blade. Extend forward with the blade hands. Stop extending and stop exhaling at the same time.

FIGURE 4.16: Begin inhaling, and follow the same arc in reverse.

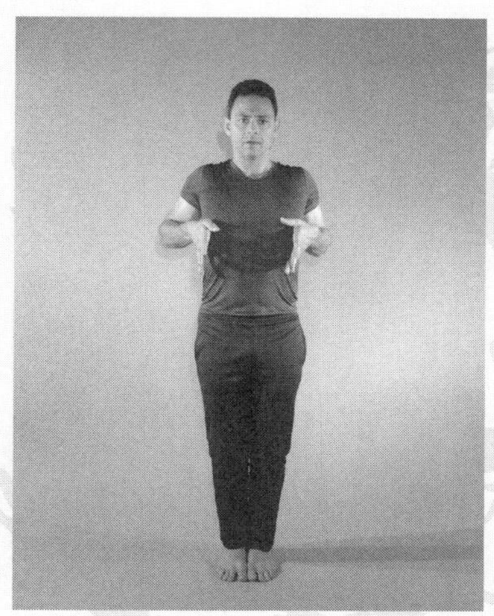

FIGURE 4.17: Continue inhaling slowly, and raise the hands up above the floating ribs.

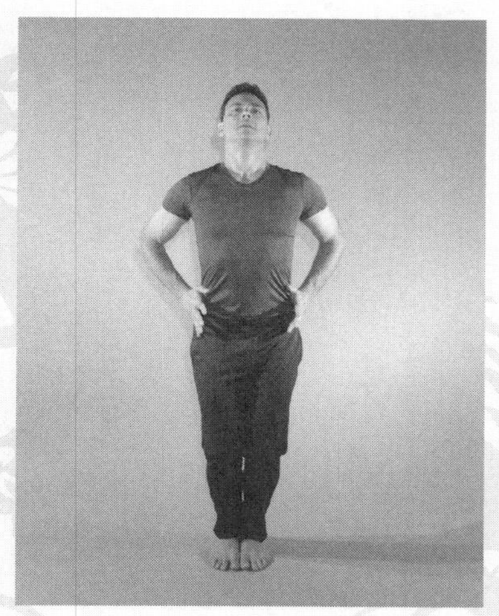

FIGURE 4.18: Continue inhaling, and slide the hands down the sides of the ribs.

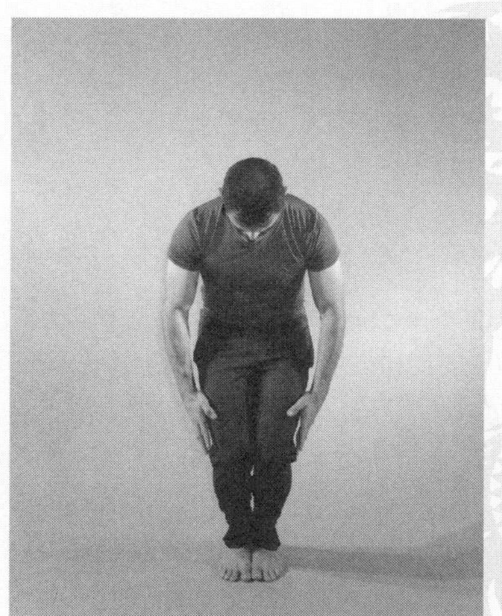

FIGURE 4.19: Exhale and empty out all breath; allow the weight of the body to curl over.

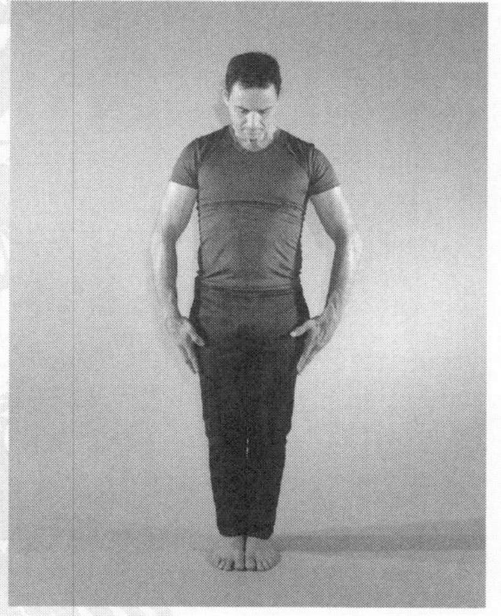

FIGURE 4.20: Inhale as you stack one vertebrae at a time, curling gradually up to a stand.

FIGURE 4.21: Stand fully straight up. Start the next bow.

FIGURE 4.22: Python forms two triangles with the arms and legs slightly apart. The first triangle goes from the soles of the feet to the groin, the second from the tips of the fingers to the crown of the head. Breathe into the bottom triangle, filling it up, then into the top. Exhale from the top down.

Step Five: Adopt the Animal Personality (Ongoing Practice)

Python listens to jazz for its intercutting rhythms and eats foods rich in oxygen content, like leafy greens. Python's meals are designed by a nutritionist, with aperitifs to maximize digestive enzyme production and the full complement of vitamins, minerals, and proteins in perfect balance; the food is cooked to bring out the harmonious composition of natural flavors, and this occurs in in a well-decorated setting. Python favors hobbies involving puzzles or collections, but whatever the hobby is, Python approaches it with a love for details. Python reads books on the natural sciences, history, murder mysteries, politics, economics, or linguistics—anything that pulls the curtain back to show how the gears work.

Python will study anatomy and kinesiology in her sport activity, with an emphasis on unlearning habits that free up the skeleton and allow the body's natural alignment to do the work. When it comes to sports in general, she favors those that require heavy lifting on strategy and planning, like sailing or trekking through foreign jungles. In martial sports, jujitsu or other joint manipulation arts are her calling card.

Above all, Python observes. Python is a tracker. All action can be evaluated in terms of timing, manner, appropriateness, or effectiveness. Watch people—what they spend money on, how they treat their superiors, subordinates, peers, children, and pets; ask what is the central axis of their psyche. Look for how much energy they spend and what they get in return. Notice the pattern of approach and avoidance between people; notice what precedes and what follows moments of communication or contact. Like Sherlock Holmes, who could identify over 140 types of tobacco, create systematized lists that you commit to memory for automatic recall. A system gives your observation traction.

Python equals camouflage. She goes undercover. You may need to abandon privilege, status, or a secure position to wade into the thicket. Keep checking your assumptions.

Python is not my natural home; I had to work at it. I want to share one practice I found productive: I self-narrate what I am noticing in a play-by-play style. The practice helps me go from merely looking or seeing to *observing*. Although Python is empirical, putting hard numbers to her observations, she is interested in the patterns of those observations. You cannot have a pattern without a story, and you cannot have a story without a perspective to frame it or context. By self-narrating, you will notice quickly the frames through which you see your stories. If they're no good, it will be easy to tell by how quickly you bore yourself with the self-narration.

And then, Python manipulates. Rivaling Tiger, Python has formidable willpower when set on a goal, but Python uses *soft* power, preferring influence to force. She wins the game by changing the rules or altering the conditions. She cares about efficiency, how to increase the energy coming in while decreasing the energy going out. Python manipulates through information and counsel, providing empowering knowledge, intelligence, or distraction, like a magician waving a wand with one hand while switching cards with the other.

Step Six: Remember Your Dreams (Daily/10 Minutes upon Waking)

If dreams are the "royal road to the unconscious," then Python paved the road and runs the traffic lights. Space precludes lengthy explanations of the major theories of dream interpretation, so I will point the reader to *Every Dream Interpreted* by Veronica Tonay,[27] which covers Jungian, Freudian, and Gestalt approaches to dream interpretation. Here are a few principles from her book to tide you over. As a Python, you want to adopt each in turn or as appropriate.

The Freudian approach looks at dreams as wish-fulfillment—secret desires you don't wish to acknowledge to yourself. The common error is to feel guilty or embarrassed, especially if the wish is racy or taboo. But the point of a dream is not to reveal the wish per se, rather to show *the kind of power it would take to make the wish come true* and the *resulting freedom you expect from making the wish come true*. As the strategist, Python wants to avoid direct confrontation by leveraging insight against power. Dream interpretation can show you how.

The Gestalt approach assumes that all aspects of the dream represent aspects of the dreamer, either collaborating or competing against each other. The Gestalt approach is particularly adept at mapping our inner landscape, the desires we strive for and the resources we bring to attain them.

Jung agreed with Freud's premise that dreams arose from unresolved issues in personal life, but he also observed recurring symbols or patterns of feelings and imagery across cultures he called *archetypes.* Archetypes appear with reliable consistency in dreams to mark important life developments. Python studies dream interpretation systems and applies them as needed.

Step Seven: Use the Plaques (Daily/20 Minutes)

Python plaque work exploits distinctions between overt and covert attention. As you do the plaque work (see appendix A), overtly (eyes move) track the edge of the triangle, while you covertly (eyes don't move) track the edge of the circle in a counterclockwise direction in time with the breath, *at the same time*. Your brain will never be the same.

Python Energy Circuit

Visualize the perceptual information of each modality flow into the corpus callosum, which shares it with both hemispheres, on the in-breath. On the out-breath, the energy flushes down into the marrow of the bones.

Python vs. Animals

Python and Boa are similar, but Boa floats with a soft breath, whereas Python rides the breath as a rollercoaster with its movement. Boa extends her empathic awareness out in all directions and waits for life to provide, while Python monitors her sense and is compelled to manipulate based on the pattern she observes. Boa is passive and content to do nothing, but Python, at some point, sets and triggers the trap.

Python Keys

Python eye gaze: The eyes fixate straight forward while you focus out of the corner of your eyes.

Python tongue position: The tongue is relaxed. Your mouth is closed, but you breathe as if it were open (this will create little eddies of air).

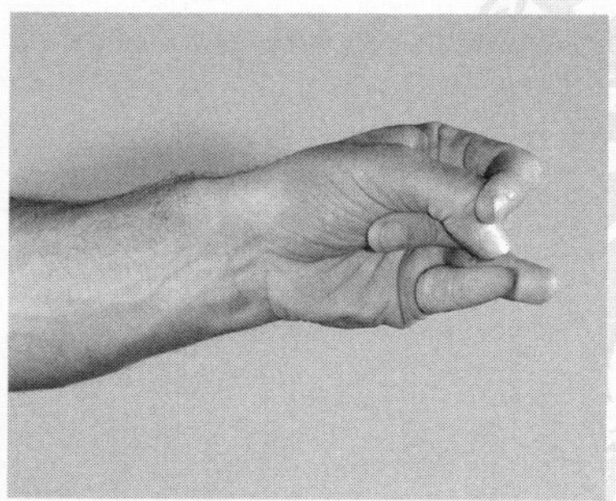

FIGURE 4.23: Python mudra: Bring the middle finger to the mound of the thumb. Touch the tip of the thumb to the ring finger, between the first and second joint. Bring the pinky below the ring finger. Touch the index finger on the thumb right between the first joint and the fingernail.

FIGURE 4.24: Python asana: Sit with the left leg crossed in front, and sit on the right foot with the heel tucked between the sitting bones.

Table 4.1 summarizes the Python archetype.

TABLE 4.1: Python Summary

Consciousness	Sensory awareness, observation, manipulation
Nature	Wherever ecosystems intersect–river bends, canyons, subterranean caves
Anatomy	Skeleton, bone marrow, corpus callosum, respiratory systems, space between the joints
Neural regions	Corpus callosum
Energetic system	Joint pumps, stored energy in the bone marrow
Favorite foods	Oxygen-rich foods, scientifically designed diets
Music	Jazz, Bach
Sports and martial arts	Jujitsu, joint manipulation
Hobbies	Chess, mystery novels, politics, history, collecting
Clothes	Whatever fits in with the locals, camouflage

BLACK PANTHER: SURVIVAL IN THE SHADOWS

As if you were on fire from within. The moon lives in the lining of your skin.

—PABLO NERUDA

THE BLACK PANTHER STEALS under the dank cloak of night, at once the hunter and the hunted, his only ally is silence. The small cat seems easy game, but nothing can prepare his would-be attacker for the onslaught of nature's drive to survive. There is no word for speed like this. The Panther's velvet fur ripples over sinews unleashing a torrent of slashes, ripping and rending the soft parts of the body rich in arteries. Instinct prevails by moonlight.

Black Panther Consciousness: Instinct, Subconscious, and Dreams

Black Panther is the cat of sensuality, instinct, and the subconscious mind; he is the master of fear and the gatekeeper to the realm of dreams. To be Black Panther is to be on the animal side of human nature, to feel like you are in the wild, at once the hunter and the hunted, every sense awake, every moment walking the razor's edge between life and death. To live Black Panther is to experience Earth as a living, sentient organism that communicates directly with you for the sake of survival. Black

Panther consciousness *receives information pertaining to survival directly from Earth.* Black Panther consciousness is immersed in the raw materials of the subconscious mind, symbols, imagery, and fairytale magical thinking, unfiltered and without the hindrance of analysis.

The proximity of death heightens the thirst to live. Fear dilates the pupils, sharpens the senses, slows down time, hastens the heart, quickens the reflexes, fuels the limbs, kindles relevant memories of similar moments in the past, and connects us to Earth. When we connect to Earth, she makes us bigger than we are. She has layered instincts atop each other over the eons of natural selection, and the rush of fear unlocks their assistance.

The power of ritual and the magic of ceremony, symbols, and emblems appeal to the Black Panther subconscious. If you have felt moved at a ceremony like a wedding, funeral, or parade, where you called the people you were with a tribe, bound together by bonds of story and myth, then you have experienced Panther's subconscious mind. The subconscious needs a tribe; it survives on mystery, magic, fantasy, and superstition.

The subconscious is the gateway to the realm of dreams. If you have ever woken from a dream exerting a strong influence on your mood, or it seemed to portend coming changes, then you have experienced Black Panther and the power of the subconscious mind. In modern westernized society, we are increasingly losing touch with the subconscious, but as individuals, none of us is untouched by it.

Black Panther Anatomy: Tendons and Ligaments, Brainstem, Roots

The Panther mythos is about *roots, recoil,* and *sensuality*. How do you tap into the alchemy of Panther? Imagine that you spill yourself into the sheaths of your own muscles, into the tendons and ligaments; imagine falling back in evolutionary history into the ancestral wired instincts of the brainstem and dropping down into the crucible basement of the groin, gonads, and tailbone. The silky sheathing of tendon and ligaments endows Panther with lightning-fast reactions and his preternatural sensuality. Rooting us figuratively to Earth are the feet, and rooting us to our evolutionary past are the gonads, groin, tip of the tailbone, adrenals, and the brainstem. These anatomical areas are important to Panther, especially when practicing moves or Panther bows, like the ones at the end of this chapter, in which you drink in the intimate alliance between sensuality and the jolting gift of fear, the sensory odd couple of survival.

When practicing Panther breathing, you focus and draw energy to the *adrenal glands*. The adrenals power up Panther's fight or flight reactions. Adrenaline shunts fuel to the muscles in preparation for fight or flight, feeding Panther's recoil. You feel adrenaline dilate the pupils to allow for more light and greater acuity; dilate the airways to let in more oxygen; shut down digestion; jump-start blood clotting to protect against injury; increase perspiration, heart rate, and respiratory rate; and clench the jaws, in readiness to bite the enemy, in a nod to our evolutionary heritage.[1]

The spring-loaded tendons and ligaments span the entire body and act like resilient rubber bands, providing the recoil we need for survival. *Tendons* connect muscle to bone, while *ligaments* tether bone to bone. Tendons and ligament are three times stronger in tensile force than muscle, and while they do not generate force, they sew the body into a lively spring, provide bounce and recoil to movement, and give motion a fluid quality. Tendons and ligaments are one tribe of collagenous fibers called *fascia,* a skin-like matrix of connective tissue that wraps around every muscle, blood vessel, and internal organ, enabling us to bounce off of our own bodies.[2] Fascia plays a large role in Black Panther's sensuality as it contains many of the sensory neurons that perceive muscle contraction or movement of the joints. Fascia provides a warm moveable support for the blood vessels and nerves and a smooth surface for muscle to slide and glide over, making such pleasurable sensation out of movement.

The Panther theme of sensuality recurs with what, in Eastern terms, is called the *yin skin,* the softer and usually less hairy underbellies of the arms, legs, torso, and neck. The yin skin is usually richer in surface blood vessels and more sensitive to touch. The yin skin does not necessarily *do* anything, but if you think about slinking, stalking, prowling, and making yourself physically smaller (things important to Panther), you do it by gliding the yin skin areas of the body close to each other.

Panther represents roots. The subconscious is the root system of the mind and is associated with the occipital lobe and hindbrain at the back of the head. The feet are the figurative roots of the body, anchoring it to Earth. The tailbone is a vestigial remnant of the tail our ancestors had, and the gonads root us to the reproductive cycle and our ancestral lineage. A student will pay attention or visualize these areas—feet, tailbone, groin, gonads, adrenals, hindbrain, the yin skin, fascia, tendons, and ligaments—when practicing Black Panther, especially, when doing the bows.

Black Panther Brain: Amygdala, Hypothalamus, Cerebellum

A man is walking along a bridge when he spots a woman looking in horror at some spot in the water. Before the man realizes what he is doing, he jumps over the railing. He swims in a beeline to the spot the woman was looking at and is wondering why, when suddenly he remembers that the woman was staring at a boy who was drowning a few yards ahead in the same direction he is swimming.[3] This is the Panther brain in action, reacting even before you know what you are doing or why. Panther is not analytical; the closest it comes to thinking is this kind of "startle-response with benefits" that comes courtesy of the amygdala. The *amygdala* (lit. *almond* because of its shape and size) regulates responses to perceived threats. The evolutionarily older amygdala gets dibs on each of the senses as information passes through the amygdala even before that same information can make its way to the cortex. This amygdala-first policy means that the beast within you reacts before the conscious part of you knows why. The amygdala fires off emotional commands with a speed that precedes conscious awareness. This is what makes Panther so powerful and so unnerving to some people—they cannot trust this part they do not have control over. Practicing the bows for Panther can help build trust in your powerful instincts.

Panther breathes through, and moves with, his fear. Imagine having a relationship to your instincts where you trust how you will react under fearful conditions. Such mastery of fear comes from not fighting fear but working with it, as Panther does. What makes fear so powerful? Part of the answer rests with the hypothalamus and the redundancy of neural circuits. The hypothalamus is a small, pea-sized organ of the brain regulating the raw appetites, called the four Fs—fight, flight, feeding, and fornication. The rest of the brain is just there to keep your hypothalamus warm, fed, safe, and snuggled. There is usually one dedicated circuit to turn something on and another dedicated nerve to turn it off. Let's take the example of eating. There is one circuit that exclusively triggers hunger and eating and another dedicated to satiety that triggers us to stop eating. But, when it comes to fear, the hypothalamus has *two* circuits to turn fear on. One circuit uses the telephone wires of the nerves, called the sympathetic adrenal-medullary (SAM), and a second, called the hypothalamic-pituitary-adrenal (HPA) system, signals fear via the "radio-waves" of hormones dumped into the bloodstream. This case of redundant circuits is a great example of a Panther hallmark, where if something is important to basic survival, then nature provides a backup or a duplicate, just to be on the safe side. Using the two systems, the hypothalamus revs up your heart, blood pressure, and respiration; it causes the pupils to dilate to take in more light; and it commands your blood vessels to constrict, shunting blood from your skin to your major muscle groups (causing the "chills" of fear). Gorged on glucose supplied to them by adrenaline, your muscles twitch with readiness, including the muscles that cause your hair on the back of your neck to stand on end and the goose bumps to rise on your skin.[4]

Muscles are controlled by the *cerebellum,* another Panther center located at the back of the head by the occipital lobe. The cerebellum (lit. "small brain") regulates movement and instinctive responses. The cerebellum is the most densely packed region of the brain. One fifth the brain's volume, it contains one half of the brain's neurons.[5] The cerebellum sends the final volley of neural signals to the muscles for contraction and relaxation. Constantine often described Panther's mind as "our primitive brain and storehouse of ancestral memories." Together the cerebellum and the brainstem are a storehouse of ancestral memory in the sense that many instinctive movements are wired here at birth: if you put a baby's feet on a hard, smooth surface, it will start to move the legs in a walking fashion—even before the body has the strength to support its own weight—with the gait and speed of your run already determined at birth. Place the four-to-six-month-old under water, and the baby will reflexively hold their breath. Other life-critical reflexes like suckling and clasping are also wired here. Alongside natural reflexes, the cerebellum is heavily involved in learning and remembering trained movements. The cerebellum stores overlearned movements—actions repeated so often that they can be triggered like a reflex—like riding a bike, playing scales, or warding off an attack. When you watch a trained dancer or see a practiced martial artist move with lightning speed, you are watching their cerebellum at work. The section on Black Panther exercises features breathing practices that circulate energy in the cerebellum.

Black Panther Personality: Hedonistic, Thrill-Seeking, Magical

Life on Mother Earth thrives at the intersections: where the ocean meets the shore, marine life flourishes; where soil meets atmosphere, plants sprout; where individuality wrestles with community or where the wisdom of the elders meets the energy of youth, people thrive. Wherever two edges rub, some form of life *will* find the friction delicious. True hedonism reminds you through flavor and touch that life thrives in the tension between opposing elements. Earth sustains life through intercourse of opposites, and things that feel good to us remind us of this. The gravitational center of the Black Panther personality is this: sensuality reaffirms that life thrives where extremes intersect.

Each of the Animals exists on a continuum of maturity, and when we find the Panther at the start of his journey, we find a person who lives life like a cabaret at its most raucous excess. "I'll try anything once," experiencing everything for the sake of the experience. At the first stage, the Panther is a warrior of hedonism and thrill-seeking. When it comes to food, the young Panther loves chewing rare, fatty, fire-roasted venison washed down with copious amounts of heady mead; Panther loves heavy, rich, and creamy foods like red, red meat and chocolate cheesecake, preferably at the same time; Panther grooves to the roots of folk music across the planet, with Afro-Cuban rhythms and drums a favorite. Folk dances around the world speak to the Panther's sense of tribe we carry with us. In clothing, Panther loves wearing skin on skin—something previously breathing—a Burning Man costume of leather, fur, feathers, wool, satin, and silk.

As the gatekeeper to the realm of dreams, Panther loves sci-fi and fantasy genres. Literature's power is to ring the bell at the gates of the subconscious, and bring to the fore what images, conjured sounds, smells, and feelings you are strong enough to handle. Bring a leather-bound tome of smelly vellum and crushed insect ink; tell tales of biblical heroes interpreting dreams; create immersive fantasy and science-fiction worlds, and Panther reads with joy. Panther will not just read those tales but explore them in dreams, going to the dreamscape of each author's creation. Panther loves the echoes of the dream world in science-fiction and fantasy and finds strength in the voices of its ancestors in folk tales, fables, and legends.

The person with a strong Black Panther affinity likes to trek through miles of trail immersed in nature and likes adrenaline-loaded extreme sports: MMA, parkour, motocross racing, or skydiving from 20,000 feet, his feet strapped into a snowboard as he lands onto a mountain slope. Panther types love to find that place where the line between pleasure and pain is blurred, and where risking their life makes the small things more beautiful.

Dana Peterson trains in Ch'ien-lung and has always been our canonical example of a male Black Panther personality. He is preternatural. He paints bridges for a living, several hundreds of feet off the ground, walking along girders nine inches wide, carrying unevenly filled canisters of paint in each hand. With his eyes closed. We performed in the 1996 Edmonton Fringe Festival, performing a piece called *Dragon Myth,* part dance and part martial arts, in which there was a demonstration segment of our blind work training. Constantine would first call for volunteers; then he would call Dana up and tie a blindfold over his eyes. Dana would spin around on the spot, hands over his ears making an "ah" sound, so as not to hear the footsteps of the volunteers walking around him at varying distances. Constantine would clap his hands cueing the volunteers to stop on the spot.

Eventually Dana, who couldn't hear the clap, would stop spinning, take his hands off his ears, and bring them down in front of him in ready position. He would then find people with his eyes closed. And I don't mean randomly bumbling—he moved directly from one volunteer to the next in smooth succession. When he tagged a male volunteer, it was not a vague gesture in the volunteer's general vicinity, but a direct punch on the surface of the volunteer's skin to a vital target or a dropping ground kick from a roll that he landed, softly, at the knee or groin. But, when the volunteer was female, he merely tapped her gently on her shoulder. With his eyes closed, Dana could distinguish between the male and female volunteers with complete accuracy. He was so good, Constantine had to ask him to make at least one deliberate error because people thought he was faking it.

He did the blind work like a Panther, and he typified other Black Panther characteristics. In physical appearance, he was akin to a Tolkien dwarf. He was a bit short, well built, more sinewy than bulky. He had a strong, pronounced chin and brows; and he was hairy—he described himself as a walking carpet. His hands had large saucer-like palms with short, thick-but-dexterous fingers, and his movement possessed a smooth grace from a frequent practice he made of doing everything as silently as possible. Black Panthers revel in fantasy and science fiction, and Dana was a member of the Society for Creative Anachronism, a role-playing festival and reenactment of medieval fares and jousts. Panthers like their toys and gadgets, and Dana made, collected, traded, and often gave away handmade period weapons. Panther types always seem to have the latest nifty gear. When you go to a Comicon (and, to a lesser extent, to an Apple store), you are watching hordes of people feeding their Panther side.

To the outsider, it may look like the Panther is getting lost in the circus of sensations, but for the Panther, Earth is gifting extreme experiences to tune the Panther toward deeper communion with life, to increase the "bandwidth" of his instinct. With every whiff, taste, snort, note, hue, shape, and touch, with every risky, near-death experience, Earth hones the Panther's receptivity to instinct with greater amperage. The same way old radios work by having a crystal diode vibrate in sympathy with transmitted radio waves, the extreme experiences create a preverbal somatosensory "crystal" in Panther that vibrates in sympathy with Earth's impulses. The Panther type seeks out extreme experiences to tune himself like a radio receiver, but here, the wavelength is instinct and the receiver is the subconscious mind.

In the second stage, with instinct more resilient, Panther finds what feels good and fulfilling in dangerous and harrowing moments, and survival begins to center around the team or tribe's needs. Panther experiences certain dreams and visions as direct communications from Earth; these confer insights, premonitions, or feelings for the benefit of the person and tribe. The healthy Black Panther type is a little more shock-resistant than his younger self. He orients a little more quickly, startling into a trained response rather than a freaked-out reaction. He doesn't ruminate over stresses—there's very little mental dialogue about his fears—once he's dealt with a fearful situation, it's done.

But Black Panther's survival mechanism makes it difficult to explain his decisions, since his way of knowing is preverbal. C. S. Nott, a British officer during WWI, told of when he and another officer were ordered to take their military companies on a ten-mile truck drive and four-mile hike to a remote site on Salisbury Plain to do some work. They left in the morning, without taking their bearings, thinking they would get home during daylight, but by the time they started their return, it was dark, frosty, and cloudy. They started hiking the four miles to their truck in the pitch black on a cloudy, February night. Nott told the story:

> *But at that moment a lost sense came into play: I knew that I knew, and went straight on. One of my subalterns began to speak of our losing ourselves on the plain, and I told him to keep quiet. For over an hour we walked, without a word, over the rolling plain, so dark that we could not see ten yards ahead. I tried not to think but to be quiet inside and to let my innate sense of direction, or "instinct," take charge. At last, I sensed that we were getting near the trucks, and in five minutes we suddenly came upon them; in half an hour we were eating hot food in camp. The other party was discovered next morning just after daybreak, wandering over the plain—cold, tired, hungry and lost.*[6]

The mature Panther consciousness means to have Death as an Advisor and Fear as an Ally. There was a time, C. S. Nott continued, when his group's survival depended much more on each other and on their connection to the planet. "We have been spoilt and deceive ourselves with a sense of superiority" with all of the technological prosthetics at their disposal. "Once, we could tell what was happening at a great distance, know what the seasons would bring, and feel enemies or allies in our proximity." He argued that modern living and technology cuts us off from this sense. Again, Nott gave a vivid illustration of instinct at play when survival is at stake:

> *Several months later I was in Somme. I was ordered to take a party at night to investigate a wood beyond the front line. I placed my men inside the wood, and went forward with a sergeant to look, or rather "feel" round. Suddenly I stopped. I could not go on. Something said "danger." The sergeant apparently felt nothing, for he was going on unconcernedly, when I stopped him. I tried one or two other points, but each time that I tried to go on, the feeling against it was so strong that it was as if I were up against a steel net. After a time, I withdrew the men, and reported back that he considered the forest to be occupied by the enemy. The next night, men from another company went into the same woods and right into an ambush and several men were killed, including the officer, and the others came running back.*[7]

Instinct is the integration of thousands of little cues in the environment too complex for conscious thought yet sorted out by the subconscious. Since the environment is always changing, so, too, are the instinctive impulses. Panther's strength is fluidity and a trusting calm in heeding those changing impulses. This requires of the Panther the hallmark of this second stage of development: the *fluidity of self.* You cannot flow with nature and hold onto your ego, the return to sender address of your identity; you have to go where you are sent. When your instinct makes itself known in a crisis, it can seem like there's a stranger in you. But to treat the stranger as an other, separate from you, will lead to your undoing. You must see the part of you in the stranger and let the stranger have a say or even take charge. In a healthy Panther, fluidity comes from being in touch with the animal nature of things—from running barefoot on the jungle floor of the psyche. This fluidity gives the Panther a wild-eyed, mad look, as each momentary impulse is king until the next impulse kicks in. All parts of life, the beautiful and the ugly, become welcome guests. You have already experienced so much that there is nothing absolutely foreign.

Cultivating the Panther's fluid sense of identity makes for an absence of hubris, where no feeling, desire, impulse, or instinct is threatening or foreign. Spend enough time listening to instinct, and it will confer a quality of humility, the sense that you are a small speck in a larger whole, open to new experiences. If you follow this path, Panther's humility sets up the next stage.

At the third stage, the Panther begins to confront what Jung called the *Shadow,* positive *and* negative (pleasant and unpleasant) attitudes, beliefs, and inclinations you possess that are on the *cusp of becoming conscious.*[8] It takes humility to walk the razor's edge of confronting the Shadow in oneself and in others. Humility allows the maturing Panther to delve deeper and face his own Shadow and to communicate with it in the pansensory vocabulary of dreams. As Panther faces the Shadow, he grows into an initiate in the world of magic, ritual, and ceremony.

At the fourth stage, the wise Panther enters a world of power dreaming and ritualistic magic. At this stage, the healthy Panther lives in a world of paradox, where every sensation meets its complement. The profane and the sacred join, pleasure and pain fuse, dream and reality are one. This paper-thin barrier between dualities allows them to delve deeper into magic and dreamwork, to be the wise shaman of the tribe. In *Cry of the Panther,* author James P. McMullen is a Vietnam vet who combs the swamps of Florida for a glimpse of the elusive Florida panther, and he captures the feeling of this stage:

> *At times like that I feel as though I am becoming part of nature around me: the trees, mud, sky, water, birds—everything. My soul seems to be cut in a million different parts, all living and breathing in the same tempo of life.... Mankind began as energy to form a molecule, and this power increased, and as it does, and probably will do forever ... until he approaches sainthood.*[9]

The Black Panther personality, when most developed, approaches the world of the spiritual medicine men and women, like Tom Brown, Jr. or Black Elk, guiding the universality of humans and animals along a sacred journey. This is shaman territory—vision quests, prophetic dreams, shape-shifting, magic, and prayer through dance and song.

The Dark Side of Black Panther: Volatile, Addiction Prone, Fearful of Abandonment

The dark side of Panther is the addict—snorting, smoking, drinking, eating, fucking, anything and everything *to feel less by feeling something else.* I am an addict. I am addicted to my anger, to my rage, and I love every small thing about it. I love how it makes my blood vessels constrict, I love the gladiator rush of energy; I love the rush of self-righteous justification. I love the aura of adamant certitude I know I exude. Yeah, it's a baseless, man-child temper-tantrum rooted in a profound insecurity about being able to fend for myself, and I know it. It has a little Tiger energy mixed in there, but what makes it Panther, and why I am sharing this, is the exaggeration of the anger. There is an overkill and a fantasy berserker bloodlust to it. But the anger stops me from feeling the other feelings underneath it. This addiction anesthetizes my instincts, it dams up the wet spout of the subconscious, and it creates a hole that I can only fill with more anger.

Giving reign to each impulse in the moment is what makes a Panther so formidable, a fluidity of identity. But when the Panther turns dark, fluidity turns to volatility. In a healthy Panther, this parliament is unified by survival and sensuality. In an unhealthy Panther, the multitude of voices run amok. The result is that the Panther may seem to change dramatically, but paradoxically, the change is always within a narrow range. A fear of abandonment is what the collective wisdom of psychology would call this, but it basically means Panther is unable to form the tribe he so desperately needs for his growth. Instead of forming a tribe, an unhealthy Panther walks an emotional rollercoaster in a whirlwind of drama. His relationships are intense, unstable, and overwhelmed with black and white thinking, which alternates, Othello-like, between adoring, worshipful idolization, and debasing homicidal hate of his Desdemona object of love. Abandonment—real or perceived—will cause Panther to frantically prevent *feeling* abandoned in any way. But in the end, the tragedy is not so much being abandoned by another as losing trust in your own instincts, thereby losing your connection to Earth.

Black Panther Movement: Slinky, Low, Fast

When a Black Panther moves, it's poetry in motion. Imagine what it would be like to move like this: layers of viscous, cross-woven fascia provide lift and shock absorption, sliding over each other with sensuous kinetic caresses; with a low center of gravity, limbs are loose but not slack, there is a springing coil in every step, each joint rolls in a small circular action to best transfer impact and minimize noise, and objects are sidestepped with ninja finesse. In mythos, Black Panther is instinct, heavy sensuality, and the subconscious, so it's fitting that the Panther ideokinetics draw on the dank, dark, loamy, and swampy places of Earth.

Panther martial artists have an acrobatic, monkey-like quality, their bodies curled and rounded by deep core-muscle contractions, their joints never quite fully extended, but they keep a slight bend of resilient tension as though they are ready to bounce or spring. They drop to the floor to roll out of harm's way or, just as easily, from a crouched position on their side or their back, they deliver a flurry of ground kicks, which in imitation of the Panther subconscious, come up from underneath like a Freudian slip. They will rebound off their own kicks, peeling themselves off the ground, to spring onto their opponent's body, climbing up limbs, to wrap both legs around a head or arm; then, using their entire body weight, they will bring their opponent down to Earth with a violent slam. Panther is a small street fighter, and because no one strike will be strong enough to take out the larger opponent in a fight, Panther uses cheap tricks and multiple dirty shots with machine-gun rapidity. Panther's logos is to land a multitude of shots, raking, cutting, and slashing, where each blow elicits a reaction in the opponent that sets up the next strike—when the opponent is struck at the head, the pelvis thrusts forward, opening the groin for a strike; then when the Panther strikes the groin, the head reflexively juts forward, open to be hit again, and so on. The reflexive back-and-forth is completely disorienting; meanwhile, the slapping speed of claws, fists, and elbows to soft tissue weakens and debilitates the opponent until they can no longer resist.

Street-smart styles like Krav Maga, LimaLama, Kuta (which reputedly has ancient Egyptian origins), and Splashing Hands (this last also has strong Tiger and Python elements) exploit this action-reaction street-smart strategy in fighting while also emphasizing a Panther quality of keeping the body loose and relaxed so that the strikes rebound off of one target to the next. These styles of ferocious speed tend toward overkill, dealing multiple devastating blows to make the outcome certain.

Like Panther, these styles use small, circular moves to roil out of the way or wrap around a limb, often moving to the inside of the body to strike soft vulnerable targets like the groin, throat, and other yin or artery-rich areas of the body. Panther's style is ideally suited to the knife, Panther's preferred weapon. The Cats go for blades, the Snakes go for sticks and staffs. Panther uses a knife like he was born with it; he uses it like he would claws, slashing the yin skin. These underbelly regions, where the skin has less hair, are part of the Panther mythos, so Panther targets them. We can only attack what we understand.

The mythos of the Animals inspires more than just fighting styles. As an artist, Panther's animal-like commitment in the moment allows him to shapeshift into a character right in front of your eyes. Once upon a time, worshippers danced, sang, and playacted the gods and spirits they wished to invoke with the hope of being possessed by an energy or wisdom that could guide their tribe. There is an ecstasy (and probably a little terror) in giving over, and the Panther in you is the crucible of sensuality that invites and morphs into the spirit it has invoked. Panther enjoys the shapeshifting. For Panther, transformation is sensuous, euphoric. That is Panther's greatest gift. Whether it's for a fighting match, a piano recital, or a CEO board meeting, when the stakes are high, your body and presence morph to meet the needs of the moment, and some part of you always enjoys the transformation; that part is your Panther.

When you are watching a Black Panther perform, his presence exudes the story of the character he is playing. I have known Panther dancers whose bodies were like subwoofer speakers for the emotions and characterizations they projected; they elicited physical sensations the way a speaker playing a loud and heavy bass makes your body reverberate. Susie, a dancer from Les Ballet Jazz de Montreal who trained early in her career with the Animal qualities, once explained that the Black Panther image had strongly influenced her sense of sensuality in her dance. From the Panther imagery, she said, she learned to allow her movement to cause and be caused by emotion and sensuality, where "the sensuality creates the movement, but then reacts off its own creation." This back and forth between kinetics and sensuality is the Panther conversation that produces microadjustments that bring life and power to movement.

Panther in movement can keep your training and performance fresh and connected. The breath work and imagery at the end of the chapter will help you do that.

This joy in embodied metaphysics, shifting your being, helps in martial training. In Ch'ien-lung classes, the instructor chooses a sparring drill—one person provides an attack, the other person redirects and counters. Invariably, they start by *bottom-lining* their practice—focusing on the drill's effectiveness (the bottom line) and evaluating their performance with all the accompanying mental chatter. Too much bottom-lining leads to *flat-lining*. Students move stiffly when working from this analytical mode. The drill is repeated ten or twenty times. They are then asked to do the same drill, but in an Animal. The instructor invokes the mythos—the part of Earth, the systems of the body, the aspects of consciousness the Animal represents—and the Animal ideokinetics. It's a scene that repeats itself every time in our classes, where embodying the Animal suddenly frees up pent-up reserves of coordination, fluidity, balance, and timing. The students are pleased as the outer form gains coherence; they can feel lines of power or a sense of control that was not there before. But it is still a drill. Then they are asked to switch to the next Animal. The drill remains the same, but because the mythos and the ideokinetics change, the movement is completely altered. They discover new timing, new angles, new brush strokes of the joints, new levers and spirals—it is like switching to a language with words for ideas you've always had but never could express. And then they switch Animals again, going through them all. By the end of the series, the drill is an afterthought, and they are struck with their own inner capacity to morph and transform by how palpable and fun it feels. It is Panther's gift, to make morphos sensual. Later, when the students recall the feeling, the movements will be easier to remember.

Panther morphos works its magic through sensuality, ritual, and tribe. Black Panther heals with sinewy sensuality. The fascia of the Panther is rich in nerves and provides much of the feedback from movement experienced as pleasure, pain, or ease. Panther healing systems, like Tom Myers' *Anatomy Trains,* focus on releasing excess tension from fascia.[10] Getting fascia to release tension produces more efficient *tensegrity*—the dynamic at work in a suspension bridge or a dome tent—and this same dynamic of tensile self-support between the skeleton and the fascia results in greater joint mobility. Although fascia release will heal the body, the tribe heals the psyche. Collective celebrations and rituals bring Panther wholeness. Barbara Ehrenreich, in *Dancing in the Streets: A History of Collective Joy,* tells that when early explorers returned from distant tribal lands, they reported all manner of different customs, clothes, foods, religions, languages, and laws, but what all tribes had in common was to celebrate collectively by dancing together.[11] To the subconscious, moving together means belonging together. There is an irrevocable feeling of being part of something greater, a sense of purpose, when we move in unison with others. That feeling makes armies and festivals and collective celebrations, from weddings to Burning Man, fulfill a powerful need: to belong to a tribe through unison movement.

Nika is a friend from college. She is now a lieutenant in the US Navy working as an anesthesiologist. She has high Eastern European cheekbones and a svelte physique, so for fun, she helps her aspiring photographer friends in NY by modeling glamorous, elegant, sexy clothing with plunging backlines that reveal her triathlon body. She's brainy, strong, and sexy. Most of the year, she wears scrubs, portioning out soporific doses to keep patients on the Panther margin between sleep and death. Then, in the summer, she doffs her uniform and scrubs, dons costumes, and does the tour-of-dance festivals like PEX, Burning Man, and Lightning in a Bottle, looking like a *Vogue* model. She lets her hair down, literally and figuratively, while celebrating with the other people she calls her tribe. She and all those celebrating may not be practicing Ch'ien-lung, but this is Panther's morphos. They are enjoying transformation through ritual, ceremony, and tribal celebration.

Black Panther Sex: From Carnal to Alchemical

Panther offers a healthy attitude toward sex and sensuality. For Panther, sex is a normal part of life to be appreciated. Panther says, "yes to the mess" of human growth and sexual expression. Black Panther's sensuality matures in stages. At first, Black Panther wants thrills for their own sake, and Panthers or the Panther part of you seeks as wide a variety of sexual sensations as possible: from tender and loving to rough and lustful, from bored routine to tempestuous makeup sex; from eating chocolate-covered strawberries off a lover's navel to BDSM roleplaying. Toss in leather, silk, satin, velour, and mink; whips, cuffs, games, and toys; do it in bedrooms, mountain-top cabins, along the ocean surf, and under starry desert nights; Panthers are not defined by hetero or homo, and they are not bi-curious—they are omnicurious, pansensual, and very limber.

Then, as the Panther matures, they make love for the transformation. Sex becomes a means to personal alchemy and to deepen their connection to the Earth. Panther makes love for the depth of insight that comes from wholly immersing himself in the reality of another. To paraphrase a line from the movie *The Opposite of Sex,* to Panther, sex is for procreation and recreation but especially concentration—a sacred crucible in which two people transform alchemically.[12]

There is a paradox to Panther's tantric alchemy. Panther uses sensuality to connect *through* the individual *to* the collective. In *Zorba the Greek,*[13] the author Kazantzakis recounts how Zorba, when making love to a woman, was making love to all women, to Womanhood as a whole. That is Panther—when Panther is intimate, it is communion with one person but also with all of life and the tribe.

Why does the Panther type or aspect actively embrace a variety in lovemaking in textures and rhythms, and why does he seek those kinds of lovers? Because the life of Earth depends on diversity. Earth has a wide range of climates, geological formations, and biological lifeforms, each with its own essential aesthetic and sensuous impression. As far as Panther is concerned, the geological formations are each a sensual expression of Earth's sentience; the soil, trees, and grass are her skin and hair; the storms, winds, rains, and cloudless skies are the moods and thoughts of a living Earth; the forms of life are her innovative artistic expressions—each possessing its own essential sensuous quality. Panther may not get to go to each clime, fauna, or monument, but through sensuous experience of his own body, he can touch on the essential quality of each, and in that way, connect to Earth more deeply and strengthen his connection to instinct.

Earth is the great teacher of texture, and Panther is a natural apprentice. As each texture, tone, or mood comes up during lovemaking, Panther allows it to have dominion in that moment, to have communion with that quality and what it represents in terms of a thought or feeling of Earth. And then, he lets it recede back into the dark. By doing the Panther bows in nature, you will learn to embody Earth's diversity, which will permeate your art, career, and relationships with the feral relish of Panther.

Panther's sexuality is an emollient to the absurdities of Puritanism and a counterpoint to the double standards we impose on women's sexuality. There is an important dimension to feminine sensuality that many men, it may be fair to say, are blind to. I count myself a member of this Brotherhood of the Oblivious, so I turned to Susie, the dancer influenced by the Animals mentioned earlier and who was considered by Constantine to be a strong representation of Panther, for insights into sensuality from a non-male perspective. In our conversation, I heard several themes that I had heard from other women in and outside of Ch'ien-lung. I mention them here bearing in mind that these experiences are not uniform to all women, nor do I imply that these experiences are somehow normative or ideal. I offer them here as important examples of Panther sensuality from the perspective of a female dance artist and mother for the benefit of other mothers and artists, of course, and also for the benefit of men looking to cultivate sensuality.

Susie echoed two themes I had heard from several female friends when she explained how, for her, feminine sensuality is deeply connected to the blood flow of her menstrual cycle. Not just the sight and smell of the blood, but the yielding to a natural force within one's own body. The days of flow are, for her, a sacred gateway to the lineage of women who have come before. She said that feminine sensuality is the feeling of the body reacting off of emotion, that emotional reactions and movement feed off each other. She believes that when emotional reactions and sensations amplify each other, everything becomes sensual, whether it is sex, snuggling, yoga, taking a bath, or watching leaves fall in November.

She also feels that labor and birth related to her sense of sensuality. In her familiarity with the archetype, childbirth was an experience of the sensuality of Panther, and as "a gate to the sacred through the place in the body where both pleasure and pain come from. It's sometimes scary being tested by your own gut, but you flow with it before coming to complete silence."

The Ch'ien-lung practice for Panther is to cultivate masculine and feminine approaches to sensuality. Although a man may not be able to get pregnant, that does not mean he cannot use his imagination to empathize with experiences like the ones Susie shared. It will round out his own carnal intelligence, where he stops thinking sex is everything, and instead everything becomes sensual.

Black Panther in the Arts

If all of human culture was arranged as an edifice, with the loftiest visions of the future like a penthouse at the top, and all the bloodiest memories of survival from the past at the bottom, then Panther would be in the basement. Looking for the Animals in art jolts them awake in you. In return, looking for the Animals in art can enhance your appreciation of an art piece in its own right. Let's start with the easier stuff—Black Panther characters.

When George Lucas set out to make the Star Wars movies, he conferred with Joseph Campbell, who was an expert on universal archetypes, to depict characters that would be recognized across cultures.[14] With Campbell's help, Lucas designed Chewbacca the Wookie as a personification (or Wookiefication) of Panther instinct.[15] Across the original trilogy, the simian-ursine Chewie is described as a walking carpet, physically powerful and prone to letting his reactions get the better of him (he's liable to tear your arms off if he loses at chess); he communicates in bear growls, "thinks with his stomach," and has the loyalty of a Labrador. Our instincts often need reigning in, and much of growing up is about integrating the Panther id with the level-headed Tiger ego. So, in this movie universe, where each character embodies parts of the human psyche, Chewie, the Panther id, is a longtime friend of Han Solo, the Tiger ego strength who directs all that wild animal instinct. Another sci-fi Panther is Lieutenant Worf in *Star Trek: Next Generation*.[16] As head of security, Worf, who is Klingon, a fierce warrior tribe, takes orders on the bridge from Captain Picard, the mature Tiger (with a blend of White Leopard). You can often catch these pairings of an impulse-driven, hulking Panther character coupled with the passionate, but disciplined, willful Tiger character.

Like all of the Animals, the Black Panther energy in a movie can be found in the writing, directing, or production values, like special effects or cinematography. The film *Pan's Labyrinth* captures the surrealistic psycho-resonance of the Panther's subconscious realm.[17] The film is about a young girl in Francisco Franco's Spain during the Nazis era, trying to escape the sadistic colonel who is courting her mother. Like an Alice, she escapes by following a guide into an underworld of fairytale creatures in a realm, it turns out, where she is actually the princess. As the plot twists and turns, you find out she has to die in the real world in order to take her throne by the side of her royal parents in the fairytale world. But aside from this story with its mythic overtones of Persephone, Oedipus, and Jesus—themes that call "Open Sesame!" to the door of the subconscious—the setting and special effects also work to invoke the Panther realm. The heroine makes her way through tunnels lined with tree roots. Again, here, subterranean is subconscious. The CGI and latex creatures she outsmarts are gruesome and protean, polymorph beasts out of dreams, which is what grownups and war look like to a child who experiences traumatic events burned directly into their psyche without the benefit of a filter.

Panther represents not only the subconscious shadow of the individual, but the shadow of the society at large, and two common dramatic vehicles are used to portray the collective shadow: crime and sex. The criminal underbelly of a city or nation is the world of impulses before rules are imposed by a law-giving analytical mind. Movies about bootlegging, Compton or Chicago gangsters, or old cowboy/bank robbery movies often pit an instinctive Panther reaction against an authority figure imposing racial or economic injustices on a societal level. The second way to talk about the collective subconscious is by portraying prudish or abusive sexual mores. Sexuality is deeply entwined with the subconscious, and the nature of lovemaking is a preverbal language of its own. Like crime or corruption, we all know it's happening, but we're not talking about it. Some movies, like *Chocolat,* for example, address the feminine issues of how male societies confuse sensuality with sexuality and enforce the shaming of female sexuality.[18] Other movies, like *Fight Club,* point to the close relationship between violence and sensuality in men with its homoerotic images of muscular, good looking, sweat covered guys stumbling over each other in bloody fights, looking for meaning and brotherhood.[19]

This analysis of movie art helps to understand Panther, but it gets in the way of enjoying art the way Panther does. The Panther is not analytical, he is visceral. He has two gears, hunt and be hunted. And, so it is with art. The Panther (and Python) use art to *stalk,* that is, they use art to understand consciousness, their own or that of others. Stalking in art is something we do naturally: you do it whenever you see yourself reflected in a play or sculpture; you do it when you watch a travel or cooking show and think to yourself, "I have to try that!" But it is not the destination or the dish that is important, rather it is the part of you waking up to learn from the journey or the recipe that's important, and that waking and learning self is the part you are stalking.

One of my Panther stalking practices, for example, involved Anthony Bourdain's *No Reservations.*[20] His was an innovative, foodie, "anti-travel show." The show and the man had resounding Panther qualities (with Python). He avoided the touristy hotspots, seeking where the locals ate: the street cart hotdog vendor, the hole-in-the-wall dive bar with a great menu—the shadow side of the food scene. His narration was poetry for Panther, sensuous yet no nonsense, talking about the conquests, crimes, natural disasters and migrations which produced the dishes he was eating. All good lessons in Panther. My wife and I would go on a trip, and I would go hunting for what I called "my Anthony Bourdain moments" I would look for a place Bourdain would visit to get a meal Bourdain would eat, with the purpose of stalking the Animals. One time it jolted my connection to Panther. We were in France, near Paris, and we went for lunch. We were seated together at the restaurant table, I bit into a tomato and started to cry. It was not just that the tomato tasted farm fresh and delicious, echoing all the clichés of French cuisine, but my whole body responded. I could taste the terroir, the characteristics of the soil and the climate the tomato came from, and it was as if my body knew where or knew it could "smell out" where that place was. It woke my Panther in a new way, maturing with me since, a new memory to invoke Panther in bows or hold in meditation. In the same way, I used culinary arts, you can use theater, dance, music, painting (or the Seven Steps at the end of each chapter) to stalk Panther, Tiger, Python or other Animals within yourself.

Becoming Black Panther

Doing Black Panther exercises should leave you feeling more connected to instinct, ancestry, and the natural world. It should make you a better whisperer of animals, plants, and soils. The healthy aspect of Black Panther within each of us craves adventures, risks, and dangers. But the Black Panther archetype is a reminder of the fuller purpose behind seeking an adrenaline rush. The well-rounded Black Panther seeks out experiences of fear to deepen his power in the realm of dreams and magic—not magic in the sense of spells and incantations, which assuage unmet childish desires for power, rather, the kind of magic that comes from cultivating a mature, deeply passionate, love for life, which allows you to apprehend the mythological in the everyday world.

The Panther Plaque

Black of night and red of blood. The Black Panther plaque (see Figure 5.1 in this book's color insert) is made up of a black triangle, red circle, and white square. The Panther's black triangle reflects the receptive nature of the Panther, the blank slate of the subconscious mind, and the small moment of surrender just before we sleep and dream—according to the sages, a surrender much like the one we need to accept our own death. The plaque's blood red circle of life reminds us that we are fundamentally a teeming bath of sensations engaged in the raw struggle for survival and that the electrifying force of fear is an alchemical gatekeeper to shapeshifting and transformation. We are meat having a dream-like experience: black and red.

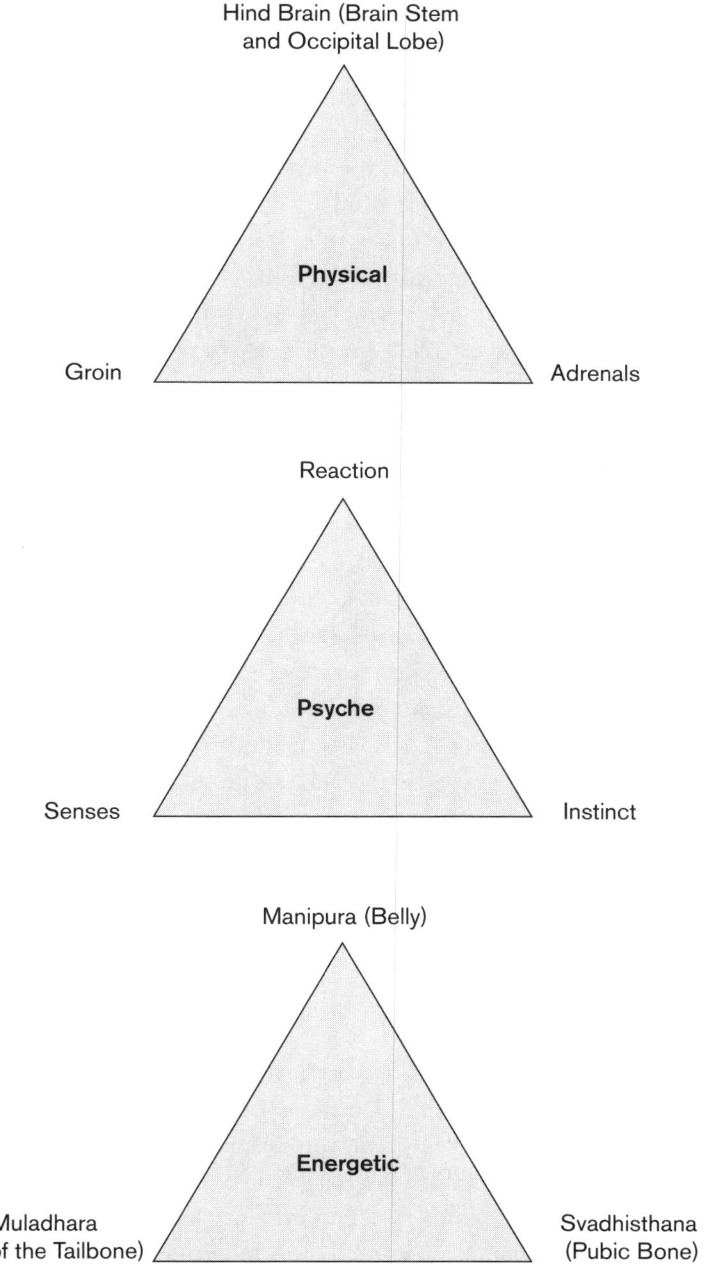

FIGURE 5.2: The symbolic meaning of the triangle points for the Black Panther

The Heart of the Panther

Constantine often called Black Panther the "Master of Fear" adding, "none of the Animals is worth a grain of salt if it is owned by fear." Panther's mastery of fear is a gift to the other Animals within you. It is not mastery in the sense of subjugation or suppression, but rather a *flow,* much like the flow of White Leopard's creativity. Fear for Panther is an existential experience. Paraphrasing Frank Herbert's *Dune,* when your fear passes through you—when you can flow with your fear—what is left afterward is you, the self.[21] Where your fear passes through you, you will be more alive and attuned to the world around you. I've often spoken to avid mountain climbers who scale cliff faces with smooth surfaces and sleep overnight thousands of feet up in hammocks fastened by steel cables of spiderweb thinness. When you ask them why, they will tell you that "facing death this way makes me feel more alive." By experiencing fear more fully, you deepen your capacity for pleasure.

Constantine often addressed dealing with fear. He explained that fear is energy to be used for the benefit of survival, but the analytical mind can interfere with the spontaneous reaction. The result is freezing in a startle-response, eyes fixed and shoulders raised, a paralysis that produces a low-grade anxiety buzz. The startled freeze becomes the go-to reaction, building up energy with each startle, like sediment over time. When people say they want to confront their fear, often what they mean is that they want to down-ramp the anxiety originating from an unresolved fearful experience that ended in a paralyzed freeze. What they do not realize is that their startled paralysis has had years to grow. If you try to tackle the startled paralysis with its massive momentum while you yourself have only a small amount of energy, you are setting yourself up for failure.

What you need is a daily practice in which you incrementally accrue energy until you possess more of it than your fear. Then, when circumstances call for you to face your fear, you do so with more energy than the fear possesses. In so doing, you discharge the energy of a painful memory and loosen its grip over your life. The memory loses its charge or taboo quality and can now be reinterpreted and integrated into a more whole and healthier narrative of your life. Lose the charge, gain the wisdom, and turn what you dread into a gift: this was what Constantine meant by making your fear your ally.

When it comes to Panther, your whole body wants to feel like *fear is what you feel when you are about to learn something new;* this is the heart of Panther. When your whole body is suffused with the feeling of fear as the herald to wisdom, then no matter what practice you are doing, you are turning it into a Panther meditation. As with each of the Animals, doing alternate nostril breathing with the plaques will help you develop the Animal quality. The "Seven Steps to Embodying Black Panther" detail how to cultivate fear as an ally along with other basic practices. But regardless of your practice, remember the heart of the Panther: fear is what you feel when you are about to learn something new.

Seven Steps to Embodying Black Panther

Step One: Follow Your Breath (Ongoing Mindfulness Practice)

Panther follows its breath because it feels goo-oood! Following your breath in Panther means visualizing you can breathe a rich, viscous energy into your

Tendons and ligaments Visualize the breath oxygenating the tendons and ligaments, from your feet up to your temples and eyeballs. Feel the breath renew the elastic recoil and viscous spring of the tendons and ligaments. The tendons and ligaments are part of a skin-like system called fascia, which includes the connective tissue for the internal organs. Feel your breath slip and slide along the fascia between the internal organs. Ideokinetics: Move as if bouncing off your tendons and ligaments. Move as if the fascia of your body wraps you like a cocoon, a sleeping bag, against which you bounce off the inside. Move as if you are a black panther. Connect to the easy coiling movement of wild animals and to the resilience of supple plants.

Peritoneum and pelvic floor The peritoneum is the large elastic sac that holds the abdomen, with smaller individual sacs for each organ. Movement promotes motility of the peritoneum, helping to circulate blood and tone the organs. Feel your peritoneum change shape as your lungs contract and expand with the breath. At the bottom of the pelvis is the pelvic floor: a trampoline-like complex of muscles and tendons that supports the internal organs. It provides shock absorption and spring in walking, running, and jumping. Feel the pelvic floor contract and expand with the breath. Ideokinetics: Move as if the pelvic floor and soles of your feet are trampolines. Connect to Earth as a base off of which you can spring.

The occipital lobe and cerebellum ("Back of the brainstem") The occipital lobe processes visual information; it is the projection screen of your visual world. As you breathe into the occipital lobe, try to see as a child does–notice objects for their tangible, physical qualities, rather than interpreting or analyzing them (Python). The cerebellum is the movement center of the brain for trained and instinctive responses. Visualize your breath flowing into your cerebellum. Imagine as you do that you are looking at the world from the vantage of your ancestors who are vested in your survival. Ideokinetics: Move as if you were an ancestor from a thousand generations ago. Connect to the records of ancient life trapped in fossils.

Tip of the tailbone Feel the coccyx as the vestigial remnant of our simian ancestry. Ideokinetics: Move as if you have a tail for counterbalance. Visualize the in-breath extending the tail, and the out-breath contracting the tail. Connect to Earth as if you have a tail to touch the ground for balance. Connect to the animal nature shared with ancient ancestors and all living creatures.

Feet From the soles of the feet, feel like you have a root system digging into Earth. Visualize the breath drawing elements from Earth to nourish you through your root system. Visualize the exhale flushing waste out the feet and hands into the soil where it will be recycled as new life. Ideokinetics: Stand as if roots extend from the soles of the feet, deep into Earth, drawing energy up. Move as if you have cushy soft pads on the soles of the feet, silencing any noise. Step through the whole length of the foot, landing and rolling on the heel to springing off the toes. Connect to Earth with every step caressing the ground.

Adrenals Visualize breathing from the soles of the feet, up the back of the legs, charging the kidneys and adrenals. After a fright or panic, breathe into the adrenals with a sense of reducing excess energy. Ideokinetics: Move as if motion originated in the kidneys, emphasizing the small, deep, stabilizing back muscles. A big one for martial artists, move as if to protect your kidneys. Connect to the struggle for survival in nature, as if Earth demanded it.

Gonads Visualize breath directly into your reproductive organs, stimulating your sense of vitality and creativity. Ideokinetics: Move as if you are expressing your relationship to sensuality and fecundity. Move as if you had a very low center of gravity located in the gonads and genitals, as if they weighed you down toward the ground. Move as if they were capable of spiraling in any direction, and movement initiates from there to the rest of the body. Connect to the procreative drive in nature, as if Earth supplied it.

Sensuality Visualize breath into your sensory organs as you savor each sensation, taking turns with each sense. Ideokinetics: Move as if your body is responding to each sensation in enjoyment, one sense at a time. Connect to Earth's sensuality in the slightest breeze, the scent of a plant or tree nearby, in the sights, sounds, and textures of animals and elements.

Instinct Imagine Earth breathes instinctual information into your tailbone, adrenals, and brainstem to let you know what's coming and how to move faster than you ever thought you could. Ideokinetics: Move as if Earth is sending you signals of where to go. Connect to Earth's way of communicating directly to you through weather and animals.

Step Two: Recall Your Day (Daily/10 Minutes before Sleep)

For Panther, review your day for sensual pleasures. Recall intense sensations that thrilled you or those sensations that, in retrospect, you could have enjoyed more. Take a moment to celebrate both.

Review your day for moments when the working subconscious was closer to the surface. Perhaps you gained a small peek into talents or attitudes that are on the brink of becoming conscious. Perhaps you noticed Freudian slips, jokes, or comments that revealed true but hidden desires.

Ritual is important to the Panther. Review your morning routine before going to work or your evening pattern when you land back home. You may think of these as habitual or routine, but start to treat them as the important moments of transition they are. Rituals conserve and reignite your focus while allowing you to shed unnecessary baggage. Bowing at the waist when stepping into the dojo; making the sign of the cross when entering a church; taking your shoes off before entering a mosque; kissing your husband or wife last thing before you leave and first thing when you get back; these rituals engage the senses in celebrating the mysteries of life and, in turn, strengthen the connection to the subconscious, instinct, and the tribe.

Panther loves tribe. Review your day for moments when you experienced a sense of tribe: a moment of community or ceremony, whether it was a religious baptism or a secular graduation.

Step Three: Scan Your Body (Daily/10 Minutes before and after Sleep)

At night before going to sleep, scan the Panther systems and anatomical areas: the tendons and ligaments, the fascia (throughout your muscles and viscera), the internal organs, the adrenals, and the brainstem.

Ping the subconscious mind by invoking mental imagery rich in symbolism, the way we read children fairytales at bedtime.

Step Four: Do the Bows in Nature (Weekly/10–15 Minutes)

Choose elements that reaffirm Panther's viscous sensuality, like a swamp or a receding lake bed, slick with mud. Affirm Panther's primitive survival instincts by doing bows in a hot, lush, tropical jungle, tuning into the surrounding sounds and smells. In Hawaii, on the fields of recently cooled volcanic rock, you can tap into the superstitious subconscious, prone to magical thinking and rituals.

Panther Bow

FIGURE 5.5: Stand with the feet together, the hands in the mudra, eyes looking out from under the brows.

FIGURE 5.6: Turn the feet out, reach the hands down to the knees, palms forward. Draw instinctive energy up from Earth.

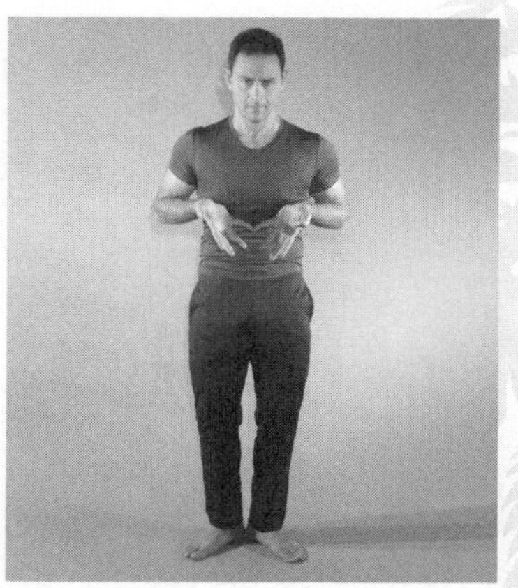

FIGURE 5.7: Inhale, raise hands up, pinky on midline of the body. Bring palms up to armpits. Draw energy into tendons and ligaments, into adrenals, groin, tip of tailbone, and back of brainstem.

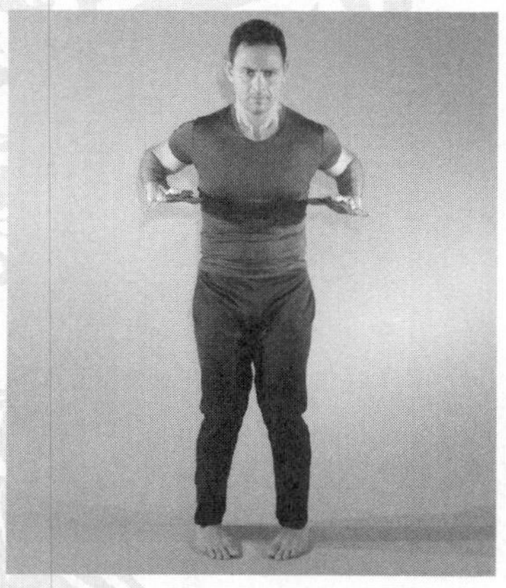

FIGURE 5.8: Hold the breath, and turn the hands over: Pack energy into Panther centers.

FIGURE 5.9: Exhale, turn feet in, press hands down to the knees, keep the thumbs pointing to the sides of the body. Finish the exhale when hands reach knees. Clear unwanted energy from Panther centers. Repeat bows.

FIGURE 5.10: After bows, make the shape of a triangle with the hands at the groin, pointing triangle down: Inhale, feet turned out, draw energy into the groin and reproductive center.

FIGURE 5.11: Exhale, feet turned in, flip the triangle so the tip points to the belly button: Pack energy into the physical center.

FIGURE 5.12: Stand neutral with mudras.

Step Five: Adopt the Animal Personality (Ongoing Practice)

One does not so much embody Panther as revel in him. Panther music can best be described as tribal and folkloric, and it is all about a deep, low bass, driving rhythm section. Foods resonating with Panther are rich, creamy, heavy, always moist, and tender—red meat and chocolate cheesecake. Have sex. Lots of it. Snuggle more. Enjoy it. Wear satin, silk, and leather; take mud baths, read sci-fi; eat, drink, and be merry. Discover your inner adrenaline junkie.

Find your sensuality. When you eat or drink, take time to savor. Let the nuances of flavor transport you to where the food came from; let food, drink, clothes, art work, and other people take you into their worlds. Experience your clothes as a second skin. If you realize you are surrounded by smells, tastes, and touches that feel flat or hollow, change them, trusting your personal taste.

To get in touch with instinct, try hunting (using a camera counts) or camping. Try walking slowly along a forest path with your eyes closed for a minute at a time. This will attune your senses, and it will allow the zombie part of your brain to take over. Seek out experiences of tribe through collective celebrations like Burning Man, Glastonbury Festival, or a Cubs game. Everyone's different (yay!), and you may find your sense of tribe with your biological family, at a professional conference, or at a music concert. Go find it.

Panther invites magic into his life with symbols and ritual. When you switch hats, take a moment to invoke an archetype relevant to the task at hand. Invoking mythological gods, biblical saints, or movie characters is fair game; what's important is that the images are larger than life so that they bypass critical reason and appeal to the subconscious.

Step Six: Remember Your Dreams (Daily/10 Minutes upon Waking)

Panther represents the subconscious, the halfway house where you can recall your dreams on waking up. With a few weeks of practice, you can reasonably improve your dream recall with a few techniques that I have found useful. First, regularly write your dreams down, and do so as soon as you start to surface from sleep, resisting the temptation to sleep for another five minutes. Nothing sends a clear message to the psyche that you want to recall dreams like repeatedly reaching for your pen and diary to write them down.

In past attempts to be a good dream diarist, I often got lost in details of a dream, losing the entire dream in the very process of writing it down. Then my wife gave me a tip she uses: write a haiku of the dream. The haiku form of five-seven-five syllables has a way of forcing you to encapsulate the essence of the dream, allowing the rest of the details to hang effortlessly.

Can you analyze dreams for symbols related to Panther? Dreams involving animals usually symbolize an instinctive impulse, a reaction or feeling you are getting ready to express. Note the ecology of any animals in your dream. Water animals, like fish, dolphins, orcas, and whales, relate to emotional impulses; birds or airborne animals reflect the mental plane of thoughts, ideas, or rationalization. If your dream contains a land animal, note whether it is predator or prey and its distinguishing feature.

Panther taps into the archetype of the Shadow. The Shadow is made of positive or negative skills, feelings, or attitudes on the cusp of becoming conscious. In a dream, the Shadow is almost always faceless and usually the same sex as the dreamer. Dreams with Shadows are intense, with the Shadow appearing as a more extreme version of a part of you. It can be disconcerting, until you realize that the dream is exhorting you to take *only a step* in the direction of the Shadow. For example, I once had a dream of a cold-blooded thug with CIA sunglasses (faceless). It did not mean I needed to join the mafia or club a seal, but I could have used a little more toughness in asserting myself in those days with friends who were walking all over me. That Shadow was shorthand for the backbone I needed without actually resorting to violence.

A *composite* is a character in your dream who has the face of one person but whom you know is someone else. We've all had dreams where "she looked like my sister, but I knew it was the milkman." These characters usually represent a combination of qualities brought together in the composite. In one dream, I was running toward a finish line with my housemate who is a marathon runner but whom I "really knew" was my graduate advisor. Analyzing their characteristics, I interpreted the dream to mean that I was feeling the endurance that completing an advanced degree requires. The dream was suggesting to me that I should take better care of myself by incorporating my housemate whom I admired for taking care of himself through lavish dinners he prepared with style and ate with gusto. The composite contained both the problem and the solution. Similarly, your psyche uses people you know in your daily life as symbols in your dreams, and deciphering their meaning is fun and insightful.

To warm up the subconscious for a night of vivid dreams, try dream incubation, an exercise developed by Jung and here adapted by Veronica Tonay. On a blank page, write down a question you are working on. It can be interpersonal, involve a creative or problem-solving situation at work, or be about developing one of the Animals. Then draw a line down the middle of the page; on one side, write down your immediate reactions in thoughts, feelings, and memories associated with that question, and on the other side, write down when you learned or who taught you to respond this way. This gives you a chance to unload your subconscious.

Step Seven: Use the Plaques (Daily/20 Minutes)

The tone Panther brings is to treat the body like a collaborator in the meditation, paying particular attention to the rise and fall of the soft underbelly as you use the Panther mudra, tongue position, and asana. Doing this exercise for twenty minutes a day for even a week will begin to create a sort of conditioned response, where seeing the plaque will elicit Panther.

Panther uses the plaque to relate to fear. You must have a strong association between the keys, plaque, ideokinetics, visualized breath, and energy and be able to articulate the Panther before actively using the plaques to work through fear.

You can accomplish this in a three-step process that you can begin by simply visualizing the plaque:

1. Identify with or put yourself in the black triangle of the plaque.
2. Visualize the feared object inside the red circle at a distance. Think of the triangle like a movie projector casting the image of the feared object onto the red circle. The distance is important; the more fearful the object, the more distance you need.
3. Infuse the projection, the distance between the triangle and the circle, with a quality of curiosity and trust in your abilities to respond.

For example, I had a fear of jumping from great heights. For this exercise, I embodied the openness to sensory experience of the black triangle and cast a beam of light on the red circle where I visualized myself safely jumping into water from a great height without hesitation. I infused the space of the projection with curiosity. A few weeks of this, then on a trip to Bend, Oregon, we stopped at a campground by a river with a thirty-foot bridge spanning it; Constantine instructed us to jump. Normally, I would have stood there for an hour, but I had done the visualization. I simply walked up to the edge of the bridge, climbed over the rail (I had always visualized hurdling it without looking … ah, well), and jumped. The last thing I heard before hitting the water was Constantine saying, "Holy shit! He did it!"

To be clear, this is not guaranteed to treat phobias or serious anxiety, for which professional help should be sought. But for me, it began a relationship with fear and reducing the anxiety from it. I still feel the *fear* from jumping off heights, but I *worry* about it less now.

Panther Energy Circuit

On the in-breath, visualize energy from Earth coming up through the soles of the feet, up the yin skin of the legs, and going to the tailbone and groin. On the out-breath, visualize energy passing from the groin to the spine, down to the tailbone, down the yang side of the legs, and out of the root system of the feet. For a more advanced circuit, imagine the energy coming up the same way to the tailbone, and then having it pass by the kidneys and go up the spine to the brainstem on the in-breath, and on the out-breath, the energy goes down the front of the spine, through the center to the groin, then to the tailbone, and down the yang side of the legs.

Panther vs. Animals

Panther and Boa are similar in that they are not analytical and feel intensely. But Boa feels emotions and sentience, whereas Panther feels sensations. Panther filters through the lens of survival and pleasure and then reacts. Boa does not give a damn about what she is experiencing unless she is getting ready to consume something; otherwise she is letting go. Panther's sensations are concrete and specific–hot, cold, sharp, soft–whereas Boa feels amorphous clouds of mood with a direction. Visually, Panther will look at the negative space around an object, looking into the shadows. Boa does not really focus with her eyes, but she feels around and moves into the negative space.

Panther and Cobra are deeply connected and sometimes difficult to tease apart. They are both privy to foreshadowing and premonitions, but

Cobra will experience a vision as removed but imminent, whereas Panther feels it viscerally in the area of the stomach or groin and the back of the head, and feels compelled to move.

Panther and Tiger have much in common, but they would get on each other's nerves; the Tiger's analytical mind would get in the way of Panther's impulses, while Panther's indulgence can come at the cost of Tiger's discipline. Panther amplifies Tiger's desires. In some ways, Tiger goes through Panther to connect to Earth. They will both tend to have hefty musculature, but the Panther's movement emphasizes the rebound of the tendons and ligaments as well as the small, deep, stabilizing muscles, whereas Tiger relies on the large, superficial prime movers.

Panther Keys

Panther eye position: Look up from under the brow to show the whites of the eyes underneath.

Panther tongue position: The tongue is pressed into the back of the mouth as if pushing it through the back of the head.

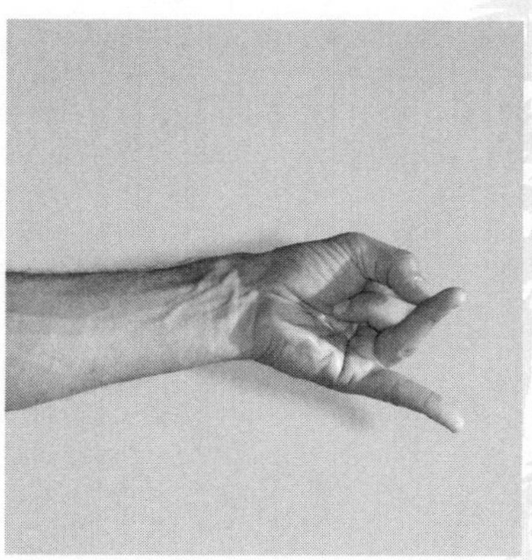

FIGURE 5.13: Panther mudra: Curl the index and middle fingers down to the life line, and touch the thumb to the first joint of the ring finger. Use the mudra in meditation or to invoke your Black Panther connection to the Earth, instinct, and the subconscious.

FIGURE 5.14: Panther asana: Bring the heel of the right foot to the groin, and put the left foot flat on the floor. The arms loop around the left thigh.

Table 5.1 summarizes the Black Panther archetype.

TABLE 5.1: Black Panther Summary

Consciousness	Senses, instinct, reaction
Nature	Swamps, caves, tropical forests
Anatomical system	Tendons and ligaments, groin, feet, back of the head, adrenals
Neural regions	Brain stem, cerebellum, occipital lobe
Energetic system	*Muladhara* (tip of the tailbone), *svadhisthana* (pubic bone), *manipura* (belly)
Favorite foods	Red meat, mead, death by chocolate
Music	African drumming, folk music, rap, hip-hop
Sports and martial arts	Extreme sports, professional team sports, fighting sports, street fighting, Krav Maga
Hobbies	Extreme sports, sex, sci-fi, and fantasy
Clothes	Leather, silk, satin, sensual costumes and couture

TIGER: THE BLAZING HEART

You gain strength, courage, and confidence by every experience in which you really stop to look fear in the face. You are able to say to yourself, "I lived through this horror. I can take the next thing that comes along."

—ELEANOR ROOSEVELT

THE MOST POWERFUL CREATURE of the jungle, Tiger has never known defeat, doubt, or hesitation. He has confronted each of his challengers head-on, directly, with a linear focus that has jaws of its own. His muscular haunches propel him relentlessly forward, almost out of habit. His roar comes from deep within, beyond even the pit of his gut; it surges from the crust of Earth and emanates from the jungle itself, knocking birds out midair and leaving even the mountain stupefied.

Tiger Consciousness: Desire, Intent, Action

Tiger is body, heart, and linear mind forged into a single-edged sword cutting through all obstacles. Tiger *is* concentration, like a magnifying glass focusing the rays of the sun. If you have ever had to exert sheer willpower in the face of insurmountable odds, if you have felt the up-swell of all your heart's passions rise in a moment of crystal clear, target-acquired action, then you have experienced Tiger. Tiger consciousness focuses the desires of the heart through the lens of reason into a single beam of laser-cutting intention, seeking and thriving under the kind of pressure that turns a lump of coal into a diamond. Tiger knows no fear, no doubt, no regret, only his indomitable force and relentless perseverance.

Tiger relishes testing his mettle through competition that grows the body stronger, the mind keener, and the heart more valiant. This is the part of you that seeks out *friction,* the character-building challenges or outright conflicts that demand grit in developing the courage of your convictions.[1]

Tiger revels in power. However, let it be known that this power is fueled by being in the service of a compassionate heart. Powerful, simple, and proactive, he lives for action that has a courageous purpose. Tiger is extremely masculine—fierce, yes—but compassionate, protective, and just. When you experience a surge of the protective masculine spirit, with a burning, linear drive, or you find yourself thriving under pressure, bending your "every spirit to its full height," then you are experiencing the consciousness and pure willpower of Tiger.[2]

Tiger Anatomy: Yang Muscles, Heart, Dantian, and Forehead

In the mythos, Tiger is the power of the body, heart, and mind as one, supported by the protective mantle of Earth's crust, where the big Cat draws his power from the friction between the tectonic plates. He calls home the belly, heart, forehead (or frontal lobe), and muscular system. The base of his power is the point three fingers below the belly button, known by various names as the *dantian* in Chinese, *hara* in Japanese, and *manipura* in Sanskrit. All of these terms refer to the gravitational center of the body, and it is from this center that Tiger's physical prowess emanates. Tiger and Panther share *manipura* in common; it is the "flower" for Panther and the "root" for Tiger. Zooming out to view Ch'ien-lung as a whole, these crossover points are the means by which you can transition between each Animal pairing, and they lend a game-board dynamic to the art.

Tiger's power and action are driven by the muscular system. In particular, they're driven by what bodybuilders with eye-popping proportions call the *mirror muscles,* the large primary movers of the glutes, quads, triceps, shoulder delts, lats, and erectus "eight-pack" abs. As the most physically and emotionally confrontational of the Animals, Tiger uses these muscle groups as *armor,* echoing the theme of Earth's mantle. Watch professional boxers as they slip punches. When the strike comes in, they shift to let the beefy muscles of the shoulders or the large latissimus muscles of the torso absorb the blow. In the East, these muscles are called *yang muscles. Yang* means active, driving, and external, and while this befits the muscles, the name actually derives from the *yang skin* that covers them; this is the hairier, protective skin on the back side of the body that acts as a shell, taking the brunt of the Sun's heat. Tiger's yang muscles provide the primary force of our motion and act as a protective body armor. They are a warrior's outer shell, shielding a vulnerable, soft underbelly and heart.

The muscles shed a metaphysical light on embodying your Tiger side: your psychological need for resistance in order to develop. Tiger has a weight-training attitude to life where character is made stronger through resistance, just as muscles are. Tiger seeks out challenges of personal will the same way a powerlifter seeks out heavier weights. Doing physical exercise of any kind, but especially resistance training, gives you the opportunity to embody the archetype by taking a moment to glory in the flint of your courage as you do the harder thing. Spending little moments throughout the day acknowledging your grit will help you cultivate your Tiger.

Constantine never wanted replicas of himself and always exhorted us to make the art our own through studying the science of the Animal anatomies. To that end, he assigned us an anatomy coloring book with the instructions to familiarize ourselves with the anatomy of each Animal and glean insights on the fit between the anatomical system and the Animal consciousness. For example, while studying musculature, I learned about *pennation,* the straight line that muscles ideally run from origin point to insertion point on the skeleton. Pennation can be composed of fused fibers, scar tissue, and knots of tension, which can jeopardize enjoyment and competitive performance.[3] I recall the moment of insight when scientific terminology gained a poetic dimension for me, when I understood, on a personal level, that just as muscle fibers must line up straight to contract with maximum acceleration, so too the Tiger must act in alignment with his values for his actions to carry weight. For Tiger, pennation was the physical manifestation of his emotional integrity. This was a sudden insight, like when you correctly interpret a vivid dream, and it made the archetype your own. In an embodied art like Ch'ien-lung, the studies of science and of the Animals enrich each other in the construction of your own mythology. The exercises at the end of this chapter will give you a starting point to enrich your own interpretation of the archetype.

Tiger may be about power, but his strength is his heart. In Eastern terms, the emotional center of energy goes by *anahata* in Sanskrit, while in Chinese, the heart is called the *middle dantian* and is personified in Chinese medicine as a good king who cultivates the qualities of love, courage, and valor, shining his compassion on all his people equally. The Western counterpart is the *vagus nerve,* a circuit that plays a big role in the physical sensations of emotions. Latin for "wanderer," the vagus is a bundle of nerves that originate at the top of the spinal cord from where they meander through the body. Passing by the larynx, this nerve bundle modulates the timbre of the voice in response to our emotions;[4] it brings a warm sense of expansion to the chest when we experience compassion, and it directs the "rest and digest" of the internal organs giving us a sense of safety or of "having butterflies." Interestingly, children with increased vagal activity will be more likely to intervene when a classmate is being bullied and will donate more of their recess time to help a child in need.[5] One of the (many) effects of (the very) complex Buddhist meditations on compassion is to ramp down anxiety by upping vagal firing.

The vagus nerve was not part of the tradition Constantine taught, but as he encouraged us to make the system our own, I found the vagus captured the mythos of emotional fortitude and vulnerability in Tiger and that it has a logic as functioning as a crossover or entry point to other Animals. The vagus nerve connects Tiger to White Leopard at the throat; it connects Tiger to Python by acting as a bridge among so many organs; it connects Tiger to Panther with the signals sent over that bridge to the organs and viscera to elicit those gut reactions and emotional feelings; it connects Tiger to Boa by the expansive feeling of openness it elicits in the diaphragm and lungs; and it connects Tiger to Cobra by simple virtue of it being a cranial nerve that is the physical counterpart to Cobra's energetic hood. The art of Ch'ien-lung is yours to personalize with imagination and discipline.

The exercises at the end of this chapter will guide you in constructing your own Tiger mythology. The principle behind the exercises is simple: Animal movement with Animal ideokinetics engages the archetype. For example, with Tiger, just before doing weightlifting, which targets the yang muscles, you trigger the vagus by recalling times when you demonstrated compassion. Eliciting memories of compassion will bring a sense of expansiveness in the chest and heart, and when you respond to these proprioceptive sensations of compassion, allowing them to influence your movement, they will cue small postural adjustments that will increase your performance and enjoyment. The effects are small but cumulative, and over time, the ideokinetics, movement, and breathing will engage each other automatically, allowing you to articulate and embody the Animal effortlessly.

Tiger Brain: Frontal Lobe

Watch a house cat hunt, locking onto a bird or mouse, getting ready to pounce, and you will see the Tiger's singular concentration. Tiger represents the frontal lobe of the brain (especially the prefrontal cortex), which is responsible for *concentration, sequential order,* and *risk assessment.*[6] The frontal lobe has several core abilities. One of its central jobs is to engage attention in goal-directed behavior. Other areas of the brain will help you shift focus and disengage your focus, but the frontal lobe locks onto a target once it is selected,[7] and the Tiger exercises engage this process.

The frontal lobe also orders sequential actions, like putting your socks on *before* your shoes. It plays a role in ordering everything from words in a sentence to recollections of yesterday's events. A patient with prefrontal cortex damage may be unable to put a set of scrambled cartoon panels back in order or sequentially list the steps involved in eating out at a restaurant. The "Seven Steps to Embodying Tiger" at the end of this chapter include practices like reviewing your day in sequential order to cultivate this ordered kind of thinking.

As with each Animal, Tiger's strength can be his weakness, and when the frontal lobe goes into overdrive, once it starts a job, it cannot stop. One of my professors once recounted a case involving a highly trained interior decorator who had sustained frontal lobe damage. The patient could not stop himself from righting every skewed picture frame in the office that his physician had deliberately tipped prior to the patient's visits. The drive to move forward, conferred by the frontal lobe, is a double-edged sword for Tiger. Forward drive can make for either inspired action or perseverating habit. On the one hand, singular focus drives Tiger's discipline, consistency, and stick-to-itiveness required for his remarkable accomplishments, while on the other, this intense focus can negate alternative possibilities, negate the perspective of others, or simply prevent Tiger from enjoying the moment.

More than any of the other animals, Tiger proactively seeks friction. Tiger *chooses the harder thing,* and the frontal lobe leads the way. Evolutionary psychologists think this area got its first big product release in predators.[8] A lioness stalking her prey must suppress the impulse to charge too soon, and this restraint of the frontal lobe *inhibits short-term impulses for longer term gains.*[9] The frontal lobe acts like the brakes on desire, helping us keep the intention while waiting for the right moment to act. With humans, the frontal lobe gets an upgrade in abstraction and goes from inhibiting pounces to assessing risk—helping us discriminate between small and immediate gains and larger, but delayed, payoffs.

Imagine being offered the choice between two decks of cards, each rigged with its own set of losses and wins. The first has a few big wins and many losses, so that over time, you end up losing; the second has smaller but more frequent wins with smaller and fewer losses, so that over time you win slowly. After playing a short while, most folks will pick the game with low risks and small but consistent payoffs that build up over time, but people with damage to the frontal lobe will reliably pick the risky deck, lured by the big but costly payoffs.

Your inner Tiger is the master of *delay of gratification,* your tolerance for putting off immediate small gains in preference of larger gains later on. Delay of gratification makes it possible for a forty-year old student to return to higher education and endure living like a pauper for a few years in order to earn a larger salary afterward. Whether it means getting up for a 6:00 a.m. workout instead of staying warm in bed or resisting the urge to slam into the back of the Pinto that cuts him off in traffic, Tiger will choose to do what is best over what is easy in the pursuit of self-determination, courtesy of the delay of gratification. To develop this disciplined side to yourself, practice delay of gratification in the pursuit of goals *you care about* (your heart has to be in it). When your efforts in delaying gratification succeed, meet the triumph with gratitude for the success rather than arrogance, so as to engage the vagus nerve. To engage the vagus nerve if your efforts do not bear the fruits you hoped for, offer yourself compassion, especially if the losses are severe, and self-respect for your efforts. These moments will become part of the ideokinetics of your personal mythology as you embody the archetype.

Tiger Personality: Discipline, Courage, Magnanimity

Healthy, Tiger is good-hearted, confident, centered, balanced, and magnanimous. He possesses a realistic sense of his limits and gives credit where due. Tiger's mere presence singes space to cut through pretense and delusion. Tiger is goal-oriented, forceful, extraverted, simple, and concentrated, with the motto "take the word *can't* out of your vocabulary."

The Tiger physique is a classic mesomorphic type, a sexy T-frame structure of broad muscular shoulders, narrow hips, and a high ratio of fast-twitch muscles that grow when they merely think of lifting weights. Tiger's facial features are open and strong; he has a square jaw, granite-chiseled cheekbones, a dominating brow with eyes that are steadfast and piercing. He is the quintessential masculine businessman or captain of the football team. The hands of Tiger are strong, the length of the fingers equal to the size of the palm. Ch'ien-lung is an embodied art, so it is not important that you possess the traits but that you *imagine what it would feel like* to possess them.

What do Tigers like? In music, they seek out the brass and rousing beat of a victory parade or the driving defiance of rock and roll; in food, they eat steak and potatoes—foods that are rich in protein to build muscles, that are hearty and substantial; in books, they prefer nonfiction material offering actionable advice or simple allegories for success; in movies, they prefer war stories or the long-shot athlete stories involving great odds, grit, and triumph over adversity. Tigers are neat and orderly; you will not find a healthy Tiger with frumpy clothes or a messy room. Tiger talks in bullet points, common aphorisms, and sports or combat metaphors. His powerful personality comes at a cost, for his fervor blinds him to the needs of others and results in perhaps the most telling feature of a Tiger: his instant karma. The consequences of Tiger's actions are immediately repaid to him with interest.

Each Animal personality progresses through stages of maturity. Tiger's personality follows an arc; he goes from basing his power on ego to basing his power on principles. At first, his willpower emanates from the self-defined but ultimately self-limited resources of his ego. Gradually, Tiger grows to recognize that will and power emanate from his alignment to a set of universal values, so his relationship to power and self-determination will mature. At the first stage, Tiger reminds me of Arnold Schwarzenegger, the great action hero. When Schwarzenegger was a bodybuilder, he was asked how he could lift heavy weights all day; he answered that he could do this because it was like having orgasms eight hours a day.

The young Tiger develops will and power for their own sake. Pushing the envelope is its own reward, exemplified by George Mallory's response to being asked why he wanted to climb Everest, "Because it's there." Tiger's discipline is the stuff of legend. He has a natural inclination for the routine of discipline, but when that routine is infused with passion, it becomes a living forge. Homer Hans Bryant is founder of the Chicago Multi-Cultural Dance Center, and not only is he a living embodiment of Tiger discipline and passion, but he also teaches a ballet floor-barre that is world-renowned for conditioning athletic ballet champions. A *floor-barre* is a routine where you do the movements of ballet, like the footwork and leg lifts, with the spine ramrod-straight in prone, supine, and lateral positions. These workouts are full-bodied calisthenics from some place near the seventh circle of hell, which you have to do while making it look pretty. From personal experience, I can tell you that they are grueling. Homer trained entire generations of young dancers by baptizing them in the fire of this discipline. In classic Tiger fashion, his school's motto, printed on t-shirts, reads

"The fun is in the discipline—the discipline is in the fun." His students trained even as their toes bled, demanding, "More! More!" "That's because they have a little bit of me in them," said Homer.

When I started training in Ch'ien-lung, my greatest strength was a Tiger's discipline. I used to work out ten to twelve hours a day, practicing forms, strengthening and stretching, doing subtle, precision-controlled alignment and coordination work followed up with meditation. I'd get up at 6:00 a.m. to meet with Connie for his early-morning classes, do dance and martial art classes in the afternoon and evening until 9:00 p.m., surreptitiously slide in breathing routines throughout the day, and round it off with more breathing exercises before bed. Tigers practice with fervor. The teacher of Ravi Shankar, the famous sitar player, is quoted as having said, "In this life, you have time for only one thing," and he would tie his long hair to the ceiling, so when he nodded off during his all-night practice sessions, he would be jarred awake by the sudden tug of his head.[10]

Even at this early stage, Tiger strives to up the regimen and seek out desirable stresses, what George Gurdjieff called *super-efforts*.[11] Super-efforts are any effort or work done above and beyond the call of duty. It's coming home exhausted from work and then going for a jog; it is doing a job that takes an hour and doing it equally well in half the time; it's going the extra mile with a roar in the belly. Near the completion of the first stage, Tiger pushes his limits through self-directed super-efforts—doing harder things faster and better. During this stage, Tiger perceives himself to be the source of his own power; his determination, discipline, and work give him a sense of control over his own life. All of this—the zeal and the go-it-alone stance—set up the second stage of development in which Tiger's actions cause ripple effects, some of which return to propel his growth.

This is Tiger, the big part of you that pushes limits that occasionally push back. Instant karma confronts Tiger with an existential obstacle or conflict. The struggle can sometimes be an internal conflict, sometimes an external conflict and, often as not, both. In the center of the campus where I teach at San Jose State University, in the heart of Silicon Valley, there stands a statue honoring two of our most notable alumni: US Olympians Tommie Smith and John Carlos, who won gold and bronze medals respectively at the 1968 Olympics in the 200-meter sprint. They received their medals while they wore beads and scarves to protest lynchings, wore their jackets open in sympathy with blue-collar workers, were shoeless to protest poverty, and raised their black gloved hands in the Black Panther salute during the national anthem. They knew that "by protesting they might lose everything," and did. They were booed and hissed during the anthem, kicked out of the Olympic stadium immediately, and upon their return to the States, they received death threats and were kicked off the US Track Team. John Carlos said, "I had a moral obligation to step up. Morality was a far greater force than the rules and regulations they had."[12] Tiger's journey is well through the second stage when he turns his power to serving others out of principle. The super-efforts of a Tiger at this second stage shift from "do more faster" to "do right better." At this second stage, the Tiger works for goals based on values which, in turn, shifts Tiger's concept of power from ego-sourced to value-based.

The burning discipline, working under conditions of friction, making super-efforts, the convergence of unforeseen external circumstances, all of this presses Tiger to develop what Gurdjieff called the *magnetic center*.[13] The language is a bit dated—it's closer to a system than a center, and closer to a mathematical attractor than to magnetism—but the magnetic center can be thought of as the sum total of insights and knowledge gained from friction and super-efforts that exert a cumulative effect upon the mind and heart to direct all your cognitive and emotional resources in one direction. The magnetic center is a way of describing the galvanization of a person's character that results in their dedicating every fiber of their body and the entirety of their faculties to one cause. The cause may be material, like finally owning a Lamborghini or purchasing an engagement ring. It may be an accomplishment, like winning a competition, dominating an industry, or acquiring knowledge through research. In a martial art life, the cause is self-mastery.

From the outside, someone with a magnetic center for self-mastery looks like they embody their values; they accurately interpret people and situations for the opportunities they offer in developing self-mastery; and they seem to have a talent for drawing people and resources to support them while skillfully redirecting their detractors. At first, the magnetic center emerges for self-mastery in oneself, and in the third stage, it emerges to support self-mastery in others, or at least to foster an environment in which greater self-knowledge for many is possible.

Thurgood Marshal is a good example of maturity in confronting limits imposed on the self-determination of the many. His steady strength of character had been shaped by his experiences of racial prejudice—he was rejected by the University of Maryland Law School because of his race, despite being academically (over)qualified. Nevertheless, he went on to argue and win the Supreme Court case of *Brown v. Board of Education,* appealing to common decency, that the doctrine of "separate but equal" is inherently unequal. In the landmark case, he confronts racism head on, saying that he

> *had the feeling that on hearing the discussion yesterday that when you put a white child in a school with a whole lot of colored children, the child would fall apart or something. Everybody knows that is not true.*[14]

He stands as one against many, placing personal experience against public myth, saying, "Those same kids in Virginia and South Carolina, they play on their farms together, they go down the road together, they separate to go to school, they come out of school and play ball together." He admonishes the opposition who, with "little pet feelings of race, little pet feelings of custom," can only uphold their arguments if they firmly believe "of all of the multitudinous groups of people in this country you have to single out Negroes and give them separate treatment," but know they cannot "stand in court and urge that."[15]

So far, he is addressing the court as a Tiger at the first level of maturity where he is directly confronting the opposition, but Marshal goes further. In a good example of Tiger at the second stage of maturity, he *makes himself bigger* than the prejudice he is fighting. He affirms that the Supreme Court "makes clear to all of these states that in administering their governmental functions ... [they must be] vital not to the life of the state alone, not to the country alone, but vital to the world in general." He deftly argues that the Supreme Court supersedes the power of the individual states, saying the Fourteenth Amendment was intended "to deprive the states of power to enforce Black Codes or anything else like it." In an example of Tiger at the third stage of maturity, he appeals directly to the collective heart, arguing for an environment in which the self-determination of the many is more likely. He affirms that the legitimacy of the individual states is based, not on the needs of the state alone, but on principles of justice recognized around the world. He drives home relentlessly that the needs of justice are greater than the "little pet feelings of custom" enforced by the Black Codes. His final remarks deal the *coup de grace*. He makes the debate about something bigger than race or class, but about human nature's tendency to degrade:

> *... It [justification for segregation] can't be because of slavery in the past, because there are very few groups in this country that haven't had slavery some place back in history of their groups. It can't be color because there are Negroes as white as the drifted snow, with blue eyes, and they are just as segregated as the colored man. The only thing it can be is an inherent determination that the people who were formerly in slavery, regardless of anything else, shall be kept as near that stage as is possible, and now is the time, we submit, that this Court should make it clear that that is not what our Constitution stands for. Thank you, sir.*[16]

At the highest level of maturity, the Animals begin to resemble their opposite. Here, Tiger almost seems like its opposite, Boa. At this fourth level, we have a Tiger like Nelson Mandela, whose directed will manifests not in monumental acts, but in a way of being. This stage is marked by a sense of purpose, what Aaron Antonovsky called *sense of coherence.*[17] Antonovsky interviewed dozens of Nazi concentration-camp survivors and was amazed to find many demonstrated fine emotional health in spite of their trials. In transcripts, he noticed that resilient survivors had three tendencies: first, a pervasive belief that problems had an explanation that could at least be understood; second, the ability to recognize resources and manage the problem; third, a commitment to meaningfulness, that is, finding the problem worthy of emotional investment. At the fourth stage, the Tiger morphos embodies Antonovsky's sense of coherence.

Dark Side: Egocentric, Love of Power, Bullying

When you learn to see Tiger personalities around you, you'll notice two paths they can take. In the first, healthy, Tiger exudes confidence, generosity, and compassion and pursues justice. He stands with others, but on his own two feet, and he places the power of his driven and directed courage in the service of his heart. But in the second, when the heart of the Tiger has been abused, shamed, or starved of reflection, then his confidence turns to arrogance, his generosity dries up into rigid rule-following, and his compassion is devoured or twisted into authoritarianism and oppressiveness.

An unhealthy Tiger, with an ego that is brittle and over-defended is, in a word, narcissistic. Tiger, unbalanced, is grandiosity personified with a need for admiration and a striking lack of recognition for the thoughts, feelings, and legitimate needs of others. The unchecked Tiger treats others as fuel to burn in the engine of his own self-aggrandizement—other people exist as the audience of his perpetual self-admiration machine. Tigers look like good leaders and are often rated as highly effective, even in instances when their poor decisions lead to poor outcomes. But followers see them as leaders because "they are sometimes wrong, but never in doubt." This Tiger self-confidence reduces uncertainty and stress in followers.[18]

It can be easy to fall into a dysfunctional relationship with Tiger. He first appears as a knight in shining armor only to reveal his inner demon later. In extreme cases, the unbalanced Tiger exaggerates his accomplishments to the point of lying, is obsessed with fantasies of unlimited fame, expects favorable priority treatment without corresponding achievement, and demands full compliance. You know you are in a relationship with one when the relationship brings about feelings of exhaustion, a sense of failure and self-blame, and when you find that you devalue yourself as Tiger finds fault with nearly everything you do.

Another dark side to the Tiger is that he makes a great foot-soldier for any army. The fierce devotion of a healthy Tiger can be turned into the *submission and obedience* of a hyper-conforming fundamentalist. They are into social domination and authoritarianism. They believe in an uncompromising dog-eat-dog world, starved of resources, where the club they belong to should maintain its power over other less morally deserving groups. They are boringly predictable in how they target women, the poor, and racial minorities, while aggressively promoting their own group or authority figure, automatically yea- and nay-saying to catchphrases and slogans borne more from propaganda than thought. Sometimes they are driven by a need for order and religiosity, other times from lust for power, and they are eager to cheat, steal, and lie. Regardless, the liberating potential of Tiger's reason is turned into a bastion for dogma, and the courage of his heart is bent toward subjugation. The best of Tiger is turned toward the worst of ends.

Tiger Movement: Tension, Centeredness, Love with Power

Tectonic plates compress and collide against each other to shape majestic peaks and jagged razor cliffs; massive glaciers pulverize and grind valleys and lakes into existence, making soft the flat, fertile plains that, for thousands of years, rebound after the ice behemoths have receded. Pressure sometimes hurts, but the payoff is definition. In the mythos of Tiger, pressure brings things into existence. Life pushes the way magma presses its way up through a volcano or a flower breaks through asphalt on a street. The ideokinetics of Tiger invoke fiery pressures that are channeled to affirm life.

When my wife and I travelled to Iceland, we went to one of the many spots where you can find the Mid-Atlantic Ridge running down the country. It looks unassuming, like a big grassy ditch with tall steep sides; on one side of the ditch is the Eurasian continental plate and on the other is the North American plate. As I often do on our travels, I do the Animal bows in a nature setting that matches the ideokinetics of the Animal, so I did Tiger here. Normally, doing the bows in nature makes me feel like less of a tourist, more of a participant, and connects me to the Animals in a deep way. But this was an otherworldly experience that brought home the power of using elemental imagery in breathing practices. Usually, with Tiger, I need to dig deep and there is a little ramping-up as the intensity builds. This time was different, and I will never forget it. The intensity of pressure was already there, and it was coming from outside of me, pressing inward. It was as though the mass of the two plates were pushing against me trying to work their way back toward each other through me. I felt an incredible surge of power doing the bows that I had never experienced before.

The Tiger mythos translates into techniques based on tension and pressure, and it begins, as it often does in Ch'ien-lung, with the breath. Walk into any karate dojo, and you will hear the high-pressured exhalation called *sanchin* or "small-aperture" breathing—it sounds like a sonic boom being forced out of a garden hose. It is performed by pushing air out as forcibly as possible while resisting it equally hard at the same time, resulting in only a small stream of air leaking under tremendous self-generated pressure. It captures the high intensity of Tiger. In many martial art styles, the self-resistance in breathing is done in tandem with what is called *high isotonic tension,* where every movement is performed against self-resistance in the opposite direction to the movement. A student performs blocks, punches and kicks under high tension, as if every limb is strapped to a cable pulling in the opposite direction. Isotonic tension forces attention to every muscle, from the big primary movers to the small stabilizers.

The Tiger ideokinetics of opposition can improve your motion in any sport. It was the first and perennial lesson Constantine gave in his classes—that we imagine ourselves inside the three-dimensional square of the plaque and extend out to each of the planes of the cube even as we were forcefully contracting the muscles toward our center. If fingers are reaching forward, reach back with the shoulder blade; pull the tailbone down and the occipital bones up; rotate the thighs out and up while you rotate the feet in and down. Someone merely standing lengthening their body in opposition along the length of their bones looks more assertive and powerful and creates more space around them through which they can move. From opposition in static stances, Constantine would then explain what he called *augmented motion* in movement, the notion that for the action of one limb on one side of the body, there was an equal and opposite action of the same limb on the other side. In a punch, for example, as one arm thrusts forward, the other pulls back; in a kick, the kicking leg thrusts forward while the standing leg presses with equal vigor down into the ground; in wrestling or a head-butt, as the torso bends down, the back arches away (like wrapping the body over a barrel). For athletes in any sport, and especially for beginners, these two principles of opposition and augmented motion will accelerate your movement awareness. They are basics that require dedicated study at first, but which then become second nature, with benefits accumulating over time. The principles of opposition and augmented motion are practiced in the Double-Wrapping and Tree Pose exercises in appendices D and E, respectively, building a bridge to other Animals and setting the stage for the Dragons.

When Tiger takes a position, figuratively or literally, the stance is as immovable as a mountain base. So, it makes sense that stance work is important to the logos of Tiger. If you have done the Chair Pose against the wall for five minutes, then you have felt your leg muscles burning and trembling and can appreciate the discipline and mental toughness required to do these exercises. Stance work is excellent practice for beginners, and while holding a position looks static on the outside, it is greatly dynamic on the inside. Stance work is not meant to be an exercise in masochism; instead, treat the stance you are holding as a snapshot *en route* between two positions, and make microadjustments as if you were still transitioning between the two poles. The microadjustments turn the stance into something of a kinesthetic test tube or a microscope under which you have isolated the principles of posture and breath to watch them interact. The secret of stance work is to treat it as though you are still moving, applying the principles of augmented motion and opposition, even though you are standing absolutely still.

In a way, Tiger meets the other Animals in the stances. Boa breathing relaxes and releases tension while engaging the double-wrapping spirals; Python facilitate microadjustments to offset muscular tension onto the skeleton; Panther's fascial tissues of tendons and ligaments get better at storing and transferring force while also tuning the brain to the proprioception of those small motions; and the stances help Cobra and White Leopard ground the energy circuits they run. You can find a list of Tiger stances with instructions included in the "Seven Steps to Embodying Tiger" at the end of this chapter. The stances can be practiced alone, but a partner who can stress test helps to identify blind spots.

In Tiger mythos, opposition is king. Tigers are wherever you find people testing their physical grit: MMA and boxing, wrestling, the Olympics, the Tour de France, obstacle course races like Tough Mudder, or paramilitary fitness programs like GORUCK. The Tiger motto is "Get Real. Fight Hard. Find Your Truth." And when embodying Tiger, the truth always has an air of simplicity, just like the logos of his movements: all blocks are performed at 90 degrees, stances have one straight leg with the other at a right angle, the hips draw simple circles to generate massive power, and the feet move along straight lines drawn on the floor in chalk.

Tiger's need for opposition is perhaps nowhere more manifest than in power training. A weight-training program for Tiger includes sets of four to twenty-one reps, with weights of between 50 percent and 110 percent of your one-rep max. Tiger makes sure to go fast on the shortening contraction to develop acceleration, the key to power, and to go slowly and smoothly on the lengthening eccentric contraction to maximize the *hyperplasia* (the production of new muscles fibers, as opposed to *hypertrophia,* the thickening of existing muscle fibers), preferably unsupported by a machine. Tiger uses free weights or kettlebells with gnaw marks on the handles to engage the core stabilizers and muscle chains. He lifts in super-sets where the contracting and relaxing muscles alternate roles in the exercises, leveraging his body's natural reciprocal inhibition in opposing muscle groups. Exercises are done on multiple planes five days a week, forty-five minutes a day, within the critical hormone window. The training is periodized over six months of the year where the strength-building phase is preceded by a stabilization phase and followed by a power phase, including interval plyometrics.[19]

Right now, true Tigers are salivating over what they just read. Whatever your sport, Tiger strength-building is the investment capital that pays dividends in acquiring new motor skills. Videos on social media today abound with body-weight or calisthenics exercises—where a ten-year-old girl phenom does one-arm pull-ups with a twenty-five-pound weight-belt or a young lady deadlifts a one-hundred-pound barbell overhead, holding it there, while she casually steps into full splits. Tigers all. But you do not have to be a bodybuilder to enjoy the health benefits of weight-bearing exercises. The Tiger's growth of muscle tissue boosts the production of hormones and antioxidants, promoting immunity and bone density, all of which prolongs longevity.

No matter the sport, though, the embodied metaphysics of Tiger is to move the body and mind together from the center. The Tiger's movement exudes power, a power generated from the hips and legs that transfers through the core stabilizers to the rest of the body. The Japanese use the term *toitsu-tai,* which loosely translates as "mind and body as one," to describe this movement. This can be clearly seen in traditional Japanese *katana* (sword, the Tiger's favorite weapon) work, where the master is not wielding a sword, but where the master *is* the sword. One of the key paradoxes in training Tiger to achieve this union of mind and body is that he needs to be taught to move the limbs, not according to the resulting outcome, but by thinking of moving the limbs relative to his center. For example, in the action of doing a pull-up, instead of focusing on getting the body up to the bar, focus instead on bringing your own hands and elbows closer to your center. This subtle mental shift in focus cultivates a mental stillness and generates full-body power.

It might be tempting to assume that Tiger looks and moves like a 'roid-raging bodybuilder, with muscles climbing over top of each other to see which will get to the head first, but this would be a sad and narrow interpretation of Tiger. In the mythos, Tiger's physical power and mental concentration serve the courageous and compassionate heart. To paraphrase Martin Luther King Jr., Tiger's power is loving and his love is backed by power. Your Tiger becomes so much more than feats of strength when you bring the full range of the heart to your prowess. This range spans from the fiery and fierce heart all the way to Tiger's soft dove heart, which makes for good sportsmanship, but also, unexpectedly, for effectiveness in life's physical conflicts.

In a story told by Sensei Robert Frager, a gentleman is in the middle of a crowd at an event in the streets of London when, in the confusion of the throngs, a young man pulls out a switchblade and orders him to hand over his wallet. The gentleman is surprised, for this young man is the same age as his own son. The gentleman feels a protective pang, imagining the fear he would have were his own son to place himself in a similar position. Without thinking, he said, "Put the knife away, son, and you won't get in trouble." The young man blinked, folded his knife, turned, and disappeared into the crowd.

The story is a great example of how the Tiger's protective and compassionate heart irrevocably shifted the frame of the conflict so that it took the young man's center with mere words. But this is not just a nice story. Ideokinetics of moving with compassion are part of the logos of Tiger. Exercise or forms done as though moving to protect out of compassion adjust posture and make the quality of *toitsu-tai* more readily available. The ideokinetics of compassion also bring intelligence and power to Tiger's touch.

Touch is intelligent, and it communicates emotion. Imagine you are seated in a psychology lab. It's at the University of California, Berkeley, and is run by Dacher Keltner of the Greater Good Science Center, whose work on positive emotions brings diamond-cutting precision to Tiger's emotional intelligence. You place your arm through a set of curtains. On the other side of the curtains is a stranger. Neither of you knows each other's sex or age. The stranger has a list of twelve words for emotions that they are supposed to communicate through touch, "in any way deemed appropriate." The stranger reads *anger,* thinks a moment and then presses, taps, or in some way touches you between your elbow and your fingers. The next word is *sympathy.* The stranger again thinks a moment and then touches or rubs your arm in some way. Your job is to choose the emotion of each contact from a list of the same words the stranger received. The list of emotions range in three dimensions from arousing (anger) to calming (sympathy), pleasant (love) to unpleasant (disgust), and self-preoccupied (embarrassed) to prosocial (generosity). If you took part in this study, conducted in the US and Spain,[20] you would not do well at identifying self-preoccupied emotions of embarrassment, envy, or pride, but you would have had a better than fifty-fifty chance of identifying arousing emotions like anger, fear, and disgust, as well as the pleasant emotions of love, generosity, and sympathy (compassionate support).

The Tiger's heart translates the feeling of compassion into a language of touch. The emotional communication happens through a combination of intensity and timing. For example, people will stroke or pat to sympathize, and use a moderate touch for a long time for love. Generating positive emotion in touch has practical application in martial arts. If you have ever crossed hands with the great teachers of a martial art, you will be surprised by the softness of their touch. In my experience, using a soft touch with a training partner makes it difficult for them to "locate" my center or anticipate my intention. It takes practice, of course, and it can be frustrating, but it is a deep communication, transforming conflict into dialogue. Directions on how to connect the heart in your physical exercises are given at the end of this chapter. From my personal experience, these exercises have practical benefits in martial practice. I have found my body recovers more quickly, my sparring is calmer, and fine-grain corrections are easier.

From logos, we turn to morphos where Tiger turns the beam of his resolute focus inward, fearlessly confronting himself. As in all things, the Tiger returns to the crust of Earth and heals by growing and building things, from farms to monuments to organizations and groups. The Tiger morphos centers on movement of the body, heart, and mind as one, in alignment with the natural laws of the Earth. Tiger finds healing through contest and competition with himself, like running marathons or rock climbing sheer cliffs. Tiger transforms by elevation. *Elevation* is doing good for others when you feel down yourself. For example, if you need a break from studying, you will be more recharged after you spend two hours helping a friend move than you will be if you spend two hours seeing a movie. In the process of healing, Tiger will discover his vulnerabilities, learn to shed his armor, and see from the perspective of others. He will learn to forgive himself and others, which will free up his energy to act, not in the pursuit of his own goals, but in the service of others.

Tiger Sex: Choosing between Love and Possession

In romance, Tiger courtship is all-consuming giddiness, and the flush of youthful love is invincible in its armor of innocence. The lovemaking of a healthy Tiger is affectionate, responsive, and responsible. With maturity, Tiger expresses more nuances in lovemaking, from tender passion to angry make-up sex, but more importantly, Tiger learns to become vulnerable and shed armor in lovemaking. The sort of textures Tiger likes in sexual intimacy are broad strokes, grabbing and kneading the muscles. When healthy, the lovemaking is a reciprocal expression of affection, based on trust, building closeness, equal parts of dare and care.

For the injured Tiger, however, courtship is more marketing and procurement, equating sex with status and power. Put crudely, when Tiger is unhealthy, sex with a partner is no different than masturbation. This kind of sexuality ends up making both Tiger and partner feel more lonely. That loneliness can push the partner away, or if the partner is an unhealthy Black Panther, it can lead to incredible dramas.

Tiger in the Arts

Every generation has its embodiment of a Tiger action hero: Douglas Fairbanks, James Cagney, Kirk Douglas, John Wayne, Clint Eastwood, Sylvester Stallone, Arnold Schwarzenegger, Tom Cruise, Liam Neeson, and Dwayne "The Rock" Johnson. Explosive, testosterone-driven, wham-bang action captures the external expression of Tiger's intensity and confrontational nature, whereas Tiger courage is celebrated in film scenes of people exercising their determination to make the world a better place against great odds, like at the front lines of a demonstration for civil rights. You hear the Tiger's roar in the come-from-behind athlete stories, especially when the competition takes on an epic conflict, like when Jesse Owens won his gold medals in the 1936 Olympics in Nazi Germany. You can also find Tiger in movies of emergence, the dawn of something new, like stories about America's Declaration of Independence.

Armor is a common Tiger motif used to mark the alchemical steps in a Tiger's development. The *Iron Man* franchise is built on the symbolism of how a Tiger will use his armor as a crutch unless he powers up his heart. In *Dracula,* to highlight the sheer willpower of his main character, Francis Ford Coppola opens with the warrior Dracula going off to crusade against the multitudinous hordes. As he bids his wife farewell, we see the young Dracula in a suit of plated armor that is sculpted to look like striated muscles, thematically amplifying the man's sheer force of will.

Becoming Tiger

Developing Tiger means thinking, feeling, moving, and breathing in the style of the archetype, adopting his favorite clothes, food, music, and hobbies. By immersing yourself this way, you gain your own personal insight into what Tiger means to you—from there, you can only grow. Tiger is made stronger by challenging the heart, mind, and body. What does not kill the Tiger makes him stronger—especially if it involves interval weight-training, punctuated by naps, charity involvement, and a subscription to *TED Talks*.

The Tiger Plaque

The plaque (see Figure 6.1 in this book's color insert) symbolizes the elements of a centered Tiger. The Tiger plaque glows the colors of his stripes: orange, black, and white. As with each Animal, the triangle represents the individual, the circle represents Earth, and the square, the universal laws. The orange triangle of Tiger represents the heart's red passion blended with the enlightening yellow of the analytical mind. The black of the circle symbolizes the world, which Tiger views as a blank slate, passive and receptive to his will, to be marked or molded by his intentions and actions. How to cultivate Tiger using the plaque is explained in the "Seven Steps to Embodying Tiger" at the end of this chapter.

Each Animal's plaque has multiple levels of interpretation: a physical level that refers to the anatomical systems important to the Animal; a psychological dimension representing its core cognitive skills; and an energetic level representing the energetic systems important to the Animal, such as the chakras or meridians. Tiger's physical triangle reflects the trinity of the body, heart, and mind, and this trinity is echoed again energetically, with *manipura,* the energetic storehouse for physical power, *anahata,* the energetic center of emotional intelligence, and, somewhat out of cadence, the energy of the frontal lobe, the center of the analytical mind. On the psychological level, the points refer to Tiger's trinity of passionate *desire,* fueling clearly defined *intention,* to be expressed as direct *action.* This is action without regret, remorse, or self-doubt.

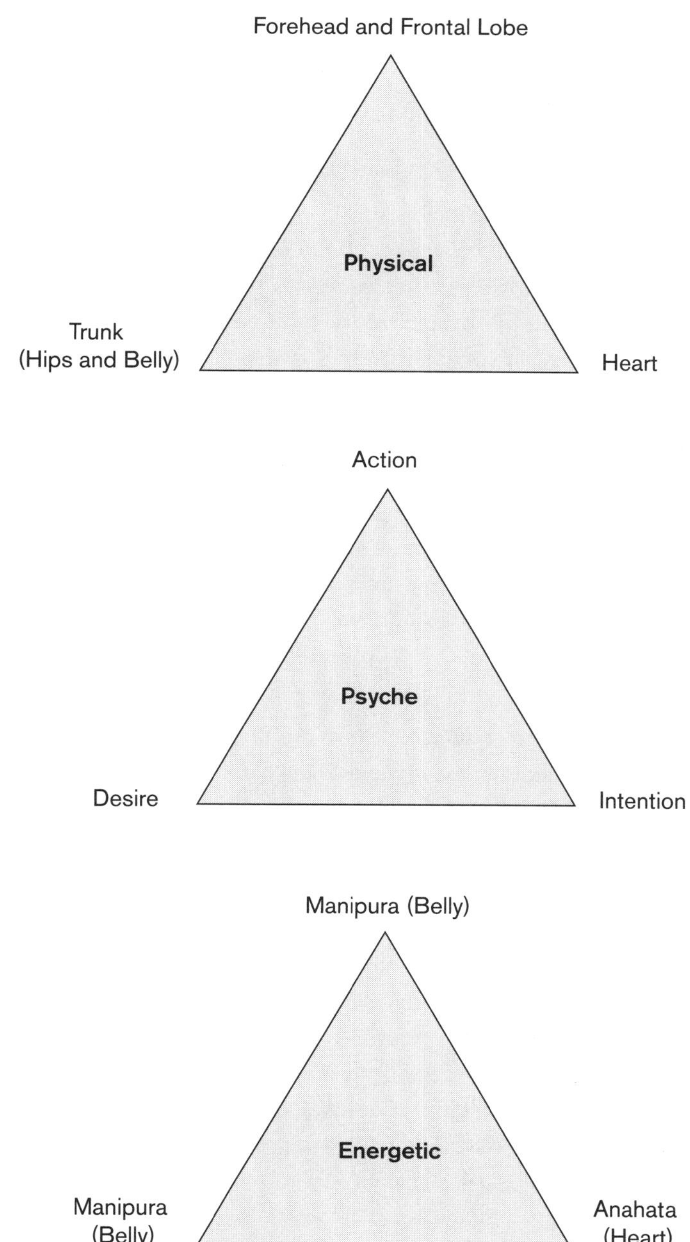

FIGURE 6.2: The symbolic meaning of the triangle points for Tiger

Seven Steps to Embodying Tiger

Step One: Follow Your Breath (Ongoing Mindfulness Practice)

Following your breath in Tiger means breathing willpower into your

Musculature Visualize breathing into the muscles, especially the glutes, quads, triceps, shoulder delts, lats, and eight-pack abs. Visualize the breath fill the muscles with a ready tension. Ideokinetics: Move as if you are a tiger. Move as if your muscles are powerful engines and plates of armor. Move like a tank. Connect to the earth's tectonic plates.

Heart Visualize breathing into the heart, softening any knots. Visualize energies of courage and compassion, justice and mercy to engage the vagus nerve—it should leave you with a feeling of having an expanded chest and an open heart, lightened of burdens. Ideokinetics: Move as if the chest was a furnace sending compressed flames through your limbs. Connect to the earth's molten heart core and the convection currents of magma driving the plates.

Belly/*manipura/dantian* Send breath to the physical center. It is critical to athletic movement. Visualize breath fanning flames an inch below your belly button, warming the rest of the body as the flame grows. Ideokinetics: Review the Melon exercise in appendix C. Move as if the melon contains a fiery pressured energy. Connect to large plains and mountain bases.

Yang musculature Feel what is called Tiger's protective mantle of the body (glutes, quads, triceps, delts, lats, and abs). Visualize the breath expanding in the body against the inside of the mantle, creating pressure and heat. Visualize energy from the pressure to pack energy and tone the body. Ideokinetics: Move as if you are using your yang muscles as armor. Connect to the intense pressure of the tectonic plates pushing against each other.

Frontal lobe Visualize breathing into the frontal lobe, increasing circulation to sharpen focus and clarify purpose. Ideokinetics: Move in a simple, linear, and clear fashion. Connect to the intense focus of a tiger.

Step Two: Recall Your Day (Daily/10 Minutes before Sleep)

Prior to going to bed, recall your day in sequential order. Tiger recalls the progression toward goals. How aligned are your goals to your values? How strongly do the goals stem from desire? How does the resistance provide you with the friction necessary to grow? Are the risks you took helping to make you or the community stronger? During the day, where could you have exercised more delay of gratification? Did any untruths burn away?

Step Three: Scan Your Body (Daily/10 Minutes before and after Sleep)

At night before going to sleep and in the morning, upon waking, scan the following systems of your body: muscular system, heart, and frontal lobe. The same way you stroke a needle with a magnet to align the atoms and magnetize it, scan your body with your Tiger awareness, asking that your body be aligned with your will.

Step Four: Do the Bows in Nature (Weekly/10–15 Minutes)

Do the Tiger bow in an open grassy plain at high noon or at the base of a mountain; a place of clear views cultivates a sense of dominion. Move in high tension, breathing in *sanchin,* as if magma is rising up through the soles of the feet, up into the belly, and the heat is contained by the musculature acting like a pressure cooker, exhaling as though venting through a safety valve.

In addition to the bow for Tiger, doing the stances in nature is a great practice. Figures 6.3–6.6 show the stances and their instructions; Figures 6.7–6.16 show the bow. Try holding the stances for incrementally longer periods while concentrating on the positive emotional values you have chosen.

Tiger Stances

Hold the stances for periods of 1, 5, 10, 15, 20, 30, and 45 minutes, and 1 hour.

FIGURE 6.3: Horse stance: Feet are shoulder width apart, toes pointing forward, knees bent at 90 degrees, the back is straight, the lower back is flat, not curved, and the torso is facing forward. Arms are out in front as if hugging a large tree. See instructions on double wrapping in appendix D to develop this stance.

FIGURE 6.4: Sumo stance: Feet are wide apart, toes pointing out, knees bent at 90 degrees, the back is straight, the lower back is flat, not curved, and the torso is facing forward. Arms are out in front as if hugging a large tree. See instructions on double wrapping to develop this stance.

FIGURE 6.5: Deep stance: Feet are wide apart, toes pointing out, weight of the body is shifted to one side 70/30 percent with one knee bent deeply and the other knee slightly bent, the back is straight, the lower back is flat, not curved, and the torso is facing in the direction of the straighter leg. Arms are reaching out in the direction of the straighter leg. See instructions on double wrapping to develop this stance.

FIGURE 6.6: Strong stance: Feet are shoulder width apart, and parallel, with one foot forward, and the other back. The front leg is bent 90 degrees, the back leg is straight. The back is straight, the lower back is flat, not curved, and the torso is facing forward. Arms are out in front as if pushing a wall. See instructions on double wrapping to develop stance.

Tiger Bow

FIGURE 6.7: Stand with feet together. Feel the mantle of the yang "armor" muscles. Bring energy up from the crust and mantle of the earth, into the belly, heart, and frontal lobe. Feel your presence cut the space like the edge of a sword.

FIGURE 6.8: Bring the hands palm up to the belly, elbows almost straight.

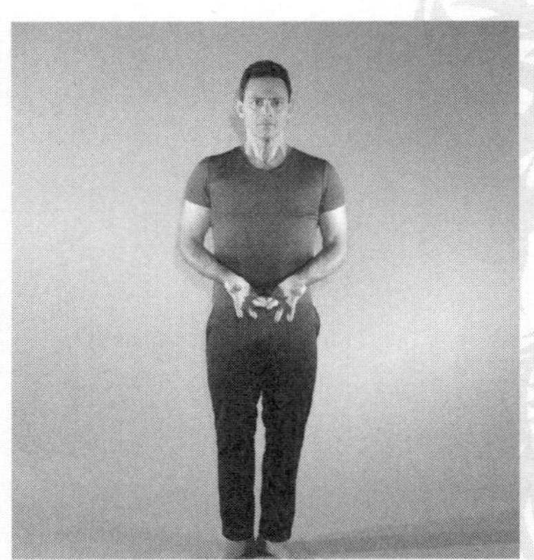

FIGURE 6.9: Inhale one short burst to fill the whole body with breath, turn the feet out, palms up, pull the hands into the belly. Super-charge the *dantian*.

FIGURE 6.10: Inhale, second short burst, super-fill, open arms out to the side, and open chest. Fill heart-center with energy.

FIGURE 6.11: Turn the feet in, exhale in high tension. Bring the hands to the heart. Focus energy out from the heart and frontal lobe.

FIGURE 6.12: Continue exhaling high tension; hands meet at heart and then push forward, making triangle shape with hands. Draw energy from tectonic plates through muscles, heart, and frontal lobe.

FIGURE 6.13: Continue until arms are almost straight. Repeat bow.

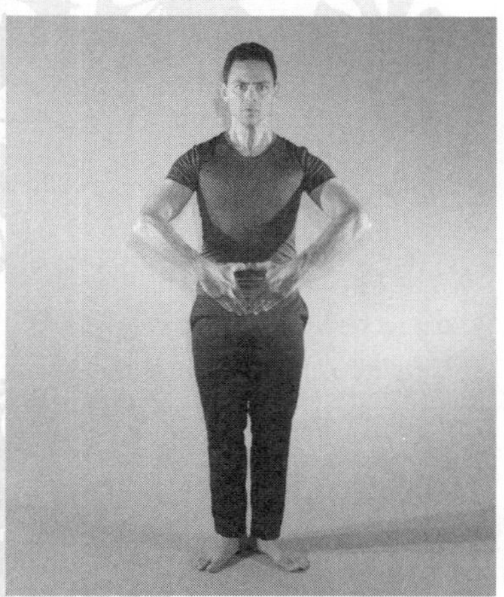

FIGURE 6.14: After bow, turn feet out, bring triangle to belly, point down, inhale. Like a magnifying glass, concentrate energy into *dantian*.

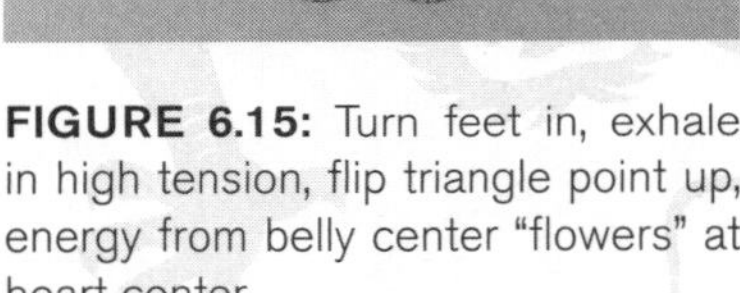

FIGURE 6.15: Turn feet in, exhale in high tension, flip triangle point up, energy from belly center "flowers" at heart center.

FIGURE 6.16: Stand with the feet together. Feel the mantle of the yang armor muscles. Bring energy up from the crust and mantle of Earth into the belly and heart and stand in neutral. Feel the mantle of the Tiger.

Step Five: Adopt the Animal Personality (Ongoing Practice)

Adopting the personality and preferences of Tiger means you must walk, talk, eat, play, and think like a Tiger. Tiger dresses neatly in conventional clothes and keeps personal affairs organized. Tiger likes brassy marches and the rousing beat of a victory parade, or the driving defiance of rock and roll. For food, Tigers eat steak and potatoes—foods rich in protein to build muscle. When it comes to books, Tigers read heartfelt stories of overcoming great obstacles against tremendous odds or concrete and practical nonfiction; Tigers watch war movies or movies about long-shot athletes and historical figures who show grit and triumph over adversity.

When Tiger walks, he projects assertive energy outward. Tigers watch and play competitive team sports and are not shy of physical contact, like tackle football, boxing, and rugby. Tiger develops a powerful muscular physique through a weight-training program that strengthens the power and integration of large core stabilizers and primary movers. Use the *sanchin* breathing technique during weight-lifting, a short bursting inhale followed by a long, high-pressured exhale. Equally important, perform your exercises with focus. The center is always at the ready to move in any direction.

If you are extroverted or want to integrate your practice with public events you can do with friends, there are obstacle course races, like Tough Mudder, or military-style workouts, like GORUCK. These popular events connect people to their Tiger nature.

One of the more intense and insightful exercises for developing a Tiger sense of ownership is to observe your use of the pronoun "I" when speaking and notice which parts of your body resonate with your words and which parts do not. This exercise provides feedback, over time, about the unity of your will, and it will give you an indication of your commitment, passion, or level of resolve moment to moment.

How do you know if you are making progress? You will notice you respect the boundaries of others and assert your own, appreciate people for their passion, and develop your own. You may become more neat and orderly; you will not find a healthy Tiger with wrinkled clothes or a messy room. You will grow more direct and to the point in communication. You will focus on getting the results. You will improve at discriminating between the problems that have a solution and those that have to be contained. When angry, you will assert your needs *and* exercise management of the problem. Tigers separate the people from the problem and focus on the interests, not the positions. You will get better at breaking up a big problem into smaller parts, and at tackling the doable pieces first. Tigers choose goals that are challenging, specific, attainable and that have deadlines or results that can be measured.

To cultivate your Tiger heart, do one thing every day, no matter how small, to work toward a dream you want to accomplish. Choose challenges that grow the heart: volunteer for a charity, take action for a cause that promotes social justice, or become a mentor to a child in need.

Step Six: Remember Your Dreams (Daily/10 Minutes upon Waking)

Tiger is not as dream-oriented as the other Animals, but you can rely on Tiger's discipline to get you consistently writing and recording your dreams. With that said, there are certain themes in dreams you can look out for that pertain to your Tiger will. Cars, trains, and ocean ships in dreams are vehicles of your willpower, the drive and passion to reach a goal. You can take a look at the kind of vehicle in which you are riding. Is the interior plush or bare? Is it reliable or does it have a faulty engine? Small details will highlight the amount of passion or clarity of strategy you have for your goal.

Success requires discipline and a steadfast "no" to distractions, at which Tiger excels. Dreams with cops, judges, or other authority figures are your own Tiger brakes, stopping you from breaking a diet, regimen, or promise. Dreams of self-prohibitions are not always fun, but they reflect deeply held values defining your Tiger commitment.

Step Seven: Use the Plaques (Daily/20 Minutes)

For Tiger, pay attention to the exhalation in the plaque work (see appendix A). Use the single-handed mudra, tongue position, and asana of the Tiger when doing the concentration exercise. Feel the mantle of the musculature compress and intensify your concentration. The eye position for Tiger is open with a clear, straight-ahead, steady gaze. The eyes of the Tiger focus unflinchingly as they follow the contours of the shapes. With Tiger, you want to feel like your mind is a *katana* cutting the edges of the shapes, with a feeling of passionate commitment, like your honor depends on it. Before starting, briefly remind yourself of a moment of courage or compassion in your life. Feel like it is this courageous and compassionate part of you that is doing the concentration exercise with the plaque.

Tiger Energy Circuit

Visualize energy coming into the frontal lobe, down into the heart, down into the belly on the in-breath. On the out-breath, visualize the energy going up through the heart, out the frontal lobe, cutting like a laser.

Tiger vs. Animals

Both Tiger and the Cobra are linear, direct, and pertain to intention. Cobra is more ethereal, concerned with karma, energy, and destiny. Constantine used to say Cobra was the "Tiger of the psychic plane." Tiger concerns itself with tangible results. The ideokinetics, breath visualization, and energy differ; where Tiger is heavy, earthen, and fiery, the Cobra is light, wiry, and electric.

When White Leopard decides to act or create, it can seem as direct as Tiger, but the Leopard strikes without warning, quickly, and is gone. You can usually see the Tiger locomotive coming; it hits heavy and it lingers. Tiger tends to attack the core of a thing, like the stomach or torso, whereas Leopard attacks the instruments, the arms. Their gazes can seem equally focused, but Tiger is concentrating on something at arms-reach while Leopard is focused intently on something in the distance.

Both Tiger and Python have fearsome will. But Python will approach a problem from multiple perspectives, playing one person off of another, allowing time to mature, looking for qualitative changes in state of mind. Tiger breaks a problem down into smaller, doable steps that are time-limited, with measurable, tangible goals, and does not care about the mental dialogue or opinions of others.

Tiger Keys

Tiger eye gaze: The eyes are looking straight forward, unwavering.

Tiger tongue position: The tip of the tongue is touching the roof of the mouth behind the front teeth.

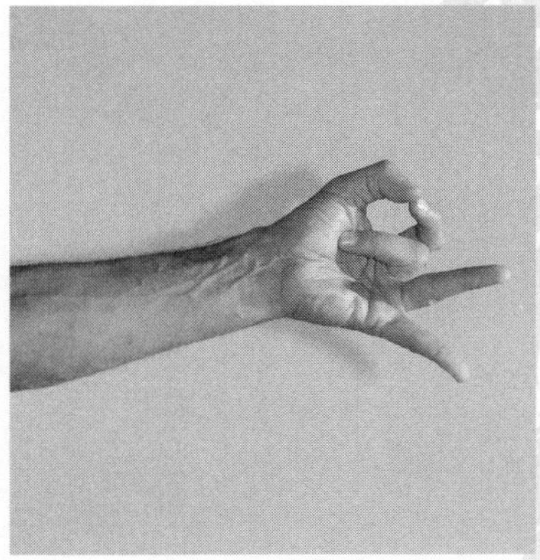

FIGURE 6.17: Tiger mudra: Bring middle finger down to life line, touch index finger to thumb. Pinky and ring finger are at right angle. Use during meditation and during the day to cultivate a linear mind and burning heart.

FIGURE 6.18: Tiger asana: Kneeling position, flat toes, and the left foot is on top of the right.

Table 6.1 summarizes the Tiger archetype.

TABLE 6.1: Tiger Summary

Consciousness	Intent, desire, action
Nature	Earth's crust/mantle, open plains, mountain bases
Anatomy	Striated muscles, heart, forehead
Neural region	Frontal lobe
Energetic systems	*Manipura, anahata*
Favorite foods	Steak and potatoes, high-protein foods
Music	Marching parade, classic rock and roll
Sports and martial arts	Australian rules rugby, karate
Hobbies	Weight training, competitive sports
Clothes	Business suit, uniform

WHITE LEOPARD: COSMIC CREATIVITY

My brain is only a receiver, in the Universe there is a core from which we obtain knowledge, strength and inspiration.

—NICOLA TESLA

HIGH UP IN THE mountains the air is so clean it makes long distances seem short. The White Leopard's speckled coat of grey and white is invisible against his rocky perch. He dreams of his prey approaching. His prey momentarily blinded by the sun, the White Leopard leaves only one paw print in the snow.

White Leopard Consciousness: Thought, Intuition, Creativity

The ancient Greeks calculated the sizes of Earth, the Moon, and the Sun and their distances with the simple geometry of the shadows cast down wells and during eclipses. The priests of ancient Egypt aligned the Great Pyramids perfectly with the stars of Orion's Belt. The Anasazi of Chaco Canyon built giant structures that cast no shadow at high noon one day a year, with walls that lined up perfectly with sister sites 500 miles away.

What else did they know? Did they know about black holes, too? That black holes can squeeze the space out of atoms until an entire planet can fit in a tablespoon? Did their visions include the white point of a black hole that emits subatomic particles, atoms, and the occasional DNA? Did they see stars compress protons, neutrons, and electrons into progressively denser atoms, including the carbon building blocks of our cells? Did their flashes of intuition show them we are stardust produced by a cosmos awesome and coldly indifferent to our existence? Have we with them known this intuitively, but unlike them, forgotten we could know in this way?

Intuition means directly channeling information from the cosmos. The information flashes through in a broad beam and possesses a dual quality of being both information and energy. The cosmos is self-aware, with its knowledge growing more complex. It transmits its cognition to us sometimes as energy via background radiation from the Big Bang, or the redshift of receding stars, and sometimes as information in flashes of genius and creative acts that move psyche and civilization. We directly perceive with intuition these bits and bytes of maturing cosmic self-awareness, the hypotheses the universe asks itself in a proto-form of energy and information. These cosmic memes are not linear like the words in a sentence or the frames on a reel—how could they be—they are dynamic. From a cosmic perspective, hieroglyphics and DNA, comets and black holes, empty space and time itself are the spectra of thoughts of the cosmos; they are forms of information as distinct from each other as Morse code, binary, and French. And the cosmos processes information, asks questions, and crunches numbers like a giant brain with every meteor collision, stock market fluctuation, dictionary edition, computer code, random combination of DNA, and every particle emission from an accelerator. The transformations of energy in these events are just another form of information processing, and information is just another form of energy, together perceived through intuition.

Leopard's abstract reasoning transposes the protean energy information perceived by intuition. Leopard's cool, objective thought does not analyze according to a preexisting checklist, but recognizes (intuits) new categories, dimensions, and continuum along which to map new ideas. Intuition listens to the latest hit songs of the cosmos, and reason transcribes them with the notes from a new language, the same way that calculus provides a mathematical language for change. The new information is also energy that fuels the White Leopard's creativity.

The Snow Leopard is our intuitive genius when, in our creativity, we do not just think outside of the box, but orbit it. This creativity gives us energy as it informs us about the nature of this very energy. It is creativity as an extension of the thoughts of the universe, and it provides context and meaning to human existence. This form of creativity has the effect of exacting a specific effect on the psyche of a people from a given culture at a given time, the same way the formula $E = mc^2$ heralded modern thought. The White Leopard's act of creativity reflects not the personal subjective issues of the artist but the objective self-aware questions the cosmos is asking of itself. For the White Leopard, creativity, information, and energy are tied together, and creativity has a specific purpose: to free up energy trapped or wasted in the social structures we create or the mechanical structures we invent in order to support the psyches of the individual and the culture in growth.

My strongest experience with intuition was at a breakfast with Constantine in the middle of a busy restaurant. He was explaining to a student that White Leopard's way of knowing is not through study or experience, but through channeling. If he, Constantine, wanted to know about the solar system, he would channel the spirits of Newton and Galileo to have a dialogue together where he could listen in on their conversation. At that moment, I had a flash of three fundamental truths at the same time that ripped through me like a bolt of lightning so that I gasped, jolting straight up and back down in my chair. First, there was a flash of the image of Constantine doing the very thing he had just described, but instead of an image mentally conjured by conversation, I had the distinct impression I had been *permitted to view it while in progress;* at the same time, as though watching a film reel in fast-forward, I relived the moments in my own life when I had done the same thing, without knowing what it was; third, there was a literal and figurative "inspiration," that this kind of communion was a natural birthright for all people—this was no mere insight, but a visceral sensation, as though I was looking at the world through the lens of another dimension. All three experiences happened at once as though in a moment of extended time.

It is for me, after all these years, a sacred experience of intuition. My body posture relaxed, my eyes widened and softened in their gaze. Constantine noticing something had happened, finished his explanation to the other student, and turned to ask me what was going on. I told him, and citing my changed countenance, he quickly paid the bill and escorted me back to the dojo, settled me in a quiet corner of the studio, and advised me to "sit with the experience in quiet mind." I later overheard him talking to others, describing it as the moment I "got plugged in" to the intuition of White Leopard.

How does intuition feel? Like broad bands of light. How does intuition change perception? Constantine once explained it saying it was like the famous visual illusion, where an image looks like a vase from one perspective and like two faces from another. The illusion is *bi-stable,* meaning you can only see one or the other, depending on the perspective. White Leopard's intuition, Constantine explained, will allow you to see both at the same time. You would see not just the forest for the trees, but the multiple lives of the forest through numerous climatic changes, as though through time-lapse photography. Intuition is an extraordinary out-of-body experience with very good CliffsNotes.

White Leopard Anatomy: Crown of the Head, Forehead, Throat

When embodying White Leopard, imagine feeling as though the crown of the head, like a satellite dish, collects broad bands of intuition from the cosmos; it's the same place where saints wear their halos, where a monk shaves his head. When the broad beams of intuition are received at the crown, White Leopard transforms their signals through the dense motherboard of circuits that is his analytical mind, sitting in the frontal lobe behind his high forehead.

Intuitive flashes can turn your worldly beliefs to ash. To expand your horizons along with the boundary-breaking vision you have glimpsed, you must put White Leopard's knack for analysis and resynthesis to work. These cognitive powers stand at the ready behind the high dome of his forehead, a second anatomy area important to White Leopard.

Leopard's mind takes methodical steps of formal logic along with gymnastic flights of perspective-taking to reach unexpected conclusions and resolve inscrutable paradoxes. He is guided by unimpeachable ethics. Indeed, at times he is coldly removed from the biases of cultural norms and local morality. You get the impression all that cognitive power waits with glowing readiness behind his shining forehead.

The throat is the White Leopard's gravitational center ... and that's as low as he goes. It's as though White Leopard has no lower limbs, only collarbones and shoulder blades. The throat is the communication center in two important ways. First, the throat communicates intuitive insights outwardly to the restive crowds. Second, it grounds intuitive flashes as the internal diplomatic back channel between the heart and intellect. While the Leopard is not emotional or sentimental, the sign of a mature White Leopard is tempering of intuition with the heart. The throat, home to the thyroid, is also the command center regulating the Energizer Bunny effervescence required for the creative flow White Leopard lives in. Regulating the body's metabolic rate, the healthy Leopard thyroid burns energy so fast, it is no surprise he prefers the cooler temperatures of higher altitudes.

Panther and Tiger anchor hard to Earth by tendon, ligament, and muscle, but White Leopard only lightly clings to Earth—and reluctantly at that—by the energy systems of the body like some electrostatically charged balloon. White Leopard represents energetic anatomy, which is illustrated in appendix B. There are the *chakras* (Sanskrit for *wheel*), which are energy centers along the spine. Each chakra stores fuel like a battery and innate knowledge like an instruction manual for life's milestones and ordeals. Although Leopard represents all the chakras as a whole, he also represents two in particular: At the crown of the head is the Leopard satellite dish, *sahasrara,* also called the Thousand Petal Lotus, which draws down inspiration and cosmic information. At the throat, matching up neatly with the thyroid, is *vishuddha,* which is the center of communication and creativity.

The *aura* is an electromagnetic field projected by the body, with each layer of the aura anchored to a corresponding chakra. Each auric layer is connected to a chakra, like a bubble on a blow-ring, changing shape or tints depending on health or personal conflicts. *Meridians* are a system of energetic rivers and lakes running throughout the body, and they generally align with major arteries and the large interstitial lines of fascia. Much Eastern medicine is based on the theory that the proper flow of the meridians results in health, while blockages or imbalances result in disease.

Leopard's energetic anatomy also includes less well-known systems. The *membranes* act as energetic diaphragms, expanding and contracting to circulate energy around the chakras, and *pumps* do the same thing for the joints of the skeleton. The *psychic meridians* are a single-line vessel of energy running down the middle of each limb and the mid-axis of the body, and they regulate the traditional meridians. Finally, there are the *streams,* ten channels of energy, one from each toe to its analogous finger. The energy systems of the streams, psychic meridians, pumps, and membranes are depicted in appendix B.

White Leopard Brain: Parietal Lobe, Myelin Sheaths, Glial Cells, Glands and the Pituitary

White Leopard's clear thinking and speed of thought rely on rapid communication among the neurons of the brain. Neural signals have an easy time traveling short distances, but signals naturally decay as they travel, which poses a problem for transmissions over long distances. Nature's solution is the fatty white insulation of myelin sheathing and glial cells. Myelin sheathing and glial cells enable neural impulses to travel further. With myelin sheathing and glial cells, neural impulses can maintain their strength over long nerve branches making possible the high-flying kicks Leopard loves as signals travel from the brain to the toes. The more insulation wrapped around and packed between the axons, the faster and more reliable the communication between the neurons, a key to White Leopard's clarity of thought. Einstein, a great example of a Leopard, possessed a brain that had roughly 15 percent more myelin sheathing and glial cells in some areas of the brain than the average person.[1]

Speedy neural transmission means the White Leopard part of the brain, the parietal lobe, can compose the panoramic satellite images we experience in intuitive flashes. The parietal lobe manufactures the perception of space. Located mostly at the back half of the cranium (the crown of the head), the parietal lobe combines torrents of bytes from parallel streams to move you and objects through space: how to pour milk from a full carton without spilling; where to run and how to reach to catch a pop fly; how to fold paper to make an origami swan. All rely on integrating multiple cues about speed, location, direction, distance, time-to- contact, orientation, weight—all calculated in the blink of an eye. The parietal lobe uses all this information to glue perception to a point in space. This gives coherence to your reality by gluing the texture of a rose and the sight of the rose to the same spot where you touch the rose. The accurate gluing of perception to space results in faster reactions. For example, when your phone display lights up, your reaction time is slower than if it lights up and vibrates, which makes no sense, if more information should take longer to process.[2] But not so. The richer the information, the faster your inner White Leopard. The perception of space lays the foundation for using space as a metaphor.

By far, the best trick the Leopard lobe pulls is the use of space as a metaphor: the parietal lobe *manufactures conceptual space*.[3] Spatial metaphors allow you to talk about rising prices, falling costs, or Tom slipping into a coma, when prices, costs, or Tom did not actually move.[4] Your imagination plays out on the holodeck of space manufactured by the parietal lobe. Space is fundamental to imagination. You can imagine the Eiffel Tower made of Jell-O, a foot high or in your backyard, but try to imagine it *not taking up space*.[5] That holodeck is housed in the Leopard's parietal lobe.

With all this information coming in, how does one disseminate or even act effectively? The endocrine system, and the pituitary gland of the White Leopard in particular, have a few tricks to teach about communication. The glands, like Leopard, remotely rouse activity in far-away places, and in this case, far-away parts of the body. The endocrine system works in a cascade fashion, with the gland at the top signaling the ones below, and it is the pituitary that sits at the (near) top of the heap (though it does take signals from the hypothalamus). The pituitary offers important lessons in communicating complex messages in complex situations. It sends messages out to the bones to grow, to the mammary glands to produce milk, to the kidneys to hold water, to the thyroid to adjust energy metabolism, to the testes to produce testosterone, to the ovaries to ready eggs, and to the uterus to labor.[6] No part of the body is left untouched. But with such a broad audience, how does the pituitary keep its messages straight? The answer is dedicated lines. For each gland, the pituitary has a dedicated messenger, with one hormone used exclusively to signal one gland whether to start and another dedicated circuit to turn things off. In this way, its lines don't get crossed.

White Leopard Personality

I once read of a film crew in Tibet making a documentary about snow leopards. The crew worked for six weeks—day and night, doing stake-outs, combing the areas they had heard of previous sightings—all to no avail. On their last day, exhausted and empty-handed, they were packing up to leave, and as some kind of cosmic parting gift, one of the guides ran into report that a yak had been killed by a leopard that had left only a paw print in the snow. The White Leopard type, like the snow leopard of this story, is rare, hard to spot, and lives in places that are geographically and spiritually rarefied. He removes himself from the world, seeking transcendence. He keeps his distance, even in a crowd. He could be in a New York subway, pressed like a sardine against other people and, still, he will preserve a sense of personal space and cool aloofness.

What does he look like? Think elf. He seems eternally youthful. His eyes may either be large and dreamy or small and beady—like he is squinting to see the distant horizon—but they will be set far apart, because the greater the distance between the pupils, the more visual power for depth perception. His forehead is prominently high, with a receding hairline, as though his hairline was obstructing his lines of sight so he had it pulled back, and his chin is narrow and pointed, in contrast with the Tiger's brick jawline. He has long, thin, almost delicate fingers, all the better to program code with, which is what he would prefer to be doing anyway. His frame is broad-shouldered and although he may have long legs, they convey lightness, like those of a gazelle; his neck, even if thick, will seem long and open.

He listens to classical music with multiple concurrent melodies because that's what intuition feels like, and he eats fruits because they are light and will not carry the karmic blemish of taking a life, which would only impede his quest toward transcending the Earthly plane. The clothes he wears are elegant and futuristic in design, including hypoallergenic natural fibers and a visor with a see-through dashboard display. For the record, his weapon of choice is the bow and arrow, which allows him lightning speed and surgical precision from a distance. He finds love in truth. He reads philosophy, revels in Socratic thought and Aristotelian logic as applied to the truth of science, the beauty of art, and the goodness of ethics. He reads anything that can be analyzed with mathematics and delves headlong into high-energy physics, deep-space astronomy, and quantum mechanics, and he loves taking long walks on the beach while doing calculus.

Whirling Dervishes spin, spin, spin because that is the best way to transmit prayers to the divine presence—through the same motion by which Earth alternates between night and day: for what is God anyway but the gradient transition between light and dark? So, the Dervishes spin. And like the Dervishes, White Leopard creates a microcosm, a small world of art, prayer, or science, which renders the higher truths he intuits on a smaller scale. In an ultimate act of the self-reflexive, when White Leopard creates, he simulates part of the mystery he worships. As far as he is concerned, he came into the world to be a clear and pure conduit for ideas. But at this early stage, he is uninterested in the grit and sweat of making things real. He is an abstract thinker. For example, although he was a brilliant theoretical physicist, J. Robert Oppenheimer, father of the atomic bomb, could not cross over into experimental physics because it demanded enduring the boring manual labor of making thin beryllium films. It was not that he was not handy—he sailed boats, corralled horses, restored his log cabin—just as long as the job was not routine, he was perfectly capable.[7]

The White Leopard personality centers on being as pure a conduit of information as possible, and the young White Leopard treats his mind as an Acropolis for the free association of ideas. You can spot the White Leopard next to you or within yourself by the sense of ethics and integrity in the pursuit of truth. It may be spiritual, artistic, or scientific purity, but it is purity with the purpose of ensuring the free flow of ideas and information. My late advisor, Bruce Bridgeman, modeled this. Bruce had a theory about how the frame of a picture influences our visual perception of the object in the frame. He ran tests, and his experiments supported his particular theory. Another researcher, Paul Dassonville, disagreed; he had an alternative theory and ran modified experiments that supported it. It happens often in science that there are two legitimate, competing theories, but what does not happen often is the collegiate collaboration between the competing researchers to determine which theory is valid. That is just what happened here in no small part because Bruce, exemplifying White Leopard, pursued the truth with purity. Bruce and Paul designed, conducted, and in tandem presented the results from the "killer study" (in Bruce's words) which, as it turned out, showed that Bruce's theory was incorrect. They presented their findings together on the same stage at a conference, and I have never seen anyone as tickled with delight as Bruce at announcing that his theory was wrong. As White Leopard would be, he was elevated by the fact that the integrity of science had prevailed and that our pursuit of truth was the better for it.

White Leopard also has a remarkable talent for getting *unstuck*—looking at a problem from novel perspectives with a childlike freshness. Creative people overcome what is called *functional fixity,* which simply means to think of using an object in only one way—basically, when all you have is a hammer, everything looks like a nail. Creative people, and the Leopard type certainly is, will generate numerous, unconventional alternatives, turning a hammer into a boomerang or a pendulum for a grandfather clock, for instance. This childlike freshness lends the White Leopard a magus-like ability in solving problems. An ordinary genius[8] takes a problem and, following logical steps, comes to a clear conclusion—as, say, Python or Tiger would. One can see the step-by-step progress and can recall them from memory later. But the White Leopard exhibits qualities of the nonordinary genius, a magus. When presented with a problem, he looks at it for a while, pinches his brows and closes his eyes in deep contemplation, then opens them and writes the solution on the board: complete, clear, obvious, and correct, and which later seems difficult to piece from memory.

In the documentary *No Ordinary Genius,* Richard Feynman gives a description of how he thinks, and it fits White Leopard to a tee. If he is standing by a pool with many people diving and swimming causing a great deal of choppiness, he will imagine himself as a very small insect seated at the level of the pool water, observing the waves, and determine who was jumping in, where, and when.[9]

Like a White Leopard, Feynman starts with a daydream where he jumps between scales of magnitude and simultaneously assumes multiple perspectives in space. White Leopard and Python are both big thinkers, but whereas Python compulsively manipulates that which she understands using skills that have a language-based flavor to them, White Leopard prefers to run spatially based simulations to refine theoretical nuances.

His pure chase of the truth, his ability to buck functional fixity, his creativity—all combine to make the young White Leopard puckishly resistant to cultural pressures. His refusal to conform to stupid rules informs his sense of distance—and he has the levels of energy to make good on his beliefs. Richard Feynman was a young man when he worked at Los Alamos on the Manhattan Project, and he resented the excessive security he felt prevented free conversations between scientists working in separate sections. To mock the sham, he went one night on a "safe-cracking spree," opening all the combination locks to the secret cabinet files. (They had been manufactured by a new company that gave the same combination to each lock.) Another time, Feynman found a small hole in the perimeter of the chain-link fence, and "he walked out the main gate, waved to the guard, and then crawled back through the hole and walked out the main gate"; he did this several times until he was nearly arrested. Whereas Panther or Tiger will run a prank strictly for the crude guffaws, and while the cleverness of the Python and White Leopard may closely resemble each other, White Leopard's pranks twinkle with an edge of higher purpose, a defiance asserting universal values and the sovereignty of the individual.

White Leopard's foresight, the ideas he channels, and the works he eventually produces may bring about the "interesting times" that propel him to the next stage of development. White Leopard has tremendous capacity to unleash forces of great scope, often just by describing them, which collide with the unprepared world. Combustible issues drive him in the only direction he knows, to abide by higher principles of harmony and interconnection—like Einstein and Oppenheimer, who turned their intellect, eloquence, and prominence to international peace in the age of atomic power, which they helped unleash. At this stage, White Leopard strives for ethical transparency that is daunting, even suffocating, to the other Animal personality types.

Another good example is Dorothy Day, the "Servant of God," an official title given her by the Catholic Church. With a deep spiritual yearning and progressive social conscience, she brought light to the plight of the poor workers in America through radio and newspaper. She described herself in *The Long Loneliness* as "disgustingly, and proudly pious." She was a passionate woman, and wrote about the ordeal of resisting the temptations of her physical passions to give herself over to the spiritual ideals of charity and justice. Like a Leopard, she sought the high vantage of other great minds, like Victor Hugo, Charles Dickens, and Edgar Allen Poe, and she read books on social justice with a voracious appetite. As a Leopard, her medium of creativity was journalism, and her oeuvre was asking in every way possible the big-picture question: "Why was so much done in remedying social evils instead of avoiding them in the first place? ... Where were the saints to try to change the social order, not just to minister to the slaves but to do away with slavery?"[10]

But those ethical standards that cause the White Leopard to seem aloof, even cold, are the ones that enable him to minimize his bias and distortion when communicating his intuition. For example, Edgar Cayce, called the Sleeping Prophet,[11] entered a dream-like state from which he predicted the fall of communism fifty years prior to its happening, described tenets of subatomic physics well before their discovery, and predicted the discovery of Judaic texts and interpretations a decade after his passing. He realized early on he could not use his gift for himself or for profit, and he awoke from his trances without memory of the counsel he had given. But when that advice was used for profit by others, even if he was ignorant of their intentions, he would become physically ill. He recovered only when, after surmising what had happened, he took some redeeming action, like giving a sum of money to charity in equal amount to that profited from the consultation.

With tempering, White Leopard matures to the third stage developing what in Ch'ien-lung is called *Higher Mind,* where intuition, ethical discipline, and vision join with the compassion, love, and courage of the heart. Here, Leopard's intuition connects with Tiger's heart. The result can be a Gandhi or a Martin Luther King Jr., who both strove for principles of nonviolent resistance and civil disobedience—high Leopard ideals—to create new paradigms out of the highest spiritual ideals of their respective traditions. Gandhi's homemade clothes, vegetarian diet, and fasts for spiritual purification spoke as eloquently as did his practices of nonviolent civil disobedience against British rule, women's oppression, and the caste system—White Leopard issues tackled in White Leopard style. Martin Luther King Jr. transcended political discourse with the poetic language of the King James' Bible and the traditions of the Baptist Church. In his "I Have a Dream" speech, America collectively shared in a White Leopard vision of history as he beckoned us high onto a mountain-top, where he showed us the long arc of history.

At the fourth stage of maturity, White Leopard retreats, and there is a sense of preparation for his alchemical encounter with Cobra to create the Dragon. If White Leopard is rare or hard to spot most of the time, at this point he is almost invisible, sitting daily in deep contemplation at the gates of death, inviting transformation in all its guises to touch the substance of the mind he shares in common with the cosmos. This is the realm of Milarepa and Francis of Assisi who, through mortification and prayer, reached a higher plane transcending the dualities of good and evil.

The Dark Side of the White Leopard

Not all is light when the White Leopard turns dark. If you clog up his channel to intuition, you turn the aloof visionary into the mad recluse: Leopard's knowledge turns to paranoia, his solitude to morbid isolation, his asceticism to autism. His love of reason now rationalizes his sadism, for which he has a talent.

With White Leopards who go dark, you get the sense that they are too smart for their own good and that they are particularly drawn to the intersection of ethics, technology, and privacy. Where the balanced White Leopard has an Essene-like belief in hygiene, the unbalanced White Leopard can no longer bear the triviality and sensory overstimulation of brushing, flossing, and wiping. And while a healthy White Leopard exhibits a playful exploration, even a jokester quality like Feynman, the unbalanced White Leopard is a Little Prince existing in his own little world—a *puer aeternus* or "eternal boy."

Going dark, inspiration turns to paranoia. White Leopard, who once saw himself as a servant of a higher message, now claims infallibility perhaps, anointment maybe, but special knowledge, certainly. His fears cut him off from the fount of inspiration he used to enjoy. Confusing quantity for quality, he now generates conspiracy theories instead of insights at a manic pace and, empty of inspiration, he projects the only thing left he finds within—his fear—onto the world. In the end, he burns out like a water pump with a blocked intake.

White Leopard Movement

In the mythos of the Leopard, the crown of the head channels broad beams of intuition, the intelligence of a self-teaching cosmos. The White Cat seeks purchase in the mountains for vantage, uncluttered by the miasma of human thought. This way he maintains the cool objectivity required to grasp the flashes of insight. *Intuition* means you know because you know. You do not have to study, you are not instinctually wired, you have not learned from firsthand experience—you know simply because the information walked in, found its reflection in you, and then stayed. In the mythos of the White Leopard, all matter is a manifestation of vibrating energy, where the body and self are composed of intersecting layers of energy, and Leopard's journey is one of purification, to allow the energy to flow as unhampered as possible. The Seven Steps at the end of this chapter will help you reaffirm this mythos.

From this mythos, White Leopard ideokinetics inspire movement up and out and ever lighter. Images that inspire White Leopard are celestial and expansive: the Aurora Borealis, the Van Allen Belt, the pattern made by metal filings around a magnet, solar flares, and the event horizon of a black hole. I was atop Whistler, British Columbia, and the wind was blowing a layer of dry snow like sand over small dunes of ski ruts. As the dry snow flowed over the wrinkles of ski tracks, it caught the beams of the setting sun, looking like ropes of golden light cascading along the surface in rivulets. Looking down, as I was, there was a moment when this scene connected to intuition for me, as though each of those golden threads was a strand of information. When I look to deepen my practice, I return to this imagery along with others included in the Seven Steps at the end of this chapter.

White Leopard moves as if wires are lifting him up by the back of the head and from underneath the brows of the eyes, and all he has to do is raise his feet in order to fly. Like David Carradine in *Kung Fu,*[12] White Leopards can walk over rice paper without leaving a wrinkle or on eggshells without breaking them. White Leopard ideokinetics emphasize a high center of gravity, working with the triangle formed by the crown of the head at the top and the collarbones at the base. Like a good aerialist, White Leopard uses this triangle to steer the body in flight, the way young gymnasts are told to look where they want to go, and the body will follow. These ideokinetics have helped me not only on the mat but on the ski slopes. One time, I was at the top of a mogul slope and did the White Leopard bows as is my practice to connect to nature through the Animals. I focused on the sense of lift and started down the slope. I usually get easily intimidated by the sheer steepness and crouch in apprehension. But this time, focusing on the White Leopard ideokinetics, I straightened myself as though I was being lifted up toward the sky by wires; I let my arms, collarbones, and head steer the direction of the rest of my body. Rather than fixating on the ground ahead of me, I looked at the view of the surrounding peaks, as if I was merely going for a zigzagging stroll down a slope; I relied on White Leopard's wide-angle peripheral vision to pick out the direction I wanted to follow, trusting my feet to negotiate the uneven terrain. The run was smooth and fearless, and it had a surfing-like quality that resonates with Leopard. The exercises in "Step 1: Follow Your Breath" at the end of the chapter and the ideokinetics they inspire will help you to embody the light-footed Cat.

White Leopard logos reflects the mythos of his psyche—the speed, clarity, and elevation of his thought. His preferred weapon is the bow and arrow, where one well-placed shot strikes from above; it flies through the air from a remote distance with a clear line of sight and ends things neatly. White Leopard martial arts involve high-flying kicks like taekwondo, where the logos of kicking up in the air reflects the mythos of moving on a higher plane, and the kicks happen at the speed of thought, fast and surgical. In Ch'ien-lung, White Leopard forms emphasize the air time, but regardless of whether you are practicing martial arts or a Fred Astaire dance, you can embody White Leopard by striving to maximize the mid-air suspension at the height of the jump. White Leopard trims friction from his natural tensile strength to allow his speed to emerge; he is fast because he is smooth and succinct. Reduced physical tension translates into a broader beam of attention, giving the big picture Leopard loves. In ideokinetics of White Leopard, you move as if you have 360-degree peripheral vision or as if you are watching yourself and your surroundings from above and behind your head.

In the logos, the Animals attack what they understand, and the tactics of the heady, aloof Leopard are to attack the head and to disable the reach of the opponent. Where Tiger will attack the core of the torso, and Panther the roots of the feet and groin, Leopard strikes the arms and works his way up to the forehead and crown. And yes, Leopard will use the force of his opponent, but whereas Python uses an opponent's force to collapse their structure in on themselves, White Leopard steals his opponent's energy to guide them along his dynamic sphere of personal space. As a three-dimensional hub from which emanate spiraling spokes of energy, Leopard guides the force of an aggressor at a safe distance along the edge of his personal space. Where Python will play more with levers and angles to turn an opponent's force against them, White Leopard triangulates his position to be off the line of attack while still remaining in striking reach of his opponent. Both Boa and White Leopard will blend harmoniously in the direction of their opponent without offering resistance to telegraph their next move. But where Boa chews up the personal space, ties (wrestles) the opponent in knots, and steals their breath, Leopard will disarm the means of his opponent's violence, and then slingshot the opponent out of his orbit, much the same way the Sun does a comet, all while seeming to have 360-degree vision.

With the logos of the Animals up to now, the explanations have been about how to embody an archetype with ideokinetics and visualized breath to affect the muscle tone and the timing of movement. It's been tangible. But Leopard requires a shift in metaphysical perspective. For White Leopard, the body, psyche, and self are the manifestation of energies vibrating at different frequencies. The logos involves the intangible, and this means working with energies of varied frequencies. Energy work is as practiced, honed, strategized, standardized, and executed as any physical skill. For many readers, this requires a shift in assumptions and adopting a metaphysical view that may be unfamiliar but that makes Ch'ien-lung an art of embodied metaphysics.

White Leopard logos includes energy work. In many tradition-based schools, this manifests as honoring the lineage, where bowing to the image of the founder or emblem of the art opens the student up to guidance from the spirits of former teachers. At a more advanced level, this is the world of extreme visualized breath and high-powered energy circuits: seated in the mountains on a winter night draped in a wet blanket that you dry out with the body warmth generated from a furnace-breathing exercise; circulating *qi* through meridians or fascia to guide energy through another person's internal organs to heal or hurt by mere touch; or projecting one of the multiple energy bodies ahead of you to see what is around the corner or on a different astral plane, now or in a dream state—a world where you guide spirits from one life to the next through the bardo states of consciousness. The visualized breath of White Leopard's energetic anatomy in appendix B is meant to cultivate a neutral witnessing of energy, a first step on the way to more advanced work. Advanced energy work is beyond the scope of this book and should always be studied with a recognized teacher who takes pains to screen prospective candidates. As an added safeguard, the Seven Steps at the end of this chapter include exercises in compassion to ground White Leopard in Higher Mind.

Energy circuits, visualized breath, and movement as prayer attract White Leopard. Leopard is naturally drawn to movement for transcendence and spiritual attunement, like Sufi dancing. Leopard explores energy work in arts like *qigong, taiji*, yoga, and aikido. Legends of masters proficient with energy pepper every martial art, stretching credulity but inspiring successive generations. In aikido, stories of the energetic abilities of the founder, Osensei, abound that capture the White Leopard energy style. Often a challenger who went at full speed to strike him would suddenly slow down as though entering a force field. By some accounts, he would sit at one end of the mat, stick his hand out in the direction of a student busily folding his clothes; the student would then find himself unable to get up, glued to the ground. Osensei would then release the student who would spring to a stand, perplexed. In Leopard style, he often went on long discourses on the spiritual makeup of the cosmos, frequently referring to guides or angels. The ability to remotely affect a person through energy captures the mythos of White Leopard.

In morphos, White Leopard integrates the narrative of the struggle by raising the ethos and creativity of a culture. With intuitive insight and clarity of thought, he forms an ethical frame that transcends both sides of the conflict, as in the dialogue of the *Bhagavad Gita* or the Declaration of Independence. From their insight, they create works that Gurdjieff called *objective art,* which is art that is based on knowledge of universal principles, and created to inspire audiences to pursue those principles, like the Taj Mahal, *1001 Arabian Nights,* or da Vinci's Vitruvian Man. These works of creativity in White Leopard culminate in new spiritual practices and ethical standards. Where Python ethics are based on a logic of evolutionary psychology—that which benefits the most people and causes the least harm qualifies as ethical in a world where life consumes other life—the Leopard standard focuses on harm to none where life consumes energy directly from the light of the Sun. Whereas the other Animals are concerned with conformity or moral laws that make life less violent and at least tolerable, White Leopard leaves behind moral and ethical guidance that aspires to a higher plane.

Whereas the other Animals have to fight every inch of the way on their journey to transformation, White Leopard sits on the cusp of transcendence. If anything, he has to work to remain neutral, allowing the process of transformation to play itself out and confer its greatest potential. In the mythos of the Leopard, all matter is a manifestation of vibrating energy, and White Leopards see themselves as on a journey to transform into pure energies, like Tibetan Buddhist saints whose bodies radiate rainbow colors when they die.[13]

White Leopard Sex: I Love You for Your Mind

White Leopard lusts for cosmic communion. Like Saint-Francis of Assisi, there will definitely be fasting, the stripping away of possessions, even a little self-immolation— all done to quell the noisy appetites of the body and to better attend the subtleties of spiritual ecstasy.

For White Leopard, carnal sex is one facet of the entire package of cosmic intercourse. Leopard seeks carnal sex as a metaphor, guide, and measure by which to know the universe. The sensuality of the White Cat is rarified. Leopard elevates touch by centering it on energy, caressing a lover's aura, loving the other person for their mind and imagination. We all do this in certain amounts, but for the White Leopard, this is the center of the sensual experience; it is what arouses them more than any kind of frottage. They may seem disconnected, overly rational, in their own little world in what should be a two-way relationship, but what they are striving for is to bring the dyad into a relationship with God or divinity.

But if all this is too abstract and you are looking for the tangible, one example of White Leopard in real physical human earthbound love is the relationship between Richard Feynman and his first wife Arline, captured in a letter he wrote to her two years after her passing. He was a rational pragmatist, at first unable to understand what good writing a letter to someone dead could do, but after two years, he realized he needed to.

> *I find it hard to understand in my mind what it means to love you after you are dead—but I still want to comfort you and take care of you—and I want you to love me and care for me. I want to have problems to discuss with you—I want little projects to do with you. I never thought until just now that we can do that together.*

He then leaps directly into creativity, asking, "What shall we do?" and recommends learning Chinese, or buying a film projector, but slowly realizes he cannot do these things without her at his side, his "instigator of ideas." As a quintessential Leopard in love, he continues:

> *When you were sick you worried you could not give me something that you wanted and thought I needed. You needn't have worried. Just as I told you then there was no real need because I loved you in so many ways so much. And now it is clearly even more true—you can give me nothing now yet I love you so that you stand in my way of loving anyone else—but I want you to stand there. You, dead, are so much better than anyone else alive.*

White Leopard in the Arts

Leonardo da Vinci's Vitruvian Man evokes universal laws of geometric proportion, the same invisible hand behind the Golden Mean and fractals. In a famous M. C. Escher drawing, Escher shows two hands drawing each other. The cuffs are two-dimensional, but the wrist, palms, fingers, and the pencil pop out of the page in three dimensions. This Escher drawing pictorially captures several White Leopard themes in art. How the hands draw each other poses a chicken-and-egg paradox, which Leopards love to contemplate. The transition from two dimensions to three conveys a White Leopard theme: the feeling of breaking out of one paradigm and emerging into another, like going from Newtonian physics to quantum mechanics. The hands duplicate not only their shape, but also their function—as though once they are finished drawing each other, they can then go on to draw other self-drawing hands, which can then go on to draw others at an exponential rate. That growth rate is what Leopards in finance know to be the most powerful force in the cosmos: compound interest.

Escher's art is a staple in classes on visual perception, introducing students to how two-dimensional cues render a three-dimensional world. He draws worlds where water flows down to higher ground and impossible triangles where the edges seem to recede backward while staying on the same plane. In White Leopard fashion, his art forces you to reexamine your assumptions about vision, to look at how you see, an act of metavision that pulls you out of yourself in order to see the big picture.

Do we truly create, or are ideas simply out there, waiting to be channeled? This is a favorite theme of White Leopard artists and a question tackled with ascetic minimalism by the reclusive Leopard Samuel Beckett in his play *Cascando.*[14] The play features the main character, a writer, who comments on the creative process while, intermittently, he opens and closes a door through which we hear The Voice. The Voice is a disembodied narrator recounting a plot. As the play progresses, the audience gradually realizes The Voice is editing and revising the plot of the story the writer is "writing." We come away from the play with the sense that stories exist, out there, spinning themselves, and authors choose when to "open the door" and write down what they hear.

Both Panther and White Leopard enjoy science-fiction, but where Panther's science-fiction is laced with fantasy and magic, White Leopard's science-fiction centers on *futurism,* tomorrow's technology intelligently extends from today's cutting-edge scientific insights, and where the story revolves around the ethical dilemmas the technology presents. It's these kinds of dilemmas that made *Star Trek* such fun to watch and authors Arthur C. Clark, Isaac Asimov, and Jules Verne so fun to read.

Once in a while you get a pure download: a White Leopard work of art, by a White Leopard artist using a White Leopard method. The poem *A Vision* is such a case. Its composition was first started by Georgie Hyde-Lees, while in a trance of automatic writing (writing with both hands simultaneously), and then continued by her husband W. B. Yeats who channeled text, glyphs, and images that would take him 20 years to turn into what some have called the greatest series of poems of the last century. As White Leopards often are, Yeats was consumed by the images from the trance, specifically the image of *gyres*—two intermeshed spirals (one stuffed into the other, perfectly out of phase, the node of one at the broad end of the other). The geometric figures were alive, as though with the DNA of unborn ideas. To Yeats and his readers, the gyres graphed the parallels between how consciousness develops across an individual lifespan and how collective consciousness develops across eons of history. Yeats spent his time contemplating how, with mathematical precision, the gyres conveyed the historical cycle by which new civilizations rise from the things rejected during the decline of the previous empire; in the gyres he saw "this pattern repeated many times in the past and [that it was] to be repeated many times in the future."[15] The poems also played a very real role in his daily life, where they acted as his own Leopard perch, holding at bay the chaos of the Irish civil wars and WWI. This is a good example of how a White Leopard will take mental distance.

The breadth of these ideas, the elevated, altered state of the writing, the geometric imagery, the scope of the ideas—all these give a flavor of White Leopard art. Leopard art often contains these kinds of geometric super-seeds that are so packed with brilliant ideas that you risk intellectual second-degree burns, much like the ideas contained in the geometry of the Tree of Life or the Yin-Yang symbol. White Leopard inspiration in art doesn't just go viral; it grows into a multitude of interdependent, self-propagating, and recombining ideas.

White Leopard Turning Toward Dragon

We all have moments of intuition when we glimpse reality as bigger and more whole, moments of oneness before the pipsqueak tyrant of the ego chops it all into bite-size morsels of dual-opposites. Tiger and Black Panther see in dualities: cause and effect, now and then, good and bad. Not White Leopards. Leopards do not see in dualities; they see in continuums, where everything from trees and rocks to ideas are in a process of becoming. Einstein placed space and time on a continuum; Carl Jung and Wolfgang Pauli conceived of causality (cause without meaning) and synchronicity (meaning without cause) as two ends of the same spectrum;[16] and the Vedic texts assert that matter and consciousness are two expressions of the same wave. White Leopard sees everything he looks at, physical or conceptual, as a moving point along a number of dimensions going off into infinity.

Of central importance to White Leopard is the spectrum between creativity and entropy. All things break down and, inevitably, are destined to degrade over time, dissipating energy, a phenomenon known in physics as *entropy*. As entropy increases, a physical structure, whether a star or cell, degrades. As the structure degrades, it causes energy to be wasted, which accelerates the degradation of the structure and so on until the energy state is completely stable and the structure is collapsed or dead. This goes for atoms, suns, and blood cells, but it also applies to housekeeping, tax codes, and fashion trends.

Entropy tends all things toward collapse, and the only countermeasures are either more energy or better information. With the first, energy must come from an outside source, like the way our Sun provides energy in heat and light for all life on the planet. The energy comes free for us, but at the cost to the star, which will eventually burn out on its collision course with entropy.

The second way to slow entropy down is by information with better distinctions. Not just the kind of information found in books or chips, but the kind of information intrinsic to basic physical reactions made by structures and organisms when they are acted upon. Structures not only react to every action but in a very real way their physical reactions process information. When a heart valve shunts blood to the brain but not to the lungs, or a stomach "decides" between digesting food and vomiting poisons, it is not just reacting physically, but processing information. Information processing allows structures to adjust the distribution of energy, making a little more energy accessible than there would be otherwise. If the information system is sophisticated enough, like a doe that can choose between two bucks, or even a culture that can debate both sides of gun control in a civil manner—then that system can deliberately adjust the distribution of its energy, making more of the energy available, which will allow the system or form of life to continue. For Leopard, the purpose of creativity is to make information more specific.

White Leopard sees information as a cosmic force pushing structures along a spectrum from the trapped energy of entropy toward the freed energy of creativity. The refining of information can happen according to the laws of physics, like with the heart valve; the dynamics of biochemistry, like with the stomach; the laws of evolution, as with the doe; or with moments of oratorical genius, as in a gun debate. In the eye of the White Leopard, these are equivalent instances of information managing energy, pushing a structure or life form away from entropy toward evolution and development. The White Leopard sees information pushing back on entropy as the creative act of an intelligent cosmos intent on self-knowledge. It's a view that leaves a narrow range in which to exercise free will, but within which we are capable of brilliance if we so choose.

But when information wins against entropy and frees up energy, it comes at a cost, and the cost is greater complexity. This tradeoff of complexity for energy is one of the explanations physicists offer for why things get more complicated over time. When working against entropy, you either get more energy, get more complicated, or just die. Whether that system is a living organism or a civilization, this up-leveling of information processing leads to greater complexity—from biological organisms that grow more complex through evolution in how they go about finding food and safety to governments that grow more complex through legislation and in how they monitor compliance and exact revenue.

White Leopard sees creativity as maximizing the use of information while minimizing the resulting complexity. To Leopard, the purpose of creative genius is to produce elegant designs that move more information with greater nuance but with less resulting complexity. A Tiger is simple, a Python is comprehensive, but a Leopard is elegant. As a White

Leopard turns toward Dragon, he sees himself and acts like a channel for information to facilitate the improvising cosmos in its self-exploration. He channels, creates, and moves on. Whether the channeling is framed in Daoist terms of guides, spirits, and bardos or in Western terms of information, complexity, and entropy is immaterial. They are all acts of creativity that release energy and reveal the big picture. It is a Leopard view useful to students of any energetic or meditative practice that you strive to cultivate in the plaque work.

The White Leopard Plaque

The square of the White Leopard plaque (see insert Figure 7.1 in this book's color insert) is colored white to represent the cosmic laws of exchanging entropy and complexity for information and energy. The square (universal laws) and the triangle (the individual) are both white. The color of the triangle and square match to reflect how White Leopard sees himself as an extension of those cosmic laws. The gold of the circle reflects the energy White Leopard looks to free up through acts of creativity by channeling information with greater specificity, as well as the high ideals and ethics his perspective demands. As with the other Animals, the shapes have layers of meaning.

One of my more vivid experiences practicing White Leopard with the plaques was an intuitive flash about calculus. I sat down one day to do my plaque practice, where I would follow the edges of the plaque in synchrony with my breath. I had been practicing regularly and was getting better at keeping the internal noise down and returning to following my breath. Well into the session, an image spontaneously popped into my perception with such clarity, it seemed to come from outside of me: on the edge of the Leopard triangle, along the line of the base, there were short marks like the intervals on the axis of a graph. The image felt like it had flashed down from the top of my head—a real "crown of the head" experience. I noticed the intervals were not regular. The distances between one mark and the next gradually increased along the line, which bothered my sense of simplicity and regularity from having trained in Tiger so much. Why were the intervals not regular? I took it as a sign of my own idiosyncrasies and went to bed.

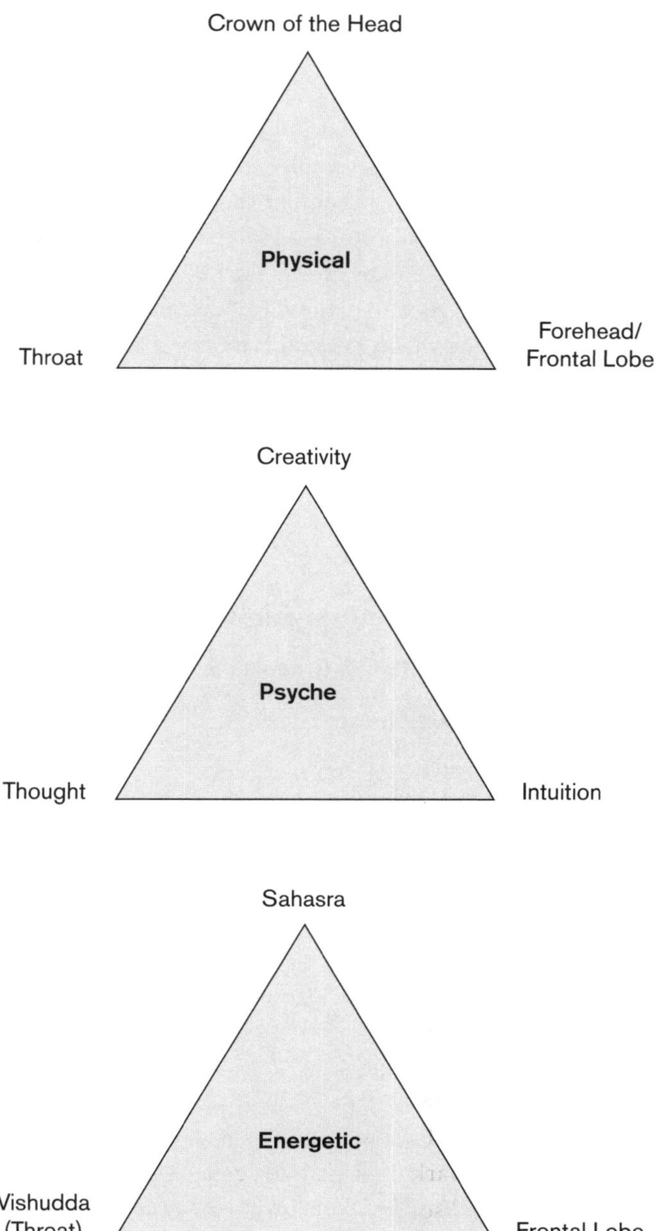

FIGURE 7.2: The symbolic meaning of the triangle points for the White Leopard

Years later, I had returned to university, opened a textbook on psychophysics, and there, I saw with a jolt, was a line on a graph with the same pattern of intervals that had popped into my mind years earlier. It was a logarithmic scale, and the intervals were exponential: it was the pattern of change found in perception across the senses, where it takes a tenfold increase in physical energy (like a number of photons) to experience one unit of increase in intensity (brightness). I sat there for a moment stunned, and had a taste of the same experience I'd had with Constantine years before in the restaurant. Of course, the flash was naked of the mathematical insight that would have made the graph practical, and I did not pursue formal calculus courses, which could have sped and deepened my studies, but for a moment, I felt part of a whole that was much bigger than me. It was humbling, but there is also a caveat: intuitive fragments are common and come cheap; to download the insight takes time and effort.

Seven Steps to Embodying White Leopard

Step One: Follow Your Breath (Ongoing Mindfulness Practice)

For White Leopard, visualize breath coming from the heavens and stars to your

Crown of the head Visualize breathing energy of the stars and heavens down through the crown of the head. On the exhale, imagine sending gratitude, awe, and curiosity back up through the crown to the stars. Ideokinetics: Move as if lifted by the crown of the head. Move as though surfing on currents of energy and information. Connect to the upper reaches of the Earth's atmosphere, and the aurora borealis, and then beyond to the stars and background radiation of the cosmos.

Parietal lobe The parietal lobe is located between the crown of the head and the brainstem–roughly where you put rabbit ears behind your friend's head. The lobe integrates information from the senses and orients us in space. It helps to disengage attention so you can change your focus. Visualize breath and energy caress over this area and pool there. Ideokinetics: Move as if information coming into your parietal lobe is guiding you. Move as though smoothly disengaging your focus, as though it were easy to get unstuck. Move watching yourself from above and behind. Move as if you can see 360 degrees around you at all times. Connect to Earth's highest mountain peaks with an overview of everything.

Throat Inhale breath from the stars through the crown into the throat, and exhale from the throat on to share ideas. Inhale into the throat and exhale out the crown to open channels of listening, the same way you would pop your ears under pressure, and then share that inspiration from the throat out to the world on the out-breath. For actors and singers, this exercise of relaxing the throat can reveal rich and nuanced vocal tones in dialogue and singing. Ideokinetics: Move as if projecting energy out from the throat. Move as if the back of the head and throat are being lifted toward the heavens while the 7th cervical sits on the 1st thoracic vertebrae. Connect to Earth's relationship to the Sun and Moon, such as with tides, solar flares, and eclipses.

Thyroid The thyroid regulates your metabolic rate, the speed at which you burn energy, and White Leopard's raised metabolism keeps him light and ready for takeoff, without burning out. Inhale energy from the stars and cosmos, drawing in a clean and bright energy, to invigorate and stabilize the thyroid. As you exhale from the thyroid, visualize letting go of impurities. Ideokinetics: Move as if the collarbones were being drawn up toward the sky by wires. Imagine they are rolling on their axis, upward when looking from the front (see Figure D.1).

Chakras White Leopard is all about the energy of the body. The energy systems include the chakras. (See appendix B for a diagram of the chakras.) Of added importance are the chakras of the throat (vishuddha) and of the crown of the head (sahasrara). To avoid spreading your focus too thin, pick one chakra. Visualize the breath spiraling out from the chakra on the exhale and spiraling in the opposite direction on the inhale for seven complete cycles before moving onto the next. Start with the inhaling and exhaling from the front of the chakra only, then from the front and the back. Build up with practice, and as you feel ready, try spiraling the breath in and out of two, three, four, and eventually all of the chakras concurrently. Ideokinetics: Combinatorial, each chakra at a time. Move as if the motion originated in the chakra. Energetically visualize the chakra changing shape, and move the body in response. Connect to places rich in energy, such the Grand Canyon or Mount Kilimanjaro.

Auras For White Leopard, the auric energy system defines its personal space, which is important in maintaining distance, clarity, and objectivity (see appendix B). White Leopard represents the aura in toto and, in particular, the outermost auric layer and the fifth auric layer from the body, corresponding to the crown chakra/pituitary gland and throat chakra/thyroid, respectively. Visualize breathing into each auric layer one layer at a time, smoothing and filling it out. Connect to Earth's electromagnetic fields that capture tiny particles from the Sun creating the Van Allen Belts. Ideokinetics: Combinatorial, one layer at a time. Move as though you do not want to tear the aura by moving too violently. Move as if the motion originated in the auric layer. Energetically visualize the aura changing shape, and move the body in response. Finally, before moving, imagine the auric body going to the place you are heading ahead of your physical body.

Membranes and pumps The membranes act as energetic diaphragms, expanding and contracting to circulate energy around the chakras. Pumps do the same for the joints. Appendix B details the instructions for synchronizing the breath with the pumps and membranes. Ideokinetics: Move using the membranes and pumps, which encourage you to contract and extend deeply from the core muscles. Note: the Leopard energy systems of the meridians and psychic meridians are not included as they not suitable to day-long activation with breath work and belong to advanced practices.

Step Two: Recall Your Day (Daily/10 Minutes before Sleep)

To recall your day in a White Leopard manner, replay the day watching yourself from a vantage point of above and behind your own head. See yourself go through your day, getting groceries, talking with people, surfing the web, as though you were watching yourself like your own guardian angel. Ask yourself what surprised you today. Certain people experience this perspective more frequently than they want; if this is the case, try the exercises in the Tiger section.

New trends in technology, thought, relationships, and communication saturate our every moment. Reviewing the day from Leopard is an opportunity to take a step back, like some alien anthropologist, and note the influences that are acting upon you from a removed distance.

But above all, feel awe. To cultivate White Leopard's elevated state of mind, review your day for moments of awe, when you experienced something that was greater than yourself, or for moments of gratitude when a boon or gift you received pointed to a bigger world. Let awe guide your curiosity.

If a moment overwhelmed you, review it to find something to be curious about—curiosity is the first step in exercising your inner Leopard's creativity.

Step Three: Scan Your Body (Daily/10 Minutes before and after Sleep)

At night before going to sleep and again upon waking, scan the White Leopard energy systems: the auras, chakras, membranes, pumps, meridians, and streams (see appendix B). If you lose focus, use the palms to glide them over your body, as though the energy from your hands is clearing and restoring the energetic body.

Step Four: Do the Bows in Nature (10–15 Minutes)

White Leopard loves mountaintop views, and the Tibetan Plateau is the consummate Leopard territory. Both the Cobra and the Leopard prefer the cold to the heat and will train gladly in snow or high altitudes. They are subtle Animals and do not like the glare of direct light, like the Sun at high noon. They prefer moonlight, but their favorite is when you can just make out the disk of the Sun or Moon behind a veil of clouds. White Leopard relates to broad bands of energy. On road trips, there have been many times when I have stopped the car to get out and do the White Leopard bows as wide sunbeams break through a ceiling of billowing clouds. The Celestial Cat loves astronomical events like solar eclipses, lunar eclipses, and planetary alignments; atmospheric effects like rainbows, sun dogs, and moon halos, with the Aurora Borealis holding a special place in Leopard's heart. Though you cannot stand on moonbeams, rainbows, or the direct alignment of Saturn with Jupiter, you can actively imagine them during the bows. Visualize drawing their energy into the energy systems of the streams, chakras, auras, pumps, and membranes.

Leopard listens to the stars. I am not an astrology buff, but I have spent time learning the astronomical facts and origin myths of the constellations. It has enriched my practice to go out under the stars and do the bows as they travel the sky during the night. It is an awe-inspiring experience; imagine the eons of navigators and stargazers the stars have stared back at as you keep time with their sacred geometric dance by the rhythmic breathing of the bow. You will feel small, yes, but somehow personally connected and enlarged by the greater cosmos and broad swaths of sidereal time.

White Leopard Bow

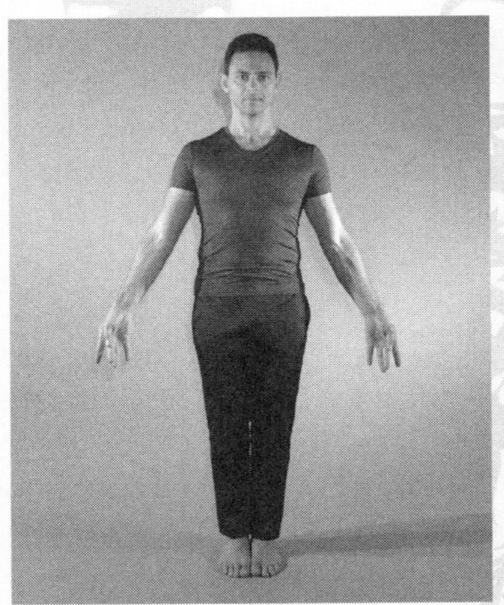

FIGURE 7.3: Stand feet together, palms in mudra turned out. Connect to the cosmos by the crown of the head, channeling energy down and out through the throat. Throughout, feel the collar-bones rolling, feel the head pulled toward the sky, the shoulder blades spreading apart.

FIGURE 7.4: Bring hands to the throat, touching it with middle fingers. Form a curled straw shape with the tongue.

FIGURE 7.5: Inhale through the curled tongue, turn the feet out and, in one action, swing the arms out to the sides as shown. Bring information in through the throat.

FIGURE 7.6: Still on inhale, continue, forearms coming up as shown. Broaden your peripheral vision, and see all around you.

FIGURE 7.7: On the second inhale, the back of the hands come down to the shoulders. Bring energy to the frontal lobe. Invoke White Leopard's speed of thought and clarity.

FIGURE 7.8: On the third inhale, move the hands as if to place a crown on your head. Bring energy to the crown and send it up into cosmos, uploading.

FIGURE 7.9: Begin to exhale, and turn the feet in. Bring the energy and information down from the cosmos, through the crown, downloading.

FIGURE 7.10: Exhaling, bring the hands down in front of the head to the throat. Bring celestial energy down, creating new concepts and perspectives.

FIGURE 7.11: Continue exhaling, pressing the hands forward from the throat. Transmit energy and information out from the throat: Repeat the bow.

FIGURE 7.12: Finish the bow, turn the feet out, and inhale. Bring the hands into a triangle shape, and point up, to the throat. Draw energy into the throat, grounding communication.

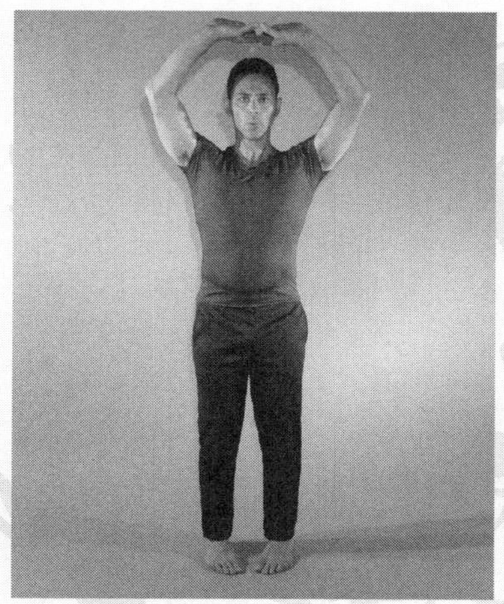

FIGURE 7.13: Turn feet in, exhale, and bring triangle-shaped hands to the crown of the head. Send energy up to and receive energy from the heavens, opening the crown of the head.

FIGURE 7.14: Stand in neutral with mudras.

Step Five: Adopt the Animal Personality (Ongoing Practice)

To make White Leopard a part of you, adopt his ways. Listen to classical music—music with multiple melodies, beatific aspirations, and intellectual lift that emphasizes the spiritual with the use of wind instruments, like the flute, invoking a light, ghostly mood. White Leopard eats light and blossoming foods—like fruit and edible flowers—that do not weigh him down; he eats the *whole* food, including the skin, like the peel of the orange or the corn husk. However, White Leopard would just as soon do a cleansing fast, preferring to live a monastic life, divesting the body and mind of the profane, in order to transcend. White Leopard dresses in natural fibers in colors of white, gold, and blue. White Leopard goes for movies that are avant-garde, depicting all of humanity in broad sweeps, and books about philosophy, probability, astronomy, high-energy physics, quantum mechanics, and wormholes. In physical fitness, the airy White Leopard practices flying kicking styles, like taekwondo, or arts that emphasize the flow of universal energy, like qigong and aikido.

To channel White Leopard within you, act on your creative impulse, keeping your tools and ideas organized with a notepad at hand to record concepts as they come to you in flashes of insight. White Leopard creativity requires you to cultivate a sense of guiding principles, ideals, and ethics, bucking outdated norms, rules, and laws that limit free thought and expression. When problem-solving, White Leopard will spend hours engaged in practical daydreaming, adopting alternative perspectives to make novel connections.

Step Six: Remember Your Dreams (Daily/10 Minutes upon Waking)

The highly creative White Leopard will frequently dream of natural environments with obstacles, like mountains to climb or rivers to raft. Highly creative people enjoy challenges, which is what these natural obstacles symbolize.[17] The White Leopard in you has problem-solving dreams. There is a history in dream literature of scientific insight garnered from dreams, like the dream of a snake biting its own tail, which helped the organic chemist Friedrich Kekulé determine the shape of the hexagonal benzene ring. Highly creative people do not dream more frequently or have more problem-solving dreams than people who do not identify as creative, but they do make more deliberate use of their dreams.

As a dream practice, you can visualize yourself in your ideal Leopard workshop. If you have a genuine, tractable problem you are trying to solve in waking-time, see it on the workbench surrounded with all the necessary tools you could wish to have at your disposal. Upon waking, remember your dreams for clues to possible solutions.

Step Seven: Use the Plaques (Daily/20 Minutes)

White Leopard's focus is like the high beams of a car, and as you follow the edge of the triangle with your eyes, you also have a sense of watching yourself do it from above and behind your own head. Even as you focus on the edges of one shape, strive to see the plaque as a whole. See the bigger picture. Use the single-handed mudra, tongue-position, and asana of the White Leopard while doing the plaque work. (See appendix A.)

Leopard Energy Circuit

Visualize breathing in through the throat, up the frontal lobe, through the crown, up to the heavens, then exhaling down from the heavens, through the frontal lobe, and out the throat.

White Leopard vs. Animals

White Leopard and Python are similar in their expansiveness and holistic view. Whereas Python comes by her scope with some talent and much study, Leopard knows because he knows. Python is compelled to manipulate, whereas White Leopard is happy to witness ideas. Usually someone who is strongly Leopard also has strong Tiger or Python in order to manifest their ideas. Both the Python and the Leopard act with subtlety, but when White Leopard acts, it is light and surgical, whereas Python leaves you feeling like you have been hit by an anvil swinging on the end of a chain.

White Leopard and Boa are both ethereal and airy, but where Boa is nebulous, Leopard is clear-sighted. In communication, Boa does not like to speak, but listens and reflects you back to yourself, whereas White Leopard may be either one of two extremes, taciturn or loquacious, as he broadens your horizons. Boa fills an expanse of space with her awareness and empathy, whereas Leopard uses space as protection and objective distance. Where Boa eats energy and does not really conceive of information, Snow Leopard channels information and guides energy.

White Leopard Keys

White Leopard eye position: The eyes look straight up as if through the crown of the head, or straight forward as though looking far into the distance.

White Leopard tongue position: The tip of the tongue is pressed at the bottom of the front teeth, while the back of the tongue is pressing where the soft and hard palate meet. You will feel a pressure at the top of the head as though you are pushing the plates of the crown apart.

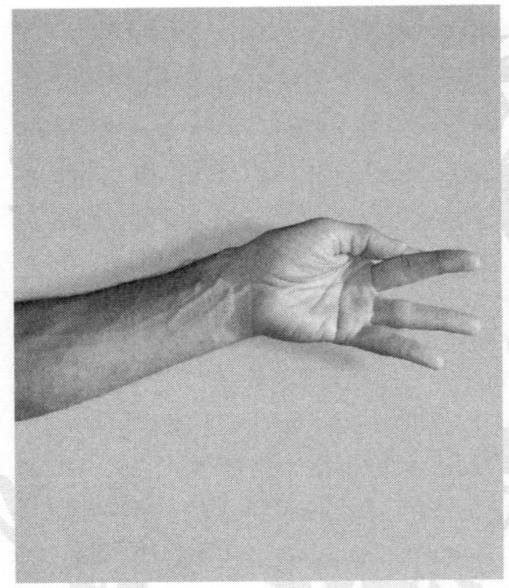

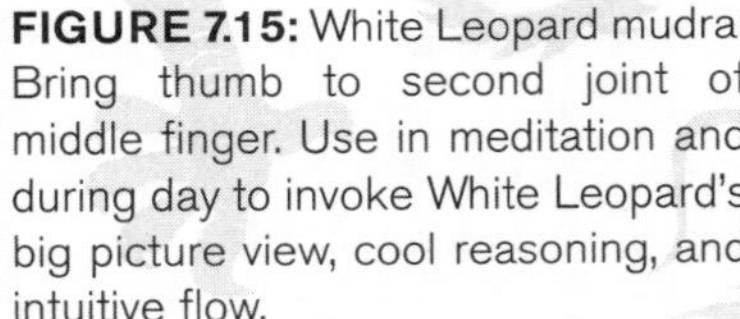

FIGURE 7.15: White Leopard mudra: Bring thumb to second joint of middle finger. Use in meditation and during day to invoke White Leopard's big picture view, cool reasoning, and intuitive flow.

FIGURE 7.16: White Leopard asana: Sit on right foot. (The photograph shows toes flexed, but can also be done with toes flat.) Place your left foot flat on the ground, knee up as shown.

Table 7.1 summarizes the White Leopard archetype.

TABLE 7.1: White Leopard Summary

Consciousness	Thought, intuition, creativity
Nature	Mountain-tops, starry night, Aurora Borealis, Tibetan plateau, Van Allen Belt
Anatomy	Throat, frontal lobe, crown of the head, auras, chakras, meridians
Neural regions	Parietal lobe, frontal lobe, pituitary
Energetic system	*Vishuddha* (throat), intellect (frontal lobe), *sahasrara* (crown of the head), auras, meridians, chakras, streams, pumps, and membranes
Favorite foods	Fruits, light foods, fasting (to transcend the Earthly realm)

Music	Classical music, high-pitched wind instruments
Sports and martial arts	Taekwondo, aikido, qigong, badminton, volleyball
Hobbies	Calculus, computer programming, astronomy, inventing, creative arts
Clothes	Natural heat-keeping fibers, white, gold, rainbow colors

8 COBRA: PERCEPTION OF ENERGY AND KARMA

If the random universe can be trusted, what then?

—VERONICA TONAY

THE QUARTZ CRYSTAL DISCHARGES a tiny pulse of electrical current as the weight of Cobra passes over it. The stepped leader of lightning strikes nearby, marking the path her prey will take. The surge of neural electricity ripples along her spine as she raises herself up to a stand. She holds open her hood to feel the heat signature of her opponent's intention. There is a gap between the intention and the action. That's when Cobra strikes, not faster, just first.

Cobra Consciousness: Psychic, Karmic, Energetic

At death, the moments of your life pass before your eyes from start to finish. It is your consciousness gathering itself. This natural concentrate made from memories and character consolidates into a flicker, summing up your psyche to prepare for its journey into the next incarnation. What if those raw elements of consciousness gave off light and heat? And what if there was a sensory modality with which to detect the luminescent warmth of the transitioning psyche? Then that modality would be the psychic perception of Cobra. Psychic perception detects any kind of intelligence capable of directed will and of evolving. Psychic perception senses the heat signature of conscious intelligence going through a growth spurt.

Cobra lives in a world where lines of intention cast threads of energy. For Cobra, intention leaves a mark. It may be in the disembodied form of a ghost; it may be in the dedicated lineage of teachers who have passed down the torch of their knowledge; it may be the creepy energy tentacle of a Peeping Tom or the straight-shooting focus of an investigating officer. Regardless, Cobra directly perceives intention as an energy, seeing lines, threads, streams, and vortices of energetic flow. When Cobra takes a martial arts class or a piano lesson, she is as much taught by the entire lineage as by the instructor currently in the room. To be Cobra is to see energy creatures visit from other dimensions, to talk to disembodied guides, to see gates and portals to other dimensions, to have flashes of a stranger's fate, and to read the Akashic records, where everything that ever was, is, and ever will be is recorded. Everything has an aura and exudes filaments of energy. Cobra detects the strands and lines of intention, and as she steps off their line of fire, she appears to stagger like a drunk, bobbing and weaving, to avoid what others cannot see.

In the realm of Cobra, the clockwork world of Newtonian physics flutters and gives up the ghost to quantum reality. At this level, energy is intelligent; that is, energy at this level of refinement carries information and possesses intention. Most folk think of these three—energy, information, and intention—as separate. For Cobra, however, energy *is* intelligent and *has* intention. Your intention is energy, and that energy contains information about you, the same way footprints can tell the size, speed, and direction of the person walking. Different cultures have different terms such as *ki, chi,* or *prana,* and although we interpret these in the West to mean *energy* in the sense of "fuel" and "force," we tend to miss the sense of "information" and "intention," which the original terms connote. The notion of an intelligent energy implies energy has a destination it is intended for and that if it fails to reach it, an overall sense of disquiet or unrest results. Cobra consciousness directly perceives the intelligence of energy. With a practice of quiet reflection, prayer, or meditation, Cobra can pass on her intelligent energy to other realms at death or in dreams.

But Cobra is not just the perception of intelligent energy; she is the *refinement of perception for the purpose of piercing into the sacred.* Cobra is an ethereal Animal (joining White Leopard and Boa), unconcerned with the physical, the material, and the mundane, but instead focused on the transcendent. As people, we experience this refinement in the spiritual practice of purification rites in religions around the world. Atonement in Judaism, pilgrimage (and pretty much everything) in Buddhism, the Five Pillars in Islam, *dharma* in Yoga, *misogi* in Shintoism, and mortification in Catholicism—all of these practices serve similar ideals: to purify our intentions and refine our perception of energy in order to prepare us for contact with the sacred. And Cobra acts to refine intention and the perception of energy even if that means the death of the current identity.

Haiku time!

Cobra's universe
Nerve, breath, destiny, subtle
Electricity.

Yes, that pretty much says it, and if you are a Cobra, the above poem would be all you need. For the rest of us, read on.

Cobra Anatomy: Nerve Endings, Third-Eye Point, Back of the Head, Hood, Tailbone

In the mythos, Cobra represents the spiritual electricity that binds consciousness to *fate,* the energy that connects and directs you from this lifetime to the next. In the Cobra mythos, neurons are the live wire of your karma, where the neural electricity is an extension of the raw energy of karma. Cobra is all things body electric—the nervous system from the tip of the tailbone to the brows of the eyes, and from the center of the spine to the receptors of the sensory organs. This is the nervous system from both the Western and the Eastern views. It is here and now, but also beyond and eternal. It is synapses and *nadis;* it's *Kundalini* and the autonomic nervous system. And, like the nervous system, Cobra comes across as an intelligent electric storm, both blistering and soothing.

Because Cobra wants to transcend and reach beyond, more than even the White Leopard, she represents the part of the body that reaches furthest out: the ends of the nerves. The ancient Tibetan called these endings *nadis* and numbered them at 72,000, which may have been a way of saying too many to count. Indeed, we have so many nerves that even if all other tissue was removed, we would still be recognizable. The Cobra pays close attention to areas that are particularly dense in the concentration of nerve endings, such as at joints, perceptual organs, and the ganglia along the spine. In the visualized breathing for Cobra, she draws breath in through *afferent neurons,* which bring sensations in through the back of the spine to the brain, and she exhales through *efferent neurons,* which send commands out through the front part of the spine.

The tip of the tailbone is the root-center of Cobra. To embody your inner Cobra, you visualize an energy circuit extending from the tip of the tailbone down into Earth, effectively grounding the Cobra's psychic circuit the same way a lightning rod grounds a bolt. The Cobra shares the tailbone as a crossover point with Panther, but whereas it acts like a vestigial root for Panther, for Cobra, the tailbone acts to dissipate excessive energy. The tailbone is also, for Cobra, an important nexus for the cerebrospinal fluid sac in which the spine and brain float.[1] *Cerebrospinal fluid* distributes nutrients, clears waste, insulates the brain, and transports hormones. Circulation of the cerebrospinal fluid throughout the sac can be increased by contracting the muscles in the area of the sacrum and tailbone. Called the *sacral pump,* its contraction shunts fluid up the spine, through the ventricles, and around the brain, sustaining and cleansing its tissues. Contraction of the sacral pump figures prominently for Cobra in the plaque work, bows, and breathing exercises at the end of this chapter.

On the opposite end from the sacral pump, and capping the spine, are the brainstem, the cerebellum, and the occipital lobe, which Cobra again shares with Panther. Whereas the back of the brainstem acts as the storehouse of ancestral memory for Panther, for Cobra, it acts like the black box for mystical experiences. A black box on a plane records all communication, mechanical readouts, and actions by the pilot and is designed to survive in crashes. The brainstem and its friends fulfill the same function for Cobra, recording and storing psychic experiences in the event of a psychological crash. Pulling back the veil and suddenly seeing clearly for miles can be overwhelming and shocking, and we may need to *not* remember until a later time when we are ready. But that does not mean the experience is lost or forgotten. As the psyche's survival mechanism, the flash of sight is simply stored at the back of the brainstem until we have matured and our skills are up to the challenges.

Just as a cobra has its iconic hood, so, too, do we have our own hoods—in fact, we have two. The first is a neural hood, and the second is an attentional hood. The *neural hood* is made of the twelve cranial nerves that sprout from the top of the brainstem and cerebellum (reinforcing their importance to Cobra) and fan out to each of the senses. The second hood is an *attentional hood,* the cone of heightened perceptual awareness around the head from the concentrated relay of sensation to the brain, which creates a kind of perceptual parabolic dish around the head. The hood is embodied in the bow by using the movement of the arms to describe its outline. As the hands describe the contours of the hood, the visualized breath fans out on the exhale through the cranial nerves.

The flower of the Cobra is the third-eye point (see appendix B, Figure B.1). The *third-eye point,* commonly called *ajna* in the Yoga tradition, is a moniker for incisive insight into the essence of a person and the locus of a kind of perception not bound by time and space. The way Constantine often described it, psychic vision is detailed but with a kind of myopic focus, vivid but without context. Psychic flashes float alone.

Once, I was driving home from work in Bay Area traffic at rush hour, a single driver in the carpool lane. Without preamble, an image arose of a highway patrol officer on a motorbike. I saw the uniform and sunglasses as though at a distance in an arid desert where the hot air caused the image to shimmer. The image appeared and dissolved, and I dismissed it as too much ham for lunch. Sure enough, ten minutes later, I was stopped and ticketed by an officer in a patrol car (no motorcycle, and no sunglasses). Now, in the Ch'ien-lung system, a premonition does not automatically mean a psychic experience. A Panther through instinct, a White Leopard through intuition, a Boa through empathy, or a Python through study can each experience a premonition or foreshadowing of the future. To tell them apart, you need to consider the quality of the vision and which part of the body responded most strongly or seemed to receive the information. In this case, with the cop, the vision was sudden, brief, vivid, and felt as though the image was located in the area of the third-eye point. The image rose like smoke or an ephemeral mirage without any kind of emotional feeling that would accompany it for Panther or Boa. Here, both the sudden, clear, visual quality of the premonition and its location centered around the third-eye point make it a Cobra experience.

In the story of the officer, coincidence and unconscious cueing cannot be ruled out, but probability is not the point here. The point is the personal meaning you make from these events and how you weave these moments into your life rather than view them as though from the other side of a museum window. We can allow these small moments to bridge us to the larger mysteries and use the Animals to embody, interpret, and enrich ourselves from them. It cannot be emphasized enough that striving for "powers" is not the objective in practicing Cobra. Rather, the practice is to simply observe these events when they occur, casting your intention toward growing more whole from them, and moving more loosely in response to them.

Cobra Brain: Pineal Gland, Parasympathetic and Sympathetic Systems, Nerve Endings

"Cobra, you are so weird!" I exclaim to my inner Cobra, trying to invoke her to write this chapter.

"What do you see?" she asks.

"I see you moving like a teetering, spastic drunk. You make no sense! You're about ESP and past lives … and yet, somehow, I'm supposed to write about what you have in common with neurons and the pineal gland! You move so fast and with pinpoint precision as you slide casually offside a line of attack, but you bob and weave like you're dodging a giant invisible hand that keeps swatting at you. You make no sense!"

"You know why, don't you?" she replies, pausing before continuing. "I am weird because I think with the pineal gland. All I do is gauge how much light there is outside, literally and figuratively, and move off the line when I am in the direct path of a beam."

She gazes intently at me, and as if with a mental finger, she probes my mind, pushing onto the three little granular facts I know about the pineal gland: where it's located (below the crown of the head, near the dead center of the brain), what it connects to (the *suprachiasmatic nucleus,* neurons that sit at the intersection of the optic nerves carrying messages about how much light is out there), and what it does (pumps out melatonin at night to induce sleep, withholds it during the day to allow wakefulness). She stares at me unwaveringly. It's like I'm missing the point, but she's gauging how much I can handle. Then, coming to a decision, she says, "If you want to see, you go to where there is light without allowing yourself to get blinded by it directly. That is why I move the way I do."

"I teeter," she continues, "because I am moving like the shifting balance point between the two opposing sides of the nervous system." She flashes images in my mind's eye (how, I have no idea) of the Parasympathetic Feed-and-Breed system and the Sympathetic Fight-or-Flight system. The two different sets of nerve start in different parts of the spine with opposing effects on the same set of targets organs. She continues, explaining that the sympathetic and parasympathetic systems are opposites in the life-force business. The sympathetic makes the person use energy to get energy from the environment, while the parasympathetic helps the person digest and conserve the acquired energy. The two systems perpetually jostle each other, pushing the body everywhere along the continuum between peace and pressure. "I am," Cobra says, "the nervous system divided in two opposing forces. One of which seeks out destiny and the other awaits it, balancing them each, one against the other, until the outcome emerges. So, I teeter."

I interrupt. "But these belong to the peripheral system, and this section is about the brain, which is the central nervous system. The sympathetic and parasympathetic systems are not part of the brain."

"To me, they are one whole. If you want to embody Cobra, you have to look at the world from the point of view of Cobra. And, I have double vision.

"I have double vision, not the side-by-side kind but the as-above-so-below kind. I wobble in my steps because the ground of perception shifts underneath my feet. For me, things are not as they are, but so much more. I see the technical, material, and physical world as a façade for the energetic and spiritual. In one moment, I may see the detailed blueprints for a laser cutter, and in the same moment, I will see the spiritual essence of the inventor's intention: to pierce the material in order to illuminate the truth underlying the manifest world. I see the material as an outer shell of karma. If you show me a sword, I look at the blade edge and see the rip in the armor of the victim whom it will cut; I look at the hilt and see the hands of the most intent warrior who will wield it; I look at the back of the blade and see the focused gaze of the artisan who crafted it. Did the victim fall at the hands of the warrior? Fate seldom reveals itself in clear memes, and besides, there is always a little wiggle room for free will. Since things are so undecided, I cannot reasonably be expected to commit. So, I teeter."

I am forming the question of what this has to do with categories of the nervous system, and before I can shape the words, she preempts.

"And so it is with the nerves. I do not just see the physiological delineations you can find in biology textbooks. I see the spiritual essence, the transcendent purpose of that tissue. The purpose of the eyes, for example, is the perception of space and time as straight lines, while the purpose of audition is the perception of space as curved and time as cyclical; the sense of smell is to know how to find God; the purpose of touch is to reach for God; and the purpose of taste is to select how to make God part of the self. When I turn to the nervous system, what do I see as its essential nature? I see that the purpose of the nervous system is to refine perception. The refinement of perception requires the whole of the nervous system—the central (spine and brain) and peripheral (limbs), the efferent (sending out) and afferent (bringing in) are equally important. How else can you refine perception but through feedback?"

In the image she flashed in my mind's eye, I see these nerves of the sympathetic and parasympathetic and how they relate to Cobra. At the top, the cranial parasympathetic nerves stretch like the ribs of an umbrella, fanning out from the top of the spine and the cerebellum to the sense organs of perception; they are the physical counterpart to the energetic hood of the Cobra. At the bottom end of the spine, the sacral parasympathetic nerves reach out to the colon (connecting with Boa) and the bladder and sexual organs (connecting with Panther). The sympathetic system is sandwiched by the parasympathetic. At each vertebra, the sympathetic nerves bring in feedback from the body, which enters through the back (dorsal ganglion), and another set of sympathetic nerves carries commands from the brain and spine to the same organs of the body through the front (ventral ganglion). And, finally, like a fireman's pole on both sides of the spine, are the sympathetic trunk nerves, which run down the spine, connecting ganglia of the vertebra above to the ganglia of the one below. The visualized breath rises up from the ground, through the tailbone, through the sympathetic and parasympathetic nerves, up the spine along the trunk nerves, to the brainstem and third-eye point on the inhale of the Cobra bow, then out from the third-eye point into Earth on the exhale, completing the Cobra energy circuit.

For Cobra, the energetic is always present. There is no separation between the scientific and the mystical where each organ has an energetic counterpart. I am feeling dizzy from seeing the world her way. I feel upright and strung-out, like a violin string stretched to the point of snapping before she plucks me one last time. Cobra flashes images of her double vision through my mind again, adding energy systems to the images of all these nerves I see in my mind's eye. Overlaying the feed-and-breed parasympathetic cranial nerves, I see the cooling and protective energetic hood of Cobra. At the bottom end of the parasympathetic system where you find the tip of the tailbone and sacral pump, I see overlaid the energy center of the *muladhara.* Along the ventral and dorsal trunk ganglia of the sympathetic nerves, I see a superimposed image of the energetic channels in Yoga called *ida* and *pingala.* In her mythos, it's like every system of the body has a corresponding aura or chakra, an energetic double to the physical. Cobra brings this twin vision of the physical and the energetic to the plaque work. In Cobra plaque work, visualized breath travels along the physical and energy systems as if they were the same. This conjoined view that Cobra has of energy and matter comes together in the alternate nostril breathing and is described in appendix A under "Part D: Energy Visualization." The connection between the energetic and the physical systems provides crossover points between Cobra and the Animals.

To my scientific training, this is whimsy—at best, a quaint representation of rigorous facts with pretty colors and energy-babble, and at worst, a consortium of sloppy thinking and unresolved contradictions: Is there a direction of causality between the energetic and the physical? Does the physical generate the energetic? Does change in the energetic cause, result from, or simply parallel change in the physical? Does the relationship between the physical and the energetic simply shift depending on context, and if so, is the shift a physical or an energetic one? All this poses more questions than it answers, and yet Cobra is happy to live with the contradictions. For her, the competing directions of causality and the different relationships between fate and free will coexist; they do not cancel each other out but create a door through which she steps to the other side.

Cobra Personality

You have met her. She carried herself with a disarming and penetrating lightness. You had a conversation, and she held up a mirror to show you your perfect flaws. You felt both invaded and grateful. She was merely candid and discerning, but on the receiving end, it felt annoyingly incisive. This is what it was like when I met my wife, a strong Cobra. And I am sure you have met someone like this at least once in your life. Like my wife, the Cobra type walked through your defenses, looked you straight in the eyes, and placed her finger right on the hot spots of your psyche. It felt like this person had a scope to see where you were evolving to and from.

How do you see Cobra within and recognize it in others? By understanding why she loves what she loves. She loves *haiku,* the Japanese poetry style that distills things down to their essence, because she is born of the ethereal, intangible, and eternal. She loves to eat seeds and nuts, honey and propolis, and wear amber beads because she lives on concentrated energy. She loves rock gardens with the thin streams of energy running around the pebbles and high-pitch string instruments like the viola because she resonates with thin lines and strands of energy. She loves acupuncture and darts and pressure points because she thrives on concentrated points of energy and directly influencing the flow of energy throughout the body. She wears scarves, shawls, cloaks, the hijab, and veils because she inhabits the mysterious dance between free will and fate. She wears the colors of gold, white, purple, and indigo because she strives for the pure, refined, and sacred.

The archetypal Cobra is wiry thin, though she will surprise you with her remarkable tensile strength. Her features are sharp: catlike-eyes, Katherine Hepburn–high cheekbones, angular temples, and pointy chin. She looks a little like a bird, tilting her head to one side then the other, as though her temples were heat-sensitive radar and she could get a better read on you by orienting her temples rather than her eyes. Her fingers are long, thin, and pointed, exquisite for pushing pressure points, and she has a gangly walk with her weight toward the balls of her feet, almost on the tips of her toes. She seems to always be on the verge of losing her balance, yet if you get in her way, she will pass around you without disturbing the air. Her interests are in the psychic side of life. She reads about Dr. Ian Stevenson, who recorded over 2,500 corroborated cases of children who claimed to have had previous lives, and *The Tibetan Book of the Dead,* Edgar Cayce, Nostradamus, Rasputin, and Joan of Arc. She learns about Russell Targ and the remote viewing ESP project at the Stanford Research Institute. She practices "ologies" from astrology and the tarot to Ouija boards to personology (reading character in facial features), studying them between classes of Kundalini yoga. (She really likes her teacher!)

Like each of the Animals, Cobra has stages of maturity. Even as a child there was something of the High Priestess about her. She was aware we all face death with nothing but a little medicine bundle of our psyche, and whenever the topic of destiny arose in polite conversation, she zeroed in with intense focus. She was neater than the other kids. She would return from playing in the woods with them, the other children's clothes torn and muddy, yet hers somehow intact and neat. Even at a young age, she showed insight into others, and more than once spoke out loud to an awkwardly hushed room about the spirits who offer her counsel. Practices of purification pepper Cobra's day; cleaning a coffee mug is cleaning the chalice of authentic feeling; cleaning windows is clearing the windows of our own perception; bookkeeping is being accountable to ourselves. When I trained with Constantine, I was poor, and he often gave me second-hand clothing of his, making sure to let me know he had "cleaned it of [his] strands" or that he was giving it to me as with a "special energy as a gift to help you." When he got in a car, he would take a moment and bless the vehicle because it was a manifestation of my will and also "to bless what could be [his] coffin." Showers were ablutions, and he said grace before each meal, occasionally sweeping his hands over the full plate of food to "clear the energy of the chef" who was having a bad day and "covered the food with negative dialogue." This mindfulness of sanctity is a central practice to embodying Cobra.

At this early stage, Cobra needs mentoring, someone who will tell her that her gifts are natural, good, and rare. The mentor will teach her to temper her powers of insight with patience in order to avoid mental errors like confirmation bias or the tricks of memory. She needs guidance so that her gifts do not turn in on themselves and so that others do not turn on her. In one sentence, her insights can turn her from a healer into a tyrant, from a friend into a traitor. The psyche illuminated is flammable. So, as she grows, she either receives guidance or she must keep herself cloistered.

The Cobra pupil has Cobra teachers who teach remotely, visiting her in dreams, in meditations, or in disembodied form. When I first started training, I would improvise visualizations of breath and energy. They ranged from cleaning out the marrow of my bones to imagining visiting the surface of the Moon. It was not until a few years later, as other students and I began to recognize Constantine's ability to visit us, adventure with us, and teach us in dreams, that I began to suspect he was far more active in guiding me in these visualization exercises. It took a while and many conversations comparing notes with Constantine and among ourselves, and while these conversations certainly did not rise to the level of objective and impartial evidence, we began to discern between thoughts *about* his lessons and dialogues *with him* about his lessons. I realized years later that those early visualizations I thought I had improvised had stemmed from his visits in energy form. His energetic form had a unique feeling, as all of ours do; his was one that was a mix of electricity and caramel, and whereas my ideas had the feeling of dialogue balloons in a cartoon, his ideas had the feeling of compact seeds.

The funny thing about this kind of nonlocal communication is that it is just as susceptible to all your petty emotions and biased interpretations. And I am not one of the best listeners. I once spent the whole day at work arguing with Constantine in my head, or so I thought, about continuing to train. By the end of the day I was leaning toward continuing. Then, as I headed back to the studio to train, all the misgivings resurfaced. When he asked me how I was, I expressed the doubts I had been wrestling with earlier, I thought, in private. I was a little shocked when he responded, "I thought we already took care of all of that," and I had a distinct impression of the energy he had expended that afternoon and that it had left a residue; I had the impression I had not been imagining him as a foil to test my arguments against, but that he had projected his energy to help me find my center in my turmoil. He promptly turned around and left me alone to decide for myself the path to take, and he barely taught me for a month until I had decided for myself to continue.

Often, the Cobra type uses another Animal as protection. Perhaps she uses Boa to compensate, to absorb the pain that comes from seeing but being unable to put words to the insights. Or Tiger, to provide her with armor and to lend her accurate irrationality a driving linear mind. This analytical Tiger-Cobra is a force to be reckoned with, bending reality by distorting the perceptions of others through Tiger's relentless confrontation and his simple rhetorical logic, which has the effect of legitimizing and normalizing the distortions. With the benefit of Cobra's insight, the Tiger element of this personality presses upon the soft spots of the opponent's psyche.

Guidance and protection allow her to mature to the second stage. Here, she grows by exploring the question: "If the random universe can be trusted, what then?"[2] She learns that events may be random, but that does not mean they are without meaning, and she learns to read coincidences for signs. Like a professor of literature who peels back the layers of symbol to reveal the hidden meanings of the author's intention, or the art historian who can extract the lines, color, and composition that draw the viewer's eyes to the artist's message, Cobra perceives aglow the minutiae that pop out as signs along the road of a spiritual journey. With discipline and acumen, Cobra has learned to filter out the tricks of the mind. In the second stage, she combines her perspicuity with interpretation. She sees memory shadows of the past, visions of the future, and works to internalize an esoteric system of symbols, like astrology or tarot. Above all, she learns to interpret moments of synchronicity. *Synchronicities* are events that, while unrelated in terms of causality, are related in meaning. Synchronicities mark milestones in the journey of a psyche toward becoming whole and can occur with a stunning improbability, like with the dream of the gold scarab.

A woman was relating to Carl Jung her dream about a golden scarab. Jung had been hoping for some kind of inexplicable event that would help the young lady overcome her heavily rigid, rational mind to let go so she could, in therapy, deal with important emotional issues. Suddenly, there was a rapping at the window pane caused by a large insect striking insistently. Jung got up, opened the window, through which the insect rushed in, and in one action, Jung caught the bug as it flew by and passed it unharmed to the woman, saying "Here is your scarab." It was a rose chafer, a sort of yellow beetle, and as close to a golden scarab as could be found in their clime. It was trying to get into the dark room, which was against its natural habit.[3] As Jung passed the woman the beetle and made his de facto statement, he worked as a Cobra, offering the woman an opportunity to perceive the synchronistic match between reality and the dream. In other words, being *psychic* is not about seeing the future per se, but about having flashes of insight about the mind and the new ways of thinking that the future will require.

And then some people just ride in on a bigger horse. In 1428, England was winning the Hundred Years War with France when Joan of Arc, the Maiden of Orleans, approached the Dauphin (title given to the rightful heir of the French throne) seeming to fulfill the prophecy that a woman would save France. Joan of Arc recognized the Dauphin, who was dressed incognito, in the middle of a crowd of courtiers and gave him the details only he could know of his earnest prayers to God from the day before to save France.[4] Stories and accounts abound of the incredible heroine of France, how she foretold blood would flow from above her breast the day before she was shot by a crossbow in the shoulder, how she knew where to find the sword she needed, and that she even recounted visions of her own fate.

But besides a string of super-coincidences, Joan of Arc makes a good study of Cobra (with strong elements of Tiger) in other ways. She possessed a blindingly clear faith in her vision that was as steadfast and resolute as her commitment to honesty, integrity, and accountability. Her devotion and her abilities lent her the *Cobra charisma,* a reality distortion field that allowed her to upend the oppressive, chauvinist customs of her time, dressing in boy's clothes and becoming the only 17-year-old and only woman in history to lead as supreme commander of a nation's army. Cobra has a charisma, a power for generating shifts in the perception of others, especially in one-on-one conversations. They also disable. Where Tiger overpowers and Python traps, Cobra has a trademark way of stepping out of the line of attack while disabling the aggression aimed at her. There is a famous account from the Maiden's trial: imagine a bevy of old, medieval priests, career interrogators, who are entrenched in the power of their country, asking a young teenage girl whether she thought she was in God's grace. The question was a trap; to answer *yes* was to blaspheme, to answer *no* was to confess heresy. But in Cobra fashion, she subtly got off the line of attack, and with an imperceptible shift in footing, replied "If I am not, God put me there, and if I am, God keep me there!"

At her last stage, Cobra is preparing to yield the world she knows for the transformation she sees must come. She does not cease to cast her intent forward in the direction of fate. For each of the Animals, this last stage presages the marriage with their opposite to create the Dragon. Of the Animals, Cobra is the one that most clearly foresees her transformation. Although by this stage each of the Animals has reached a level of maturity to accept the changes the Dragon symbolizes, Cobra, more than the others, can see and is, for lack of a better word, keen on her approaching transformation.

The Dark Side of Cobra

Being this sensitive is taxing, especially in Western societies. The West is not kind to this kind of sensitivity. There is no vocabulary for it. The Cobra in need of help is overwhelmed by her perception. Her interest in mysticism—potentially healthy in stimulating the imagination and cultivating humility—becomes unbalanced. She becomes uncritical in her reasoning, prone to wishful thinking and paranoia. The stress of matching up what she psychically perceives with what she sees in the physical world makes her vulnerable to breakdown. The unbalanced Cobra uses her perspicuity as a way of avoiding reality, and she is easily capable of creating an aura of mystery or power, preying on the wishes and insecurities of the vulnerable, like a Charles Manson or Hitler. A little darker, the Cobra tarries more and more in the realm of delusion. The refined perception of the Cobra makes her susceptible to psychological breaks from reality—going from psychic to psychotic.

Cobra Movement

The ideokinetics of Cobra are invocations of electricity, rarified gold, and delicate flowers blooming amid thorns in the desert.

Once, a group of us were walking at night toward the Havasupai Falls of the Grand Canyon, instructed by Constantine to do bows by the waters. We were nearly there when the stepped leader, the leading edge of a lightning bolt, flashed down in front of us not 50 yards away. Dana had been in the lead, and he had to rub his eyes from the glare while we stood stunned. When I need to invoke Cobra, I recall this memory as well as the image of other electrical phenomenon, like electrical fireballs and the blue glow of St Elmo's fire. Imagine doing Cobra bows in the caves of the Grand Canyon, which are rich in piezoelectric crystals, where you can imagine the discharge of current under the pressure of your foot, or draw on the image of the Naica caves, in Chihuahua, Mexico, with its selenite crystals measuring 50 feet in length.[5]

Cobra ideokinetics connect her to the desert. She loves the desert because all noises are silenced by its austere severity. The desert allows Cobra to tune into subtle energies and contemplate intention and fate. It is one of the reasons tens of thousands of people love to go to Burning Man. For all of the music and noise, when you walk out onto the playa, you cannot escape the complete nothingness that brings in sharp relief the pulses of our intentions manifested as art cars and fairy costumes. All these costumes and giant art installations are extensions of our psyches but only visible when there is nothing in the background but sheer existence itself. People go to the playa to have their intentions reflected back to them by the desert.

In mythos, Cobra strives for transcendence, so her ideokinetics reflect flowerings, the blossoms casting their seeds to create the next generation, like the century plant with its serrated leaves and pointy tips that produces flowers once every ten to thirty years, often blooming only once before it dies.[6] She also resonates with the desert plants and animals that must adapt to extremes by drawing and conserving every iota of energy and moisture. Her ideokinetics draw on the refined concentrates of nature—like honey, amber, and silk—sensations, and imageries to invoke during the Cobra bow. Energy is part of her ideokinetics. When she goes for a walk in nature, she feels energy drops dripping from the tips of fern leaves and the streams of energy flowing amid the trees in a glen, or the upward and downward swirling vortices of Sedona. This was what it was like to do a nature walk with Constantine who pointed out these energy flows.

The weirdest of ideokinetics is that Cobra moves as though in response to synchronicities. I sat down to write about how Cobra moves when, synchronicity would have it, a young man embodying the style happened to walk that way by my coffee table. He was a young security guard, narrow in frame—you could slide a narrow hoop over his whole body—and when he walked, his heels never touched the ground, and he seemed to spring off the balls of his feet. His limbs were loose, and he looked like he could be blown over by a breeze. Someone who was not watching where they were going was about to collide with him. He moved out of the way without skipping a beat. He simply swished out of the way and swished back. Not only was it a lesson on how to embody Cobra, but the fact that I recognized it at the precise moment I sat down to write about Cobra (and they are rare to spot!) elicited a sense of wonder. Wonder can cue variations in movement, and doing the bow while recalling such a moment or while contemplating its synchronicity is a way of embodying the metaphysical perspective of Cobra.

So, how do you begin to embody this weirdest of sisters? Imitate the action of a cobra about to strike. From slithering on the ground, it lifts itself up, stacking one vertebra on top of the other, without the help of hands, which requires a massive effort. The cobra then opens its hood to reveal pigmentation in the pattern of two large eyes to make the snake seem larger, and these eyes invoke a hypnotic mix of awe and dread. It teeters as it waits, then with a weirding sense of timing, it cuts a slice right through defenses like they were mist. In the mythos, Cobra perceives the lines of energy formed by our intentions and moves to avoid them, lending the Cobra a drunken style, moving as though to avoid the direct blasts of intention from others. It is loose, top-heavy and light, like a hot air balloon. Though Cobra looks like a gawky wraith, when she lands, it is with her full weight, like a petite lady stepping on your foot. She rides the edge of balance and somehow manages to keep her head up. Embodying Cobra is about the fine art of getting out of the way of the opponent's strike, without looking like you're getting out of the way; it leaves an attacker feeling like they have been fighting a ghost.

The neural mythos of Cobra translates into a logos of debilitating precision strikes to to the literal and figurative nervous systems of a body or institution. The Animals attack what they understand, and whether it is in hand-to-hand fighting or as a general strategy or tactic, Cobra delivers debilitating precision strikes to the nervous tissue of an individual or the metaphorical nervous system of an organization with mind-numbing effectiveness. In a set of pinpoint strikes, she uses each blow to fulfill a distinct purpose: one to stun the mind, a second to stop the breathing, a third to stop the heart, and all mediated through the nervous system. The knobstick is Cobra's favorite weapon. The *knobstick* is a pen-length weapon with a sharp point for stabbing on one end and a bulbous knob on the other for jamming into nerves. However, Cobra does not need a stick. Cobra (Tiger, too) practices *iron-palm training* to make the hands and fingers hard enough to karate-chop a brick and finger-spear a watermelon and yet soft and sensitive enough to guide energy for healing. In the hands of a master, iron-palm strikes can range in severity from paralysis without damage—you're just done—to deadly arts like *dim mak,* a sort of pressure-point art for wizards where tightly guarded techniques of applying the correct amount of pressure, in the right direction, upon a specific combination of points, with precise timing, will result in delayed death accompanied by symptoms of organ failure or changes in mental state.

In Cobra ideokinetics, you move on the edge of your balance; this drunken style offers a gift for the athlete, dancer, or yogi. There's a myth of a young kung-fu student who, after years of drilling the same techniques, wants to learn new styles. He expresses his desires to his teacher, who dismisses him. In frustration, the student goes to a tavern and gets drunk. His teacher finds him and tries to take him back to the school, but the student refuses. In the ensuing fight, Drunken Monkey style is born. The student is loose and relaxed, and with his extensive training as a foundation, he moves in a completely different, uninhibited way, baffling his teacher. Drunken Monkey or Drunken styles exist for the purpose of breaking students from self-imposed habits that hamper them from reaching the next level.

There are also practical advantages to moving like a drunk. Drunks are relaxed. A drunk who falls down a flight of stairs walks away without a bruise because he does not stiffen or brace against the fall, which is what causes the injury. Drunks are minimalists of effort. Why jump when startled when you can just step to the side? Drunks have to move from their center as alcohol inhibits fine motor control, and when drunks lift their arms, they do so not with the puny muscles of the shoulder, but with the large brutes of the back muscles, getting the weight of the whole body behind the arm. This does not mean you need to drink before you practice, but there is something about perpetually losing your balance, and using the body's natural rotations, spirals, and calm in order to regain your center.

You cannot fight your way out of losing your balance. Although Tiger holds his center like a rock, this is too brittle for Cobra, who prefers to bend like a willow, out of the way of the main line of force, and then to bounce back from an unexpected angle. Instability exercises, from wobble boards and fitness balls to elastic bands wrapped around the knees, condition a relaxed and responsive way to recover balance. You can bring Cobra into your own practice easily. Choose a fundamental and stable move or stance to your sport or activity. If mimicking a drunkard is too much of a stretch, challenge your balance by binding your knees so your feet are no more than 6 inches apart at any time. For example, to find Cobra in my surfing and skiing, I practiced pop-ups (for surfing) and two-foot jumps (for moguls) on solid ground with my knees bound together by a rope or belt. You cannot fight against the belt or the ground; you need to relax and turn the vestibular reflexes of the limbs into a flowing movement that helps in regaining your balance.

Cobra moves in response to the intentions of the opponent. Stories abound in martial arts lore of masters who respond ahead of their opponents' attack. The master can feel the intention of the attack before it takes place. Not necessarily faster, but first. In Japanese arts like kendo, aikido, and iaido, this is called *sen no sen* (literally "before the before"), and it requires extensive practice in emptying the mind and perceiving the whole of the opponent and in avoiding fixating on the weapons or eyes of the opponent. We all get glimpses of this on or off the mat when we preemptively act in a decisive way. Embodying the Cobra by walking as if you are avoiding being in the line of fire of the intention of others' will not develop psychic perception per se, but it will attune you to shifts in people's focus, adding nuance to your connection with others.

In morphos, whereas White Leopard sits on the cusp of transformation, Cobra, as though fly fishing for transformation, casts a line into a new realm without any chance of reeling it back. The Cobra psyche is that part of ourselves that actively wants to transform. The transformation

Cobra seeks may be a transformation of the psyche, from an old to a new you; however, it is also a transformation from this life into the next. In morphos, Cobra integrates conflict into a meaningful narrative by doing contemplative and energetic practices like yoga and qigong. She meditates, performs purifying rituals, and contemplates the synchronicities of the journey that have brought her to the cusp of transformation.

Cobra will need much energy in her coming transformation. Through her ritualized sacred practices, she will grow more powerful and nuanced in energy work, conducting it, healing with it, and clearing it where blocked. Like a bee, she runs abundant but diluted energy from nature along the energy circuits of her body to concentrate the refined fuel, honey-like, into different energetic systems. These practices develop Cobra's metaphysical double vision, which can be disconcerting to consider, and definitely dizzying to embody. In many psychic and esoteric systems, there are practices to refine the intelligence of energy, making each energy system intelligent, possessing its own information and intention. In these metaphysical practices, Cobra can, for example, make the astral body go one place while making the dream body go somewhere else. The energy systems are bound by the same identity but are capable of independent action and learning. The interdependent energy bodies seek out knowledge and experiences that support the person's overall intention to transform.

People who can do this are few and far between, and they have usually experienced a profound, mystical, out-of-body, near-death, or dream-body experience, usually following extreme danger, fear, or pain. This multidimensional perception of the body is otherworldly and can be alienating, but the time to transform always comes. And when it does, it is part of the Cobra morphos to cut off all ties holding her back in this world, severing any strands of ownership and attachment held onto by others, so she may cast her intention unimpeded into the next realm.

Cobra Sex

For Cobra, sex is a sacred, energetic practice, a gateway to refining vital energy. When exploring sex, Python, Tiger, and Panther focus on the carnal side: what to touch, how to kiss, where to stroke, when to tease—all the wet, warm, fleshy notes in the music of lovemaking. But Cobra, and likewise, White Leopard, finds meaning in sex when it includes directing energy and breath during lovemaking. In this way, they recruit the physical to cultivate the spiritual.

Both Cobra and White Leopard approach sex with a view to cultivate energy. They differ in the texture of energy. Cobra likes refined thin lines of energy and precise energy points. A Cobra having sex focuses on pressure points of the nervous system, playing with points that cause a pleasurable, but sharp, sensation. White Leopard prefers broad beams and fields of energy, and in lovemaking he focuses as much on the mental presence as the physical responsiveness. By including the aura of their partner's body, both Cobra and White Leopard maintain that spatial distance and awareness they prize so much. Cobra energy work makes life hyperpersonal, and White Leopard energy work connects you to cosmic awareness and the big picture.

Mantak Chia's *Taoist Secrets of Love* and James W. McNeil's *Ancient Lovemaking Secrets* present the classical tenets of Taoist and Chinese lovemaking. There is not enough room in this book to go into all the detail, but to give you an idea of the tenor of the exercises that Cobra and White Leopard like, here is a broad outline. The practice consists of running energy along precise circuits, in time with breathing, while in the act of making love. Taoist lovemaking starts with drawing energy up along a circuit at the back and down the front of the spine, called the *microcosmic orbit.* The orbit line goes up the central line of the spine from the peritoneum, up the sacrum, to the crown of the head on the in-breath, and then down the midline of the body on the front, down the belly, through the pubic bone and the genitals, to the peritoneum (for males where the blood vessels of the penis go up into the body, for females the halfway point between the anus and the vagina). The tempo is one full cycle approximately every 7 seconds.

The Tantric breathing can be practiced alone or with your partner during lovemaking. Couples synchronize their breathing during coitus so that as one exhales, the other inhales, while circulating one's own *and the partner's* microcosmic orbit. Tantric sex practices are entirely consistent with how Cobra and White Leopard approach sex. At first pass, this seems awkward, taking the natural spontaneity of sex and imposing rules worthy of Texas Hold 'Em, but Cobra (and White Leopard) enjoy the added dimension of breath awareness in sex; it has a liberating effect for them.

Cobra in the Arts

Alex Grey produces quintessentially Cobra art. His paintings are filled with energetic and otherworldly content. In the piece entitled *Painting,* he portrays a painter at work … and that is the only normal thing about it. Everything else about the painting takes you into Cobra's reality: the painter has transparent skin, through which you see the major blood vessels, brain, and skeleton. The eyes of the painter are fixed on the canvas—you can tell because of the light beams projecting from his eyes and charging the canvas with a golden glow of intention. His heart is obviously in his work, because the chakra is lighting up the canvas like a high-beam. In this Kirlian-enhanced x-ray, you see the meridians, the layers of the aura; and off in the corner are the spirits of famous painters, Vincent Van Gogh, Frida Kahlo, and others, looking on as they watch approvingly. Grey shows sperm-shaped ideas swimming down from above, competing to be part of the work. At the painter's back is a light-being of inspiration guiding the painter by virtue of more light beams coming out of more eyes; and down at the rear lurk the ever-present demons of doubt and fear that wait to devour any artist. Grey paints the world as Cobra sees it with a gothic level of detail and, in subject material and style, produces a strong example of Cobra art.

If Cobras are psychic, then do Cobra authors write prophetic fiction? Such was the case with Morgan Robertson.[7] In 1898, Robertson wrote the science-fiction novel of his day called *The Wreck of the Titan* about an impossibly mammoth ocean liner that's in its fictional maiden voyage, struck an iceberg, causing a massive loss of life due to the drastic shortage of lifeboats. At the time, his story was fantastical. However, fourteen years later, in 1912, the *Titanic* tragedy replicated the disaster of Robertson's fiction with uncanny detail, down to the tonnage of the ship and the number of passengers, with the added touch that a copy of his novel was included on the mantelpiece of the *Titanic*'s dining room.

Stories that reaffirm this aspect of psychic experience can be sensationalistic and easily dismissed with a dozen plausible explanations: the fourteen-year span was close enough in time that the author could have been privy to the plans of the designers of the *Titanic,* or maybe the shipbuilder's designs were inspired by the book and hence placed with reverence on the mantle shelf. Both are very reasonable possibilities. But this is not about choosing one perspective over another—when you practice Cobra, you do not choose between rational analysis and irrational transcendence—it is about holding both together, because we pay a spiritual cost when we do not.

If we do not heed the wisdom of holding both views with humility, then we run the risk of making Cobra's least favorite mistake, as Carl Jung said, of meeting our destiny on the very road we take to avoid it. The allegory of the prince and the horse makes this point. There once was a Russian prince who, the soothsayer foretold, would be killed by a newly born foal in his stable. The prince gave orders that the horse was to be allowed to live a natural and healthy life, free to roam in the pastures and return to the stable as it pleased. The horse lived out its days and died a natural death, its body left out in the pastures it loved. One day, the prince came to view the remains of the horse. In a moment of triumph, he kicked the skull of the horse, under which lay an adder, which bit the prince, killing him later that evening. Fate met.

The prince symbolizes Russian culture emerging with its rich history and traditions of mystery and standing on the cusp of the industrialized West's age of rationalism. The prince respects the past but holds it at bay. He gives it a wide berth and the freedom to roam, but he refuses to make direct contact with this mystical strain in the psychological DNA of his people, represented by the horse. When the prince encounters the mystery of the psychic, he does so as a small part of himself, his analytical reasoning. He is without the psychic vitality that gave soul to his people. With the pipsqueak of the rational intellect, he meets his own giant irrational side, and when the empty shell of a man kicks the empty shell of the horse's skull, he inadvertently unleashes the suppressed psychic vitality, the adder, lurking below.

Yes, the story is about prophecy and linked to Cobra that way, but in a deeper way, it is about the reader's grasp of free will. Although Tiger, Panther, and Python may look at this as a simple moralistic warning against hubris or question the role of free will, Cobra sees it as an instruction on the mutual influence of one's psyche and actions. Cobra sees the exercise of free will as always coming with a cost to the psyche. For Cobra, it is not that we do not have free will; it is that free will is, well, not absolutely free. All acts come at a cost, and at best, free will allows you to choose the price you will pay for the intention behind your actions. Each Animal has its own way of appraising the consequences of its actions: Tiger looks at tangible results from exercising power; Black Panther gauges enjoyment in the struggle for survival; Boa feels the emotions as she yields and surrenders. Cobra sees the costs incurred by the psyche when we pursue a goal with great or petty intentions.

The prince, after a life of bringing rationality to his people, likely improving their material and political life, was confronted at the end of his life by the old roots of the Russian psyche that his work was supposed to serve, but which he had pushed to the side. From the Cobra perspective, the story is not about what strategy the prince should have used with the horse—put it to pasture, slaughter it, ride it like the other horses—or whether he even could have avoided his fate at all. From the point of view of Cobra, the psychic lesson is that the progress made in the realm of the rational and linear, represented by the prince, was incurred at a cost to the spiritual and transcendent aspects of the psyche, represented by the horse. For Cobra, especially, effort in the irrational, through ritual or art, needs to match the investments in the rational. This balance is what brings wholeness to a person's psyche. Otherwise, the spiritual debt accrues, and mysterious forces will claim their share.

Cobra in movies goes beyond the mere mention of telepathy or clairvoyance, with characters like Jean Grey or Francis Xavier in *X-Men*.[8] A film can have a Cobra feeling to it even if no one is using psychic ability per se. The eerie, personal quality of the psychic is often portrayed in stories with an intelligent animal, which possesses overtones of magical or charmed qualities and responding definitively to the deep psychological needs of a character. In *Into the West*,[9] the memory of his wife who perished during the birth of their younger son haunts an alcoholic father. The younger son only knows his mother through the stories his grandfather tells him of a queen in a magical fairyland. Into their lives comes a mysterious horse that, Bucephalus-like, can only be controlled by the young boy. Following a series of events, the young brothers steal the horse back from an underhanded tycoon and ride him west, back to their home and away from the city slums and their father. At the climax, as the boys and horse are escaping, the young son nearly drowns and is saved by the horse, which appears to him as an apparition of his mother. The way the movie is made, the horse is an embodiment of the mother's spirit. The boys' ordeal acts like a psychic shock that breaks the father from the shackles of alcoholism. The film has many elements of other Animals, with Tiger races against the clock and bawdy Panther jokes, but what makes it good food for your Cobra is the portrayal of how each character chooses to see magical forces, premonitions, and synchronicities, the fodder for psychic life. This, in turn, provides an opportunity for the viewer to do the same in their own life.

Cobra Turning Toward Dragon

There is a nearly 100-volt-per-meter difference between the ground and the top of the atmosphere. It is the kind of charge that is strong enough to raise your hair on end like when you rub it with a balloon, and it can be felt by the hairs of a spiderling.[10] When a baby spider needs to commute, it climbs to the top of a plant or tree where the charge differences are greatest, it raises its abdomen, and it releases several gossamers from its spinnerets. It casts a thread, and the negative charge in the atmosphere repels the negatively charged gossamer, pushing it along the electrostatically charged currents.[11] Slight shifts in electrostatic charge carry the spiderling sailing, called *kiting*, on windless, clear skies.[12] Spiderlings have been recorded landing on ships a thousand miles out to sea and on weather balloons as high as two and a half miles up, all after following airborne currents of electrostatic charges.[13]

Like the spiderlings, Cobra turning toward Dragon casts her gossamer of intention into the unknown to be carried to her encounter with her transpersonal complement, the White Leopard. They focus on the transcendent, but like two master painters from radically different schools. Whereas the White Leopard sits neutrally on the cusp of transformation, Cobra casts her intent over the edge and waits to be pulled. Both Animals focus on energy, but whereas Cobra likes thin lines and concentrated points of energy, Leopard likes broad beams and planes of energy. The White Leopard looks at the time course of a person's life and sees all the possible paths, taken and not taken, mapped out by satellite. Cobra sees, from a first-person perspective, the precise exit ramp to change from one trajectory to another. White Leopard apprehends the meaning of a person's life as though the universe were using that life to explore a question. Cobra sees the meaning of a life as defined by the person's deepest-held intention, as though the person was using the universe to answer questions. Whereas White Leopard creates to free energy, Cobra refines perception to harness and manipulate energy. Where Leopard channels information to make structures in the world more specialized helping the cosmos hone itself, Cobra refines her perception to make her psyche more specialized so she may hone her intention to move through the cosmos. Both perspectives complement each other.

Cobra turning toward Dragon enjoys being energetically double-jointed. She plays with articulating her energy body with the same reticular control a snake has of its spine. This is the weird land of esoteric practices that Cobra calls home: Cobra develops multiple energy systems through which she projects her consciousness in order to travel, gain knowledge, and enjoy experiences separate from the physical body. Names vary, like the astral body, etheric body, dream body, spirit body, and the like, with differences of energetic makeup and ability varying from person to person as much as the individual differences in physical appearance and athletic ability. Cobra exercises volition over the energetic systems through a symbolic language composed of imagery, breath, and energy. Disciplines like Wicca, Daoist alchemy, Christian esotericism, Tarot, the Kabbalah, and Ch'ien-lung use languages made up, not of words, but of imagery, breath, and energy, each one with its own flavor or emphasis, but the practices amount to the same thing: have aura, will travel. Contemplation and ritualized repetition internalize the imagery and ideokinetic and visualized breathing to the point where they act like buttons on a touch-tone phone, opening a line of communication to the energy bodies. This requires a blend of grounding and openness. So, blind games, like the ones in the Seven Steps at the end of this chapter, along with blind card games like the one described in the upcoming section, "Card Games for Cobra," are used to anneal the psyche, to retain its strength while making it more flexible.

But blind work by itself is not sufficient. Cobra's transformation requires her to *construct a personal mythology*. Cobra builds her mythology on the back of the metaphysical systems she has learned. The symbols, breath, and energy work are first internalized. Cobra must then use the language she has learned to reflect on her own life. She contemplates the synchronicities of her life and explores the question, "What is my why?" When Cobra personalizes her mythology connecting it to her psyche's deepest intention, she stamps her energy with an individuality rooted in her tone of meditation, which propels and aids her transformation.

The shapes, colors, and triangle points in Ch'ien-lung's plaque work are intended to be used to help a person cultivate their own personal mythology. Although concentration exercises with the plaques will benefit the mind by increasing calm and focus, it is by contemplating the meaning of the symbols, like the colors discussed in a moment, in connection to the synchronicities of your own life that personalizes this work and empowers the connection to the energy systems.

The Cobra Plaque

The triangle of the plaque represents the person, the circle is Earth and the world (as seen through the eyes of the Animal), and the square represents cosmic laws. For Cobra, the triangle is gold, while the circle and the square are both white (see Figure 8.1 in this book's color insert).

What do these colors signify? Gold, across cultures and ages, is an alchemical symbol for transformation, where crudeness turns to refinement, and perception becomes more accurate. It is the color of being true to your highest qualities. Cobra strives to refine and purify herself so she can perceive more accurately. The white represents the constant and unchanging laws of the universe. That the circle and the square are the same color white signifies that Cobra sees higher laws as bleeding through her everyday world. In my own practice with Cobra, this "looking behind the veil" has helped me become a more insightful person. I can honestly say that this practice has made me a better husband, teacher, and researcher. As I have matured through mid-life, I seem to be getting more comfortable with having my worldview tilted but without the fear of losing my balance.

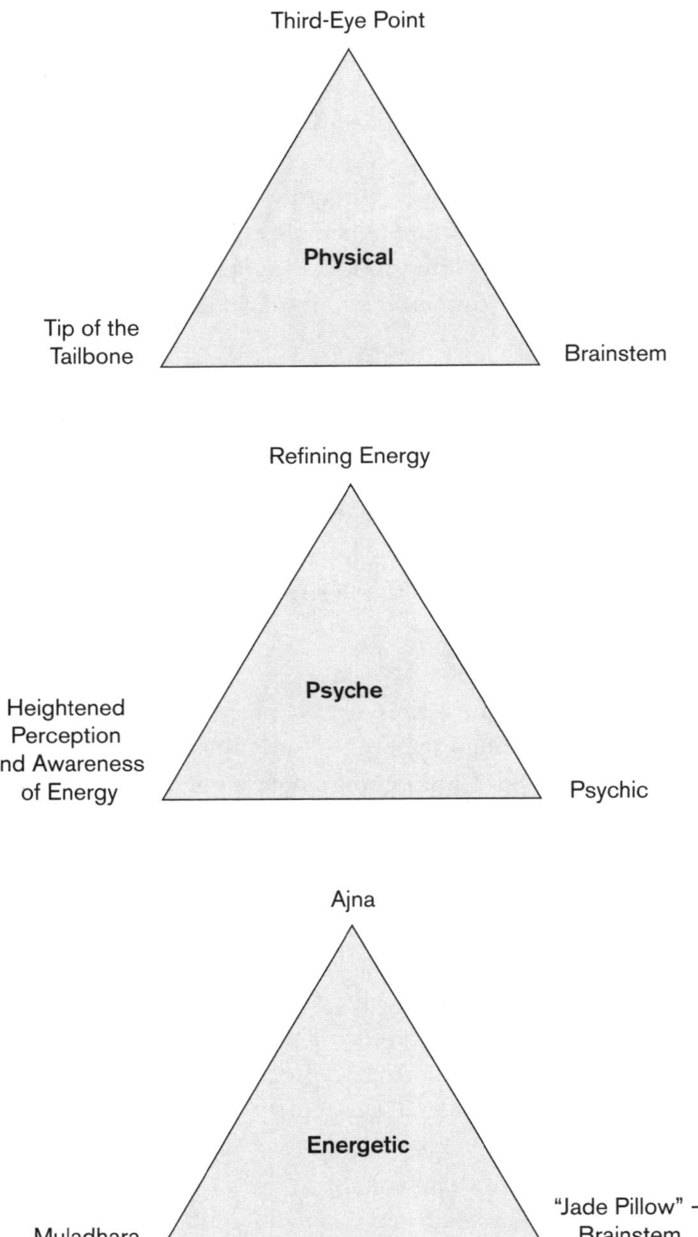

FIGURE 8.2: The symbolic meaning of the triangle points for the Cobra

The Cobra plaque holds multiple levels of interpretation. At the physical level, the points of the triangle refer to the key anatomical points of Cobra: the tip of the tailbone, the brainstem, and the pineal gland located between the brows of the eyes. At the energetic level, the three points of the triangle represent the energetic points corresponding to the anatomical Cobra areas, with *muladhara,* the energetic grounding of psychic energy to Earth at the tailbone; Jade Pillow, the energetic center at the back of the brainstem; and *ajna,* the energetic center of the third-eye point. On the psychological dimension, the three points of the triangle reflect how Cobra sees and acts in the world—where the first point stands for energetic awareness, the second point stands for psychic perception, and the third point stands for refining perception.

Psychics and Research

Russell Targ is a great example of a Cobra-type person: he cofounded the Stanford Research Institute (SRI) remote viewing program, is legally blind, wears thick glasses, and was an early pioneer of the laser (the refinement of electromagnetic energy). He discovered his own psychic ability in a way that typically sets Cobras on their journey. He started off as an amateur magician and would do a card trick where audience members would write down information on a piece of paper. During the trick he would surreptitiously get a peek at what they wrote and then bring the envelope up to his head to continue with the mind-reading act. When he did so, however, he would have the experience of seeing things that the trick did not allow for, thus gaining more information than he could have surmised from the writing in the envelope.

These experiences later prompted him to found the ESP program at SRI and develop a set of standardized methods for guiding everyday normal people with no previous experience in transpersonal perception to have psychic experiences. I have included some of his recommendations alongside the psychic games Constantine organized us into playing. Russell Targ and Jane Katra portray their research in their book *Miracles of Mind.*[14] This research was funded by several government organizations including the CIA, NASA, and the US Army, with details that have been released under the Freedom of Information Act. In the book, they talk about experiments that touched on psychic healing and remote viewing with everyday people. One of their research subjects was Pat Price.

In 1973, Pat Price, a police commissioner from Burbank, California, participated in remote viewing experiments at SRI, in Palo Alto. He sat down in a Faraday cage, a room shielded from all radiation, where he relaxed and tuned in to a location researchers Hal Puthoff and Bart Cox had randomly selected from a previously composed set of possible places. One such place was a large pool at Rinconada Park in Palo Alto; the actual pool was 110 feet in diameter, but Price described it as being only 100 feet in diameter; Price also described in detail another smaller, 60×80-foot, rectangular pool of water that had a concrete block house he described as a water purification plant. He drew both pools, water storage tanks, and rotating machines that went with the second smaller pool. Although Hal and Bart did indeed visit this pool, there was no water purification plant there—at the time. Pat Price participated in several other psychic experiments before he passed away in 1975.

It was not until 1995 that the *Annual Report of the City of Palo Alto,* with its centennial celebration, published some of the historical changes in Palo Alto—including, in 1913, the replacement of the waterworks with the municipal pool. The photograph of the waterworks included in the report matched the details of Price's sketch. It had been assumed that Price simply had gotten the water purification plant wrong, when in fact he had not only visited the plant at the correct location, but had "gone into the past" to view the same location at two different times.

Card Games for Cobra

We practiced psychic push-ups with Constantine using the face cards of a regular deck. A sender holds the image of the card in mind, while a receiver focuses on perceiving the card. Rather than the whole card, the sender focuses on one attribute at a time; for example, with the King of Hearts, they focus on the masculinity of the King, then the red of the suit, and then the roundness of the heart. The receiver builds on these incremental impressions before calling the whole card. The sender responds by simply saying "Good," regardless of the receiver's accuracy, leaving the results for after the exercise, and keeping track of the answers on a piece of paper. Doing this card exercise is surprisingly tiring, making a slow regular pace important. After each transmission, let the receiver rest a moment by taking seven regular breaths, allowing them to clear their mental slate.

My wife and I played psychic games for fun using objects from around the house. We followed the same principle Constantine taught of building up basic features, and it made sense to pick objects with distinct parts, like our cat or a pair of glasses rather than a plate or a bowl. To embody Cobra, it is important to avoid interpretation and just report on the perception. If the receiver reports seeing "a metal rod with hooks … maybe a shower curtain" help by saying, "You don't need to guess what it is, just tell me what you see." We found it useful to keep the size in the range between a golf ball and beach ball, and the psychic impact of the object around the level of "requires attention but does not cause tension," so, for example, a butter knife is better than a steak knife.

Seven Steps to Embodying Cobra

Step One: Follow Your Breath (Ongoing Mindfulness Practice)

Following your breath in Cobra means visualizing you can breathe into your

Nervous system Visualize breathing into the nerves. Breathe into the areas dense in nerve tissue, like the joints; the sensory organs of the eyes, skin, ears, mouth, and nose; and the ganglia along the spine's sympathetic system, controlling excitation, and the parasympathetic, controlling calmness. With practice, visualize breath and neural signals traveling, on the inhale, from the body to the brain through the dorsal (back) of the spine, and on the exhale, from the brain to the body through the ventral (front) of the spine. Ideokinetics: Move as if the nerves were jolted by small electrical pulses coming up from the ground. Move as if there was an electrical grid over the whole earth and you follow the wires like a cable car. Connect to lightning and the path of least resistance the stepped leader will follow.

Nadis A non-Western category of neurons, nadis refers to the neurons that are connected furthest out–that is, the muscles, the organs, and the sensory receptors of the perceptual organs. If all other tissue were taken away, because of the nadis you would still be recognizable. Visualize breathing into them. Ideokinetics: Move as if you are drawing refined energy into the *nadis.* Move as if they are cups holding energy you do not want to spill. Connect to Earth's crystals, especially, large crystal caves, like those of the Naica caves.

Pineal gland The pineal gland is located dead center in the brain, and it gets signals from neurons atop the optic chiasm that tell it about changes in daylight. These signals enable the pineal gland to regulate your circadian rhythm, the daily rhythm of sleeping and waking. Visualize breathing into the pineal gland. The pineal gland cycles through firing rates over the course of a day–it fires most quickly at around 2 p.m., when your reaction times are fastest and your oxygen consumption is highest, to its slowest rate in non-REM sleep (sleep without visual dreams), at night around 2 a.m. Notice how your breath changes as a result of your circadian rhythm. Ideokinetics: Move as if you are trying to avoid bright beams or strands of light. Connect to subtle forms of light, such as starlight, moonlight, and the Sun behind a veil of clouds.

Back of the brainstem Breathe into the back of your head, into the brainstem, the cerebellum, and the occipital lobe. This area is like the Cobra equivalent of a black box on a plane; it records everything. Cobra is concerned with the energetic, subtle, and refined, and these areas of the brain help to ground the insights you gain from paying attention but that you may not be ready to fully grasp. When you experience an insight or a premonition, breathe into this area, relaxing it and allowing the impact to settle. Ideokinetics: Move as if the back of your head is making you top-heavy, making you teeter.

Tip of the tailbone The brain and spine float in a sac filled with cerebrospinal fluid (CSF). The sac envelops the entire brain and extends down the spine. To enhance the circulation of your CSF, imagine that your tailbone slightly lengthens out and curls in as you inhale and exhale, pumping CSF around the spine and brain. Energetically speaking, the tailbone acts as the energetic equivalent of the grounding prong on a plug–it helps to protect against sudden discharges of energy. If you feel overwhelmed, on the out-breath, imagine you are sending surplus energy into the ground through the tailbone. Or inhale, up from the ground, via the tailbone, up the spine, to the brainstem and occipital lobe, to the third-eye point, and direct the energy straight into the ground. Ideokinetics: Move as if you were bottom-weighted like a Bobo doll, and every time you teeter you get drawn back upright. Connect to Earth through the tailbone, sending excess energy down for grounding, and drawing energy up for guidance.

The Cobra's hood Energetically visualize the oversized Cobra hood, extending from the base of the neck to above the head, which is sensitive to energy. Visualize the energy of other people's intentions as they give off heat. Imagine you can detect this heat with the hood. Visualize energy into the hood and exhale, directing a beam of energy into the ground. Ideokinetics: Move as though you are top-heavy and trying to dodge the linear lines of the intentions of others, bobbing and weaving like you are about to lose balance. Connect to Earth by casting open your hood and kiting like the spiderlings on currents of energy.

Step Two: Recall Your Day (Daily/10 Minutes before Sleep)

Your day is filled with work, jobs, errands, and chores. Yet, mundane habits carry a dimension of spiritual growth: baths can be baptisms or ablutions or purification; coffee is a reminder that sometimes the good things come with a little taste of the bitter earth. There's always some part of our routine that makes us muse about the big questions. In reviewing your day, notice when you were mindful of these higher purposes.

There will be moments when you lapse, when you go into automatic pilot, or when you just indulge in your lesser angels. There will be many of these moments, and they will result in wasted energy. As you review your day, feel like you are gathering back the wasted energy of those moments and storing them for use the next day. At first, it will be nearly impossible to even recall what happened during those zoned-out moments. But with practice, you will gradually be more present, notice you are wasting less energy, and spend more time in a mindful state that makes recall at the end of the day easier.

Step Three: Scan Your Body (Daily/10 Minutes before and after Sleep)

Scan your nervous system prior to and upon waking from sleep. I find it natural to do the nerves of the limbs (feet to hips then fingers to shoulders) before starting on the spine and brain. Strive to be sensitive and detailed in your scan.

Step Four: Do the Bows in Nature (Weekly/10–15 Minutes)

Choose places that reaffirm the spiritual purity and the subtle energetic awareness of this electric Animal. You can do the bows in (careful) view of a lightning storm, using your hood to feel the path the lightning bolt will follow as it looks for conduction. The natural cave of giant quartz crystal in Naica, Mexico, is an ideal spot for Cobra. Quartz is *piezoelectric,* meaning it discharges a tiny electrical pulse when placed under pressure (*piezo* = foot) and returns the favor by vibrating when an electrical current is run through it.

With Cobra's sensitivity, it can be exhausting to be around people and their conflicting intentions. She seeks refuge in the desert. The desert imposes an economy of effort and quiet. There she can reclaim her sense of purity, which allows her to see clearly. The Cobra is easily over-stimulated. She avoids direct light, enjoying the Moon, and her favorite is when the Moon or Sun is veiled behind a thin layer of clouds, muted, with a just-discernible outline.

When performing the bow for Cobra, take three small sipping in-breaths as you direct energy up from Earth in a circuit to the tailbone, up the spine, through the brainstem, to the third-eye point. On each sipping breath, touch Cobra's three energy centers in order–tip of the tailbone, third-eye point, back of the brainstem–before holding your breath as you describe the shape of the Cobra's hood. On each sipping breath, contract the sacral pump lightly. The sipping breath, touch, and sacral contraction occur together, as you feel energy pulse through the parasympathetic and sympathetic trunk ganglia. On the exhale, produce a *hssss* sound, and send energy from the tip of the hood and the cranial nerves, through the third-eye point into the ground, contracting the sacral pump during the entire and continuous out-breath. You can also work with incoming energy entering through the dorsal (back) of the spine and outgoing energy exiting by the ventral (front) of the spine.

But more importantly, it's how you relate to the *energy* of a place that matters to Cobra. Constantine would take us on walks through the ancient rainforests of British Columbia or on the trails at the bottom of the Grand Canyon. In Cobra style, he would point out all the different energy currents: small thin rivulets through the salal, the droplets falling of giant ferns, geysers of energy spiraling or pouring down, and the small slip streams animals follow as trails or paths. The Cobra opens up to streams of energy.

Cobra energetically sees and moves in response to lines of intention of precise and direct purpose. To foster this sensitivity, and to get people out of their heads, Constantine had us play blind games in nature. An important part of our Ch'ien-lung practice, we played the following games where one or both people have their eyes closed as a way of cultivating Cobra sensitivity to energy and the intentions of others. Although I am certainly not the most adept person, I have enjoyed greater perceptiveness because of these exercises, both on and off the mat. I am listing them here under Cobra, but they can be adapted to the practices of the other Animals, as well.

Hunter-seeker: Like Blind Man's Bluff, four or more people stand stalk still, while the blind seeker tries to find them. Those standing still cannot move until tagged, and once tagged, they move out of the play area. The seeker tags them with a soft punch or kick (when played with a martial emphasis).

Blind sparring: This is just like it sounds. Either one person or both people can have their eyes closed. Go slowly, continuously, and smoothly. If you find yourself accelerating, slow down. Strikes will get through, and when they do, it is a valuable opportunity to turn or roll with the strike, letting it provide the impetus for the counter, allowing the strike to help you reposition yourself.

Blind walk: Blind walks through the woods or a nearby park are done with a guide who has their eyes open, while you follow, blind. The guide snaps their fingers as they walk ahead, ten feet or so, while the blind person follows in the direction of the sound. The guide makes sure the blind walker is safely on the path and gives verbal cues to avoid falling off small cliffs or negotiating minor obstacles.

Blind punch-block: This is blocking punches with the eyes closed. The blind person has their hands out to the sides, as though they are ready to catch a big beach ball. The other person, with eyes open, throws arrhythmic, slow punches at the chest, head, or belly. The blind person is to block the strikes before they touch the skin. This is a sensitivity exercise. The puncher is to match their speed to the ability of the blind blocker. After each individual block, the blind person returns their hands to the neutral starting position.

Kodak Moment: Senses are heightened just after blind work. In this game, intersperse blind work with moments of opening the eyes to gaze upon something beautiful. Stop the blind walker or the blocker, place your fingertips on their forehead and press lightly, which is their cue to open their eyes and look at whatever you have lined them up to see. The person keeps their eyes open for as long as they feel the pressure, which should last no more than a second. The exercise has a way of refining perception by highlighting defining characteristics of people, objects, and landscapes.

Cobra Bow

FIGURE 8.3: Stand with feet together. Hold mudra. Connect the tailbone to Earth, feel hood of the Cobra.

FIGURE 8.4: Release mudra, and place middle finger over index finger (Cobra fangs).

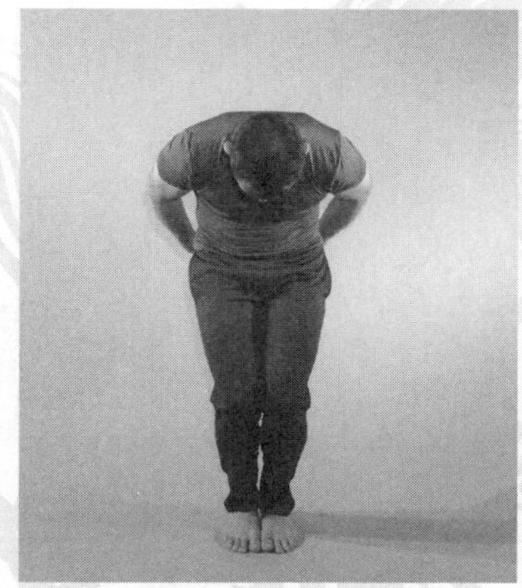

FIGURE 8.5: Curl over to push air out of body. Touch fingertips to the tailbone and take a sipping in-breath. Bring an electrical jolt to the tailbone from Earth, and connect to the electrical planetary grid.

FIGURE 8.6: Curl up, turn your feet out, and touch your fingers to the third-eye point, taking a second sipping in-breath. Energy rises up the spine to stimulate the black box of cerebellum and occipital lobe. Breathe jolting energy into the third-eye point.

FIGURE 8.7: Touch the fingers to the occipital lobe, taking third sipping in-breath. Energy flows directly from the back of your head to the third-eye point. Breathe a small jolt of breath directly in the back of the head.

FIGURE 8.8: Hold the breath while your hands go out, describing the contour of Cobra hood.

FIGURE 8.9: Your hands draw a circle in the air above your head and join above the third-eye point.

FIGURE 8.10: Turn your feet in, and exhale, sending energy out the tips of your fingers, into Earth.

FIGURE 8.11: Your fingers come palm down to your third-eye point, drawing a small loop as your palms turn open to the face.

FIGURE 8.12: Exhale, and lower the hands.

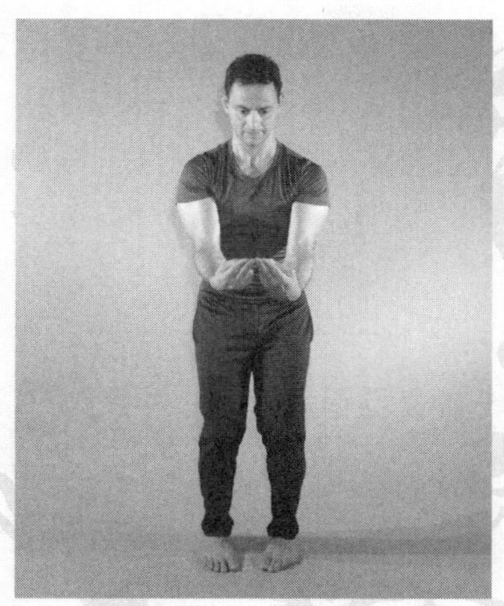

FIGURE 8.13: Exhale, continue to lower the hands.

FIGURE 8.14: Exhale, and finish lowering your hands: Repeat the bow.

FIGURE 8.15: Finish the bow, inhale, and place your hands in a triangle position, tip down, at the tailbone. Turn the feet out.

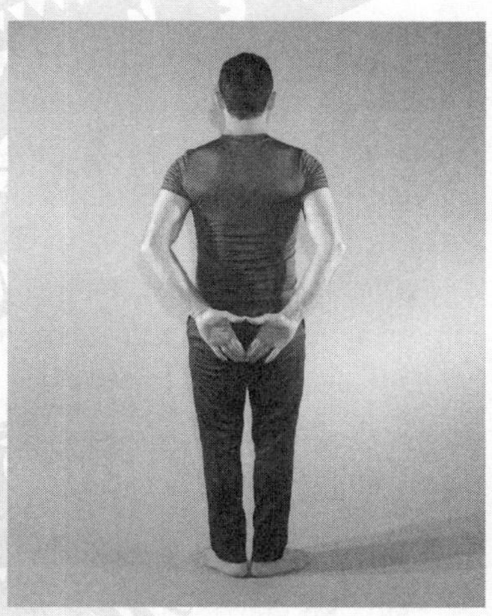

FIGURE 8.16: This is the rear view.

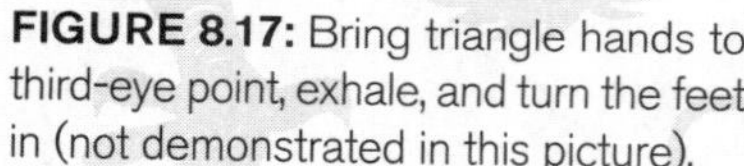

FIGURE 8.17: Bring triangle hands to third-eye point, exhale, and turn the feet in (not demonstrated in this picture).

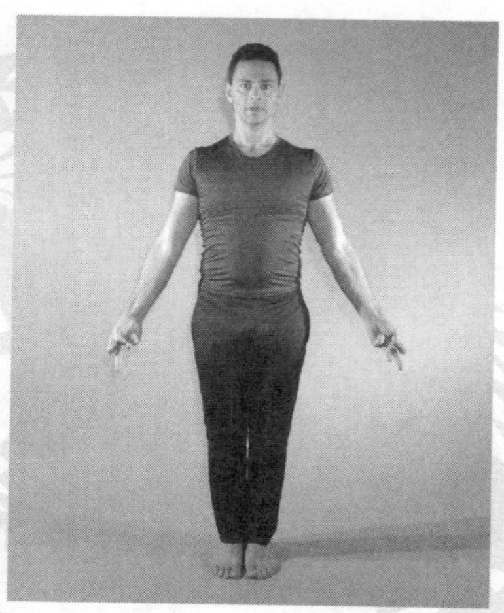

FIGURE 8.18: Stand in neutral, with mudras.

Step Five: Adopt the Animal Personality (Ongoing Practice)

When it comes to food, Cobra eats seeds or nuts. These are foods concentrated with energy, like the nerve points she breathes through.

Listen to high-pitch string instruments and sounds that pierce and resonate in the area of the third-eye point. Truth wears a veil, and so does the Cobra wearing shawls, scarves, saris, hijab, and veils, in colors of purple, gold, white and indigo, and vermillion. Jewelry, especially over the third eye, is worn to remind the wearer they are striving for the rare gem of spiritual sight.

If reading tea leaves is asking too much, read books and watch movies on the topics of psychic perception, delving into arts like astrology or tarot with a transcendent system that contains iconic symbols. Endeavor to give gifts that reflect the spiritual essence of the recipient.

Every person's day is filled with work that Cobra infuses with spiritual meaning. The Japanese call it *misogi*, or purification; but whatever the label, there is a sense of carrying out a task for an elevated purpose: to cleanse one's soul and raise mankind. Do housekeeping as prayer. Before starting a task, can you associate the mundane action with a sacred equivalent? Can you turn housekeeping into a sorting of the self, a bath into a baptism, morning wash into ablutions?

Step Six: Remember Your Dreams (Daily/10 Minutes upon Waking)

Being psychic, Cobra's dream work involves prophetic or precognitive dreams. Psychic dreams emerge spontaneously, are vivid, and are imbued with import. Such dreams are more of a gift than a skill, but practicing Cobra tones the system to handle them.

A practice to cultivate such openness is to take a piece of paper and draw a line down the middle. On one side of the line, write down your reactions to a problem in the dream as well as how you learned in childhood to respond this way. On the other side, write the qualities required to resolve the problem. Think of things that embody those qualities, preferably people you know and trust, or animals, or meaningful objects. By thinking of your history, you give your subconscious a chance to unload, as in the dream incubation. By thinking of the people, animals, or objects, you are creating a personal arcana of symbols for the qualities of the psyche you wish to cultivate. Those people, animals, and objects become living symbols, a psychic alphabet making future dreams easier to decipher. As the symbols gain strength, visualize yourself and the symbol inside the golden triangle of the Cobra as you drift off to sleep.

Step Seven: Use the Plaques (Daily/20 Minutes)

See appendix A for instructions, and follow the breathing pattern common to all Animals. When doing Cobra plaque work, visualize the breath as a thin but concentrated strand of gold light. The more refined, the better. Think laser!

Cobra Energy Circuit

On a small sip of in-breath, visualize electrical energy coming up from Earth to the tailbone; on the second sip of breath, imagine it moving up the spine to the brain stem; on the third sip imagine it moving through the pineal gland to the third-eye point. On one continuous out-breath, direct energy from the third-eye point into the ground. This energy circuit is visualized in the bow as well. Contract the sac of cerebrospinal fluid using the same force as when you pucker your lips to hold a straw, on each sipping in-breath and on the duration of the exhale.

Cobra vs. Animals

Cobra, White Leopard, and Boa are part of what Constantine called the *ethereal triad,* while Panther, Tiger, and Python were the *physical triad.* Embodying an ethereal Animal means looking at energy differently. For all three, energy is more than fuel. For Cobra, energy is thin, spider web threads formed of intention. For White Leopard, it is broad beams of information. For Boa, energy is an amorphous cloud of feeling.

Cobra and Python can look a lot alike. They can both leave you feeling manipulated. But where Python manipulates the 'hard' structure, Cobra manipulates the 'soft' communication lines. Where Python studies the structure and levers, often letting plans mature, Cobra perceives the sensitive hotspots, striking with no need to study. Like Python, Cobra's actions can have a domino effect, but where Python uses your structure to implode on itself, Cobra overwhelms the circuits, causing a fuse to blow.

Like Tiger, you are struck by how direct Cobra is. But where Tiger is direct, like with a hip-check or a head-on collision, Cobra is more subtle. She's direct by being straight in front of you but not quite in your line of fire. She side-steps with a nearly imperceptible shift, as your shot grazes by her. And somehow that has placed you right in her strike zone, where with timing, and even tact, she presses on a combination of hotspots to create a cascade of reactions.

Cobra Keys

Cobra eye position: The eyes are looking up as though to the third eye.

Cobra tongue position: Place the tip of the tongue behind the front upper teeth, pointing to the third eye.

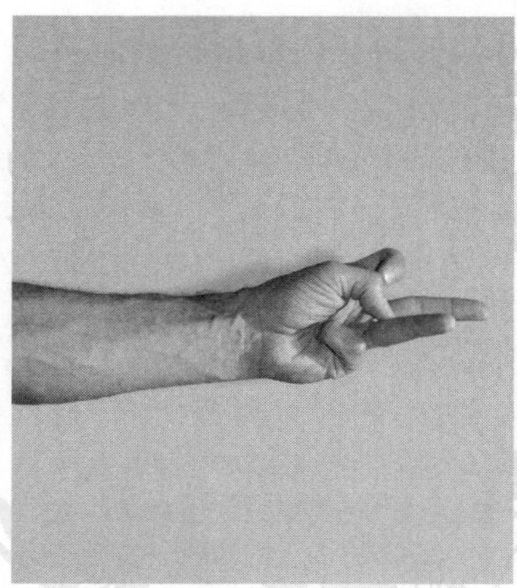

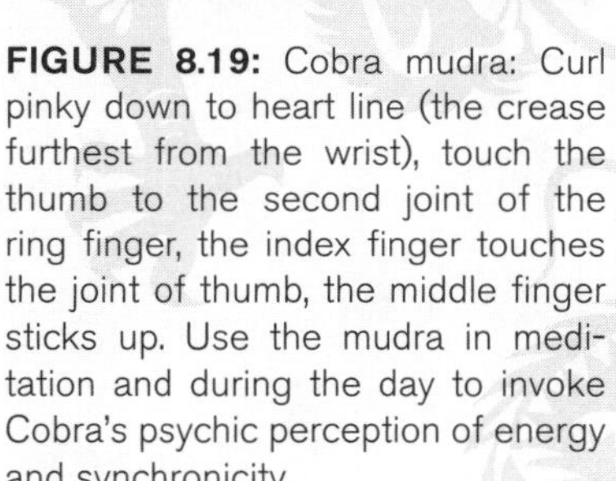

FIGURE 8.19: Cobra mudra: Curl pinky down to heart line (the crease furthest from the wrist), touch the thumb to the second joint of the ring finger, the index finger touches the joint of thumb, the middle finger sticks up. Use the mudra in meditation and during the day to invoke Cobra's psychic perception of energy and synchronicity.

FIGURE 8.20: Cobra asana: Kneel, but balance on the toes, the knees out to the sides. If too unsustainable, kneel on shin bones, toes flat, knees pointing to the sides. The mudras interlock, the middle finger points to the third-eye point.

Table 8.1 summarizes the Cobra archetype.

TABLE 8.1: Cobra Summary

Consciousness	Transmission and receptivity of energy, psychic awareness, refinement of perception
Nature	Deserts crystal caves, where lightning is about to strike
Anatomy	Nervous system, tip of the tailbone, brainstem, third-eye point
Neural region	Pineal gland
Energetic system	*Muladhara* (tip of the tailbone), Jade Pillow (brainstem and cerebellum), *Ajna* (pineal gland), *Nadis*

Favorite foods	Seeds, nuts, spices (foods highly concentrated in energy)
Music	High-pitched string instruments
Sports and martial arts	Pressure point control, Drunken Monkey
Hobbies	Esoteric studies (e.g., astrology, tarot)
Clothes	Veils, flowing robes, colors of gold, white, purple, indigo

BECOMING DRAGON

THE TIGER WALKS ALONG the path. His whole life he has known only victory. But today, he senses something is different. Unable to discern what it is, the Tiger moves forward out of habit.

THE BOA RESTS IN a tree, confident that life will bring her what she needs. Predators normally cull the weakest of the herd, but Boa is interested only in what has the most energy, the greatest vitality.

THE TIGER PASSES BENEATH the branch where Boa is resting. The Boa, roused by the Tiger's life force, drops from the branch, onto the Tiger, and they begin to fight.

THE TIGER HAS NEVER encountered such an opponent. For every strike the Tiger makes, the Boa seems to avoid, absorb, wrap and coil the limb away. The Boa is amazed at the power and perseverance of the Tiger as they fight for three days and nights.

THEIR CONFLICT TURNS TO admiration and attraction. Clouds descend upon the two, cloaking them. The Tiger, with the will to be part of something greater, surrenders himself. The Boa consumes the Tiger whole, becoming pregnant. Lightning and thunder fuse them together, and in that moment, the consciousness of the Earth Dragon is born. Not wanting to be born of a mother and thereby bound by the laws of the Earth, the Dragon tears its way out of the Boa, fully conscious.

Playing with Dragons

Dragons play in the weirdest way: they chase the pearl. In most images depicting a dragon, you can easily find the pearl, and always the dragon is chasing or clutching it as if spellbound. The pearl is a symbol of the treasures we create when we meet adversity with our humanity. Consider how a pearl is formed. Deep in the ocean, the symbol for the unconscious, a grain of sand enters an oyster. The sand irritates the oyster's soft flesh. To relieve itself from the irritation, the oyster bathes the grain in its own essential juices. Over time, it turns the invasive irritant into an iridescent jewel. The pearl is a symbol of us drawing on our essential nature to turn adversity into redemption, to transform hardship into beauty.

The Animals are fun, yet for all the energy expended in writing about them, Ch'ien-lung is not about the Animals. Ch'ien-lung is not about the Dragons. Or even about the Pearl. Ch'ien-lung is about *the dance between the Dragon and the Pearl,* a journey in creative resilience. In the dance, the complementary but diametric qualities of the Animals combine to create the Dragon, a state of flow where you creatively turn weaknesses into strengths, as you turn adversities into opportunities for growth in affirming humanity. In the dance between the Dragon and the Pearl, you choose how to be before deciding what to do.

The Dragon Cycle: Lather, Rinse, Repeat

A full description of the alchemy of the Dragon is a topic for a future book, but a simple outline will give you an idea. Dragon is not so much an end product as a continuous process of skillfully becoming. Whereas practicing the Animals is like playing scales on a piano, the Dragons are akin to improvising melodies with chords. Becoming Dragon has three main practices: *purifying, refining,* and *energizing.* Each phase is focused on separately, but with time, they flow together, overlap, and combine.

Purifying

The goal of purifying is to *articulate* the Animals. This means you can visualize breath and energy in the Animal anatomy, brain areas, and earthly power spots; evoke the Animal's favorite sensations and adopt its personality; visualize and mentally manipulate the plaques; identify relevant symbols from your dreams; and recognize Animal themes in art and your daily life. The goal of the articulation is to bring all of the aspects of the Animal up to a working baseline. To articulate Tiger is to make the heart equal in strength to the mind and the body; to articulate Panther is to make enjoying sensuality equally strong as enjoying fear and surrendering to dreams; to articulate White Leopard is to make the play of intuition equal to the rigor of moral reasoning. Each of the Seven Steps will help you accomplish this articulation.

The word *purify* is used because you are confronting your bias toward an aspect of an Animal in yourself. We've had many students come through our classes and use the bows and mythos of one Animal to round out their own. One person was a natural Tiger but was allergic to strong passions and emotional vulnerability, while another Tiger was disgusted by physical competition; a natural Python was very observant but did not follow through on her insights to satisfy her own needs. A Panther student was judgmental of sensuality, numb to the soft needs of his own body, and hated sleep because it felt like death. A White Leopard found intellectual play frivolous, not appreciating that play was how the colleagues he admired developed their best ideas. The students started by learning about the mythos of the Animal they wished to embody, practiced the visualized breathing, embodied the movement along with the keys, contemplated the psyche of the Animal symbolized by its plaque, and observed their prejudices toward the second-class parts of their psyche. One young lady with strong Tiger realized she had always been rewarded for her open heart but not for her physical prowess in a family where the boys were celebrated for their athleticism. Gradually, as this student practiced, the habits of tension and anxiety began to unravel, and her Animal emerged well rounded and articulate, seeking affirming experiences. After she witnessed herself shying away from the Tiger practices enough times, she allowed herself to embrace the bows and the Tiger in herself. She has since gone on to win podium in semipro women's cycling.

The Animals offer psychological distance, objectivity, leverage, and fun in recognizing these deep biases, and each of the Seven Steps plays a role. It is much easier to ask, "How can I strengthen my Tiger's musculature?"

than "Why are my muscles so weak?" When a question is posed in a positive way, the Animal psyches (especially Panther's subconscious, Boa's unconscious, and White Leopard's intuition) have no choice but to work on it and find a solution. The Seven Steps help them along. When you adopt their personalities, you will be surprised to discover the number of knee-jerk biases you carry. Recalling your day develops memory- and perspective-taking as you review the causes and effects of those biases. Biases and prejudices cause the instruments of attention to play out of key, so the plaque work tunes them. Finally, recalling your dreams builds a symbolic language of insights into the origins and expressions of these biases, all of which simmer in the cauldron of the bows.

The deep biases make attention narrow and breathing shallow. The Basic Breaths are breathing exercises to restore attention and breath; they run across all the Animals and are detailed in appendix C. In the end, the essential self in its purest form is where breath and attention meet. The Basic Breaths reaffirm the essential nature of the self, the alchemical backdrop from which the Dragons emerge.

Part of the purifying work is learning to not abuse your Animals. The term *abuse* here has less to do with cruel mistreatment and more to do with inappropriately using an Animal for a problem it was not meant to solve. You cannot use your Tiger's linear mind on a problem that can only be solved by your Tiger's heart or your Panther's instinct. You cannot use your Boa's empathy to gather the hundreds of threads of your White Leopard's intuitive thoughts or use your Python's analysis to manipulate your way to your Panther's sensuality. The same way it is abuse to force a child to act like a surrogate parent, so is it abusive to have one type of intelligence do the job of another, whether it is to analyze with your emotions or to feel with your analysis.

During the purifying phase, correcting postural alignment parallels the work on attitude alignment. The body is designed to self-correct if provided with a chance to relax and articulate a joint's full range of motion in each plane. During purification, which is sometimes called *dredging* in Daoist alchemy and *rectification* in Taiji, students relax and release tension by practicing alignment exercises, like the skeletal alignment exercises in appendix C, including the Rock 'Round the Clock (the exercise done with Mary-Anne in chapter 2), the Melon, and the

Standing Pose. Whether you are a dancer, yogi, athlete, or actor, these postural exercises will improve your responsiveness.

How do you know the purifying work is progressing and you are articulating an Animal? You experience a *morphological shock,* a sense of disorientation when transitioning between Animals. I still recall when it happened to me. I had been practicing Tiger intensely, working hard at all Seven Steps, for several months. I lived, breathed, and moved Tiger. It got to the point where I was scaring some of the younger students. Then, halfway through a class, Constantine instructed me to shift right then and there to Boa. I did, and as I focused on embodying Boa, I experienced a wave of nausea, like I was seasick on an ocean of moral outrage. Baffled at first, I realized later it was because I had so intensely internalized Tiger that I had tied my sense of self-worth to him, framing my outlook of the world through his eyes. So, when I shifted to Boa, it was like I had pulled a psychological rug out from underneath myself, leaving me without an equally strong frame to replace the one I had developed with Tiger—a self-induced culture shock. It was as if by doing the Tiger work, I had quarantined all the other Animals. Then, when I suddenly let Tiger go, the other Animals expanded to reclaim their space with all the psychological subtlety of an airbag.

It is natural to need time to switch between roles, like taking ten minutes of silence when first arriving home from work. But what makes this type of shock odd is that it is completely self-generated and rooted, not in roles or jobs, but in how we choose to be who we are. You will likely experience it early on—depending on the thoroughness, intensity, and duration of your training and the element of surprise when you shift Animals. You are apt to experience a disquieting, visceral reaction for no other reason than that you have shifted your viewpoint. It will feel awkward, but paradoxically, this will be a sign that your work is bearing fruit and that the Animals are developing a life of their own. At this stage, it is important to continue because this shock will subside in intensity in the future, but only with practice.

The goal of purifying is the articulation of all the Animals, marked by an absence of morphological shock, and a skill in adopting their character and mindset. But the practice of purifying, especially facing biases and guarding against abuse, never really ends. Doing the work of confronting biases, practicing the bows and the Basic Breath yields powerful results, lasting a lifetime, and supports the next phase, refining. There is nothing to stop someone from skipping the basics of purifying and its Seven Steps and jumping right away to the refining phase, but what I have seen is that the work does not stick for those who skip ahead. You want your mindfulness of the Animals to sink into your cells. The self-observation of the Animals within you is foundational to this embodied art.

Refining

When you can articulate each of the Animals, you can move onto the work of refining. The purifying stage is very much like learning the basics of how to drive a car. The next stage, refining, is like learning to take apart and rebuild the engine—blindfolded. During purification, you become familiar with all the Animals within you. During the refining stage, you are integrating elements of the Animals. The best way to do that is to practice the Dragon bows, the Warrior exercise, the Tree exercise, and the Sun-Moon exercise. The Dragon bows combine the bow from one Snake and one Cat, with a synthesis of the textures from both Animals. At first, the Dragon bows involve a simple alternation between a Cat and a Snake, but with time, a synergy emerges where the extreme end of one Animal's breathing quality is the starting point of the next. In Earth Dragon, for example, which is created by combining Tiger and Boa, Boa expands and expands until she collapses on herself. The implosion begins Tiger's contraction, which tightens so intensely, he explodes, which begins Boa's expansion, and on it goes. During the purifying stage, the Animals are practiced in contrast to each other to define the boundaries of the archetypes. But in refining, the Animals in the Dragon bows resemble two poles of the same cycle.

The Warrior exercise in appendix D teaches you how to take the engine apart. In the Warrior exercise, you describe the idealized expression for aspects of consciousness separate from the Animals. For example, what does intellectual integrity mean, whether it is for Python or White Leopard; what does physical intelligence mean to Tiger and Panther? Describing the aspects of the psyche in your own words makes you take ownership. Each Animal has one or two elements that overlap with another: Tiger's physical prowess intersects with Panther's; Panther's comfort with the subconscious meshes with Python's; Python's reach into the unconscious connects it with Boa. It's like a metaphysical game of snakes and ladders where you can get from any Animal to any other Animal by a crossover point. Describing them makes it easier to change between and combine them in the Dragons.

Although the Warrior exercises deconstruct the Animals, the Tree and Sun-Moon exercises deconstruct your history. *Deconstruction* means to reevaluate behavior, whether deliberate or not, which preserves power and inclusion for yourself *while withholding these from others.* The Tree and Sun-Moon exercises provide a glimpse at the assumptions of power and privilege that may be present in your practice of the Animals and Warrior exercises. Seen through the lens of the Animals, power comes in many forms and can be used for benefit or for harm. The degree to which we know ourselves determines how much good and how much harm we can do. The Tree and Sun-Moon exercises (described in appendix D) develop that self-knowledge.

The Warriors, the Tree, and the Sun-Moon are psychological exercises of the refining stage, and double wrapping in Appendix D is the physical counterpart. The Double-Wrapping exercise promotes the opposing spirals that naturally occur in dynamic movement. It benefits dancers, yogis, athletes, and martial artists, supporting the learning of movement where you will not just be imitating the gross outer shape, but seeing each joint contribute to the overall flow and grace. Double wrapping can be practiced when you are simply standing or when you are doing the Tree Pose.

Energizing

The third stage, energizing, involves higher-level energetic and sacred work. Space precludes going into these practices in detail, but the exercises associated with such practices are called Core Energetics and make up a regular part of our in-class curriculum. These exercises, like the bows, which include movement, visualized breath, and energy, are similar to exercises found in other traditions of Chinese or Daoist healing arts. One such exercise is the Tree Pose in appendix E; it incorporates the energetic anatomy of appendix B and the postural directions of the Standing Pose and the Melon exercises in appendix C. Core Energetics are designed for people practicing and not practicing the Animals. They are easily accessible for beginners, promote health and well-being, and support the Seven Steps.

Concentration, Meditation, Contemplation

Meditation. You may say you do it, would like to do it, have a friend who does it, do it sometimes, wish you did it more regularly, did it once and freaked out, or did it once and fell asleep. You can get quiet, you can pray, you can do a moving meditation, you can recite a mantra, you can concentrate on a mandala with one-point focus. You can flow with the universe, you can be at one with everything, or you can let your ego dissolve into nothing. Which one of these is meditation? Will the real meditation please stand up? What are you doing when you are humming your favorite Sanskrit lyric in one spot or staring at a blank wall, thinking about Buddha? Is praying the same as meditation, and who needs to meditate when you can ski off cloud-crowned cliffs into deep pillows of white powder?

We are plagued by rooftop chatter, our minds run rampant, and worries topple over each other faster than players in a rugby skirmish. We live immersed in the noise of our own minds, and this is accentuated, if not directed, by carefully planned media ad campaigns. Those of us drawn to martial arts or yoga usually do it to quiet the ruckus. We get flexible, we get strong, and we learn about resilience and respect, but first and foremost, we learn to turn the volume down.

In Ch'ien-lung, the words *concentration, meditation,* and *contemplation* have specific meanings and are important to know by the time you begin work with the Dragons.

Concentration requires focusing on a predefined set of objects or ideas to the exclusion of others. When most people talk of meditation, they are referring to concentration. Concentration can be reciting a mantra, counting during inhalation and exhalation, playing a musical instrument to get sound clear, or praying to Jesus for forgiveness. In concentration, there is you and the object, nothing else. Besides showing you how subtle and difficult the simplest of things can be, concentration is great for stimulating and articulating a sense of identity: you and your boundaries. In concentration, you teach yourself what you can and cannot control, defining the limits of agency. It gives you a nose with which to sniff out the thoughts you are actively generating and the ones that are simply byproducts of being on mental autopilot. It creates a sense of identity based on willed attention and choice-making, a profound thing when you consider how often folk base their identity on feelings or circumstances.

Here is my favorite quote on the difference between concentration and meditation: "Prayer (i.e., concentration) is talking to God. Meditation is listening." In *meditation,* you stop worldly mental activity; there's no preset focus or task. In meditation there is no you. No object. Just a simple, pure awareness without direction. There is no sense of identity, no you "doing" it, and no "it" to be done, but you are not sleeping or drifting. Instead, you are perpetually doing nothing and being none of the roles you play in life, none of the labels you ascribe to yourself. Your breath is breathing you, your organs function, and your brain is quiet without mind patrol policing for rooftop chatter.

Contemplation is a paradox. There is awareness with direction, but you are not the one directing it. There is a sense of self, but it is dynamic, and there is an object, but you are neither separate from nor lost in it. You are a process of being, and you allow something in the world to come in for a visit. You and the object are one. In contemplation, the self becomes a lens through which to perceive the essential nature of things, resulting in an existential "Ah-ha!" of profound insight.

Each Animal has its unique approach to concentration, meditation, and contemplation, where concentration is developed first for meditation to be viable, but contemplation grows on its own. Each Animal has their own way of concentrating. Python will concentrate on a pattern, while Tiger will focus on one point. Concentration can have an external focus, like the plaques, making it easier to notice lapses, or an internal focus, like a mantra based on the triangle points. In a way, the Warrior exercise is a concentration game for each sense.

It may be more difficult to understand how each of the Animals has its own way of meditating. If meditation is not thinking, then not thinking is not thinking, whether it is Boa, Panther, or Tiger. Here, Ch'ien-lung has something to offer. Meditation is awareness without direction, judgment, or task, but although there are no words, there is a *tone,* a quality of the person's presence that permeates their awareness. Each of the Animals has its own tone. Boa is quiet and absorbing, whereas Tiger is loud and full. Panther is liquid alive, and space is made orderly by Python's stillness. White Leopard is light and expansive, and Cobra is intensely sublime. As you embark on your own practice, you will discover your own tones.

Although a healthy concentration is a prerequisite to deliberate meditation, contemplation can occur independently, although a concentration practice will strengthen it. Each Animal differs in its object of contemplation. Leopard channels cosmic insights, and Cobra sees the karmic. Tiger contemplates the fruits of will, whereas Boa delves into the lifecycle of sentient things. Panther contemplates in a dream-like state, whereas Python uses contemplation to delve deeper into the reality of material world.

That's Not What They're For: The Dragon's Gift

One of my most vivid dreams happened before a descent down into the Grand Canyon, after I had been working to raise sponsorship for the trip. In my dream, I am standing in front of a Dragon, and I ask it for sponsorship. The Dragon looks at me for a second, and then Whoosh—burns me to a crisp! I woke up laughing at myself. I started telling the story to Constantine (who finished my own story by filling in details I had forgotten). I asked him if the Dragon was angry that I had asked it for sponsorship, and he answered, "No. It's just not what they're for."

The Dragon's gift is not in what you get, but in what you can be. Wealth comes from the mind seeing deeply into things by the light of the heart. We understand those things we recognize in ourselves, and the more we expand our understanding of who we are, the more we can embrace a wider world. I am not the most mindful Zen person, and I couldn't win a fight with a tangled garden hose, but playing with Dragons and Animals has helped me reach out to others from a more substantial, authentic center. It has given me more presence of mind in the moment, all the better to dream what the future can be. It has allowed me to reflect more deeply and accurately, and the contemplated life is lived twice.

This generation and the ones to come will be forced to tackle the problem of a growing peoples on a shrinking planet without sacrificing either the people or the planet. It is my belief that all martial arts have a role to play in this. The masters have always taught that conflict is dance in another form. The point is not to find the ultimate or best style, but to find better ways to resolve conflict. It is not always possible to avoid conflict, but we can get better at how we resolve it, and the first steps have always included breath, movement, and taking the perspective of others. We can foster a better world when we remember we are the ones who choose to foster it. We either choose the world as we envision it could be or we must resign ourselves to the accidental one we stumble into. The difference depends on whether we remember to choose. And so I write this book: to remember.

PLAQUE WORK: BREATHING PATTERN FOR ALL ANIMALS

The plaque work draws from alternate-nostril (also called *nadi shodhan* or *anulom vilom*) breathing exercises, also called *pranayama,* and forms a cornerstone in Ch'ien-lung training. There are four parts:

A. The breathing cycle, which includes the use of the hands to open or close the nostrils.

B. Embodying the Animal psyche.

C. The timed gaze of the eyes along the edges of the shapes.

D. The visualized energy circuits.

The components are modular, like building blocks, and are described in this appendix followed by an explanation of how to combine them and why.

Part A: I Got Rhythmic Breathing and Nose-Pinching

The breath cycle consists of four stages: The *inhalation,* the *hold,* the *exhalation,* and the *pause.* Inhaling and exhaling are self-evident. The hold is a voluntary holding of the breath *in,* while the pause is a voluntary holding of the breath *out.* The hands are used to pinch the nostrils closed.

Hand Position

The hand position is a "hang loose" for yogis (see Figure A.1). From a closed fist, raise the thumb, pinky, and ring finger. The index and middle finger are curled over, touching the heart line (top line) of the hand.

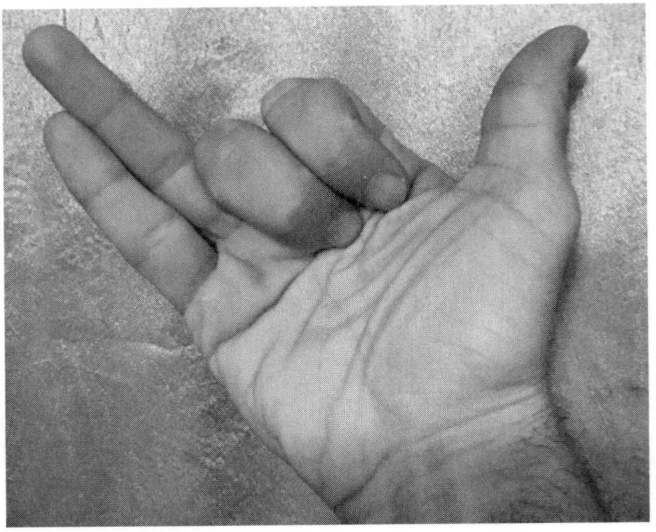

FIGURE A.1: Finger position for alternate-nostril breathing

Breathing Cycle

Alternate-nostril breathing is so called because you alternate the breath between nostrils. The fingers stop up one nostril while you breathe in and out from the other. A full breath cycle consists of one in-breath and one out-breath from both nostrils. Make the hand shape described in Figure A.1 and sit comfortably. Bring the thumb of the right hand to the right nostril, closing off the air passage. Prior to starting, blow out residual air through the left nostril.

1. **Left Inhale:** Keep the thumb on the right nostril, and inhale through the left open nostril.
2. **Hold:** Finish inhaling, and use the pinky and ring finger to close off the left nostril. The right nostril is still closed by the thumb, pinching your nostrils shut as you hold your breath.

3. **Right Exhale:** At the appropriate count, remove the thumb from the right nostril and exhale.
4. **Right Pause:** After the Exhale, Pause, keeping the breath out. Feel the gap between cycles, using it to relax tension and focus, feeling the impulse for the next in-breath. Try to wait for the count, but if you feel an overriding impulse to breathe before the count is done, respect it, and inhale.
5. **Right Inhale:** There is no change in finger position from the Pause.
6. **Hold:** Finish inhaling, pinch the right nostril with the thumb, and hold the breath.
7. **Left Exhale:** Release the ring and pinky fingers from the left nostril and begin exhaling.
8. **Left Pause:** Complete the exhale, and feel the pause before the impulse to inhale again.
9. **Repeat.**

The Count

Beginners: The basic in-hold-out-pause rhythm of 4-4-4-4 is appropriate for all levels, including beginners.

Intermediate: The intermediate rhythm follows a (in-hold-out-pause) count of 4-8-8-4. This an intermediate rhythm in *pranayama* for those with more experience or for those with an intense athletic, especially endurance, background.

Advanced: Experienced students can increase the hold and exhale and decrease the inhale and pause. An extreme version of difficulty is a (in-hold-out-pause) 4-10-16-2 count. You can vary the values of the components for each session, but do aim for consistency in the practice, and pick counts where the *exhale equals or is greater than the inhale,* to which Constantine often added, "you are giving more than you are receiving."

Seven full breathing cycles make a full set, which you do with your chosen Animal's plaque. Beginners should use an actual plaque, while advanced students can try visualizing it.

If you lose track because you get lost in thought or your feelings, return to your breath with an attitude of suspending any critical self-judgment.

When you can complete a set of seven cycles, without being derailed by lapses in attention, you are then ready to add the next element. It should feel like you can keep track of the breathing and the count with the same level of attention as riding a bicycle. After extensive practice, you may even experience a sense of "starting the machine" by merely placing your fingers to your nostrils. The amount of time it will take for this level of proficiency will vary from one to six weeks depending on the person and the intensity of the practice. You can do the exercise one to four times a day. Once a day is a maintenance level, twice will allow you to begin to build momentum, and three times and above are intense levels of practice. It is advisable to practice under the guidance of an experienced yoga teacher if you practice more than four times a day regularly or for sessions that last longer than an hour. Remember: go at a pace that feels natural; more is not always better.

Part B: Animal Tone, or How to Unleash the Meditation Beast Within

The timed-breathing and hand shape of Part A should feel second nature before adding on Part B.

The second element is unique to Ch'ien-lung and involves embodying the Animal by generating the Animal tone. Called the *hedonic tone* in psychology and the *feeling tone* in Buddhism, tone is intrinsic to meditation, the active generation of presence. Indeed, the meaning of the word *mantra* in its Sanskrit root does not only refer to the repeated phrase, but also to the underlying emotional or attitudinal tone the phrase evokes. You can find a short description in "Step Seven: Use the Plaques" of the Animal for its tone, and you can read the rest of the chapter for additional ideas. Identify a quality that makes sense to you as the gravitational center of the Animal psyche—an attitude, a quality of consciousness or texture from nature that resonates with the Animal for you—and incorporate it into your plaque work. Your goal is to have the feeling pervade the whole body while doing the plaque work.

For example, on certain occasions when I do Tiger, I choose *manipura* as its center of consciousness, the storehouse of its physical power, and I will feel a sense of willpower that I associate with the base of a mountain, as though that feeling starts at my bellybutton and emanates outward. On another occasion, I may choose Tiger's analytical mind, which I associate with the steel edge of a samurai's *katana,* and imagine that feeling starting at the frontal lobe and spreading from there. Finally, I may choose to focus on Tiger's courage, which is captured by the quality of a torch, and imagine the heat of its light centered at my heart, spreading and warming my whole body.

Your goal is to generate the feeling tone of the Animal as though it is emanating from one of the Animal's centers, spreading from there throughout the entire body. To know where the feeling should be centered, look at the points of the Animal's triangle (its plaque) at the end of the chapter. For example, the Boa triangle points represent the respiratory system, the lymphatic system, and the skin. I will generate the meditative tone of Boa's soft, healing empathy and feel it start to grow throughout my skin. From there, I imagine the feeling growing throughout my respiratory system. Finally, I allow the feeling to grow through my lymphatic system and ventricles. The amount of time required will again vary depending on the person, but it usually takes an absolute beginner three to six weeks to reliably generate a feeling tone from one Animal center and approximately three to four months to generate it from all at the same time. I recommend practicing to generate the tone for one Animal before jumping to another. When you reliably generate the feeling at multiple centers, then you can move on to adding the timed gaze and the visualized energy.

Take at least a month to read about the Animal you are interested in prior to embodying it in the plaque work. You want to have a sense of the Animal and, importantly, a reason for practicing. What larger purpose are you fulfilling by drawing on the Animal? Ask yourself what quality about the Animal you find most intriguing. It may be White Leopard's subtle thought or Cobra's soulful insight. Then explicitly ask yourself which places in your body most resonate with the quality, and be sure to have that area in your awareness while breathing.

Part C: Timed Gaze

In the Ch'ien-lung plaque work, you shift your gaze along the perimeter of the shapes in sync with the breath. There are two patterns: Shift on Pause and Fixate on Pause. The Fixate on Pause is used with the energy visualization (described in Part D). Let's start with the Shift on Pause pattern.

Shift on Pause

In Shift on Pause, you move the eyes as if following a bead of water rolling along the edge of the shape (in the Animal's plaque) on the exhale, hold, and pause, and you fixate on the inhale. It so happens that with the triangle and circle, the Inhale occurs at the same point.

Start at the top point of the triangle (see Figure A.2). Empty all your breath, and then begin with the inhale, keeping the eyes fixed on the top point. Finish the inhale, pinch the nostrils, hold the breath, and with your gaze, travel clockwise from the first point to the second point along the edge of the triangle. (This can be done with the square at the corners, and with the circle at the points where it intersects with the triangle.) Time it so that you arrive at the next point ready to exhale. As you exhale, travel along the next segment to the third point. Arrive at the third point. At the third point, pause—that is, keep the air out. As you keep the air out, continue shifting your gaze along the edge of the triangle, returning to the initial point to inhale. During the exercise, run the eyes *as smoothly as possible* along the perimeter of the shape as if following a ball rolling around the edge.

Fixate on Pause

The second synchronized pattern is used when you add on the visualized energy. This pattern is nearly identical to the previous one, with the exception that you fixate the gaze during the inhalation *and* the pause, smoothly pursuing the edge of the shape with your gaze on the exhale and the hold.

Plaque Work: Breathing Pattern for All Animals

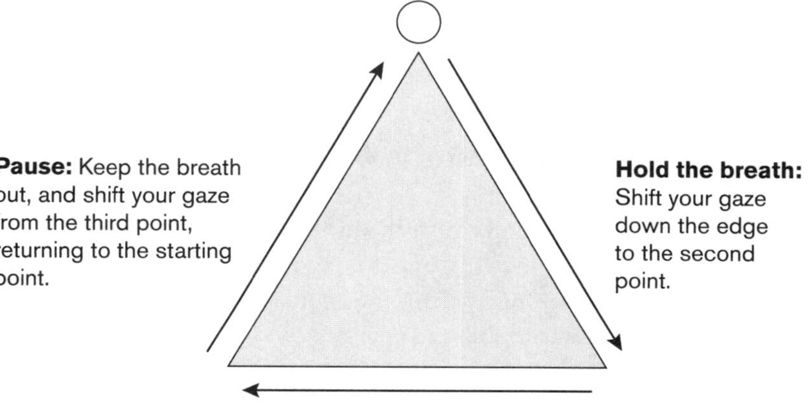

FIGURE A.2: Plaque work diagram: shift on pause

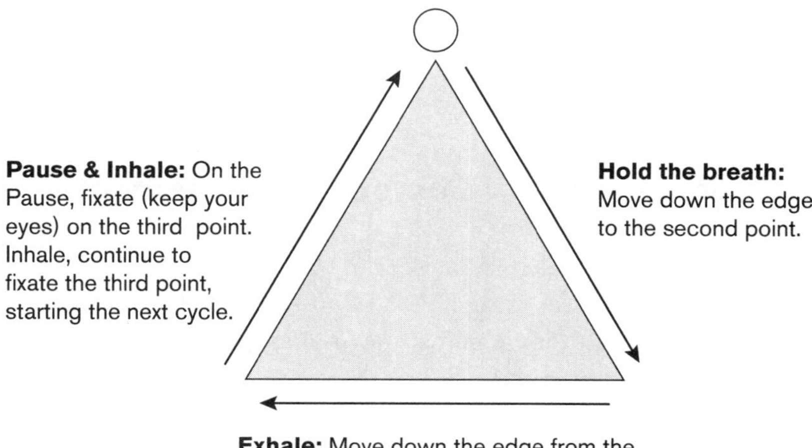

FIGURE A.3: Plaque work diagram: fixate on pause

It will take between four and six weeks of consistent practice each day to run a set of seven alternate nostril cycles without serious lapses of concentration while embodying the Animal tone. Take your time before adding on the last part.

Part D: Energy Visualization

Visualize guiding lines of energy with your spotlight of attention. As you inhale, visualize a light drawn from the plaque to the right nostril, up over the head and down the back on the right side of the spine to the tip of the tailbone. At the tailbone, the energy rounds the corner and travels up the front of the spine to the energy center or chakra of the Animal. On the hold, spin the energy in the chakra clockwise for males or counterclockwise for females. On the exhale, send the energy along the same circuit in reverse on the left side of the spine, over the top of the head, and out the left nostril to the plaque. Repeat the cycle on the other side.

Do not just imagine *seeing* the energy; imagine how it would *feel* if the energy were running this circuit. Start with thick lines of energy in bold colors, and with practice, make the lines thinner and more translucent, imagining the distinct feeling of these subtle lines. It usually takes four to six weeks of regular practice to sustain energetic visualization without lapses in concentration.

Bringing the Four Components Together ...

When we first learned the plaque work, it was taught with all four components at once. You can imagine the effort it demanded and what an effect it produced! But while going to extremes is fun for some, others do better starting simple and building over time. So, the plaque work is broken down here into four parts to make it more accessible. It is best to practice one element for a month to six weeks before adding on another element. Begin with the breathing cycle. When your count and hands are automatic, add the Animal tone.

Next, add on either the timed gaze or the visualized energy. The timed gaze component exercises involve external focus, whereas the energy visualization is more internally focused, and your decision on which to do should be influenced by the Animal you want to practice. Tiger, Panther, and Python are more externally focused, whereas Boa, Cobra, and White Leopard focus more internally. But individual preference and personal goals have a say, so pick the one that seems appropriate. Practice the third add-on until you can complete a full set of seven cycles without lapses in concentration. You can then choose to do all four together.

... And Why

The four components work the four basic elements of embodying the Animals: paying attention outwardly, paying attention internally, taking action outwardly, taking action internally: 1) the timed-gaze of the plaque works the Animal's outward focus, 2) visualizing energy cultivates the Animal's internal focus, 3) voluntary rhythmic breathing is an outward action everyone is capable of, and 4) generating the tone is an internal action—it is the active choice to be something. By combining all four elements, you are practicing the basics of any metaphysical art, which are internal attention and action, and external attention and action.

Energetic Anatomy

The Chakras Figure B.1 shows chakras, which are energy centers corresponding to a type of intelligence and which are associated with glands of the endocrine system. From top to bottom, the chakras are as follows:

Sahasrara: White Leopard's intuition, big picture, creativity.

Ajna: Cobra's psychic insight and energetic perception.

Vishuddha: White Leopard's communication center and energy regulation.

Anahata: Tiger's heart, and the full range of its emotions.

Manipura: Tiger's and Panther's center of physical power.

Svadhisthana: Panther's sexual center, procreative and alchemical cauldron.

Muladhara: Panther and Cobra's vestigial tail and grounding rod.

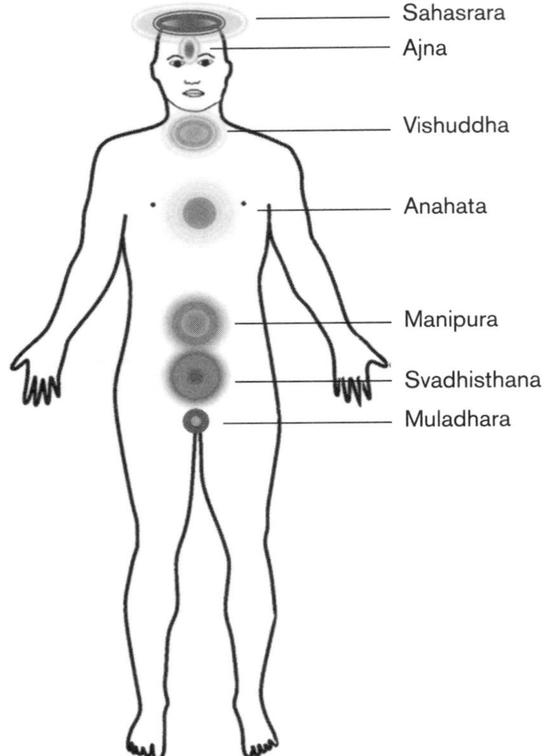

FIGURE B.1: The chakras

The Auras Figure B.2 shows the auras. Each layer corresponds to a chakra, where the top-most chakra is associated with the outer-most layer, and so on. As a crossover point between White Leopard and Boa there is an interstitial layer between each aura which Constantine called the empathic membranes.

Membranes and Pumps Figure B.3 shows the membranes and pumps. The membranes are like energetic diaphragms, working like billows to clear stagnant energy. The pumps do a similar job for the joints. The membranes move with the breath. From the bottom, the 1st, 3rd and 5th membranes expand down on the inhale, and contract up on the exhale. The 2nd, 4th, and 6th (at the crown) membranes expand up on the inhale and contract down on the exhale. The spaces between the membranes are called the membrane packages. Feel the packages expand and contract with the breath. Focus on membrane 1-3 for Panther, 2-4 for Tiger, 4-6 for Leopard. On the inhale, contract your muscles to elongate and deepen the pumps of the joints drawing energy in; on the exhale, relax your muscles to let the pumps "snap back" which propels energy out.

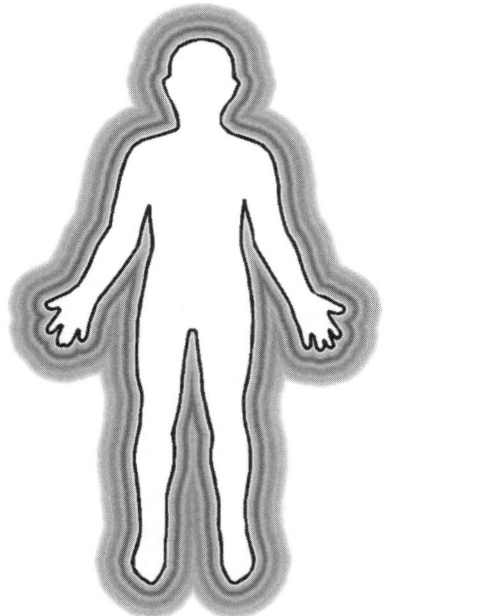

FIGURE B.2: The auras

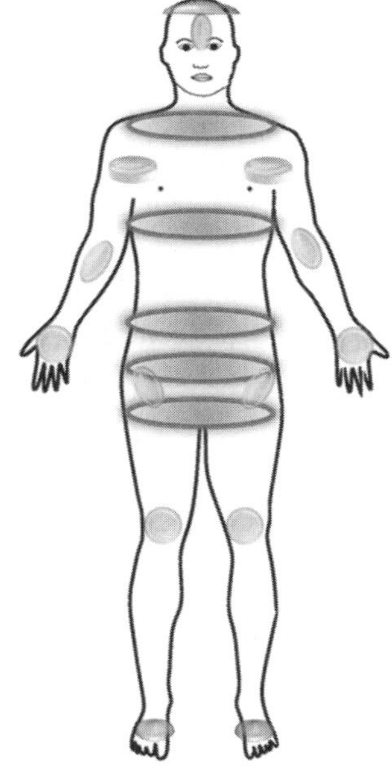

FIGURE B.3: Membranes and pumps

The Streams Figure B.4 shows the streams. The ten streams are distinct from the meridians and the psychic meridians. They support the transport of energy and information throughout the body, propelled by the pumps and membranes. Like the meridians, there is one set on the yin skin and another on the yang. Visualize energy running up the streams of the yin skin on the inhale, and down the streams of the yang skin on the exhale. You can run energy along the streams during bows, stances and the Tree Pose in appendix E.

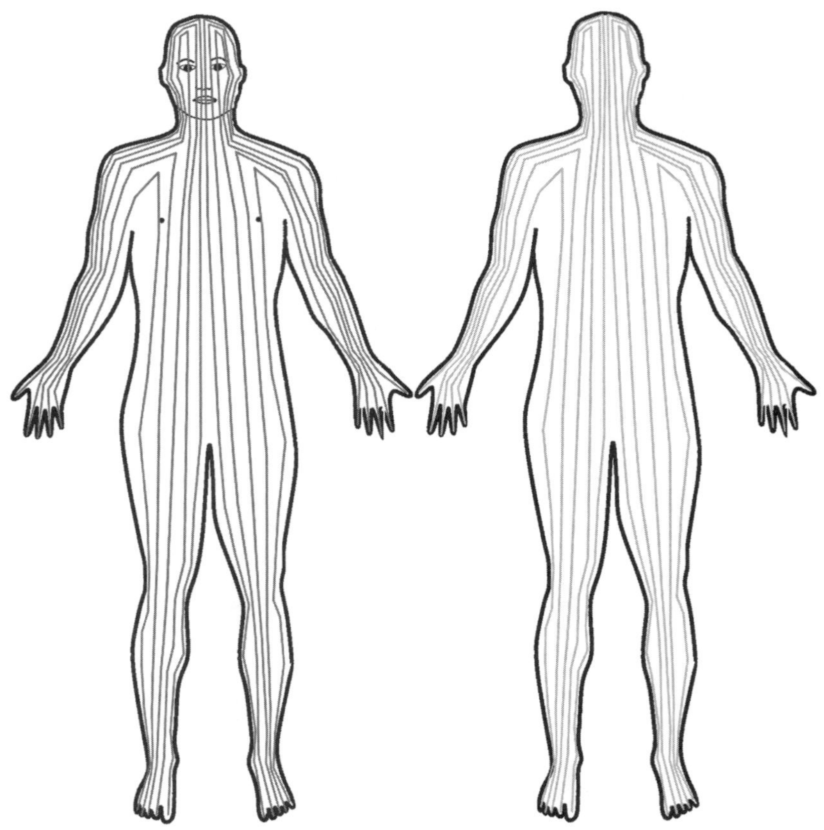

FIGURE B.4: Streams

The Cocoon The Cocoon (Figure B.5) is not a part of the energetic anatomy; rather, it is an energy visualization practice.

Feel a ball, formed of earth, wind, water, and fire energies 1½ feet below the feet. From that ball, spiraling up from right to left, 1½ feet out from the body, see/feel a golden strand of light weaving to another such ball, 1½ feet above the head. Send your consciousness to the first ball and begin a new strand spiraling upward in the opposite direction, from left to right; the second golden thread intermeshes with the first thread.

Now endow the strands of the Cocoon (also known as the Dragon's Womb) with the capacity to attract and keep in positive energies, while drawing out and keeping out unnecessary energies. The Cocoon stretches and shifts, so no matter your motion, it enwraps the whole body 1½ feet away from the skin. Begin by visualizing the balls 6 feet into Earth and into the sky, and then from the center of Earth to the edge of the atmosphere. Finally, dispense with the balls. Using the Cocoon will offer a practice in physical awareness as well as emotional, psychic, and energetic protection, helping you conserve your force for other endeavors in self-development.

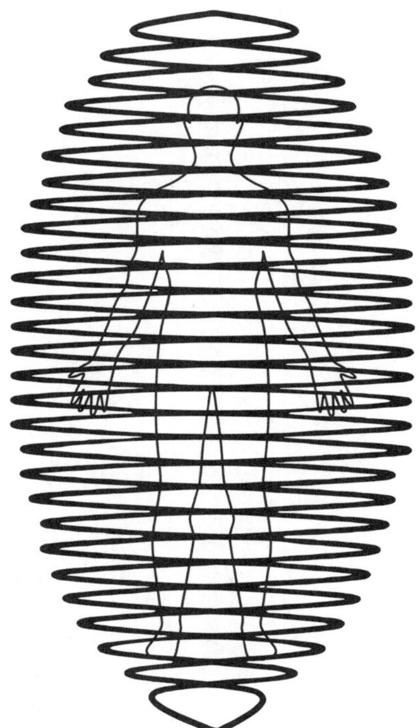

FIGURE B.5: The Cocoon

The Golden Spiral Form the same elemental balls as formed for the Cocoon. Imagine a plumb line going from the top of the head down to the floor. The line follows a functional path, intersecting organs and tissues. See/feel a pencil-thin spiral of energy rising up this center line of the body from one elemental ball 1½ feet below Earth to the other ball 1½ feet above the head. Once formed, with each in-breath, the whole length of the spiral broadens in diameter. Maintain the new expansion during the out-breath; meanwhile, the spiral is rotating on its axis, very much like a brush-spinner in a car wash, dislodging and cleaning any unwanted waste. Keep expanding the diameter of the spiral until it reaches the inside surface of the Cocoon. After practicing for a while, as in the Cocoon, extend the Golden Spiral (Figure B.6) from the center of Earth to the edge of the atmosphere.

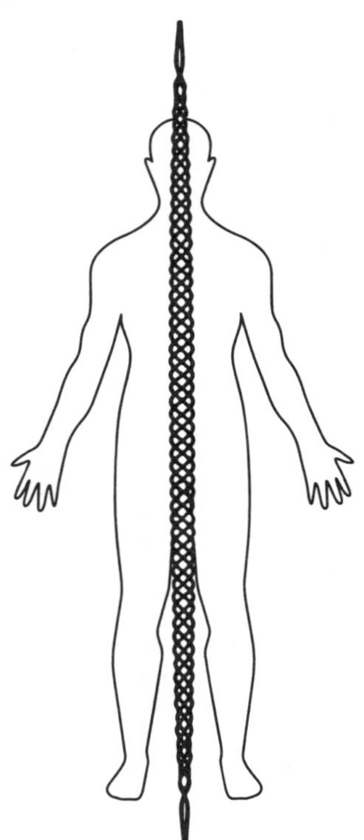

FIGURE B.6: Golden Spiral

FIGURE 3.2: The Boa Plaque: Empathy, the Acceptance of All Things, Yielding and Absorbing.

"Do not speak unless you can improve the silence."—Proverb

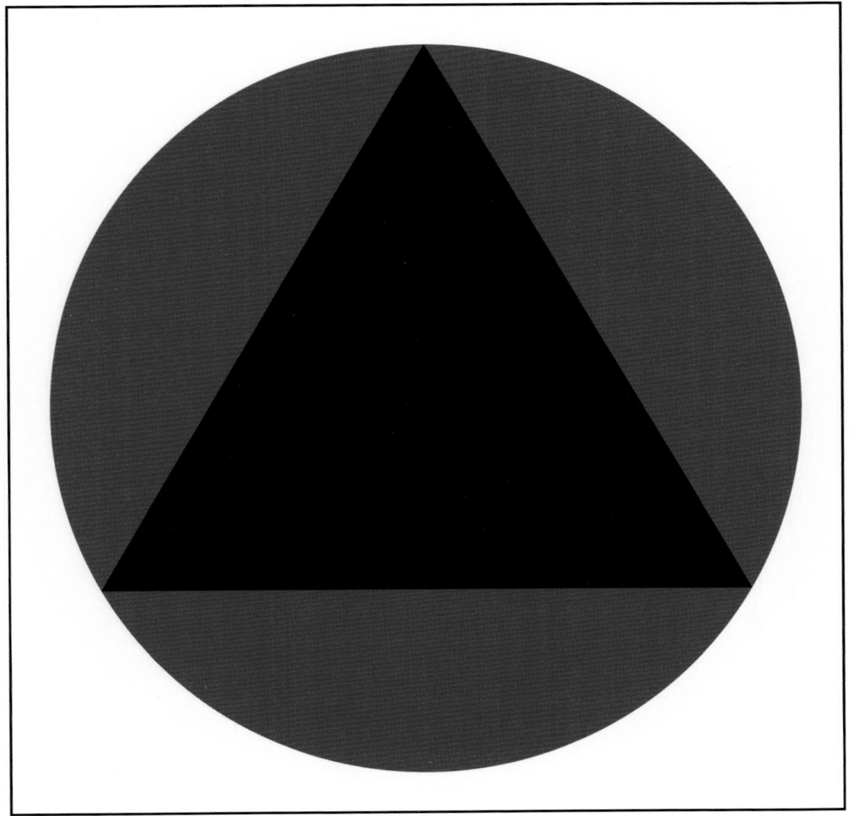

FIGURE 4.1: The Python Plaque: Awareness, Observation, Manipulation.

"The more I study religions the more I am convinced that man never worshipped anything but himself."—Sir Richard Francis Burton

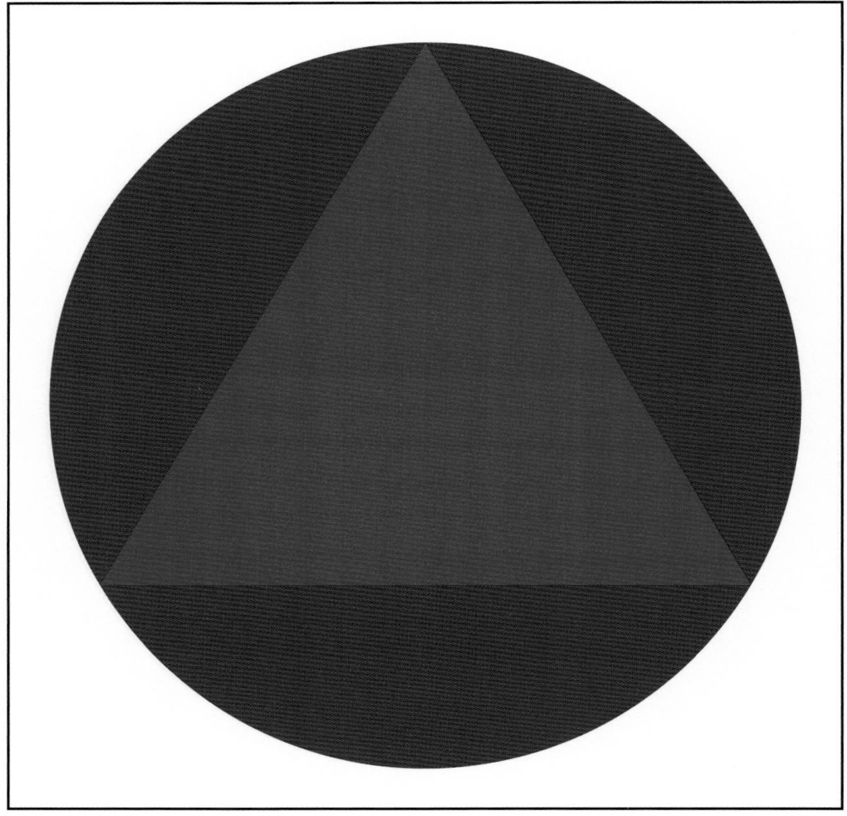

FIGURE 5.1: The Panther Plaque: Senses, Instinct, Reaction.

"The world is so rich, simply throbbing with rich treasures, beautiful souls and interesting people. Forget yourself."—Henry Miller

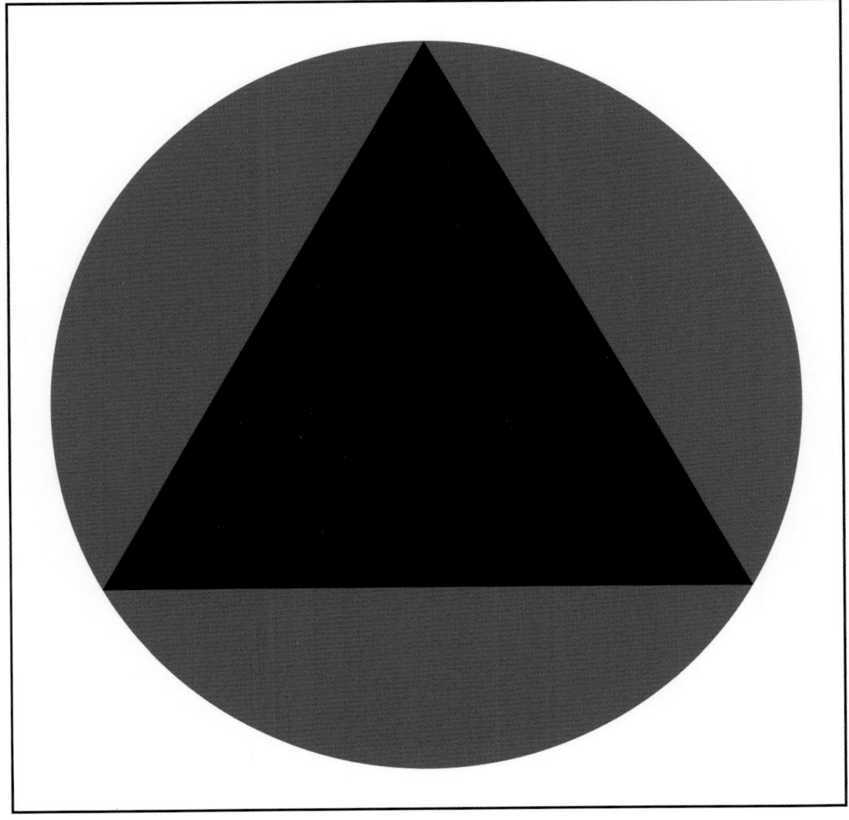

FIGURE 6.1: The Tiger Plaque: Desire, Intent, Action.

"We make a living by what we get, but we make a life by what we give."
—Winston Churchill

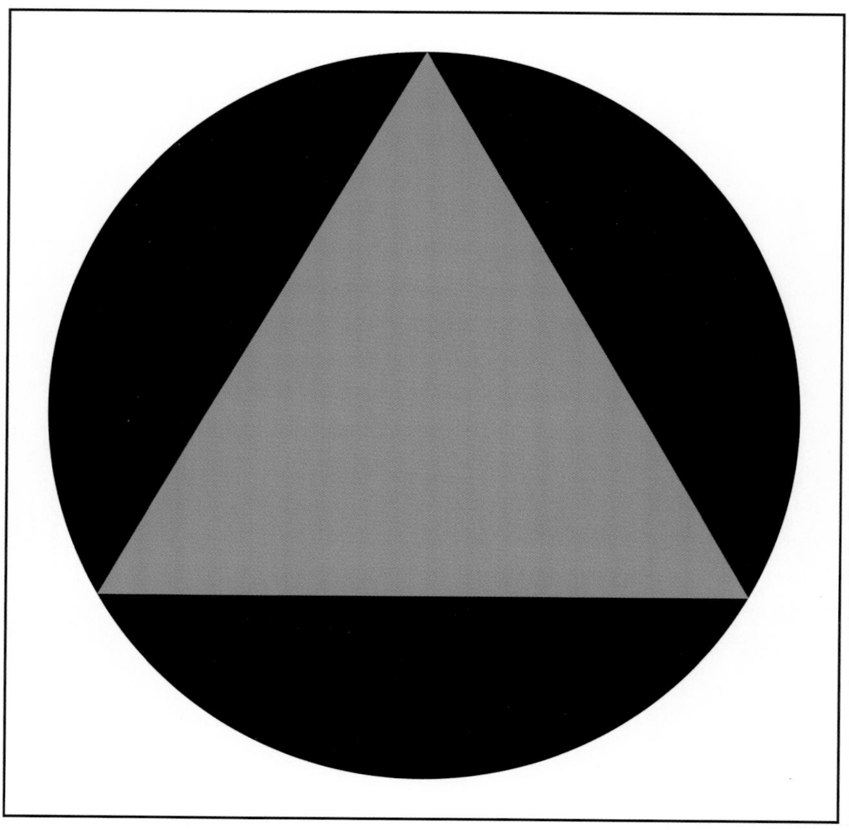

FIGURE 7.1: The White Leopard Plaque: Thought, Intuition, Creativity

"Imagination is more important than knowledge."—Albert Einstein

FIGURE 8.1: The Cobra Plaque: Energetic Awareness, Refinement of Energy.

"If coming events are said to cast their shadows before, past events cannot fail to leave their impress behind them."—H. P. Blavatsky

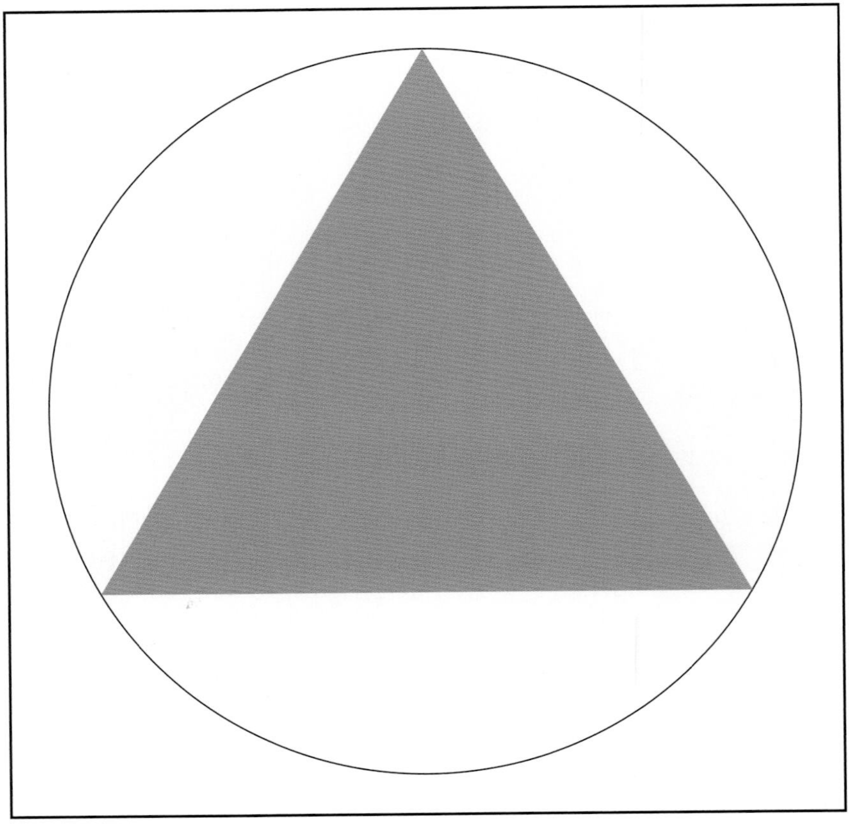

Author performing a standing side thrust from the Dragon form.

Sifu Constantine Darling, 2008, while hiking in the Grand Canyon.

Constantine practicing the quiet mind of Boa at the edge of the Havasupai Falls, Grand Canyon. He never missed a chance to infuse internal work with joy and playfulness.

Constantine practicing a Ch'ien-lung form with students by the Mooney Falls, in the Grand Canyon. There's no app for the personal, immediate, and soul-soothing feeling of invoking energy through movement and breath in nature with friends.

Constantine Darling (center), and Ch'ien-lung instructors, the author (right), and Alisoun Payne (left).

Psychic Meridians Figure B.7 shows the psychic meridians. Called Golden Brocade in other systems, these rivers run up the center of the major limbs and regulate the traditional meridians. They are not included in the Seven Steps as they are part of an advanced seated-practice for Boa: on the inhale, visualize a breeze spiraling in tighter arcs into a psychic meridian, then on the exhale, spiraling outward in the opposite direction. Repeat for each meridian, then for all simultaneously.

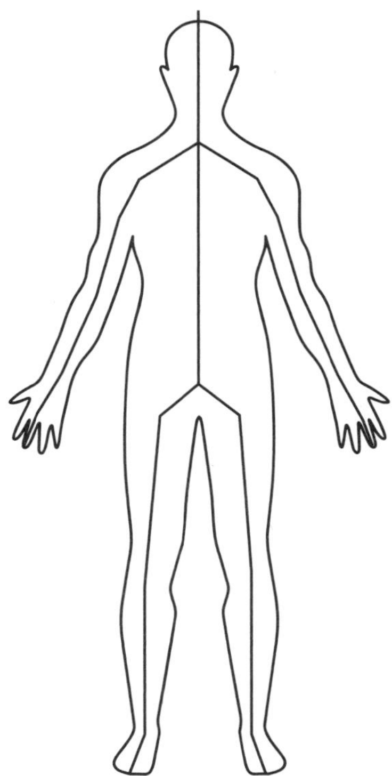

FIGURE B.7: Psychic meridians

PURIFYING

Basic Breaths

The Basic Breaths of the purifying stage reduce tension stemming from poor physical or emotional "posturing." The practice benefits all the Animals, and especially Boa. The Basic Breaths consist of the retention breath, the cleansing breath, the rejuvenation breath, and the *prana* shake.

All Basic Breaths start the same: knees slightly bent, body curled over, head falling comfortably, lungs empty, palms facing forward. They differ in what you do on the inhale, but the pattern of the inhale itself is the same.

1. Fill the lower back, middle back, and upper back with breath.
2. Then fill the lower abdomen, the middle torso sideways, and the upper chest forward and upward.
3. Lift the head upward, as if by a string attached to the back of the head, while the breath pushes the plates of the skull apart.

Retention Breath

From the starting position, begin to inhale, curling up, keeping your head over the pelvis—avoiding strain on the lower back, slowly straightening the knees and letting your head be the last thing up. At the same time, imagine tree roots extending from your feet into the Earth, drawing water and earth energy up both legs. They meet at the belly button, combining into a single line. At the same time, imagine drawing fire and air energy through open channels in the fingers and palms, up both arms. All four lines converge at the manubrium (collarbone junction), and rise up and out through the crown of the head (see Figure C.1).

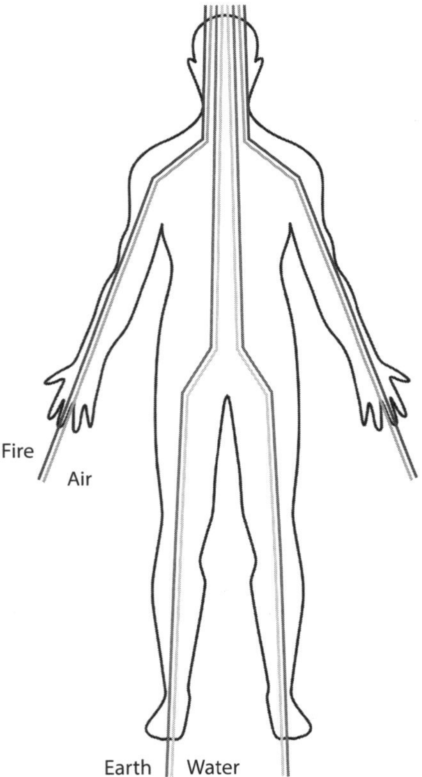

FIGURE C.1: Visualize the elements running along the psychic meridians, with fire and air entering through the fingers, while water and earth rise up the legs.

From the crown of the head, direct the combined energies into the sun, and hold the breath. While holding the breath, visualize it being cleansed and rejuvenated in the sun. When ready, begin to exhale, see/feel the energy descending from the sun, back down through the crown of the head.

On the out-breath, let the chest cave in first, slightly tilting the face to the sky, and keeping the lips pursed, exhale from the mouth. When it feels natural let the head fall towards the chest and curl down, bending your knees. The earth/water energy flows down the arms, while the air/fire energy flows down the legs and out the roots of the feet. The energy brought up the legs goes out the arms and vice versa.

Cleansing Breath

The breath comes in the same way you inhaled for retention breath. On the out-breath, exhale in seven short, forced-out breaths (like blowing out a candle from a distance—seven times). Each out-breath cleans out a chakra: The first clears *sahasrara,* the crown of the head and the center for intuition; second, *ajna,* the third-eye point, the center of psychic awareness; third, *vishuddha,* the throat, center of communication and creativity; fourth, *anahata,* the heart, the emotional center; fifth, *manipura,* located just below the belly button, the storehouse of physical energy; sixth, *svadhisthana,* just behind the pubic bone, the storehouse of sexual energy; seventh, *muladhara* at the tip of the tailbone, the instinctive connection to Earth, functioning very much like a ground in an electrical socket. With each out-breath, you roll down the spine a little until you are hunched over as before, knees bent, head above the pelvis so as not to strain the back.

Rejuvenation Breath

As you inhale, drawing up energy the same way as you did in retention breath, tap the ribcage and abdomen with the tips of the fingers, letting the reverberations resonate through the internal organs, dislodging any stuck matter or energy. When you have filled up with breath and can no longer inhale, cup the palms so the hands make a hollow sound as they continue to strike. Let the sound permeate the skeleton and the internal organs, like an ultrasound massage. As you exhale, bring the hands in front of the face and throat area, casting the out-breath like a waterfall, as your body slowly rolls down one vertebra at a time.

Prana Shake

Inhale, drawing energy in as you did in retention breath, but this time your hands start with the palms turned to the back, and as you inhale, the arms rise so that when you are filled with breath, they are zombie-like straight out in front of you, parallel to each other and to the ground, palms turned down. As the arms rise, the palms, like magnets, attract the energy of the elements into the body. Then hold the breath, turn the palms up, make fists (close the circuits) to lock in the energy. Then, as the name suggests, shake the arms vigorously back and forth by bending and straightening at the elbows. Make sure that when you push your fists away, your elbows are straight and wrists are extended. When you pull your fists back, flex the wrists, and bend the elbows. Let the legs be involved naturally. Do this breath as if you intend to shake the muscles off your bones. Done with focus, this exercise will pack energy into the muscles, skeleton, and internal organs and circulate your cerebrospinal fluid.

Skeletal Alignment

These are not aerobic exercises. This is an unlearning process. Take your time. As you get better, do not go faster, go smoother. Rest before changing directions. After completing an entire exercise, stand and feel your body, and then walk around naturally, being aware of your body. Walk around naturally, noting differences in posture and movement compared to before. What shifts in attitude and focus seem to accompany the physical changes? This is a proprioceptive workout.

Rock 'Round the Clock

Lie on your back, knees bent, feet flat on the floor, with your arms resting at your sides. Imagine the top of the sacrum is 12 o'clock, the tip of the tailbone is 6 o'clock, the right side is 9 o'clock and the left side is 3 o'clock. Rock around the clock:

1. Rock from 12 straight across the clock to 6.
2. Rock from 9 straight across the clock to 3.
3. Rock from 12 o'clock to 3 o'clock.
4. Rock from 12 o'clock to 9 o'clock.
5. Rock from 6 o'clock to 9 o'clock.
6. Rock from 6 o'clock to 3 o'clock.
7. Rock from 9 o'clock through 12 o'clock to 3 o'clock.
8. Rock from 9 o'clock through 6 o'clock to 3 o'clock.
9. Rock around the clock clockwise and then counterclockwise.

Spinal Roll

Lie on your back, knees bent, feet flat. Imagine a tennis-sized ball at the base of your spine. It is heavy enough to press each vertebra into the floor. Roll the ball up and down your spine, pressing one vertebra at a time into the floor. Rest. Repeat five to seven times. Then stand up.

Standing Pose

Figures C.2–C.4 show this pose from the front, side, and back view.

1. Stand feet parallel, shoulder-width apart. Imagine a thumbtack under the sole of each foot, but you cannot step off it, so you lift up the arch of the foot as much as possible.
2. Point the shin bones (and knees) in the same direction as the feet.
3. Straighten the legs without locking the knees, but keep them slightly bent (so you could suddenly squat if you needed to).
4. Align the hips, knees, and ankles in a plumb line.

5. Pull the tailbone straight down so that it flattens the curve of the lower back.
6. Press the hip bones toward each other at the front.
7. Press the iliac crest sideways at the back. Feel the melon at the lower back.
8. Press the pubic bone up toward the sternum.
9. Press the joined ribs toward the sternum.
10. Press the sternum up toward the back of the head.
11. Pull the back of the head straight up toward the sky.

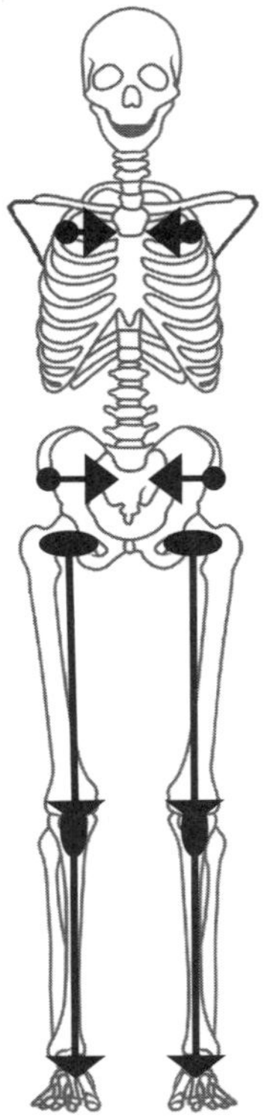

FIGURE C.2: Standing Pose, front

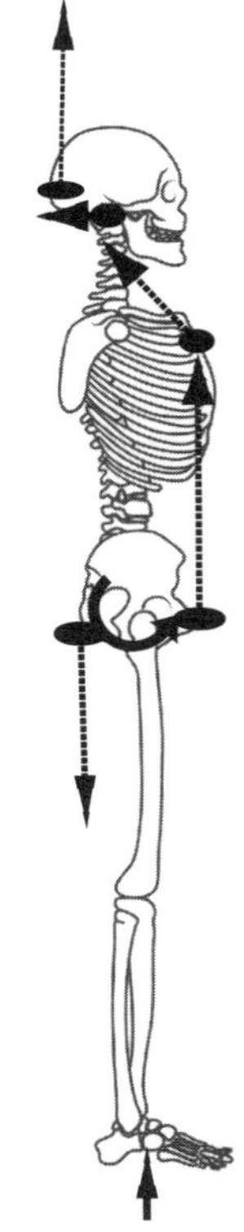

FIGURE C.3: Standing Pose, side

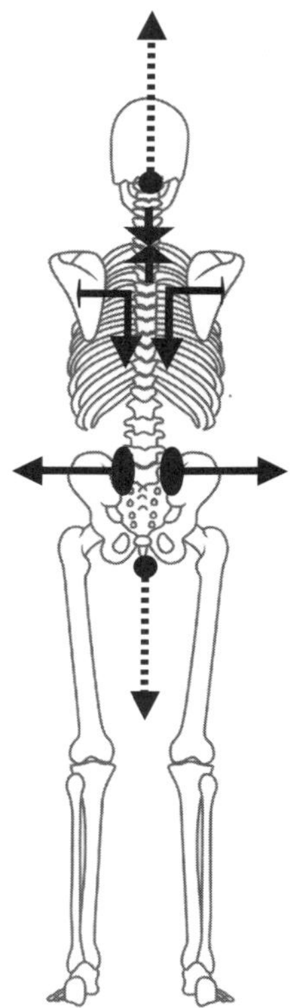

FIGURE C.4: Standing Pose, back

The Melon

Imagine you have a ball of air in the shape of a watermelon located in the pelvis, the narrow ends of the watermelon pressing the hips from the inside.

Breathe deeply, and fill the melon with air. It bulges outward, pressing your hips out sideways, your pubic bone and lower belly forward, and the sacrum and lower lumbar backward.

As you exhale, empty the melon of air, but keep the expanded feeling of the melon—like letting air out of a tire but without letting the tire shape collapse. Keep inhaling and exhaling in this manner.

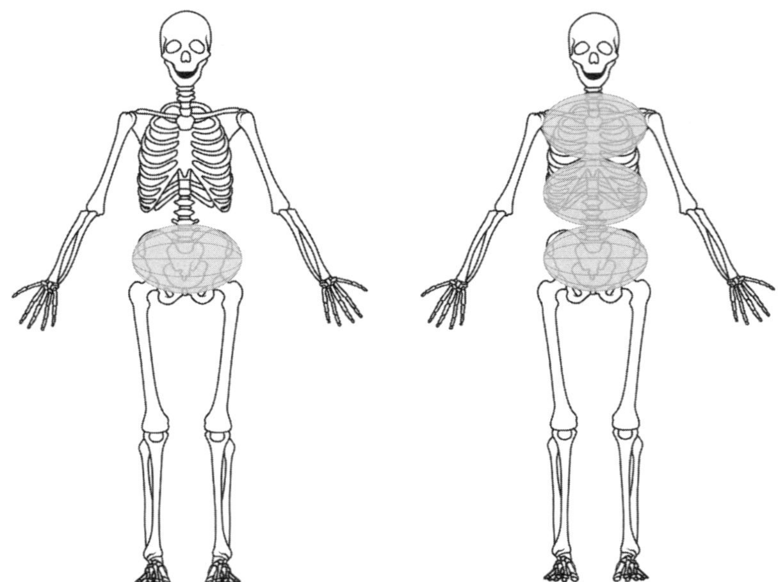

FIGURE C.5: Melon: Visualize a melon-shaped and -sized volume of air between the hips, pushing out front, back, and side to side. Then feel the melon spinning on its axis, going down the back and up the front.

FIGURE C.6: Stacked melons: With more practice, you can visualize three melons, stacked on each other.

For beginners, especially, you can use your hands to provide feedback, placing the hands to feel the expansion of the lower abdomen and back. Finally, doing the melon while lying on your back, using the floor for feedback, is perhaps the most productive exercise in improving movement quality that you will experience.

If you feel competent in creating the melon at the level of the pelvis, then focus on rolling the melon up and down the body. Inhale to fill the melon, and then roll the melon up the body from the base of the spine to the base of the neck. Hold the melon there, and then roll the melon back down as you exhale.

After you practice rolling the melon, practice stacking three melons. The first melon is located between the hips and reaches up to the level of the belly button. The second melon is stacked on top of the first, from the level of the belly button to the heart. The third melon is stacked on top of the second going from the heart to the collar bones. The melons swell, pressing the torso out in each direction, front, back, side, up, and down.

Finally, if you are comfortable with stacking the melons, imagine the melons *spinning*. They spin in places as though they are getting ready to roll up the body. They roll *up the front* and *down the back*.

Scan your body as you do the melon exercises, and watch how you want to adjust your skeletal alignment (Python), your musculature (Tiger), fascia and tendons and ligaments (Panther), nervous energy (Cobra), breathing (Boa), and energy (White Leopard). The Melon breath visualization is excellent for working on power and posture in any sport. Focus on the fundamental skills and postures of your sport, practicing them while incorporating the Melon visualizations, and your body will incorporate the benefits of a martial artist's power posture.

REFINING

Warrior Exercise

For each aspect of consciousness listed, generate a *mudra,* eye-position, tongue position, *mantra, asana,* imagined taste, imagined smell, and imagined sound that, for you, is natural to associate with that aspect of the psyche. You are constructing a personal mythology.

In addition, write one paragraph describing the function or job of that aspect of consciousness and the subjective experience (what it feels like). For example, what is the purpose of the intellect, and what does it feel like to use it well? Then write a paragraph describing how a warrior would use and relate to that facet. For example, what does it mean to be an intellectual warrior? For each facet of the psyche, there is a warrior. Be sure to connect the warrior to its corresponding Animals.

- Psychic
- Intuitive
- Karmic
- Creative
- Physical
- Emotional
- Empathic
- Intellectual
- Dream
- Unconscious
- Subconscious
- Instinctive

Sun and Moon Exercise

This is a group activity, lead by a competent facilitator. The group provides one individual thoughtful reflections on how the person presents themselves outwardly (Sun) and on qualities about themselves they may not be aware of (Moon).

Tree Exercise

This purpose of this exercise is to look at the sociological and psychological influences that made you who you are. Draw a tree, where the soil represents the social and historical influences that acted on your family, such as migration, class struggle, war, and economics. The trunk represents your parents and the psychological dynamics that brought them together. The branches are qualities you possess which you may have inherited or learned from them. The right side of the tree is for the father or the masculine parent, and the left side is for the mother or the feminine parent. The fruits of the tree are the decisions or outcomes along those paths.

Double-Wrapping Exercise

Double wrapping (see Figure D.1) reaffirms the natural opposing spirals of body movement and can be incorporated in the Tree Pose.

Start standing, with feet together and arms down by your side.

1. **Feet:** Imagine that you have a thumbtack under the sole of each foot; you cannot step off of them, so you lift up the arches of the feet as much as possible.
2. **Ankles:** Press the joints of the big toes toward each other, as well as the ridges of the instep and ankles.
3. **Shins:** Line up the ridges of the shin bones with the gap between the big toes and second toes.
4. **Knees:** Press the knees together.
5. **Thighs:** Rotate the thigh bones away from each other.
6. **The Serape:** Feel as if two rubber bands crisscross up the front of the torso and down the back, intersecting at the level of the heart on both sides. The bands are in constant tension, so rotation in one direction causes a slight resistance in the opposite direction.

Review the alignment for the hips, iliac crest, upper ribs, sternum, pubic bone, tailbone, back of the head, and shoulder blades from the Standing Pose in appendix C for additional posture tips.

7. **Armpits:** Deepen the pits of armpits as much as you can.
8. **Collarbones:** Spread the collarbones sideways, and roll them upward along their axis lengthwise.
9. **Upper arm:** Rotate the bone of the upper arm outward without pinching the shoulder blades.
10. **Elbows:** Deepen and lengthen the inside of the elbow joints, and get them to point toward the back and down toward Earth.
11. **Palms:** Deepen the cups of the palms like you are holding a bowl.

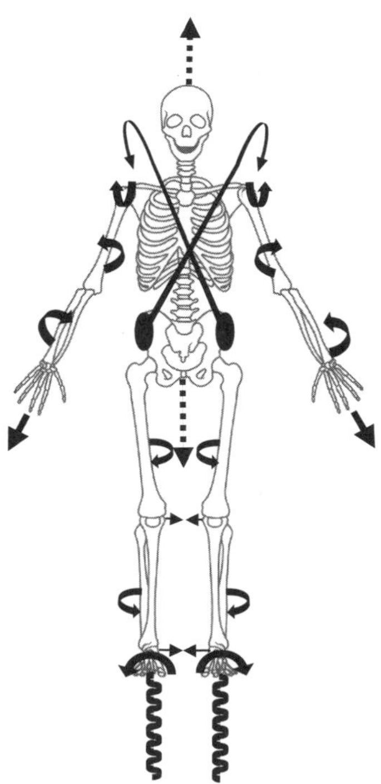

FIGURE D.1: Double wrapping: The body moves in opposing spirals. In static position, rotate the upper limb in the direction opposite the lower limb.

ENERGIZING

Tree Pose

Static exercises like the Tree Pose (see Figure E.1) are not tests in muscular endurance. They are used to train the mind to use breath to dissipate tension and cultivate energy. Small postural adjustments in tandem with the breath redistribute stress, and visualized breath focuses the mind and guides energy.

1. Place your feet shoulder width apart, feet parallel. Imagine the soles of your feet are springing roots that drive deep into Earth. (Or, as an alternative image, imagine the soles of your feet are like drill bits driving into the floor.)
2. Point the shin bones (and knees) in the same direction as the feet.
3. Bend the knees slightly.
4. Pull the tailbone straight down so that it straightens out the curve of the lower back.
5. Press the hip bones toward each other at the front (see "Standing Pose" in appendix C for steps 5–13).
6. Press the iliac crest sideways at the back; feel the melon at the lower back.

7. Press the pubic bone up toward the sternum.
8. Press the joined ribs toward the sternum.
9. Press the sternum up toward the back of the head.
10. Pull the back of the head straight up toward the sky.
11. Press the last cervical vertebrae down onto the first thoracic vertebrae.
12. Press the mandible joint back toward the spine.
13. Slide the shoulder blades down the back and toward the spine.
14. Raise the arms as if hugging a tree or large beach ball. The hands are at the height of the cheek bones, the elbows at shoulder height, bent and pointing toward the floor.
15. Deepen the cups of the armpits (see Figure B.3, Membranes and pumps, in appendix B for steps 15–17).
16. Deepen the inside of the elbow joints, and point the elbows down to the ground.
17. Deepen the cups of the palms.

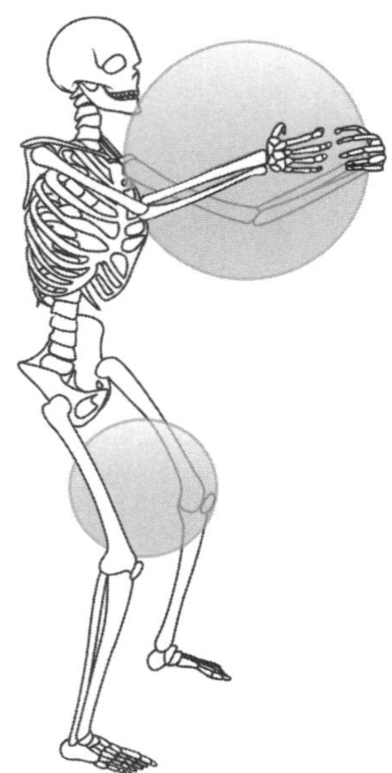

FIGURE E.1: Tree Pose

Energy Visualization

The Tree Pose gives you a chance to explore and steep in the synergy of posture, breath and energy. You take the static pose, then combine it with the energy visualization or ideokinetics of your choice. The possible combinations are endless. Below are a few of my favorites. The practice is life-long and so are the health and wellness benefits.

1. Run energy up the yin skin from the soles of the feet, up the inner thighs, up the midline of the body, the neck, the face to the ears, then down the inside of the arms, focusing on the soft, less hairy skin. Run the energy down the yang skin, going up the arms to the shoulders, to the trapezius, to the back of the head, then down the back, down the legs and feet, following the thicker, hairier skin.
2. Run the energy circuit of the Animal you are practicing.
3. Feel energy run up psychic meridians and down the limbs in the layer between the skin and muscles.
4. Breathe into the anatomy of one Animal at a time.
5. Hold the position while feeling the Cocoon and Golden Spiral, separately, and then together.
6. Breathe, contracting the pumps and membranes going up the body on the inhale and down the body on the exhale.

NOTES

Chapter 1

1 The White Leopard, as it has been called so long as I have been practicing, refers to the snow leopard species in Central Asia. For consistency I use the term White Leopard, alternating on occasion for variety's sake with Snow Leopard and Leopard.

2 Similarly, I will be alternating between Black Panther and Panther, but both terms refer to the same archetypal Animal.

3 The name Ch'ien-lung, Constantine often claimed, meant "celestial" or "heavenly dragon." And, if so, would have used the characters 天龍 (T'ien-lung), which we used originally. He then added that it was named, too, for the reign title (Qianlong) of Aisin Gioro Hongli, the Manchu Emperor during the Qing Dynasty who reigned from 1735–1796—where the namesake origin implies that the martial art was offered as a gift to the Emperor. But this name uses the different characters 乾隆 which mean "Heavenly Prosperity," or "Era of Strong Prosperity." There is simply no known documentation to support either of these claims, and because it is impossible to reconcile the different characters which happen to have similar sounds, it leaves little else to say except that it is a kung-fu. I have chosen to stick with the Wade-Giles form, and leave to later the problem of tracking the lineage. My goal with this book is to present the system as it was taught to me.

4 The Japanese term *budo* is 武道, "the way of war, or of the warrior." The term migrated to China in the early twentieth century using the same characters and meaning, pronounced *wudao. Wushu* in Chinese is 武術 and translates as "warrior arts" or "martial arts." *Budo* and *wushu* are not strictly equivalent; however, they share the 武 character.

5 Constantine Darling, informal conversation, at the bottom of the Grand Canyon at the Havasupai Campground, Thursday July 3, 2008.

Chapter 2

1 Visit www.sixanimalskungfu.com.

2 Vandana Shiva, *Staying Alive: Women, Ecology, and Development* (Oakland, CA: North Atlantic Books, 2016). Gloria Orenstein, Doretta Zemp, and Judith Auerbach, "Rethinking Environmental Choices: The Intersection of Feminism and the Environmental Movement, or What Is Feminist about the Feminist Perspective on the Environment," *American Behavioral Scientist* 37, no. 8 (1994): 1090–1103. "[B]asically it talks about reclaiming what they named the *feminine principle* in India. This has nothing to do with the way we describe the feminine principle ... We in the West tend to associate the feminine with intuition, passivity and submission. In India it is an active principle, not a passive one, and it has to do with the creation of the Earth. In India, the Earth, which is conceived as feminine and therefore creative and intelligent is conceived as having Her own will and will not necessarily yield passively to developmental projects imposed on the land by Western capitalist investment companies. This is called mal(e)development."

3 Orenstein, Zemp, and Auerbach, "Rethinking Environmental Choices." "Ecofeminism is a new movement ... from its outset, included men and women together ... Ecofeminism is the movement that rethinks everything from a completely new perspective of the earth and the cycles of nature."

Chapter 3

1 Davis Guggenheim, *An Inconvenient Truth* (Hollywood, CA: Paramount Pictures, 2006). DVD.

2 Shiu-sing Tong and Pak-ming Hui, "The Last Breath of Caesar," *Physics World*, Accessed September 4, 2013, www.hk-phy.org/articles/caesar/caesar_e.html.

3 Ewald R. Weibel, André Frédérick Cournand, and Dickinson W. Richards, *Morphometry of the Human Lung*, Vol. 1. (Berlin: Springer, 1963).

4 Jason Lederman, "You Can Taste Garlic Through Your Feet." *Popular Science*. December 9, 2016, www.popsci.com/you-can-taste-garlic-with-your-feet.

5 Giuseppe Di Pellegrino, Luciano Fadiga, Leonardo Fogassi, Vittorio Gallese, and Giacomo Rizzolatti, "Understanding Motor Events: A Neurophysiological Study," *Experimental Brain Research* 91, no. 1 (1992): 176–180.

6 Evelyne Kohler, Christian Keysers, M. Alessandra Umilta, Leonardo Fogassi, Vittorio Gallese, and Giacomo Rizzolatti. "Hearing Sounds, Understanding Actions: Action Representation in Mirror Neurons." *Science* 297, no. 5582 (2002): 846–848.

7 Jean Decety and Philip L. Jackson, "The Functional Architecture of Human Empathy," *Behavioral and Cognitive Neuroscience Reviews* 3, no. 2 (2004): 71–100.
8 Andrew N. Meltzoff and Wolfgang Prinz, eds. *The Imitative Mind: Development, Evolution and Brain Bases*, Vol. 6. (Cambridge, UK: Cambridge University Press, 2002).
9 Giacomo Rizzolatti, Leonardo Fogassi, and Vittorio Gallese, "Neurophysiological Mechanisms Underlying the Understanding and Imitation of Action," *Nature Reviews Neuroscience* 2, no. 9 (2001): 661.
10 Sarah C. Nuding, Lauren S. Segers, Kimberly E. Iceman, Russell O'Connor, Jay B. Dean, Donald C. Bolser, David M. Baekey, et al. "Functional Connectivity in Raphé-pontomedullary Circuits Supports Active Suppression of Breathing During Hypocapnic Apnea." *Journal of Neurophysiology* 114, no. 4 (2015): 2162–2186.
11 Jan G. Veening, Trynke de Jong, and Henk P. Barendregt, "Oxytocin-Messages via the Cerebrospinal Fluid: Behavioral Effects; a Review." *Physiology and Behavior* 101, no. 2 (2010): 193–210.
12 Edward Bradford Titchener, Lectures on the Experimental Psychology of the Thought-Processes. (New York: Macmillan, 1909).
13 Peace Pilgrim, *Peace Pilgrim: Her Life and Work in Her Own Words*, (Hemet, CA: Friends of Peace Pilgrim, 1994).
14 Adam Mizner, "Lessons on Song." YouTube. Accessed May 18, 2018. Address N/A.
15 William Blake, "Auguries of Innocence," Accessed April 4, 2017, https://allpoetry.com/Auguries-of-Innocence.
16 *X-Men*, directed by Bryan Singer (2000; Los Angeles: Twentieth Century Fox, 2000).
17 *Phenomenon*, directed by Jon Turteltaub (1996; Burbank, CA: Touchstone Pictures, 1996).
18 *Star Wars Episode IV: A New Hope*, directed by George Lucas (1977; Los Angeles: Twentieth Century Fox, 1977).
19 Ben Brantley. "Mother, Courage, Grief and Song," *New York Times*, August 22, 2006, E1, Arts section, East Coast Edition.
20 *Big Blue*, directed by Luc Besson (1988; Los Angeles, CA: Columbia Pictures).
21 Fynn, *Mister God, This Is Anna* (NY: Ballantine Books, 1978).
22 Peter Wohlleben, *The Hidden Life of Trees*, Translated by Jane Billinghurst (Berkeley: Greystone Books, 2016).
23 Veronica Tonay, *Every Dream Interpreted* (London: Collins and Brown, 2003).

Chapter 4

1 Helen Keller, *The Story of My Life* (New York: Doubleday, 1903).
2 Crystal Heather Kaczkowski and Laura Jean Cataldo, *The Gale Encyclopedia of Fitness, Vol. 2, Skeletal System* (Detroit: Gale, 2012.)

3 Katherine, Tucker, L Kyoko Morita, Ning Qiao, Marian T Hannan, L Adrienne Cupples, and Douglas P Kiel, "Colas, but Not Other Carbonated Beverages, Are Associated with Low Bone Mineral Density in Older Women: The Framingham Osteoporosis Study." *Journal of Clinical Nutrition* 84, 4 (2006): 936–942.

4 Thomas Merton, *The Way of Chuang Tzu* (New York: New Directions, 1969).

5 US National Library of Medicine, "Bone Marrow Diseases," Accessed April 21, 2017, https://medlineplus.gov/bonemarrowdiseases. html.

6 Sergey Makarenko, "Strikes and Kicks, Essentials and Variables" (Lecture, Systema Norcal Seminar, Sacramento, CA, March 24, 2018).

7 Sergey Makarenko, "Parameters of Power" (Lecture, Systema Norcal Seminar, Sacramento, CA, September 23, 2018). Junling Gao, Jicong Fan, Bonnie Wai Yan Wu, Zhiguo Zhang, Chunqi Chang, Yeung-Sam Hung, Peter Chin Wan Fung, and Hin hung Sik. "Entrainment of Chaotic Activities in Brain and Heart During MBSR Mindfulness Training." *Neuroscience Letters* 616 (2016): 218–223, https://doi.org/10.1016/j.neulet.2016.01.001.

8 Erika Erdmann and David Stover, *Beyond a World Divided: Human Values in the Brain-Mind Science of Roger Sperry* (Lincoln, NE: iUniverse, 2000).

9 David Wolman, "The Split Brain: A Tale of Two Halves," *Nature*, 483(2012): 260–263.

10 Edward Rice, *Captain Sir Richard Francis Burton: The Secret Agent Who Made the Pilgrimage to Mecca, Discovered the Kama Sutra, and Brought the Arabian Nights to the West* (New York: Scribner, 1990).

11 Leonard Charles Smithers, ed. *The Book of the Thousand Nights and a Night*, Vol. 10 (London: HS Nichols and Company, 1894).

12 J. R. R. Tolkien, *The Fellowship of the Ring* (New York: Houghton Mifflin Company, 1994); C. S. Lewis, *The Lion, the Witch, and the Wardrobe* (New York: Macmillan, 1950); Frank Herbert, *Dune* (New York: Chilton Books, 1965); J. K. Rowling, *Harry Potter and the Sorcerer's Stone* (New York: A. A. Levine Books, 1998).

13 *Star Trek*. Season 1, Episode 20, "Court Martial." directed by Marc Daniels, aired February 2, 1967, CBS.

14 Paul Ekman, *Emotions Revealed: Recognizing Faces and Feelings to Improve Communication and Emotional Life* (New York: Henry Holt Books, 2007).

15 Sigmund Freud, *Beyond the Pleasure Principle* (London: Penguin, 2003).

16 Robert J. Richards, "Why Darwin Delayed, or Interesting Problems and Models in the History of Science." *Journal of the History of the Behavioral Sciences* 19,1 (1983): 45–53.

17 Robert D. Hare, *Without Conscience: The Disturbing World of the Psychopaths among Us* (New York: Guilford Press, 1999).

18 Michael I. Coates and Marcello Ruta. "Nice Snake, Shame about the Legs." *Trends in Ecology and Evolution* 15,12 (2001): 503–507, Print, DOI: 10.1016/S0169-5347(00)01999-6.

19 Sergey Makarenko, "Fists and Blades, Anatomy of Efficiency" (Lecture, Norcal System Seminar Sacramento, CA, June 30, 2018).
20 Daniel C Dennett, *Consciousness Explained* (New York: Little, Brown and Co, 1991).
21 J. R. R. Tolkien. *The Hobbit* (Boston: Houghton Mifflin Harcourt, 2012); J. R. R. Tolkien, *The Lord of the Rings: One Volume* (Boston: Houghton Mifflin Harcourt, 2012).
22 Herbert, *Dune.*
23 Rowling, *Harry Potter and Sorcerer's Stone.*
24 Sir Arthur Conan Doyle, *The Adventures and Memoirs of Sherlock Holmes* (London: Wordsworth Editions, 1992); *The Usual Suspects,* directed by Singer, Bryan (1995; Universal City, CA: Gramercy Pictures).
25 *The Silence of the Lambs,* directed by Jonathan, Demme (1991; Los Angeles, CA: Orion Pictures).
26 A. P. Orage, *Psychological Exercises* (New York: Red Wheel/Weiser, 1976). By George Gurdjieff's student, A. P. Orage, this is a compendium of concentration exercises to make a Python drool.
27 Veronica Tonay, *Every Dream Interpreted* (London: Collins and Brown, 2003). Full disclosure, she is my wife and, of course, the best dream interpreter I have ever met.

Chapter 5

1 John P. J. Pinel, *Introduction to Biopsychology* (New York: Pearson Higher Education, 2015).
2 James Edward Gordon, *Structures: Or Why Things Don't Fall Down* (Boston: Da Capo Press, 2003).
3 Daniel Goleman, *Emotional Intelligence* (New York: Bantam Books, 1995).
4 Arthur S. P. Jansen, Xay Van Nguyen, Vladimir Karpitskiy, Thomas C. Mettenleiter, and Arthur D. Loewy, "Central Command Neurons of the Sympathetic Nervous System: Basis of the Fight-or-Flight Response," *Science* 270, no. 5236 (1995): 644–646.
5 John Dobbing and Jean Sands, "Quantitative Growth and Development of Human Brain," *Archives of Disease in Childhood* 48, no. 10 (1973): 757–767.
6 Charles Stanley Nott, *Teachings of Gurdjieff, the Journal of a Pupil* (Abingdon-on-Thames, UK: Routledge and K. Paul, 1961).
7 Nott, Teachings of Gurdjieff.
8 Anthony Stevens, *Jung: A Very Short Introduction,* Vol. 40 (Oxford: OUP Oxford, 2001).
9 James P McMullen, *Cry of the Panther* (New York: McGraw-Hill Book Company, 1985).

10 Thomas W. Meyers, *Anatomy Trains: Myofascial Meridians for Manual and Movement Therapists* (New York: Churchill Livingstone 2001), 280.
11 Barbara Ehrenreich, *Dancing in the Streets: A History of Collective Joy* (New York: Macmillan, 2007).
12 *The Opposite of Sex*, directed by Don Roos (1998; Los Angeles, CA: Rysher Entertainment).
13 Nikos Kazantzakis, *Zorba the Greek* (New York: Simon and Schuster, 2012).
14 *Star Wars Episode IV: A New Hope*, directed by George Lucas (1977; Los Angeles, CA: Twentieth Century Fox).
15 Joseph Campbell and Bill Moyers, *The Power of Myth* (New York: Anchor, 2011).
16 *Star Trek: The Next Generation*, Season 1, Episode 1–2, "Encounter at Farpoint," directed by Cory Allen, aired September 28, 1987, CBS.
17 *Pan's Labyrinth*, directed by Guillermo Del Toro (2006; Los Angeles: Warner Bros).
18 *Chocolat*, directed by Lasse Hallström (2000; Los Angeles: Miramax Films).
19 *Fight Club*, directed by David Fincher (2000; Los Angeles: 20th Century Fox).
20 *No Reservations*, produced and created by Zero Point Zero Production, aired 2005–2012, on Travel Channel.
21 Frank Herbert, *Dune* (New York: Chilton Books, 1965).

Chapter 6

1 Peter Demianovich Ouspensky, *In Search of the Miraculous: Fragments of an Unknown Teaching* (Boston: Houghton Mifflin Harcourt, 2001).
2 William Shakespeare, *Henry V* (Boston: Riverside, 1973).
3 Wynn Kapit and Lawrence M. Elson. *The Anatomy Coloring Book* (New York: Harper and Row, 1977).
4 Jennifer E. Stellar, Adam Cohen, Christopher Oveis, and Dacher Keltner, "Affective and Physiological Responses to the Suffering of Others: Compassion and Vagal Activity." *Journal of Personality and Social Psychology* 108, no. 4 (2015): 572.
5 Jennifer E. Stellar and Dacher Keltner, "Compassion in the Autonomic Nervous System," *Compassion: Concepts, Research and Applications* (2017): 120.
6 Michael S. Gazzaniga, *The Cognitive Neurosciences* (Cambridge, MA: MIT Press, 2004); Jamie Ward, *The Student's Guide to Cognitive Neuroscience* (London: Psychology Press, 2015).
7 John P. J. Pinel, *Introduction to Biopsychology* (New York: Pearson Higher Ed, 2015).
8 Steven Pinker, *How the Mind Works* (New York: W. W. Norton and Company. 1999).

9 Duane E. Haines, *Fundamental Neuroscience for Basic and Clinical Applications E-Book* (Elsevier Health Sciences, 2006); Chad E. Forbes and Jordan Grafman, "The Role of the Human Prefrontal Cortex in Social Cognition and Moral Judgment," *Annual Review of Neuroscience* 33 (2010): 299–324.
10 *Raga,* directed by Howard Worth (London: Apple Films, 1971).
11 Ouspensky, *In Search of the Miraculous.*
12 DeNeen L. Brown, "They Didn't #TakeTheKnee: The Black Power Protest Salute That Shook the World in 1968," *Washington Post,* September 24, 2017, https://www.washingtonpost.com/news/retropolis/wp/2017/09/24/they-didnt-takeaknee-the-black-power-protest-salute-that-shook-the-world-in-1968/
13 Ouspensky, *In Search of Miraculous.*
14 Josh Gottheimer, *Ripples of Hope: Great American Civil Rights Speeches* (New York: Civitas Books, 2009).
15 Gottheimer, *Ripples of Hope.*
16 Gottheimer, *Ripples of Hope.*
17 Aaron Antonovsky, *Unraveling the Mystery of Health: How People Manage Stress and Stay Well* (San Francisco, CA: Jossey-Bass, 1987).
18 Emily Grijalva, Peter D. Harms, Daniel A. Newman, Blaine H. Gaddis, and R. Chris Fraley, "Narcissism and Leadership: A Meta⊠analytic Review of Linear and Nonlinear Relationships," *Personnel Psychology* 68, no. 1 (2015): 1–47.
19 Michael Colgan, *The New Power Program: New Protocols for Maximum Strength* (Vancouver: Apple Publishing, 2001).
20 Matthew J. Hertenstein, Dacher Keltner, Betsy App, Brittany A. Bulleit, and Ariane R. Jaskolka, "Touch Communicates Distinct Emotions," *Emotion* 6, no. 3 (2006): 528–533.

Chapter 7

1 Marian C. Diamond, Arnold B. Scheibel, Greer M. Murphy Jr., and Thomas Harvey, "On the Brain of a Scientist: Albert Einstein," *Experimental Neurology* 88, no. 1 (1985): 198–204.
2 Charles Spence, "Multisensory Attention and Tactile Information-Processing," *Behavioural Brain Research* 135, no. 1–2 (2002): 57–64.
3 Steven Pinker, *How the Mind Works* (New York: W. W. Norton and Company, 1997).
4 Steven Pinker, The Stuff of Thought: Language as a Window into Human Nature. (New York: Penguin, 2007): 45–47.
5 Steven Pinker, How the Mind Works (New York: W. W. Norton and Company. 1999): 291.
6 "The Pituitary Gland," YouTube Online Video 21:25, Posted by Ray Cinti, October 7, 2013, www.youtube.com/watch?v=f6x_p666Vm4&t=1s.

7 Kai Bird and Martin J. Sherwin, *American Prometheus: The Triumph and Tragedy of J. Robert Oppenheimer* (New York: Knopf, 2005).

8 James Gleick, *Genius: The Life and Science of Richard Feynman,* (New York: Vintage, 1992).

9 *No Ordinary Genius,* directed by Christopher Sykes, produced by Christopher Sykes Productions, aired January 25, 1993, BBC.

10 Dorothy Day, *Long Loneliness* (San Francisco: Harper, 1997).

11 Jess Stearn and Dan Lazar, *Edgar Cayce, the Sleeping Prophet* (New York: Doubleday, 1967).

12 *Kung Fu,* created by Ed Spielman, Jerry Thorpe, Herman Miller, produced by Jerry Thorpe, aired October 14, 1972–April 16, 1975, ABC.

13 Sogyal Rinpoche, *The Tibetan Book of Living and Dying: A Spiritual Classic from One of the Foremost Interpreters of Tibetan Buddhism to the West* (New York: Random House, 2012).

14 Samuel Beckett, *Cascando and Other Short Dramatic Pieces* (New York: Grove Press, 1968).

15 Neil Powell, "Yeats, W. B. (1865–1939)," In *British Writers, Retrospective Supplement 1,* edited by Jay Parini (Detroit: Charles Scribner's Sons, 2002) 325–339, www.cengage.com.

16 Mary H. Guindon and Fred J. Hanna, "Coincidence, Happenstance, Serendipity, Fate, or the Hand of God: Case Studies in Synchronicity," *The Career Development Quarterly* 50, no. 3 (2002): 195–208.

17 Veronica Tonay, *The Creative Dreamer: Using Your Dreams to Unlock Your Creativity* (Berkeley, CA: Celestial Arts, 2012).

Chapter 8

1 Leon Chaitow, *Cranial Manipulation: Theory and Practice—Osseous and Soft Tissue Approaches* (New York: Elsevier Health Sciences, 2005).

2 Veronica Tonay, *Every Dream Interpreted* (London: Collins & Brown, 2003).

3 Carl Gustav Jung, "Synchronicity: An Acausal Connecting Principle," from Vol. 8. of the *Collected Works of CG Jung* (Princeton, NJ: Princeton University Press, 2010).

4 Biography.com Editors, "Joan of Arc Biography," Biography.com, April 2, 2014, www.biography.com/people/joan-of-arc-9354756.

5 Juan Manuel García-Ruiz, Roberto Villasuso, Carlos Ayora, Angels Canals, and Fermín Otálora. "Formation of Natural Gypsum Megacrystals in Naica, Mexico." *Geology* 35, no. 4 (2007): 327–330.

6 Chicago Botanic Garden, "Century Plant," Chicagobotanic.org, accessed October 2, 2018, www.chicagobotanic.org/plantinfo/century_plant.

7 Morgan Robertson, *The Wreck of the Titan or Futility* (New York: MF Mansfield, 1898).

8 *X-Men,* directed by Bryan Singer (2000; Los Angeles: Twentieth Century Fox, 2000).

9 *Into the West,* directed by Mike Newell (Los Angeles, CA; Miramax Family Films, 1992).

10 Erica L. Morley and Daniel Robert, "Electric Fields Elicit Ballooning in Spiders," *Current Biology* 28, no. 14 (2018): 2324–2330.

11Gabriel S. Weyman, "Laboratory Studies of the Factors Stimulating Ballooning Behavior by Linyphiid Spiders (Araneae, Linyphiidae)," *Journal of Arachnology* (1995): 75–84.

12 Gorham, Peter W. "Ballooning Spiders: The Case for Electrostatic Flight," arXiv preprint arXiv:1309.4731 (2013).

13 Ed Yong, "Spiders Can Fly Hundreds of Miles Using Electricity," *Atlantic,* July 5, 2018, www.theatlantic.com/science/archive/2018/07/the-electric-flight-of-spiders/564437/.

14 Russell Targ and Jane Katra, *Miracles of Mind: Exploring Nonlocal Consciousness and Spiritual Healing* (San Francisco: New World Library, 1999).

INDEX

Italic page numbers indicate illustrations. "i-" before a page number indicates the color insert.

Symbol

A

B

C

E

F

G

H

I

J

K

L

N

O

P

Q

R

S

ABOUT THE AUTHOR

© copyright SJSU, photo by Robert C. Bain

STEVEN MACRAMALLA, founder and chief instructor at Six Animals Kung-Fu in Santa Cruz, California, has over thirty years of experience in practicing Ch'ien-lung. Holding a PhD in Cognitive Psychology, Steven previously worked at NASA Ames before joining San Jose State University as a lecturing professor. He lives with his lovely wife in Santa Cruz.

About North Atlantic Books

North Atlantic Books (NAB) is an independent, nonprofit publisher committed to a bold exploration of the relationships between mind, body, spirit, and nature. Founded in 1974, NAB aims to nurture a holistic view of the arts, sciences, humanities, and healing. To make a donation or to learn more about our books, authors, events, and newsletter, please visit www.northatlanticbooks.com.

North Atlantic Books is the publishing arm of the Society for the Study of Native Arts and Sciences, a 501(c)(3) nonprofit educational organization that promotes cross-cultural perspectives linking scientific, social, and artistic fields. To learn how you can support us, please visit our website.

To Reva Noel,
May you be blessed
during you retirement,
you have served the
CASA well, now
enjoy!

your CASA friend
Bonnie L. [illegible]

703 Wagner St.
Elkhart In.

Reflections of Perseverence

by

Bonnie R. Clark

Bloomington, IN

Milton Keynes, UK

AuthorHouse™
1663 Liberty Drive, Suite 200
Bloomington, IN 47403
www.authorhouse.com
Phone: 1-800-839-8640

AuthorHouse™ UK Ltd.
500 Avebury Boulevard
Central Milton Keynes, MK9 2BE
www.authorhouse.co.uk
Phone: 08001974150

First published by AuthorHouse 3/29/2007

ISBN: 978-1-4259-6819-9 (sc)

Printed in the United States of America
Bloomington, Indiana

This book is printed on acid-free paper.

This book is written in memory of my dear mother, the late Daisy M. Burson, who is the source of my existence and the coming about of this book.

Acknowledgements

Thanks are given to my late mother, late step-father and brother. Also, I give thanks to my sister and brother for the experience of 703 Wagner. I also thank the many people who helped me to write this book. I give a huge thank you to my husband who tried to be patient with me and my children who always encouraged me along the way. I love you all very much. Without all of your help this book would never have been possible. Finally, Thanks be to God who has kept me focused when I thought it was impossible. I've always known but have truly experienced that trusting in God makes all things possible. This book is also for my grandchildren to allow them to know and remember how I grew up and survived in the early days when living as an African-American was more of a challenge and held more struggles than they currently have to face.

Forward

It all began when I was four years old in 1939. I was told we were moving from St. Joe Street, which was predominately African-American, to 703 Wagner. My mother, Daisy Lyons, was a domestic worker on Goshen Avenue and my step-father to be, Austin B. Burson, was a carpenter. One day while my mother was working on Goshen Avenue, Austin was working across the street building bleachers at what would become Rice Field and he came to the house on Goshen Avenue seeking to fill his water jug. Daisy was working that day and she answered the door. Thus begins the friendship that would lead to Wagner St.

Chapter 1: From St. Joe to Wagner

Months later after the friendship between Daisy and Austin began my mother told us we were going to be moving. St. Joe St. I knew, but Wagner I knew nothing about. I had never even heard of that street. I lived in the 400 block of St. Joe in a house where I was also born. I survived this street and was blessed for when I was a baby my two brothers set fire to the couch by taking coals out of the stove, playing cowboys and Indians, starting campfires and silly boy games. My mother told me how she had to rescue me from my crib.

After a long courtship with Mr. Burson my mother fell in love with Austin when I was 4 years old. She told us she was getting married to a carpenter by trade, although in the 1930's Blacks were not issued a journeyman's card and were not allowed to be members of the union. Our house at 703 was directly in front of the New York Central Rail house where trains would be lined up out front. There were only four houses on Wagner Street due to this. The four houses in this area were all occupied by white families except for the second one, which would be our residence. The rest of the area was empty lots and an alley. On the block behind us, lived two old sisters named Ms. Mary Ann and Ms. Vester. They had no electricity and dipped snuff. I can remember Ms. Vester's out house always had an odor and my step-father was always after her to keep it from smelling. He would get so angry and sometimes curse her out. I liked it when he did this.

I didn't like the house when we moved into it. I found that it had an old fashion sink in the kitchen that I could not reach. To get a glass of water I remember crying a lot so my step-father finally made a stool for me so I could reach the sink. Unlike many of the other families we had running water but it still felt like we were living in the country because Wagner was a dirt street, unpaved like St. Joe Street. We had a pump in the back yard when we first moved in and we had to pour water down it to prime it before we could actually pump the water out. I could hardly wait until I was old enough to pump it because it always looked fun. Since we had running water Austin made us a bathroom but before this we would have to take our Saturday night bath in a No. 2 tin tub in the living room by the stove. My sister, Phyllis and I had to bathe together and our mother would have to heat our pail of water on the stove in the living room. In the summer months we used the gas stove to heat the water. We kept a little bottle of gas because there were no gas lines on the street until years later. This is not to say that we were unclean, we washed up everyday but Saturday was bath day. This may seem rather primitive, the way we had to live, because we were up north and not down south where these living conditions were normal. Mother had to wash our clothes in a big black pot in the back yard because we had no washing machine. Then one day we got a washing machine, a Maytag, with a ringer on it. We had to have two tin tubs to rinse the clothes in. Mother let me shake the bluing in the first tub to whiten the clothes. Sometimes she would let me put them through the ringer. This was fun until I got older and it became a chore, not a choice. Phyllis got to help mom more often than I did and I never understood why. I guess it was because she was a year older and I was always referred to as the baby.

As we were growing up some of the things we did was listen to the radio on Saturday and Sunday nights. The one program we looked forward to was the Shadow Knows. This was a big hit in our house but I found myself afraid to go to sleep in the dark. I tried to be the first to get to bed so I didn't have to turn off the lights, but this didn't always work because my sister caught on to what I was doing and she would beat me to bed. I soon grew out of the fear. We would also sit and listen to the Grand-ole Opera and Randy Record Shop would play the blues and gospel. This was always a marvelous time. My mother loved to sing gospel music and she could sing like a bird. Our radio only got turned on during these times or on special occasions because we had to keep the electric bill down. On some good days our step-dad would tell us stories about growing up in the Mississippi Delta. I loved to hear him tell these tales for I was glad I didn't have to grow up there. Times then were much harder than when I was growing up. He would tell us how they had to pick cotton and say "yes sir" to children their own age.

The day came when we no longer had the stove in the living room because our step-dad had received a used furnace and installed it in the basement. He had to dig out the basement in order to fit it into the house. My brothers helped him to do this and boy was that hard work. After that our house became the spot to be at. People wanted to come over to see what it looked like to have a furnace and no stove in the living room. We were the only family on Wagner Avenue to have a furnace and indoor plumbing. Dad had to cut a hole in the living room floor to install a register which was large enough to heat our seven room house. We had what you call a Michigan type basement which means we had a dirt floor basement. In the winter mother would dry our clothes over the register on a wooden rack. She would also use the clothes line on the back porch in the winter. On cold sunny days she would hang them outside and bring them inside while they were frozen and stand them by the register to thaw them out. It was amazing how the clothes would be dry in no time.

Now as far as our bathroom goes, my step-dad installed that off from the porch and this was without heat. When we went in there we had to use the kerosene heater to take a bath. We also moved our No. 2 tin tub in there. He installed the sewer line and then put a toilet in there. We had to draw water to pour into the toilet to flush it because there was not a water line yet, that came later. We got a used bathtub from a construction site my step-dad had worked and he bought it home to replace the tin tub. The water issue stayed the same but at least now we had a 'real' bathtub. Later my dad got a tank and installed that and somehow rigged a line from the furnace to the tank so we had hot water in the winter. This only worked in the winter because that is when we would use the furnace. That water was so hot in the winter that it could burn you. When we told our friends about our bathroom and hot water they were fascinated and we were proud. The bathroom remained un-insulated so we still had to hurry out of the bathroom to dry off and get dressed.

Chapter 2: My Journey Begins

I am the youngest of four children and I have two older brothers, Curtis and Fitzhugh, and Phyllis my sister. My bothers went to a private school called St. Vincent before we moved to 703. After the move they had to attend a new school called South Side which was located on Cleveland Avenue. This was an all black school. At that time integration was not an option and not heard of. Phyllis was in the first grade and I was left at home because of my late birthday. Since I was left at home I would have to go to work with my mother or if my step-dad didn't have work I would stay home with him. I thought that was fun.

By now we had a regular little chicken farm in our backyard. Dad had made a chicken house and would order chickens through the mail and when they arrived my sister and I would help him count them and pick the peak off their bills. We would give them medicine with a dropper and I remember squeezing them and how soft they felt. I sometimes squeezed them too tightly and they would die after a few days and my dad never knew why. Next we got a banny rooster to be with the banny chickens so they could lay eggs. We had another rooster for the hens to keep them laying eggs. I used to stay outside and watch the chickens and hens because I hated to stay inside the house because I never really liked that house. The banny rooster didn't like us so I had fun teasing him and he would chase me up to the back porch. He would spread his wings and run like hell at me. Phyllis would sing this song called, "You gotta stand the test in judgment" and this seem to make the rooster even angrier. I would call for my dad to save me from his attack. This rooster was so bad that he would flare up at my dad too so he would shoo him back to the hen house. When we wanted to have more fun we called our friends to come over and join in. All the chicks and hens ran loose in the back yard unless they got into trouble. We kept plenty of fresh eggs and I had entertainment. In the winter the chickens would be brought inside to keep them from freezing. We bought in about eight chickens and one rooster. They would lay their eggs in the ledges and Phyllis and I would gather them up. In order to keep the basement clean dad would rake the basement floor getting the chicken droppings up and haul them outside in a bucket. Believe it or not this did not smell, or if it did we were too used to it to notice. This also kept us with fresh chickens for Sunday dinner.

Curtis and Fitzhugh had the job of killing the chickens for dinner. Dad taught them how to do it and it wasn't long before Phyllis and I were involved in the often challenging task of catching the chicken and trying to kill it. To kill the chicken you had to catch it, hold it down on the chopping block while the other person got the ax and chopped the head off. The first time Phyllis and I did this she thought she had the head off and I let go of the chicken and the chicken took off with its head half off so we had to catch it again and finish the job. Until then I didn't know a chicken could run with its head cut off. After the slaughter we would put the chicken in a tub of scalding hot water in order to pluck the feathers so that mother could clean the chicken. This was never fun or my choice, but we had to eat.

My mother kept her vegetables on a ledge downstairs that was left from the digging out of the basement furnace. This area kept all of her vegetables and canned fruit cold. My dad kept his homemade wine down there and grape juice. I was not allowed to go down there by myself. We had a cold cellar outside of the basement where we would store our cabbage, carrots and beets in there in the winter. Getting back to the beverages stored in the basement, Fitzhugh often thought it fun to play church down in the basement with him being the preacher and Phyllis and I being the congregation. Of course we would only do the communion service so we could partake of the grape juice. One time we got the wine instead of the juice and we thought the taste was different but we kept drinking it anyways. Little did we know this would make us sicker than dogs and by the time we were done playing church we were a little tipsy! Boy did we get into trouble. Needless to say we did not play church anymore.

When winter rolled around this time we had a man who would dump coal through a window in the basement that was our coal bin. Dad kept the pipes from freezing by wrapping them in rags. Isabel Coal Company was located right down the street from us and they made the deliveries every 2 weeks in the winter. Sometimes we would run out of coal if it was extremely cold and dad would have to stroke the fire in the furnace during the night to keep the heat going or sometimes dad would have us sneak out at night and go across the street to the rail yard and pick up coals and fill our buckets. If we couldn't get enough off the ground, Fitz would climb in one of the engines and toss down coals to us. It took two of us to carry one bucket home. We knew stealing was wrong but sometimes there is a fine line between survival and greed. This happened about twice a week. Curtis and Fitz learned how to stroke the fire too. One night Fitz forgot to stroke the fire and dad cussed him out because he had to re-start the fire and it was already cold. I didn't like to hear my brother being cussed out and I began to think and feel that our step-dad was mean to us.

Living close to the railroad inspired a love of trains. Inside the railroad house was a turn table. This table was located in the center of the yard and Mr. Jackson, a member of our church, operated the little house. I would often times sit on our steps and watch him operate it when they would bring the trains out of the roundhouse. The turn table would turn the trains in the direction they were to travel because the trains could not turn around on this. Mr. Jackson would come over to the house and eat his lunch while visiting dad and one day I asked him if I could go for a ride one day in his little house and he said yes. One day during his lunch break he came and got me and I was so happy, I had dreamed about doing this. Being on the site was overwhelming. The old locomotives were so huge and I just loved to see them back onto the turn table and watch Mr. Jackson turn them around to the tracks they were to be stored on at the rail yard until their journey. It was so much fun to be there to see this take place. The railroad was exciting but it had some disadvantages too.

It wasn't always nice living across from the round house because very often they would not give you notice and start their engines which created a lot of black smoke. My mother would get furious when this would happen because she would have clean laundry on the line and the smoke would dirty it up again. Of course this meant work for Phyllis and me. We finally learned the schedule so it would not keep happening. Our metal blinds on our wraparound porch required much dusting and washing which added to our chore list. All we needed was something else to add to our chore list which we had to start working on at 5am in the morning. Our hard work would pay off on the weekends.

Saturdays was our day to take the little money we earned and go to the picture show. We could go to the matinee at the Bucklen Theater and watch a movie, get a tub of butter popcorn, a soda pop and penny candy. That was a lot back then. We had fun walking up Main Street with our friends. No one would bother us kids then because people used to look out for each other. It was nice to feel and know that people cared about us and our actions be it good or bad. If we got out of line or was spotted doing something wrong then our parents would know before we got home and they would take care of the issue by spanking or some sort of discipline. If you were well behaved your parents were also told and you were bragged upon by people in the community which always made your parents feel they were doing a good job. Growing up on 703 Wagner and in our small town community was full of work and sometimes fun.

Chapter 3: Death Comes to 703 Wagner

Now I am seven years old, the war is just about over and the year is 1944. We have cousins serving in the war and they are on their way home and everyone is happy from the outcome of the war. The only unpleasant thing going on in our lives was that my eldest brother, Curtis Arthur, had taken sick and he was only 11, almost 12 years old.

Early one Saturday morning Curtis was helping our step-dad work on his Model-T Ford and something happened out there. Some stated our step-dad struck him with a metal part from his car.

This was believable because our step-dad had a bad temper and could be quite mean at times, especially when he had been drinking. He could also be quite nice and because of this I used to call him Dr. Jekyll and Mr. Hyde. Curtis came into the house and told mother that he had been hit by our step-dad so mother checked him over and he appeared not to be hurt too bad. Curtis and Fitz got cleaned up and off they went to enjoy the Saturday matinee at the Bucklen Theater. After the shows were over they were on their way home and Curtis was complaining that he did not feel well. They stopped at our step-brothers barber shop, Rev. Burson, to get hair cuts on 221 St. Joe St. and when they got there Curtis told him how he felt. Rev. Burson checked Curtis and found that he had a fever so he called mother and brought them home. When they arrived at 703 Wagner Curtis was feeling worse. Mother and Rev. Burson got into the car and rushed Curtis to the hospital where they admitted him right away. Doctors ran several tests and he was finally diagnosed as having lock jaw. I was so worried and sad because we were so close and I was afraid of what was happening to him and what could happen to him. Curtis would only survive for one more week. I will never forget his last day with us; we all went out to the hospital to see him. Curtis was a very spiritual young man this mostly due to us being raised in the Methodist faith at St. James African-Methodist-Episcopal Church and attending St. Vincent Catholic School. With all of us there Curtis repeated the 23 Psalm and told us all how much he loved us. He spoke to Fitz and told him to take care of mother like he had planned to do when he got older. He spoke to mother and told her to be forgiving and that God will take care of everything. After these words Curtis passed away. He was such a kind-hearted and loving person who did not like to hurt anyone or see anyone be hurt. He taught me so much even though he was so young and he was so very wise for his age. It was like God was directing Curtis every move. When step-dad was on the rampage Curtis would keep us all at peace. The day he passed was the darkest day of my life up to that point. I thought I couldn't make it without him but then I remember what he told mother and I knew everything would be alright.

After word of Curtis's death got around the neighborhood people came from all over to offer their support. They showed support, love and caring in many ways. They would bring over full meals, keep us children entertained and keep mothers spirits lifted. There would be so many people at the house that people were inside as well as outside. We lived in such a loving community in the 1940's. This helped me to forget the sadness for a moment for I loved being around people. We all grieved for some time but mother worried us the most for she would not eat or could not eat and I was afraid she may die too. Finally after about 3 days she began to eat and Phyllis and I explained to her that she had us to think about and care for and we reminded her that we needed her too. So being believers in God we grieved for a season and overcame our grief with knowing that God is greater than all things. Mother came back to herself and sorrow turned into joy.

At an early age I learned that there are some sad days and some happy days in life. I had to grow up at an early age and take on the regular duties of our home. I began to be shown how to do the chores properly by mother that included making our beds after we got out of them, sweeping the floors, dusting, mopping the floors on our hands and knees, washing windows and picking up trash from the yard. We were kept so busy that there literally was no time for us to get into trouble. I used to think that mother was tough on us, making us do all of those things, but as I grew older I was glad of the lessons I learned. We had the cleanest house in the neighborhood and people would often make the comment that "you can eat off Daisy's floors". I know this to be true because

I was the one cleaning, and waxing the floors until they shined from the sunlight coming in from the window. Mother expected perfection and perfection is what she got.

Chapter 4: Grade School Years

I'm in the fifth grade at South Side elementary school and times are changing and this is being signaled by the integration of the schools. Our school which was located in the black neighborhood on Cleveland Avenue had only had all black students in attendance. We would now be assigned to different schools which were called Samuel Strong, Rice, Roosevelt, Hawthorne, Lincoln and Beardsley. I was excited about this change until I fell ill.

The first semester of the school year I got sick. I was often plagued with frequent nose bleeds but on one Saturday it was worse than normal. I was coming home from the movies that afternoon when my nose started to bleed but this time it began to hemorrhage and no one could stop it. Neighbors would come over to the house to give mother suggestions on how to get it to cease. They ranged from telling her to put salt in both of my hands and for me to squeeze it tightly to putting a pair of scissors down my back to lie on. Needless to say these remedies did not work. Mother called the hospital and an ambulance was sent to get me. I was afraid because this was my first ride in an ambulance. Upon arrival at the hospital the Dr. packed my nostrils and later cauterized them. The bleeding finally stopped and I thought that after being in the hospital for a week I would be able to go home but to my disappointment I had developed a fever which led to pneumonia. My high fever made me go into shock and I ended up having double pneumonia. I was rushed into an oxygen tent for one of my lungs had collapsed. I don't remember much after that, but I do know I could hardly breathe. Mother sat with me day and night praying for my recovery. This was so hard for her because she had just lost Curtis and losing another child seemed unimaginable. The medicine didn't seem to be working so the doctor ran tests and found out that I was allergic to penicillin. They didn't know how to treat me and everyone was becoming frustrated but no one gave up hope. Then in comes Dr. Compton from the research lab at Miles Laboratories and his staff who had made a formula that worked and saved my life. After I received my treatment I was extremely weak and had to miss the entire school year. My immune system had become compromised and I could not be around anyone who had a cold. I lost a lot of weight and I hurt emotionally because I couldn't go out to play like the other children, I could only watch from the window. Phyllis would play with me but I would tire very easily. I must say to this day I still thank God for the miracle of my life for I know there was a guardian angel watching over me and God had saved me for a purpose and that would remain to be seen.

Mother went to the school to tell them of my illness and to ask if the lessons could be brought home for me to work on and they told her no. So I couldn't do any curriculum that entire year. I had to repeat the 5th grade and would be assigned to Hawthorne for integration had been passed into law. I thought that would be good because I enjoyed getting to know other children.

The summer before school started mother asked me which school I would like to attend but to me it really didn't matter because I was already told I had to go to Hawthorne because of our address, 703 Wagner. I became one of the trailblazer for the black community by being the first Black child to attend the school. I can remember my very first day, walking into the school and the principal Mr. Otis Lamier standing there waiting for me. He was very nice to us and we registered and got everything we needed to start that Monday. Mother had warned me on how to conduct myself which I already knew because she was a very strict disciplinarian. I was glad mother taught us to treat ourselves with respect as well as others. She often told me that you need to love yourself then you can love others as you would have them love you. My mother was so full of wisdom and I loved her for that.

Chapter 5: Integration in progress

We had to walk to school from Wagner to Lusher Avenue which was about 8 blocks and arrive at 8am. There was no type of bus transportation for us. The Caucasian children were watching me as I entered the building. Some of them sneered at me and some of them spoke to me. I said hello to the ones who spoke and told them my name. I got my room assignment and found my seat. Some of the girls in my room ignored me and some were nice to me. The boys were nicer than the girls at first and after the girls saw this they came around and started talking. One of the first girls to talk to me was Jeanne Hertzel who lived behind us on Indiana Avenue. There was also Maryland Bryant who lived further down on Indiana and after about a week of school they told me that they were afraid to talk to me because their parents told them that the Black children would beat them up and that we carried knives. I was so surprised that they had been so misled about us and I assured them that I was not that kind of person. I told them that I was a Baptist Christian and I did not believe in violence. After that everyone began to like me they started asking me to sit with them at lunch at their table.

I had began to settle in okay except for a few teachers who I would consider prejudice against Black people or Negroes, as we were referred to back in the 40's and 50's. They tried to discourage me in everything that I wanted to do so I told my mother and she had to come to the school and talk to Mr. Lamier about the situation, I could never understand why. This treatment was stopped immediately. Mr.

Lamier was a very stern principal and he didn't stand for one to be treated unfairly. He encouraged me to participate in everything that the school offered. I joined the choir for I loved to sing and I sang in the children's choir at church since I was very small. I also ran track making the hurdles my main event. I would go on to learn the violin and be in the orchestra. The rental fee for the violin was $7.00 and this was more than mother could afford so at first I thought I would not be able to participate because the director said if I couldn't come up with the money I could not be in the orchestra. When Mr. Lamier found out about the situation, he waived the fee and allowed me to continue. Boy was I glad because that would have been my first major disappointment. Well like mother would say, "What's for you is for you and no one can stop it from happening." When I got that violin I practiced like an Olympic athlete would and after I learned the fundamentals of the strings and chords and reading the music, I was unstoppable. I became quite good and one day I tried out for first chair. This was not without some trials. The director had me practice a piece of music that was much harder than that of my white classmates in the hopes that I would not be able to perform well. Well little did she know of the determination that was inside of me, I practiced those pieces over and over until I had them perfect. The day of tryouts came and the director had the others go first and then she called me up by my last name, Lyons. I played so well that I never made a squeak and in front of the principal I played perfectly. To the directors surprise no doubt, but she did tell me that I played the pieces perfectly and beautifully and told me that I had won first chair. When it came time for the first concert all the other parents were shocked and surprised to see a Negro child sitting in first chair of the violin section. To set it off the director would have all the first chairs stand so the parents and audience members could applaud us. Many were slow to applaud because of me but some kept clapping until the entire gymnasium was clapping. My mother was so proud for she had to work hard for the other rental fees that needed to be paid and she was glad to see that all of my practice paid off. I learned then that one has to spend lots of time on something that you want to be perfect at and learn to give our 100% plus. After this I was treated very nicely and with respect. One of my friends enrolled at Hawthorne and joined the orchestra and took the first chair of her section.

The next year came and more Negro children poured into our school so that took us up to six students. Sixth grade was a great year for me and my class was called the best disciplined class that the school had had thus far. We did have one bully, a girl, who came and would scare the white girls especially. I had a friend come to me one day and ask me to talk to her so she would stop. She was a large girl for her age and had just moved up from the South. Of course I wasn't scared to talk to her so I went ahead and talked to her about the way she was conducting herself and I told her that no one should be treating people like that. She was mad at me at first and accused me of thinking that I thought I was better than her. She even challenged me to a fight. I told her not to let the fact that I was nice to the white kids fool her and that I was not scared of her just because she was bigger than me. I told her I do not fight and won't start now just to prove a point. I finally got her to calm down. She got better but ended up dropping out before the year was over.

Our sixth grade class was so great that we were honored by the planting of an oak tree on the front east side of the school. I had the honor of shoveling dirt with the rest my classmates. The tree still stands there today. I give thanks to Mr. Lamier for making my years at Hawthorne one of the best years of my school career. I will never forget these formative years of my life.

Chapter 6: How Life in Elkhart Changed

I was promoted to the seventh grade at Roosevelt Junior High School and I did not know what to expect of this school because it had a larger Black student population than Hawthorne. Once I started the school year I really liked my homeroom and saying the pledge of allegiance and a prayer before listening to the morning announcements on the p.a. system. I was eager to learn all I could in this new school year and I was happy to meet lots of new friends, some that I would have life long relationships with. At this point in my life my mother had gotten away from domestic work and had employment as a custodian at the junior high I was attending. Sometimes after school I had to stay and help mother wash the blackboards before going home and I thought of this as fun, not like a chore.

Walking was still the only transportation we had to get to school, we had no buses to transport us and in the winter months I can remember how extremely cold it was to walk from Wagner to Indiana Ave. where the school was located. We didn't have what is known today as snow days, we had to go to school whether there was an inch of snow or five feet of snow on the ground. In this climate no boots helped. We had on snow pants, scarves, boots, gloves and hats we kept the scarves around our mouth so we could breathe without the cold air whipping our faces. This was fun sometime too because everyone had to walk so we could laugh and joke along the way and play in the snow. Back then the winters were long and hard but somehow we made it. God was good to us.

School had a lot more discipline than in the modern schools of today. No fighting was allowed and I mean no fighting was permitted. Students were more respectful of the teachers because they knew their parents would get them if they did any form of disrespecting to anyone in control. Parents in the 1940's & 1950's did not tolerate disrespecting of any adults no matter what. This helped in others getting along but didn't make people blind to realities of behaviors kids would display.

Seventh grade was a great year for me I participated in choir and orchestra. In orchestra I switched from the violin to the viola, which was a little bigger than the violin and had a deeper sound to it. I would often play solos at church on Sundays to participate in the service and for practice in front of others. After school I would stop at my cousin's house for a snack before going home. She lived on Maryland St. in the housing projects and she had little girls I loved to play with. Sometimes I would take them home with me and they had gotten used to me coming over that if I didn't take them with me they would cry. Mother put a stop to me bringing them home almost daily because she noticed that I wasn't getting my chores done at home because I was occupied with the girls. It was fun while it lasted. This year was great, but next year would bring more of a challenge.

I found eighth grade a bit more challenging and I had to study a great deal more than what I had been accustomed to. I did all the necessary things to maintain my good standing as a good student. Since reaching the eighth grade I was now able to travel with my church to attend the conventions. I really enjoyed the conventions because this allowed me to travel and meet new people and learn more things about God. I attended different classes at the conventions that would help me in my spiritual growth. My love of reading helped out greatly in experiences like this.

My love of books also led me to help out in the school library. Ms. Banter, the librarian, would let me help file books during my study hall period. I thought this was the next big thing besides going to church conventions. I was good at working in the library and she told me I could sign up to be a library assistant and help the students in the library to find their books, periodicals, etc. One of my biggest assignments as an assistant was to draw a map of the floor plan and place the right books on the correct shelves. This was a challenge for me but I finished it on time and unknowingly had been nominated for an award at the school awards assembly program. I received a letter, "R" with the word librarian written across it. I was surprised and happy knowing my hard worked paid off. This made going into ninth grade something to look forward to.

During ninth grade I began to feel sad for it had been a wonderful three years at Roosevelt were there weren't really any race issues and life was fun, exciting, and smooth. I had learned that if you respect yourself others will respect you also. I made a lot of friends both black and white and had been involved in a young women's group called the Y teens. We were founded out of the YWCA. We had fun doing crafts and things and mostly learning about each other. I was the only Black girl in the group so I learned a lot about the White girls and they learned a lot about me. I experienced tremendous growth during this time.

Elkhart was gradually changing as far as race relations. Of course we were still predominately racist and prejudice, but the Black youth were starting to excel in sports and music. Black youth were becoming more involved in athletics and were joining choir. The choir director, Mr. Ulm was so great. He was so good and treated everyone fairly. This was one of my favorite courses along with science and history.

I enjoyed science because of all the different things to learn about nature and going on the nature trips was fun. Mr. Baker made the class so interesting that you couldn't help but learn. On the way home from school I could apply the things I learned to what I would see going home. I could also share this with the children I would baby sit in the neighborhood. I loved children and everyone knew this so I was always watching after someone's child. They knew they were safe and I enjoyed watching them. 703 Wagner was a good place to be.

Chapter 7: Dark Days Again

Life again at 703 Wagner is changing and this time it was through our step-dad. He was getting older and the older he got the meaner he got. Mother was getting older too and she was beginning to wear down and dealing with all the confusion she was being dealt was getting harder. She was a firm believer in her marriage vows but now it was getting a little too much for her to bear. Step-dad was getting to the place where he would bring his drinking buddies to our house after a drinking frenzy at the local bar, The Cozy Corner. This was making my mother mad and sick. They would be sitting on the front porch talking loud and cussing each other out. Of course we kids heard all this and sometimes we would be scared and thought that a fight was going to break out at our house. I was beginning to hate people who drank thinking that they were all bad. Step-dad was what you would call a weekend drunk. All week he would be sober then as soon as Friday night got here he stayed drunk until Saturday night. He was the chairman of the deacon board at church so by Sunday, for the most part, he would have sobered up enough to go to church.

It amazed me how he could get up there with his black suit and tie on and lead devotions and take the offering like he hadn't been out doing anything wrong. For the most part he played this role well but one Sunday it was too much for him to handle. One Sunday morning during offering time the ushers would collect the offering and then they would bring it up to the tithe table and the deacons and step-dad would stand in front of the church and count the money. Well step-dad was in charge of this and on this particular Sunday a deacon by the name of Mr. Ed had counted the money and told step-dad that his count was wrong. Now first of all let me say that step-dad didn't like for anyone to tell him he was wrong when he was wrong, so naturally step-dad didn't like what Mr. Ed was saying. So as they were counting the money on the table in front of the pulpit of the church Mr. Ed told step-dad again that his count was wrong. Well before Mr. Ed could blink, with a few choice words and a balled up fist, step-dad had hit him in the face and knocked him out in front of the whole church. Our pastor, Rev. Mayes, stood up and ordered step-dad out of the church. This was so embarrassing for our family and that day many of mother's friends were finally encouraging her to leave this evil hateful man. They knew that mother was of better standards than what this man was displaying. This wasn't the first incident of his foolishness, just the worst.

The family stayed at the church, except for step-dad. He tried to get mother to leave but she was a strong willed woman and stayed at her church with her dignity still in tact. Step-dad started to study with the Jehovah's Witness group every Saturday night. I didn't like to study with them so mother never insisted that we kids had to sit and listen. Phyllis and I had to sit on the front steps but sometimes just out of curiosity we would sit in and listen to see what the differences was between our religions. Step-dad studied with the Jehovah's but never joined them and he never came back to our church. You may have thought this would have changed step-dad but I guess the old saying is true, "you can't teach an old dog new tricks". Step-dad continued to drink, actually a little worse than before, and he began to become abusive to us kids. We tried to be nice to him but he always found a way to not be thankful and to be cruel. I can remember one Father's Day in particular when Fitz, Phyllis and I had saved our movie show money and bought him a nice hat for Fathers Day and we gave it to him and he never once said thank you. He just looked at the hat and put it down on the table and when we asked him did he like it he just grunted. I couldn't hold my piece and had no choice but to be disrespectful and I told him how we saved our money to buy him this hat and how we were trying to express our love for him and that he could at least acknowledge that. This still didn't help. He was too evil and drunk to care. Mother would give him chance after chance and for short periods of time he would be nice and then Mr. Evil would return and the mean behaviors continued.

Chapter 8: Time to Leave 703

Step-dads drunkenness, mean-spirited ways escalated to the point that mother had finally had enough. The last straw was the constant cursing out she would receive on a daily basis. He called her every name but a child of God and he started throwing things at her and locking her out of the house at night, making her sit out on the front or back steps. Fitzhugh was 15 years old and becoming a man, came to mothers rescue one morning. On this morning we were all sitting at the kitchen table eating breakfast and step-dad started in on mother cursing at her and he lunged at her to strike her and

Fitzhugh and I jumped up from the table and mother ran out the backdoor. She didn't want to fight him. Fitzhugh grabbed step-dad by the collar and pinned him against the refrigerator and I was ready to help him beat him down. Fitzhugh told him he had better not ever hit our mother or he would be sorry. I was standing right there waiting to let him have it. Because of how mother had raised us we didn't beat him down. He was old and we probably could have killed him.

After this mother came back in the house and called his son, Rev. Burson, to the house to come and quiet his dad down. When he got there he wouldn't even listen to his own son. Rev. Burson talked to mother and us and told us he would not hold it against her if she left him. This might seem trivial or silly but back then you didn't leave your spouse and if you did you often sought approval from your pastor or clergy or circle of friends. Fitzhugh left the house first and stayed with a family friend until he found us a house.

Fitzhugh was working at a local ice cream plant so he had income and he found us a house on St. Joe St. It was my God mother's mother-in-laws house. The new address was 310 St. Joe and the house sat where the Benham Street underpass is currently. We rented the house and God was again good to us for allowing us to leave that horrible situation without physically getting hurt and keeping our good name.

Chapter 9: Moving On

The move and drama happened during my ninth grade year so I finished that year living at 310 St. Joe St. Mother was stilled married to step-dad and she would still cook him meals and have me take them to him. I hated this because it was a quite a walk from St. Joe to 703 Wagner. One day I was feeling quite evil toward this man who had caused my family so much pain and mother had me fix his plate. As I was on my way to take it to him I felt like he didn't deserve the two pieces of chicken she had sent so I took one out, the breast and left him the chicken leg. It made me feel good to do this, but unknowingly to me he had had the nerve to call mother up and ask her why she only sent one piece of chicken instead of two. She told him she had sent two and this idiot tried to call her a liar. Mother had figured out what I had done and she talked to me and told me that I should not have done that. I confessed and she didn't get upset but she asked me never to do that again and that if I did she would have to punish me by way of the switch. I can remember the way those braided peach tree limbs felt so I never did that again.

We had a good life at 310 St. Joe St. I learned that you don't have to stay in a bad situation for there is always a way out if you trust in God he will deliver you out of one thing and into something better. Fitzhugh was my hero for he looked out for our family as he had promised our brother Curtis. We received some bad news that the house we were currently in had been sold but to no dismay Fitzhugh, with God's guidance, found us another home. This one was located at 341 Chapman and we could buy this house with only $500 down. We were happy again but to our surprise mother had asked Fitzhugh if we could move step-dad in, for he was ailing and mother had pity for him, but Fitzhugh said no. He didn't want this because he knew step-dad would come in and try to lord over us again and we no longer were his prisoners. Mother understood and was so happy. She still worked hard to help Fitzhugh out and I got a babysitting job so I could buy my school clothes and I joined this Cinderella Club where you could lay-away sweaters for school and get them out in September. Phyllis did this too with the money she earned from working.

We had finally begun to live and mother had taught us well giving us the tools we needed to persevere in all conditions. I thank God for my mother and when I look back I don't think I could have endured the things she had to endure from our step-dad for our sake.

Chapter 10: High School Days

Now it is 1954 and Phyllis is about to graduate from high school. Fitzhugh will graduate in 1955 because he had to drop out of school to work and buy us a home. I will graduate in 1956. I am now a sophomore at Elkhart High School and I still have to walk to school in all kinds of weather. The walk is longer now because the high school is downtown on Third Street in all climates. So in the winter I was still bundling my self up and walking to school. I had snow pants but they had to come off once I got to school because girls were not allowed to wear pants. We had to wear skirts, sweaters, bobby socks, saddle shoes, penny loafers or felt skirts with the crinoline underneath. I remember having a black one with a poodle on it that I bought with my babysitting money. I really enjoyed my sophomore year. Once again I met many new friends and enjoyed my classes. My favorite class was sewing class. I was good at this I even got an "A" on a dress that I had made for our class project. I didn't care for cooking class though. I always got into disagreements with the teacher over how many spices to add to the food. I figured if I had to eat it I wanted it to at least taste like my mothers cooking. Needless to say I only received a 'B'. I was counting on these skills to transition me into adulthood in the community and at home.

Times for the Black race were getting a little better in terms of places we were now allowed to live. We were now allowed to branch out a little further like to the upper part of Hickory St., Chapman Ave, Maryland Ave, Park Ave and Benham Ave. On Sixth St to Indiana Ave there was a dairy called Wambaugh

Dairy and a few houses were available for us to purchase. I was glad that being Black didn't prevent us from driving an automobile.

Being fifteen and a half I was anxious to get my drivers license. I would turn sixteen in December and had been bugging my brother to teach me how to drive. Fitzhugh never had the time to teach me so mother let me sign up and take drivers education at school. She went ahead and paid the small fee and off I went to driver's education. My instructor was Red Buttons and he did a good job and I passed with flying colors and got my license at fifteen and a half. Fitz let me drive and I really thought I was something, I could drive and Phyllis couldn't. I was the baby girl so this was a grown up thing for me. Phyllis wouldn't learn to drive until she got married years later. Now that I was gaining more responsibility I was more helpful to mother.

Mother had such a sweet soul and spirit and this often times left me wondering how she could be so giving to someone who didn't do the same. I am referring again to step-dad. He had gotten much worse now and could not take care of himself so Fitz allowed mother to bring him to our home so she could take care of him. The sad thing was that he had three daughters, two who lived in Buffalo, NY and one in Cairo, IL and they refused to take care of their dad. Fitz and I had even visited Leo and Rose in New York and had a good time but they didn't want to have anything to do with their dad. I know why this was and I really couldn't blame them because even now he was still hateful. He had the nerve to yell at me one day. This man just never knew how to ask for some water in a nice way so I would take my time and he would even have the nerve to shake his cane at me. I was getting fed up with him and I told him to shut up. I know this wasn't very nice to him and I thought I was getting back at him for the abuse he rendered to mother and us. It was the least I could do. I knew it wasn't nice so I made sure I didn't do it often, just when he had pushed me to the limit.

One day I got home from school mother had to take him to the hospital. That day we found out he had been diagnosed with psoriasis of the liver and they said it had turned into cancer. I guess those years of heavy drinking, Old Grand Dad liquor straight or mixed with cola, caught up with his body. From the hospital he went to the nursing home where he had a stroke. One day I came home from school and mother told me he had passed away. I was sad for him because I was afraid he was not going to be with the Lord because of his being so mean and on the other hand I was okay because he had been so mean to mother and she would finally be free of him. So you see she did honor her vows, 'until death do we part'. I really respected her for being faithful. Fitz and mother had to bury him because he drank up all of his money and his children didn't even want to help with that, such a sad way to leave this earth.

Fitz gave him a proper burial; he bought him a suit, shirt and tie and sent him back to the earth.

Chapter 11: Getting Close to Finishing High School

I passed the tenth grade and am now a junior in high school. Finally I am no longer an underclassman and junior year started with a blast! My favorite subject this year is art. I found that I love to draw abstract art and paint. Mr. James was my teacher and he brought out creativity in me that I did not know existed and this led to me earning A's in art. Typing was a good class too and of course I excelled in choir. I took algebra but didn't really apply myself like I should have. I only took the course because it qualified as a college preparatory course and I wanted to go to college and you need three units of math to qualify. After school activities became more fun now that I was older and could drive.

I was driving Fitz's car and I would take him to work after school and keep his car so I could go to the skating rink in South Bend. I loved to roller skate! I would go skating and then grab a bite to eat at a local restaurant. There was a young man in South Bend who I liked at the time so this made skating more fun. He taught me how to skate backward and we had great fun. I got so good that the owner of the rink asked me to be a monitor and gave me a whistle in order to keep the skating flow nice and in order. I really loved my brother for letting me use his car to go skating. I had enough time to have fun and be back to pick him up from work, at Whitehall, before 11 pm. Mother wasn't happy with me being up so late but she trusted me to do the right thing and I did obey her. She had instilled listening skills in me through discipline when I was a young child. She defiantly taught me by age 13, my last spanking, how not to spare the rod and spoil the child. Mother's lessons help shape me into a responsible young teenager and soon to be adult.

The school year was going extremely well so to keep the fun going I joined the girls club, Y-teens, at school. This was a group that got together at the YWCA after school to talk about different issues around being a young Christian girl. Our instructor was Ms. Thomas and she really helped change my attitude and the way I carried myself as a young lady. This was a positive environment for all girls, but outside of school, circumstances were not always that positive.

Being Black was still something to deal with. We had two drug stores in the area on Main St. that did not allow Blacks to come in and sit at the counter to have a soda out of the soda fountain. I can remember youth staging a sit-in to try to get the store to let us sit and have a soda but this failed. Needless to say, the drugstore removed their soda fountains from the store so Blacks could not come in and get one. There was also a sweet shop in the same block that wouldn't allow Blacks to come in and sit down, but we could come in and carry our food out- just not to sit. One day after Y-teens my White friends and I went to the sweet shop for sodas. Once we got there the manager told us we could not sit in there and have our sodas. My White friends got upset and told him that they would not come back if he made us get up and leave. The manager in all his ignorance then told us we could stay but we had to go sit in the booth in the back so none of his customers could see us. We ended up staying, but I was afraid because I didn't know what to expect from him. He told us not to be too loud so we respected his wishes. If I had not been so naïve I would have not stayed to be put into the back corner of a shop who didn't think I was good enough to be there. I did end up being the first Black to sit in the shop to have a soda but not in the way that would have been proper or beneficial for others. I was afraid to tell my mother when I got home because I thought she would be angry with me for putting myself in danger, but she took it pretty well when I told her. It really was a dangerous thing for a Black person to be in an all white establishment, where they were not allowed, at that point in history. It's ironic because it wasn't long after that the sweet shop went out of business. I did miss it because they had the best homemade ice cream and would serve the biggest ice cream cones for five cents.

Chapter 12: All Grown Up

My last year in high school, senior year, it's hard to believe that I've finally become a young adult. Senior year was the most challenging of my school years. I encountered the most racism thus far in dealing with adults. It first started with my counselor advising me that there was no need for me to take U.S. Government because Black girls didn't need the course because after high school we would be domestic workers so the class would be a waste of time. In 1956 Elkhart that's what Black women were domestics because they were not allowed to work in the factories. The counselors or teachers never even entertained the thought of Blacks going to college or trying to take courses to enhance their knowledge. They told this same story to every Black female and told the Black males that it wasn't necessary so this left me as the only Black in my U.S. Government class. My teacher was the worst of all. She was a racist White woman who spoke rudely to me and ignored me in class. She would never call on me when I raised my hand and would never give me a grade higher than a 'B'. I remember her asking me why I even signed up for the class and I remember being shocked to even be asked such a question. I was getting tired of her rude unfair treatment so one day I asked her point blank what she had against me and she replied, I quote, "I don't see why you have the need for this subject on government for all you will ever be after graduation is a domestic." I was livid. I thought she had better be glad I was raised to respect my elders because I could have retaliated in an awful way. I maintained my composure and told her, "I am not going to be a domestic worker cleaning someone's house for the rest of my life." She didn't like my reply and we continued to have problems and she continued to grade me unfairly. She taught me that in life people will try to throw stumbling blocks in your way but you have to keep stepping over them or walking through them. One has to persevere through life's situations in order to get where they want to be.

My other classes went well and as graduation neared it was time to order the commencement announcements. I was so excited to be graduating so I could move on with my life. Economic times were still difficult for us so I had to go without my announcement cards, mother just couldn't afford it. This disappointed me a little because I could not exchange them with my classmates. I did get the opportunity to attend the Senior Girls Tea. It was a lovely affair and we looked so nice in our dresses and hats. In our graduating class there were only six

Black females and two Black males out of a class of three hundred students. That prints a clearer picture of what it was like being a minority in an all white school during the most racist and segregated times in America. Even though those times were tough I met a lot of friends from all walks of life from Hawthorne to Elkhart High School. I was blessed to graduate from high school because of the obstacles and situations I had to overcome to even get there. It was rough for me growing up and accomplishing this proved that you can make it no matter what.

Upon graduating from high school I became the superintendent of our Sunday school classes at church and teacher of our primary class. This allowed me to attend more conventions and to be more active in participating in leadership in the church. In a short period of time I was promoted to teaching the adult class as the assistant teacher. I maintained this position for about a year until I moved to San Francisco, California.

Moving to San Francisco was a beautiful experience. I had family friends who lived out there and they were asking me to come out and go to college. They were more like family than friends and they let me stay with them while I attended San Francisco State College. It was very exciting to be living in a new environment but also a little sad because I had never been that far from my mother and family and I missed them dearly. My San Francisco experience was a great one. I was going to school majoring in sociology and I had found a church to be active in. I united with Third Baptist Church under the leadership of Dr. Frederick Haynes. I joined the choir under the direction of the famous organist the late Earl Grant's sister, Mrs. Graham. Our choir was so great that we were asked to open at a concert at the San Francisco Opera house where the late great gospel singer Mahalia Jackson was in concert. Singing for Mahalia and then meeting and talking to her was the biggest thrill of my life. I had a chance to speak with her after the concert and she encouraged me to keep singing for the Lord and not give into secular music. It was hard for me to believe I was actually in her presence but I took her advice and kept signing praises to the Lord for I knew if I kept the Lord first in my life all other things would be added unto me.

To make my San Francisco chapter complete I found the love of my life, my husband, Roy. We fell in love quickly and married within 10 months. Roy was in the Navy and was originally from Alabama. He was the nicest man I had ever met and the only serious boyfriend I would have. This union has proved to be a blessing and an addition from the Lord blessing us with 47 years of marriage and four beautiful children.

Life is an awesome journey that takes many twists and turns. It can start out a little rough and then somehow work out for the best. Beginning at 703 Wagner I learned that you must not be afraid to venture out in your life, that nothing is more important than family and that all things are possible through Jesus Christ.

About The Author

Bonnie Ruth Lyons-Clark was born in Elkhart, IN, to the late Daisy Mae Austin-Lyons. She lived all her life in Elkhart, IN. except for the three years she lived in San Francisco, CA. While in San Francisco she attended San Francisco State College. She then moved to Cornada, CA after her marriage. She is a born again Christian who has a special love of people and justice. This love led her to become a volunteer worker in 1995 for an organization called CASA which is a court appointed special advocated for abused children. She enjoys helping these children and parents in these tough circumstances. She has been a Sunday school teacher since her high school years and has served on boards including being president of the Meadow Oak Subdivision for 20 years. She has been married to her husband Roy L. Clark who she met and married in California. They have been blessed with four children, Cedric, Corwyn, Cameron, and Crystal. Their youngest son Cameron is deceased. Bonnie and Roy now reside in Bristol, IN. God has richly blessed them and they are ever grateful.